INTRODUCTORY MACROECONOMICS

SECOND EDITION

INTRODUCTORY MACROECONOMICS

SECOND EDITION

MICHAEL VESETH
UNIVERSITY OF PUGET SOUND

ACADEMIC PRESS, INC.
(Harcourt Brace Jovanovich, Publishers)

Orlando San Diego San Francisco New York
London Toronto Montreal Sydney Tokyo
São Paulo

Academic Press, Inc.
Orlando, Florida 32887

United Kingdom Edition published by
Academic Press, Inc. (London) Ltd.
24/28 Oval Road, London NW1

ISBN: 0-12-719570-X
Library of Congress Catalog Card Number: 83-71285

Printed in the United States of America

CONTENTS

PREFACE

THIS MAY be the most important book you read (and the most important course you take) in your college career. You live in a world of economics—of inflation, unemployment, interest rates, exchange rates, fiscal policies, budget deficits, taxes, and international trade. Most people have only a general (mis)understanding of how the economy works. This is an important gap in their education because economics is not just some esoteric theoretical fantasy (although you may question this later). Economics is the study of the world you live in. If you don't understand economics, you are ill-prepared to deal with that world.

Let's get something straight right from the start. Economics isn't very hard. The word economics, for example, comes from a pair of Greek words that, roughly translated, mean "management of a household." Chances are that you already know something about how to manage a household—after all, what does this involve? Balancing the checkbook. Making sure that the right things are in the right places. Keeping the roof patched and the lawn mowed. Getting the laundry done and meals cooked at the right times. Nothing to it, right?

Well, maybe it's a little more complicated than this—just take a look at your room, for example. Some mess, huh? Although the basic principles of this "home" economics are pretty straightforward, the realities of it are a bit more complex. Each task is simple by itself. Managing it all at once is the real trick. (The economist Kenneth Boulding has the solution, however. Boulding says that, "Housekeeping is a snap—if you set your standards low enough!")

This book isn't about cooking and cleaning, but the basic principles of this home "economics" apply. Economics is made up of a few basic ideas (often called "models") that are simple and easy to grasp by themselves. When we put them all together, the analysis that results is more complex, but more interesting, too. Since we can't make an omelet without breaking a few eggs, let's get cooking.

What Is This Book About?

This book introduces you to macroeconomics—the study of how the nation's house is run. In studying macroeconomics you will see both how the economy is constructed and, more important, how you fit into that structure. The economy, you see, is not just a bunch of nameless guys in New York or Washington, D.C., busy passing laws, selling bonds, or trading stock. It isn't a system of impersonal numbers, indexes, and charts, either. The economy is a collection of people like you. Your actions influence the way the economic world works and you and your future depend on outside economic events. It is important that you see how you fit into this puzzle so that you can make wise economic decisions as a consumer, a producer, and a voter.

Features of This Text

This book has many built-in features that should make the study of macroeconomics more interesting and more rewarding for you. These features include:

UNDERSTANDING CURRENT PROBLEMS. Economics students generally have only a general understanding of the nature of economic problems. What is unemployment? Why is inflation so important? How are things different today from past years? This text puts the current situation in perspective by looking back at the past and puts today's problems into focus by thoroughly examining the consequences of economic ills.

FOCUS ON CURRENT EVENTS. Economics is alive and living all around you. This text tries to bring this point home by applying timeless theories to a timely analysis of today's headlines. You need only to pick up a copy of a newspaper like the *New York Times* or the *Wall Street Journal* to discover how useful the ideas developed in this text are.

ANALYSIS OF INFLATION. Inflation is economic Enemy #1—it is the most important and misunderstood phenomenon of the 20th century. You'll find that the discussion of inflation ranges throughout this book. Every chapter discusses the way that inflation, its causes, economic effects, and potential cures affect us all. One major goal of this text is for you to finally understand the peculiar consequences of this invisible enemy.

MODERN ECONOMIC THEORY. To understand how the economy works we need to develop a theory of the economy and a model of the economy itself. This text presents the most modern and useful, yet most easily grasped theory of the national economy—the aggregate demand-aggregate supply model of macroeconomics. Since the tools of this theory are not particularly difficult to use, we can devote our time to using those tools to see why economists and policy-makers disagree about how the economy works.

EMPHASIS ON ECONOMIC POLICY. Economic theory is important, but it gains significance when it helps us understand how economic policy can be used to deal with our current ills. The primary focus of this text is on policy—the way that government tools can be applied to making economic conditions better and the problems that economists and politicians face in using those tools.

INTERNATIONAL ECONOMICS. We live in an interdependent world, a world of exchange rates, international trade, and finance. It is important that you understand how the rest of the world affects our national economic policies and you as an individual. The heavy emphasis on international economics found here is designed to make you fluent in a vocabulary that can only grow in importance.

EASY READING. Economics has a vocabulary all its own, and learning how to speak this foreign tongue is difficult enough without a textbook that also tries to make the ideas harder than they really are. This book is written in a clear, somewhat jovial style that you'll find easy to read, understand, and remember.

Built-In Study Aids

You are probably reading this book because you are taking a course in macroeconomics. You want to learn the material, but you also want to get a good grade in the course. Several built-in features of this book are designed to help you in both tasks. Each chapter includes several features to help you learn more and get good grades, too.

PREVIEW AND REVIEW. Each chapter begins with a Preview section, a set of questions that the chapter answers. Be sure to read these questions before you read the text itself. Studies show that reading comprehension improves when the reader goes into the material with some questions or ideas in mind. The Review section at the end of the chapter provides a quick check to see if you've understood the main points covered in the text.

DISCUSSION QUESTIONS. Several discussion questions appear at the end of each chapter. These questions range from simple checks of the facts to some difficult applications of the concepts the chapter presents. Be sure that you can answer each of these questions before you go on to the next chapter.

TEST YOURSELF QUESTIONS. Each chapter also includes objective questions of the type you might encounter on examinations. In answering these questions you should be sure to know what the right answer is and why it is correct and why each of the wrong answers is wrong, too. The correct answers are provided in an Answer Key in the back of the book, but the whys are left for you to supply.

ECONOMIC CONTROVERSIES. Each chapter also includes an Economic Controversy section. These readings present both sides of an economic debate. They give you a chance to see how well you understand and can apply the text material to real-world problems. Since both sides of the debate are presented but no answers are given, you'll have to make up your own mind on these issues. You'll find this a difficult but fascinating problem.

SUGGESTIONS FOR FURTHER READING. Any textbook can only get you started on a topic as large as macroeconomics. A section in the back of the book supplies suggestions for further readings for each chapter. You are encouraged to take advantage of this list and explore the economic landscape far beyond the little patch of ground we will clear together here.

Acknowledgments

This book benefited from the contributions of many individuals whose names, alas, do not appear on the cover. My colleagues at the University of Puget Sound supplied both encouragement and constructive criticism as the second edition of this text was written. The University of Puget Sound provided me with the time to undertake this ambitious project. Several professors, known for their excellence in teaching, provided comments on drafts of this book that were useful in final revisions. Susan Elliott Loring provided editorial leadership at Academic Press. I thank my wife, Sue Trbovich Veseth (who is a very much better writer than I am) for giving love and encouragement while probably preventing our divorce by refusing to read a single page of the manuscript!

Thanks go, finally, to my students at the University of Puget Sound. They have put up with experimental material and some reasonably bizarre lectures as this second edition was prepared. I dedicate this book to my students, past, present, and future.

TO THE INSTRUCTOR

THE FIRST thing that instructors ask when they pick up a new text is, "What's so new about this? Why do we need another macroeconomics text when there are so many around already?" These are good questions and they deserve good answers.

A macroeconomics text should be able to really explain the problems that face the economy today. It should deal clearly with the problems, policies, and theories that are current to the discipline and it should do this in a way that pleases not only the instructor choosing the text, but also the student who reads (or, too often, does not read) the book. Most of the textbooks currently on the market fail this test. This book was written in an attempt to remedy this problem.

The typical macroeconomics text presents a traditional Keynesian picture of the economy. The principal economic model used is the well-worn 45-degree line picture with occasional brief excursions into the dynamic world of the IS-LM curves. These models are useful and informative to the economist—indeed, all the information and theory contained in these models is included in this text. But it is important to realize that the ideas of Keynesian economics are not identical with a 45-degree line figure. That is, it is possible (even easy) to teach good economics without also teaching the particular geometry embedded in that model.

The Keynesian 45-degree line model was designed to show how macroeconomic equilibrium is reached and how that equilibrium can be changed to fight unemployment. It says little, if anything, about inflation or the relationship between inflation and unemployment rates. Today's students want and need to understand today's problems. They become quickly disillusioned with a macroeconomics course that fights unemployment for the most part, gives lip service to the problems of inflation and then finally, and briefly, treats the relationship between the two as a back-of-the-book chapter. They come away with little more than a Phillips Curve view of the world. This is not good enough.

Does this mean that we must scrap Keynesian economics? Clearly not! Economics courses have traditionally limited themselves to discussion of aggregate demand, but Keynes didn't. Keynes held that aggregate supply was also important and that, in times like these, both sides of the economy should be dealt with.

The problem we face is that the teaching of macroeconomic principles has failed to keep up with the principles of macroeconomics. That is, teaching at the introductory level has lagged behind the profession in its understanding of the causes and cures of inflation and unemployment, not to mention the problems of economic policy and international economics. While instructors and textbook authors have sought out new gimmicks to better explain the traditional models, economists and policy-makers have found that different models are needed to deal with our changing economy. These more realistic and useful pictures of the economy have trickled down to the many excellent intermediate-level macroeconomics books.

The first goal of this book is to bring better economics to the principles-level course by introducing a simplified version of the aggregate supply-aggregate demand model of the economy found in intermediate theory texts and in Keynes' General Theory, too. The wide acceptance of the first edition of this book suggests that this attempt was not altogether unsuccessful. This second edition continues along the same path.

The second goal of this text is to make macroeconomics as understandable and exciting for students as it always has been for professors. Many texts make the error of assuming that students need only to be prepared for intermediate-level courses where they will learn "real" economics. They spend too much time on the specific geometry of the Keynesian models and too little time on the economics of the macroeconomy. This method may benefit the tiny minority of students who go on in economics, but at a high cost.

It is the philosophy of this text that the goal of the first macroeconomics class ought to be to prepare students for life, not just for more economics. Most students take only one class in macroeconomics. They will have just one chance to really understand how the economy works and how it affects them. This text makes the most of that one chance. Macroeconomics here is presented in a clear, readable form. The stress is on policy and applications while presenting a modern theory background. Tools and theories have been consistently questioned—if they teach more geometry than economics they have been scrapped, revised, or rethought. The simplified structure of the economy that results contains more economics than is found in many more theoretically elegant treatments. The time saved in explaining geometry is efficiently used in explaining important current topics.

This may be good for the student who does not go on in economics, but what about the student who decides to major in our field. Doesn't this training harm the potential major in future classes? Clearly not, based on the experience of many instructors. Students exposed to this approach end up with a sound intuitive feel for the economy and so are better able to see where intermediate-level models are going. It is not, after all, the quality of the geometry that is ultimately important, it is the quality of the economics and the depth of understanding that makes the good economist. This text represents no handicap in this area.

Organization of the Text

This text is divided into four parts. Most instructors will use material from all four parts, although individual chapters may be deleted and extra material added to fit the needs of particular students or courses (sample course outlines are found in the *Instructor's Manual* available from Academic Press).

In *Part I: Tools and Problems*, the reader is exposed to a discussion of national economic problems and equipped with the basic tools of supply and demand for use in analyzing those problems. Chapter 1 presents an overview of macroeconomics and recent economic history, focusing on the changing relationship between inflation and unemployment. Chapter 2 develops the supply and demand model of market activity with emphasis on particular applications seen again, in a different context, in later chapters. Chapter 3 applies the supply-demand analysis to a discussion of unemployment, then focuses on the labor market aspects of this problem. Chapter 4 ends the first unit of the text with a thorough discussion of the economic effects of inflation.

Part II: A Simple Model of the Economy constructs a simple but effective framework for analysis of the national economy. Chapter 5 develops an understanding of aggregate analysis by analyzing the gross national product definitions. Chapter 6 presents the essentials of aggregate demand by working through a simple Keynesian model (the 45-degree line ideas are developed in the main part of the chapter, while the geometric model itself is presented in an appendix). Chapter 7 adds aggregate supply to the analysis and begins to unravel the causes of stagflation. Chapter 8 examines fiscal policy and applies aggregate demand–aggregate supply to an analysis of government economic policies.

Part III: Money Credit and the Economy looks at the role of money and credit in a modern economy. Chapter 9 presents the basics of money, interest rates, and fractional reserve banking and introduces the Federal Reserve System. Chapter 10 looks at the credit market and shows how interest rates are determined through the interaction of demand and supply. Students find this analysis particularly useful and interesting, now that interest rates are big news. Monetary and fiscal policies are developed and compared in Chapter 11 and the problem of financing government spending is discussed. Finally, Chapter 12 presents alternative views of the economy. A monetarist model of economic policy is introduced and the Keynesian versus monetarist versus supply-side versus rational expectations versus disequilibrium points of view are discussed and compared.

Part IV: International Economics takes a good long look at the international forces affecting individual and national economic policies. Chapter 13 looks at international trade and payments. Comparative advantage, tariffs and quotas, and the balance-of-payments problems are discussed here. Chapter 14 introduces the exchange rate and develops the foreign exchange market. Students (and the professor!) are fascinated by these concepts that are really just simple applications of demand and supply. Chapter 15 looks at monetary and fiscal policy from the perspective of an open economy. Chapter 16 ends the text by glancing backwards at the goals of the economy and the problems, tools and trade-offs that have been discussed in the text. The problem of making economic policy provides the focus here.

Special Features of the Text

This text has several special features designed to make it more useful for both the instructor and the student. These important features include an expanded number of *Economic Controversies*. These special sections debate major economic issues and problems, but leave the final answer up to the student. These sections are particularly well-suited for class discussion.

A *Preview* precedes the text of each chapter, a *Review* follows the text. These brief units help students see what they will read about and check their reading comprehension. Chapters end with a variety of questions that have proven useful to students and instructors. *Discussion Questions* provide topics for both classroom discussion and for essay-type homework. *Test Yourself* questions give students a chance to see how well they have mastered the material and to find weak spots. The True/False questions of the first edition have been replaced with a series of multiple-choice questions that are both more demanding and less ambiguous. Answers to these questions are found at the back of the book. *Suggestions for Further Reading* are also found at the back of the text, as is a complete *Glossary* of economic terms.

These features make this text a self-contained guide to macroeconomics that can be used in a wide variety of classroom situations.

New for the Second Edition

Students and instructors who used the first edition of this book have been kind enough to provide feedback used in drafting the second edition. As a result, ambiguous language has been cleaned up and better examples found where required.

Important changes in this second edition include a more thorough integration of the Keynesian analysis into the main body of the text. This was accomplished without loss in readability. If Keynes gets more visibility, so do alternative schools of economic thought. Supply-side views are more visible here as are the influential ideas of monetarists and the rational expectations theorists. Even disequilibrium macroeconomics gets a mention. The general aggregate demand–aggregate supply theory has been strengthened while the discussion of fiscal policy has been reworked to lean less heavily on multiplier analysis and more on the policies themselves.

In making these changes, the real strengths of the first edition have not been forgotten. The reasons that professors and students both have been drawn to this book have been its readability, the focus on aggregate demand and supply, the strong treatment of the credit market, the emphasis on international economics and, finally, the discussion of economic problems that makes it clear that we are dealing with an economy of people, not numbers, charts and graphs.

I cordially thank everyone who has commented on the first edition of this book and look forward to future discussions of introductory macroeconomics.

INTRODUCTORY MACROECONOMICS

SECOND EDITION

I

TOOLS AND PROBLEMS

1

MACROECONOMIC PROBLEMS

Preview

What is economics? What is macroeconomics?
What are our national economic problems?
What are our national economic goals?
Have we been successful in achieving those goals?
How have our economic problems changed over the past decades?

MANY OF our most difficult individual and national problems are economic problems. To understand the world and make intelligent choices, therefore, requires that we understand something of economics.

It is astounding to consider how much economic events have come to monopolize our time and influence our lives. The federal government was once mostly a referee (making and enforcing criminal and civil law) and a guardian (protecting us from foreign powers). Now Congress and the President seem to spend most of their time fighting economic fires—battling inflation, unemployment, and budget deficits. Newspapers used to count on stories of fires, murders, and kidnappings to increase circulation. Now taxes and interest rates make the headlines and sell papers.

Businesses that once were preoccupied with the difficult matter of making a profit, now worry, as well, about investment tax credits, gross national product, and exchange-rate policies. People who, 10 years ago, did not know the difference between prime rib and prime rate, now think more about the latter than the former. They know that they must master some pretty sophisticated economics if they are to make even simple personal and business decisions with confidence.

Economics is important stuff and this book is designed to help you understand economic theories, policies, and news. It is the goal of this text to increase your EQ (Economics Quotient) by leading you through a discussion of economic theory, the nature of our current ills, and an analysis of some of the frequently prescribed cures. Strong medicines, however, often have undesirable side effects; as a result, a perfect prescription for the economy may not be found. Policies that reduce one economic problem inflame another, are politically impossible, or have unacceptable social consequences. Pat answers are hard to come by, but an understanding of the problems and trade-offs that we face helps us make better decisions. Throughout this book, we look for answers to our questions. What we find, in the end, is simply a better understanding of the questions themselves.

This chapter answers some basic questions that students have regarding economics, macroeconomics, and the nature of our national goals and problems. We will take a brief trip down memory lane to see where we have been so that we can better understand where we are going.

What Is Economics?

Suppose you were to pose the question "What is economics?" to a hundred average college freshmen in an attempt to find out what economics is all about. What response do you think you would get? The answers might look something like those listed in Table 1-1.

Most of the students in our sample group did not have a clear idea of what economics is all about. But, as luck would have it, one economics professor

TABLE 1-1 WHAT IS ECONOMICS?

Response	Percentage responding
"Economics is the study of the production and distribution of goods and services in a world of scarce resources."	1
"Economics is like business—how to make a buck."	37
"Economics is all about inflation and unemployment and stuff like that."	23
"Economics is a bunch of charts and graphs."	18
"I really don't know."	15
"Leave me alone or I'll call a cop."	6

accidentally stumbled into our survey to give us the textbook definition: "**Economics** is the study of how society chooses to produce and distribute goods and services in a world of scarce resources." This really says a lot. Economics is about choices, choices that are made necessary because we live in a world of scarcity. Since we cannot have everything we must choose between competing alternatives. We need to decide how to use scarce resources (production choices) and who is to receive the fruits of the economic tree (the distribution choice). Economics helps us understand these choices and the **trade-offs** that are necessary whenever a choice must be made.

economics: a social science dealing with the production and distribution of goods and services in a world of scarcity.

trade-off: the situation where one good or goal must be given up to gain another.

Many of the students in our sample thought that economics is the study of business. This answer, while not as elegant as the professor's response, is also correct. In a **market economy,** like the United States, most of the production and distribution choices are made by individuals and business firms buying and selling goods in free markets. If people want video games instead of ballet, the market sends a message to business firms. The profits available in video games and the losses found in ballet production force private firms to re-allocate society's scarce resources. We use dollars to vote for what we want in the free market.

market economy: an economic system where production and distribution choices are made by individuals acting without government direction.

Basic economic decisions are made in a different way in a **command economy.** A command economy, like the USSR or the People's Republic of China, is one where fundamental economic decisions are made by a centralized group of planners, not by individual buyers and producers acting in their own self-interest. Needs and choices are determined by a central authority and businesses act merely to carry out the government's commands.

command economy: an economic system where production and distribution choices are made by central planners.

No economic system is entirely governed by either the market or by planners. Most countries really have some form of a **mixed economy** where some choices are made by individuals and others by government authorities. The real difference between market and command economies is less a matter of black and white than one of different shades of gray.

mixed economy an economic system where some choices are made by individuals and others are made by central planners.

Several of the students polled said that economics is the study of inflation and unemployment. This response is partially correct, too. Inflation and unemployment are the two most visible national economic problems. Much of this book is devoted to an analysis of the causes and cures of inflation and unemployment. This study is termed **macroeconomics.** It is an important part of economics but not all of it. Equally as important is **microeconomics,** the other side of the economic coin.

macroeconomics: the study of the functioning of the national economy.

microeconomics: the study of how individual economic choices are made, focusing on producers, consumers, and markets.

models: simplified descriptions of real-world processes that increase the understanding of the real world.

Some of the students responded that economics is just a bunch of charts and graphs. These poor folks must have already taken an economics course somewhere along the line. Economists love charts and graphs because economists love to use **models.** Economists use models to make the world more understandable (although you might not think so for awhile). A model is just a simplification. By taking a complex process and reducing it to its simplest forms, we gain a level of understanding that would not otherwise be possible. Sometimes less is more.

This book uses several models to examine how the national economy works. The first one is the market model of supply and demand that you will read about in the next chapter. Our models, because they are simplifications, cannot hope to embody all the detail of the real world. Something must be lost in the translation. However, we build on this simple framework, adding realism as we go along, until finally a simple but useful model of the national economy is constructed.

Macro- Versus Microeconomics

Microeconomics and macroeconomics are not two opposing schools of economics. They are simply two different ways of viewing economic events. Microeconomics focuses on individual decisions. Microeconomics asks questions such as: What determines the price of pizza? How many donuts should an individual bakery produce per week? How many engineers will be employed next year? How do consumers decide how much to spend and how much to save? The emphasis here is on individual choices, the factors that influence these choices, and the trade-offs that must be weighed.

Macroeconomics, on the other hand, looks at the broad issues of the national economy. Macroeconomics looks not so much at individual actions as at the combined consequences of those actions. Instead of asking how much an individual firm sells, macroeconomics looks at the total production of the economy. While microeconomics might be interested in what forces affect the price of pizza, macroeconomics is more concerned with those forces that affect many prices, that bring on inflation or deflation.

Macro- and microeconomics have much in common because they both look at the same scene, but they focus on different aspects of the landscape. Microeconomics examines the individual trees, macroeconomics looks at the health of the forest as a system. Each view is informative and important. This book concentrates on macroeconomics.

Macroeconomic Goals and Problems

Congress officially put the nation into the macroeconomics business when it passed the Employment Act of 1946. This Act set macroeconomic goals for the nation and made the federal government responsible for achieving these goals. The act reads:

> *The Congress hereby declares that it is the continuing policy and responsibility of the Federal Government to use all practicable means . . . to promote maximum employment, production and purchasing power.*

These goals are difficult to achieve and may be mutually exclusive. Nevertheless, we can restate these fundamental goals as:

GOAL 1: FULL EMPLOYMENT. The first aim of national economic policy is to attain high levels of employment (in other words, low unemployment rates). This is a difficult goal because unemployment is not a one-dimensional problem. The predicament of an out-of-work machinist is different from that of an unskilled laborer or a recent college graduate. Each is unemployed, but each suffers unemployment for a different reason. Unemployment is really many different problems, not just one; consequently, it requires many different solutions. We will look closely at unemployment and the goal of full employment in Chapter 3.

GOAL 2: ECONOMIC GROWTH. Full employment is a useless achievement if resources are not put to a productive use. The Great Depression make-work schemes (like digging holes and then filling them in again to give desperate workers a job) increase employment but add little to the economy. The economy must grow and production must rise, Congress tells us, if we are to sustain our level of economic well-being.

Economic growth is important, too, because it could be the best way to improve the economic position of low-income groups. Giving the poor a larger slice of the economic pie is easier when the pie itself is growing. Some must lose so that others may gain, however, in a stagnant or shrinking economy. Achieving economic growth in the long run means increasing the economy's ability to produce goods and services—increasing what we will later call aggregate supply. Much of this book concentrates on the problem of economic growth.

GOAL 3: STABLE PRICES. High employment and rising production mean little if inflation erodes our gains. Stable prices (that is, low inflation rates) are necessary to achieve maximum purchasing power.

Inflation is a serious problem because it affects us all. Inflation creates winners and losers and causes us to waste time trying to protect ourselves from its ravages. Inflation is all the more important because many of its consequences are hidden. Sure, we all see inflation at the grocery store or the gas pump. But this is only the tip of the iceberg and, like an iceberg, it is the part that you cannot see that can kill you. Inflation is discussed in detail in Chapter 4.

OTHER ECONOMIC GOALS. Congress expanded this list of economic goals with the Full Employment and Balanced Growth Act of 1978 (often called the Humphrey-Hawkins Bill). This act added new goals and spelled out strategies to use in achieving the old ones. The new goals this act introduced are important. They include a balanced federal government budget (in other words, government spending is not to exceed tax revenues) and an economy that is better able to compete in international markets. The act suggests that these goals be achieved by stimulating capital formation (through the construction of new factories and machines), providing full-employment opportunities for all, and reducing the presence of the federal government in the economy (through both fewer regulations and relatively less government spending). The act also charges the President with developing a plan for obtaining all of these goals.

real gross national product (RGNP): a measure of the total annual production in an economy, adjusted for inflation.

How well have we hit these economic targets? Let us look at the record. You can trace the course of economic history through Figure 1-1. This figure shows the **real gross national product (RGNP** is a measure of the total annual production for the economy). When this curve rises, incomes increase and jobs are created. When the curve falls, even a little, the result is increased poverty and millions made jobless! This is a little figure that means a lot!

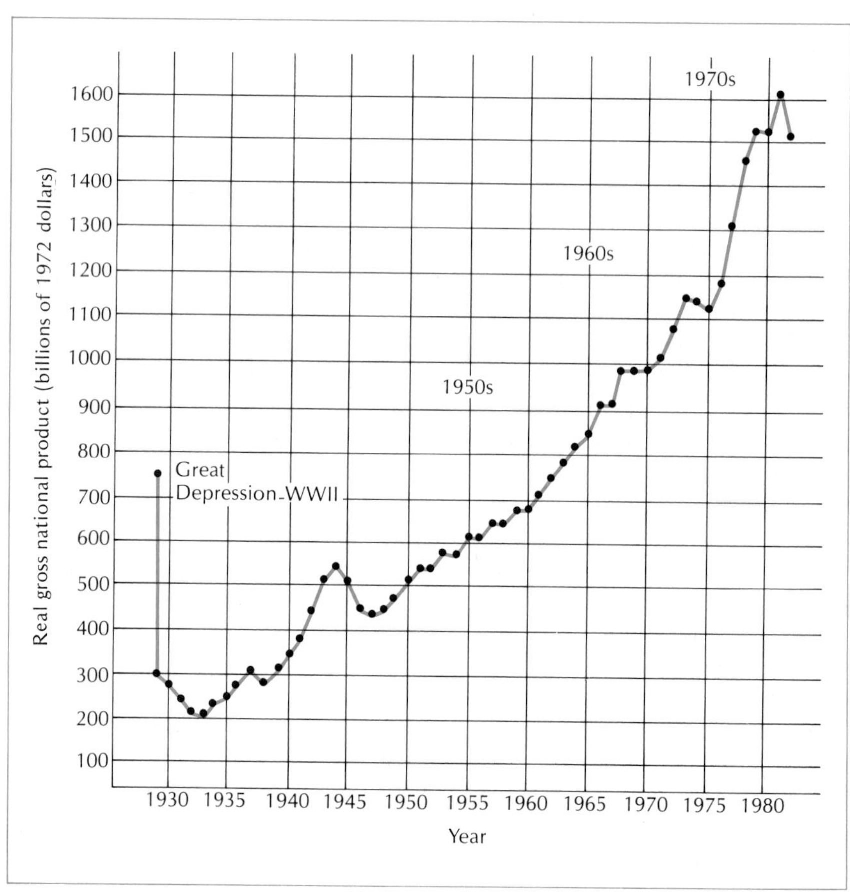

FIGURE 1-1 REAL GROSS NATIONAL PRODUCT, 1929–1982. Total production (measured in billions of 1972 dollars) increased dramatically over the period from 1929 through 1982, but not without periods of decline. The depression of the 1930s is clearly evident, as are the recessions of the 1940s, 1950s, 1970s, and 1980s. Only the decade of the 1960s provided uninterrupted economic growth.

The Great Depression

Our look at economic history begins in 1929. Despite a cushion of over 50 years, the year 1929 still brings to mind a vision of grief and desperation. Financial panic! Investors leaping from skyscrapers! Riots in the streets and on the stock exchange.

The year 1929 began the long period that we have come to call the Great Depression. Production in the United States fell by nearly a third between 1929 and 1933. The unemployment rate for the nation rose from just 4 percent to over 25 percent. Twenty-five percent!

The Great Depression is an important landmark for us because it was not until this time that macroeconomics was taken seriously by economists and policymakers. Before the Great Depression, many economists (the so-called classical economists) thought that prolonged severe unemployment was impossible in a market economy since any idle worker could always find a job by simply offering to work for a little less than the going rate. The national economy, economists thought, was pretty much self-regulating. Macroeconomics really did not even exist.

With the Great Depression came the realization that the economy was not automatically drawn to full employment. The British economist John Maynard Keynes (pronounced like "canes") invented a theory that said prosperity and poverty were equally likely in the absence of government action. Much of this book is based on the principles that Keynes expounded.

What caused the Great Depression? The causes are many and economists still debate them. It really took a combination of events to so shake the world economy. The stock market crash was part of the problem. Wall Street speculators had purchased millions of dollars of stock on credit. They planned to pay back the loans with profits from rising stock prices. This scheme had often worked during the 1920s. The only problem was that if their speculations did not pay off, they had nothing with which to pay back the loans. As stock prices began to fall in 1929, these "margin" buyers found that they had to unload piles and piles of stock to pay their debts. This made stock prices fall further, creating even more problems.

Falling stock prices meant that stock traders could not pay their debts. This pushed shaky banks over the brink. Nervous savers started bank "runs." Since the banks did not have enough money to pay off all their depositors, the banks themselves failed and closed.

People's stock was worthless. Their life savings were gone. So they tightened their belts and spent less on everyday goods. But as spending fell, even more workers were laid off. This created still more poverty, resulting in a vicious circle that lasted for several years. Unemployment rates hit new peaks and, with no one to buy, prices fell.

Bank failures and stock panic are not the only reasons for the Great Depression. Crop failures deprived the economy of a good deal of its income. And, in a grim move, nation after nation enacted steep barriers to international trade. These protectionist moves were supposed to keep the depression disease from spreading from one country to another. Alas, with less trade there were even fewer jobs than before and the Great Depression got even worse.

Herbert Hoover (the first economist-President) presided over this descent into the depression's depths. Popular belief has it that President Franklin D. Roosevelt was responsible for leading the nation out of these dark regions. Roosevelt closed the banks for seven days in 1933 so that they might reopen on a more solid footing. He gave the unemployed hope and what little confidence they could have that things might get better.

As is usually the case with popular beliefs, however, the view of Roosevelt as hero of the Depression is somewhat misleading. He continued and expanded many of the programs begun under Hoover and followed the policies of Keynes to a certain extent. But the activist role of government under Roosevelt was more modest than many remember. Congress and Roosevelt worked to keep a balanced federal budget (taking in as much in taxes as they spent) because they felt a sound government would inspire a sound economy. Most modern economists (following Keynes' theories) suggest that the government should run a budget deficit (spending more than is received from tax revenues) during depressions. Under this approach, higher government spending should be a substitute for lower private-sector purchases.

Under Roosevelt, unemployment fell, but idle workers still amounted to 13 percent of the labor force in 1937. The Great Depression did not go away overnight. Indeed, it might have lasted even longer had it not been for the unfortunately stimulative effects of the Second World War.

The 1940s: War and Inflation

The 1940s brought a different set of economic problems to the nation. Unemployment disappeared with the military activities of World War II, but inflation reared its ugly head. Virtually all workers not in the armed forces were employed producing guns, tanks, planes, and other goods. Real gross national product shot up as more and more goods came off the production line. Workers found themselves with lots of money to spend but little to buy, since most of the goods they produced went to the war effort. What little remained for civilian markets was quickly bought up at rapidly increasing prices. Scarce items, such as meat, gas, and tires, were in such short supply that the government instituted a system of rationing to handle the shortages.

Government price controls were imposed (economist John Kenneth Galbraith was head of the control agency) and people were issued coupons for meat and windshield stickers for gasoline that entitled them to purchase fixed amounts of these items. Rationing and price controls kept prices from rising as fast as before, but they left consumers with a pent up demand for consumer goods. When the war ended and controls were phased out, this demand made itself felt with the result of another bout of inflation in the late 1940s.

The 1950s: Business Cycles

The 1950s are full of interest to economists. The thirties and forties showed us that consistently too little spending or consistently too much spending spells trouble. The fifties showed us that the **business cycle** of boom followed by bust was not much better. You can see the business cycle at work in the ups and downs of RGNP in Figure 1-1. The overall trend of the 1950s was economic growth, but recessions interrupted to drive down RGNP in 1954 and again in 1958.

business cycle: periods of economic expansion followed by recession.

The business cycle is reflected in another set of economic statistics. Figure 1-2 shows the cycle of economic events by plotting the inflation rate in each year (measured on the vertical axis) against the corresponding unemployment rate (measured on the horizontal axis). By plotting each year in this way, we can see how the relationship between inflation and unemployment changed over this period.

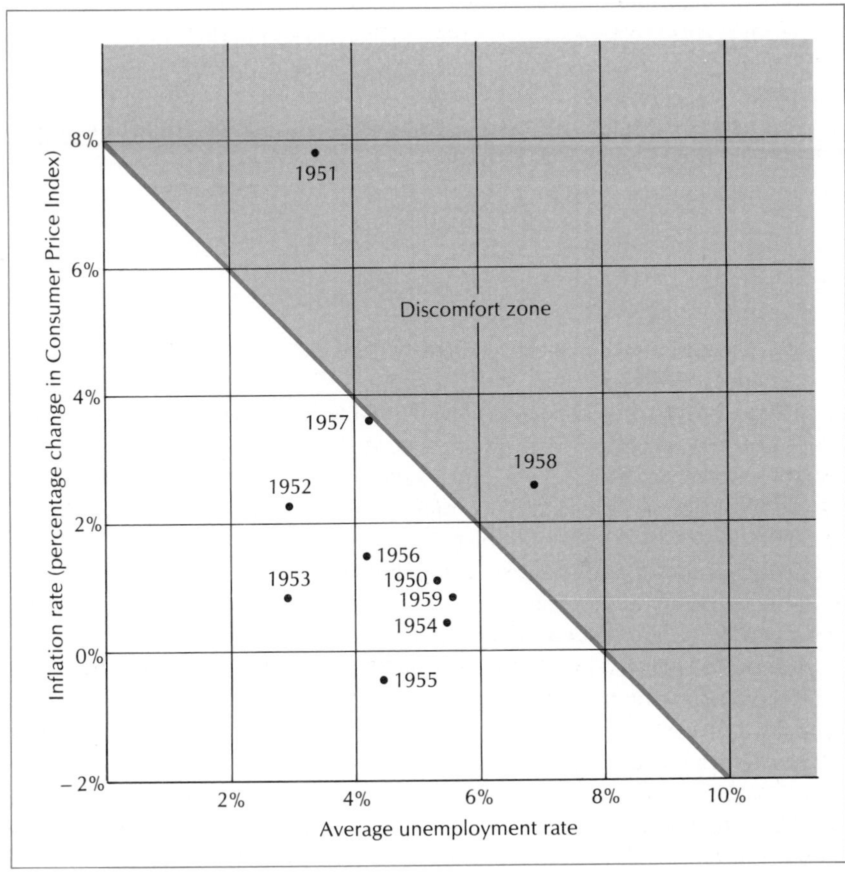

FIGURE 1-2 INFLATION AND UNEMPLOYMENT, 1950–1959. Unemployment was high during much of the 1950s, as the economy twice hit the bottom of the business cycle. Inflation was generally low (prices actually fell in 1955). The Economic Discomfort Index only entered the Discomfort Zone twice: in 1951 and 1958.

Economic Discomfort Index: a measure of the magnitude of national economic woes; the sum of the inflation and unemployment rates.

Economists use something called the **Economic Discomfort Index** to get an idea of how severe a nation's economic problems are. Meteorologists have a Weather Discomfort Index found by summing the temperature with the relative humidity—it tells you how "sticky" it is going to be. Similarly, the Economic Discomfort Index adds together the inflation and unemployment rates to give us a feel for how much "heat" economic storms generate.

Figure 1-2 is divided into two zones according to the value of the Economic Discomfort Index. The area beneath the diagonal line marks off an area of acceptable economic performance where the sum of the inflation and unemployment rates is less than 8 percent. This definition of "acceptable" is purely arbitrary and open to debate, but it does give us a convenient point of reference for the discussion that follows. The second area—the Discomfort Zone—indicates years when inflation and unemployment summed to more than 8 percent. When the economy moved into this range in the 1950s, the Discomfort Index was high enough to cause economic and political unrest.

Figure 1-2 shows that inflation was low and unemployment high during much of the 1950s. Twice, in 1951 and again in 1958, the economy moved into the Discomfort Zone. The cause in 1951 was the high inflation of the Korean War. The cure to bring inflation down to an acceptable level was a dose of wage and price controls. In 1958, a long steel strike created high levels of unemployment. The discomfort caused by this event did not completely disappear until well into the next decade.

The period of 1950–1959 was a time of cycles and uncertainty. The RGNP rose and fell. Inflation turned to unemployment as the economy moved in and out of the Discomfort Zone.

The 1960s: The New Economics

The 1960s present another picture entirely. The sixties were the longest period of sustained economic growth in U.S. history. Figure 1-3 shows that RGNP grew every year during the period from 1960 to 1969. The real gross national product grew by a total of over 46 percent during the decade. Production rose to satisfy a variety of wants. Consumer spending was high. Government spending on defense (for the Vietnam War) and social programs (John Kennedy's New Frontier followed by Lyndon Johnson's Great Society) grew at record rates. The unemployment rate fell to, and then below, the target of 4 percent.

The economy also managed to stay out of the Discomfort Zone for most of the decade. Economists thought that they were finally able to accurately apply Keynes' theories. The "New Economics" that they practiced was given credit for the growth and stability of the economy. Only in 1969—when the combination of high consumer, military, and social spending brought on high inflation—did the Discomfort Index exceed 8 percent. The stock market soared during this period and the Dow Jones average finally broke 1000.

Economic policymakers observed a peculiar phenomenon in the sixties. Take a pencil and roughly sketch a curved line through the points in Figure 1-3. Notice that most of the years fall close to this line. There appears to be a

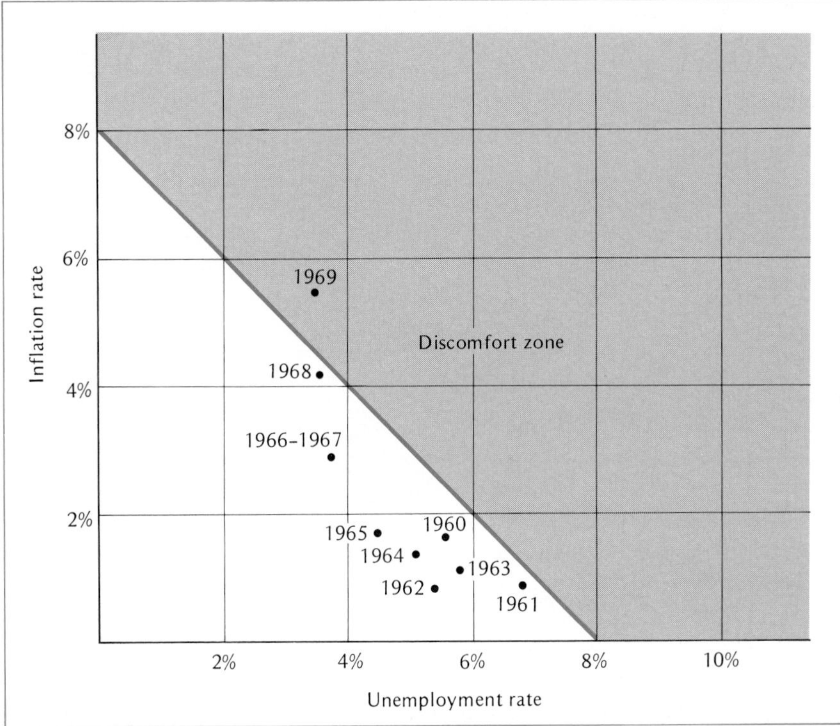

FIGURE 1-3 INFLATION AND UNEMPLOYMENT, 1960–1969. The 1960s demonstrated the trade-off between inflation and unemployment. The first half of the decade exhibited relatively high unemployment with moderate inflation. As the unemployment rate fell during the period from 1965 through 1969, the pace of inflation quickened.

stable inverse relationship between inflation and unemployment in the 1960s. This relationship (first noticed in the late 1950s) is called the **Phillips curve** after its discoverer, British economist A. W. Phillips.

Phillips curve: a curve showing an inverse relationship between inflation and unemployment rates.

The Phillips Curve

The Phillips curve, illustrated in Figure 1-4, suggests that there is a predictable short-run trade-off between inflation and unemployment in a modern economy. When you try to reduce unemployment, you cause inflation. But inflation can be fought by raising the unemployment rate.

The idea of the Phillips curve relationship, along with the evidence that it worked in the 1960s, gave policymakers the idea that they could fine tune the economy. Playing inflation against unemployment does not cure both economic problems, but it might assure us of only moderate levels of each. This might be an acceptable compromise, especially if rapid economic growth is part of the bargain. Figure 1-3 shows how well this idea worked during the 1960s. The economy slowly climbed up the Phillips curve—unemployment fell but inflation worsened—during most of the decade. The problems changed, but the Discomfort Zone was generally avoided.

Figures 1-3 and 1-4 tell us what the Phillips curve looks like, but they

FIGURE 1-4 THE 1960s PHILLIPS CURVE. The Phillips curve describes the inflation/unemployment trade-off that economists observed in the 1960s. Policymakers thought that they could "fine tune" the economy and avoid the Discomfort Zone by trading inflation for unemployment.

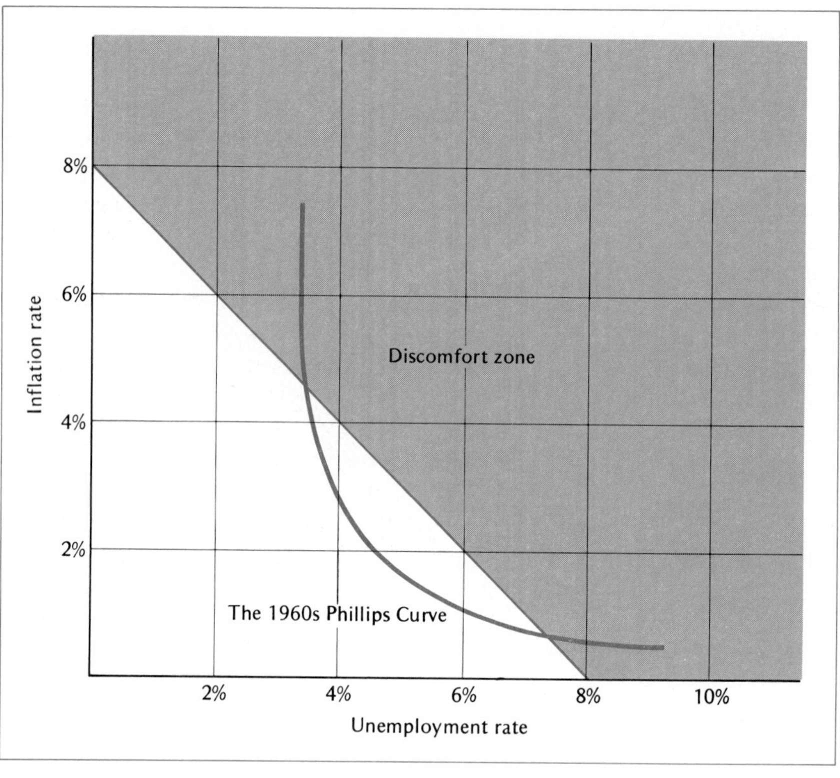

the 1960s? Was there some reason for this relationship between inflation and unemployment, or was it just an historical accident? There is a strong correlation between unemployment and sunspots, but that does not mean that sunspots cause unemployment or that unemployment causes sunspots. What is the theory behind the Phillips curve?

Economists disagree about both the Phillips curve and the theory behind it. We will talk more about this debate in future chapters, but for now let us look at just one possible explanation for the Phillips curve: the **wage-lag theory.** According to this theory, higher inflation rates reduce unemployment because of a surprise effect. When prices go up, this theory holds, wages generally lag behind for a few months or longer (until, for example, a new labor contract is negotiated). Higher selling prices and constant wage costs temporarily generate added profits for employers who greedily try to get even more by cranking up production and hiring more workers. Inflation, it follows, causes more people to be hired, reducing the unemployment rate.

wage-lag theory: an hypothesis concerning the cause of the Phillips curve that holds that inflation can temporarily increase business profits and so cause firms to increase employment.

If you believe in the wage-lag theory or some other explanation of the Phillips curve, then the higher and higher inflation rates of the 1960s logically bring with them reduced unemployment.

The 1970s: Stagflation

The 1970s spelled the end of blind faith in the Phillips curve. The 1970 **recession** proved that high inflation and high unemployment rates could occur simultaneously. The Economic Discomfort Index rose to levels not seen since 1951. High inflation rates refused to fall even in the face of heavy unemployment. President Richard Nixon responded to these problems by announcing a radical change in economic policy. His August 15, 1971, edict provided for a 90-day freeze of all wages and prices, followed by programs of wage and price controls. Many prices and wages could only be increased with federal government permission. These controls caused inflation to moderate during 1972, as Figure 1-5 shows, but did little to alter the public's expectations of inflation. When people expect inflation, they tend to get it (see Chapter 4 for more details on inflationary expectations). Inflation returned in 1973 at a rate of over 6 percent.

recession: a sustained period of declining production and income.

Stagflation, which is the combination of high unemployment and high inflation, hit the U.S. economy with full force in 1974. Many factors contributed to the rise of stagflation. The devaluation of the dollar made imported goods more expensive. Worldwide crop failures drove up the prices of agricultural products. And, not coincidentally, the Organization of Petroleum Exporting Countries (OPEC) boosted the world price of crude oil and imposed an embargo on oil shipments to the United States.

Stagflation: high inflation rates accompanied by high unemployment rates; a stagnant economy with inflation.

Any one of these events could shake up the economy. Taken together,

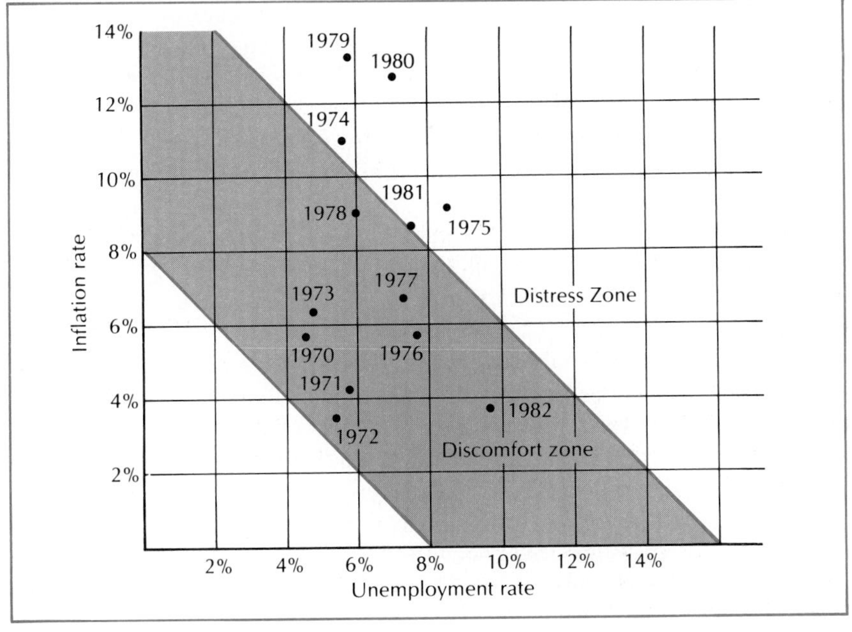

FIGURE 1-5 INFLATION AND UNEMPLOYMENT, 1960–1982. The Phillips curve seemed to disappear in the 1970s. Both inflation and unemployment rates increased. If you were to connect the dots in this picture, the result would be a confusing tangle. The Economic Discomfort Index zoomed repeatedly into the Distress Zone.

the result was nothing short of devastating. Prices rose and they kept rising to previously unseen heights. The Consumer Price Index jumped over 10 percent in 1974—into the dreaded "double-digit" range. As prices rose, consumers found that their incomes were not keeping pace with the price increases. Consumer purchasing power declined considerably and people cut back on spending. Cars were fixed up to last one more year. Heavy coats were made to last one more winter. Purchases of durable goods like freezers and furniture were also put off.

Industry sold fewer goods because of the spending cuts, so they laid off workers. Higher unemployment rates meant that even fewer goods and services were purchased, compounding the problem. In this instance, high prices caused recession, not the economic growth of the Phillips curve.

OPEC's actions in 1974 not only sent prices skyrocketing, they also caused physical shortages of oil and oil-related products. Long waits in line for gasoline were only a small part of the problem. Plants and factories were forced to shut down for lack of oil to use as an energy source or as raw material. Coal mines had to halt production because they did not have enough fuel to run mining equipment. At hospitals, some surgery was postponed or canceled because latex tubing (made from oil products) was not available. In 1974 America learned that it was a land of shortage and scarcity and this knowledge changed the economy.

The stagflation caused by rising prices coupled with physical shortage pushed the economy out of the Discomfort Zone and into the Distress Zone (going nearly into the Twilight Zone). The Economic Discomfort Index topped 20 percent in July, 1975. Something had to be done.

President Gerald Ford fought inflation with his Whip Inflation Now plan (everyone wore little WIN buttons for awhile) and hit back against unemployment with a tax rebate program that sent every taxpayer a $100 to $200 check. These programs helped a little, bringing the United States back into the Discomfort Zone, but the economy was still in a shaky condition.

The decade of scarcity continued under President Jimmy Carter. Carter's economic policies never seemed to get off the ground, but perhaps this was in part because the economic climate changed too much and too quickly during these years. Another oil crisis—this one triggered by Iran's seizure of American hostages—brought back the gas lines and pushed inflation rates in 1979 and 1980 to new heights. The inflation rate for 1979–1980 averaged more than 13 percent.

This period also brought with it a different kind of shortage and a presidential election. The shortage this time was not of oil but of money. The Federal Reserve System controls the availability of money and credit in the United States and, in October, 1979, the Fed (as it is affectionately called by bankers, bond traders, and other sentimental types) put a lid on loans for the economy. People who could not get loans to buy cars or build houses simply did not buy cars or build houses. While this policy might deserve credit for the subsequent decline in the inflation rate, it might also deserve the blame for the rise in unemployment that followed.

What Happened to the Phillips Curve?

The comfortable policy recommendations of the 1960s Phillips curve seemed to stop working for much of the 1970s. What happened to the Phillips curve, anyway? There are many possible explanations, but let us consider just two of them to get a feel for how the economy changed during the 1970s and how that change affected macroeconomics.

One theory for the disappearing Phillips curve holds that the 1970s gave us a new kind of inflation. The inflation of earlier days, the argument goes, was an inflation of prosperity. People had higher incomes and they used the money to buy more goods and services. All this spending created even more prosperity (as factories hired more workers to meet rising demand), but it also bid up prices (in the next chapter, we will refer to this situation as "demand-pull" inflation). These rapid increases in spending generate the Phillips curve phenomenon observed in the 1960s.

The inflation of the 1970s was caused by scarcity, not prosperity. With oil—then oil and credit—scarce, prices pushed up, forcing consumers to cut back spending. This "cost-push" inflation gives us both inflation and unemployment. The Phillips curve formula breaks down.

A second explanation of the Phillips curve's demise is based on the wage-lag theory discussed a few pages ago. This theory suggests that wages tend to lag behind price increases, generating short-term profits that encourage businesses to hire more workers. This explanation of the Phillips curve only holds, however, if wages do, in fact, lag behind prices—if inflation is a surprise. If workers are sophisticated about inflation, the Phillips curve stops working. Workers negotiate higher and higher wage increases in anticipation of higher prices at the grocery store and gas pump. Wages no longer lag behind prices. Indeed, it might work the other way, forcing business firms to lay off workers if prices do not rise fast enough to cover contractual wage increases.

The Phillips curve is down, but it is not out. It is easy to find phantom Phillips curves in the 1970s (look, for example, at the period of 1977–1980 in Figure 1-5). The only thing clear here is that there is more going on than just the Phillips curve. The trade-off between inflation and unemployment is not as clearly defined as economists once thought.

The 1980s and Beyond

Ronald Reagan became the second U.S. president with an economics degree (of course, he went to college a *loooong* time ago). President Reagan pledged to fight both inflation and unemployment through a "supply-side" policy that would stimulate economic growth and balance the budget. In short, he promised to achieve all economic goals at once. Reagan's record is mixed. Inflation has been stopped dead in its tracks but at the price of much higher unemployment rates and falling RGNP. And the budget is as far from being balanced as it has ever been. The economy moved back into the Distress Zone in 1981. President Reagan is fond of sports stories, so let us compare him to a baseball player. He has picked four goals and has managed to hit only one of them. It is still too early in the season to draw firm conclusions, but a .250 batting average is not going to get him into the Hall of Fame!

The economy is not so easy to manage as it once was. The magic formula of the Phillips curve has lost its sure power. Consumers, investors, and workers are more sophisticated. They hedge, act, and react in response to news, expectations, and government policies. The international economy is more important than at any previous time. What happens in Tokyo, Bonn, or Tehran affects us in Tulsa, Boston, and Tacoma. Inflation and unemployment are both serious problems that will not line up to be handled one at a time. Political decisions about the economy are even more difficult to make after a decade of declining purchasing power.

Macroeconomics in the 1980s and beyond is the study of a complicated and interrelated world trying to achieve goals that may be mutually inconsistent. Stagflation is the enemy and understanding is our best weapon. It is in this setting that our study begins.

ECONOMIC CONTROVERSY:

Another Great Depression?

The 1930s taught economists, politicians, management, and labor that a modern economy is not immune to severe economic problems. Catastrophic levels of unemployment are possible. Nothing automatically assures full employment. The economy has experienced several smaller economic downturns in the fifty-odd years since the Great Depression, but none of these recessions has been as devastating as the disaster of the 1930s.

Can we manage prosperity? Is another Great Depression possible? Is it likely? Can it be avoided? These are questions that economists have often debated. In these Economic Controversy sections we will look at both sides of important economic issues and then leave it to you, the reader, to make up your own mind.

Is another Great Depression around the corner? Let us look at both sides of the controversy.

The Coming Bust

Here is how many people see this issue: Cycles of boom and bust may not be inevitable, but they have been a frequent landmark on the economic scene. Recession has been as frequent a visitor as prosperity, except in war years. A major depression in the future is likely. There are many reasons for this view.

Economic policy in the United States practically invites a Depression. The President, Congress, and the Federal Reserve's decision makers are just reactors, not actors. They do not take actions designed to influence coming economic events. Instead, they wait until problems are upon us and then try to fight the latest fire with short-term policies. This creates a dangerous policy lag. Instead of taking actions to prevent inflation, for example, the President waits until inflation is rampant and then tries to push the economy into a recession to get rid of it. When the recession hits, Congress tries to spend its way out of it, causing a renewed burst of inflation. This gives us the boom-bust cycle that has become so familiar in recent years.

Recently the booms and busts have gotten bigger. The dizzying inflation rates of 1979 and 1980 were followed by the frightening recessions of 1981 and 1982. We are riding an increasingly unstable roller coaster of economic policy. It is only a matter of time until it jumps the tracks, tossing the economy into the void of hyperinflation, the dungeon of mass unemployment, or, more likely, an economic black hole combination of the two.

If this scenario is not enough to make you nervous, recent economic events (calls for balanced budgets, protectionist moves to keep cheap imports out of the country) mirror, in many ways, the events that helped launch the Great Depression of the 1930s.

It would not take much to push this unstable economy over the brink, and there are many forces pushing. OPEC almost did it in the 1970s. Even a tiny country like Iran seems able to thoroughly disrupt the big U.S. economy. What is next? Will it be the last straw?

Another Great Depression is our historical fate. The Russian economist Nikolai Kondratieff discovered a 50-year cycle of massive boom and bust in the capitalist world. The Kondratieff Long Wave is just now reaching its bottom—exactly 50 years after the last big bust. Is the capitalist system doomed to massive depression every 50 years? Nothing in today's headlines suggests otherwise!

A final reason for believing that depression is just around the corner is that inflation is still a major economic problem. Inflation presents two dangers. First, governments are tempted to throw the economy into recession to fight price increases. Who knows how deep this Phillips curve recession could be? If inflation is left unchecked, however, depression is still likely. Inflation has a tendency to feed on itself, eventually becoming hyperinflation where prices double or triple in a single year. When inflation is left to compound rapidly, money becomes worthless, making work a fruitless exercise. With no incentive to produce, the economy could quickly reach a critical mass and literally explode. It has happened before in other countries and it is not unreasonable to suppose that it could happen again here.

Does anyone take these arguments seriously? You bet! The *New York Times'* best-sellers list is frequently crowded with books telling readers how to save themselves from the coming bust. Buy land, they say. And gold, too (since paper money will not be worth anything). Build a cabin in the hills full of gold and guns and grits and move to it when the economic world falls apart. If we can judge what America thinks by what it reads, then this is the future.

We Can Manage Prosperity

If the first speaker in this debate has succeeded in frightening you, perhaps you should read on to hear the other side of the issue. The prophets of gloom and doom are wrong. To paraphrase Mark Twain, the rumors of the economy's death are much exaggerated. We can manage prosperity, and there is no reason to believe that another Great Depression is on the way.

We should not judge our ability to meet today's economic problems by what happened in the 1930s. Economic policies were flawed then, but we have learned from them. We have read our history books and need not repeat past errors.

We are now better able to deal with economic ills. Economists these days have more sophisticated tools to diagnose economic diseases. Econometric computer models of the nation tell us in advance what is going to happen and how economic policy will work so that we can deal with problems before they reach critical mass.

You do not have to look far to see that the economy has learned from the Depression experience. Many government programs have been enacted that automatically work during hard times to prevent them from becoming worse. Bank accounts are now insured by government agencies, making bank runs a thing of the past. We have social security payments for the elderly, unemployment benefits for the jobless, and welfare payments for the poor. All sorts of social programs are on the books now that did not exist in the 1930s. These "automatic stabilizer" government programs adapt quickly to changing economic circumstances and thus dramatically reduce the odds of another Great Depression.

The growth of government is itself an argument against a repeat of economic collapse. More and more workers are now employed in more recession-proof government jobs. This firm base of safe jobs helps protect the entire economy against mass unemployment.

Sure, it's easy to criticize economic policy. Our economic system is not perfect; it is not fail-safe by any means. But it is unlikely to plunge us into another Great Depression. Economic doomsayers do not give policymakers enough credit for knowing what they are doing. Neither do they give the economy enough credit for its inherent stability. Our economy is strong and growing. Even if policymakers were as ignorant as the doomsters suggest, the strength of the economy would probably prevail anyway.

In any case, it is hard to believe a Great Depression is just around the corner when people are able to spend $20 on books that tell them how hard life is. That looks more like a sign of prosperity!

SUMMARY

1. Economics is the study of how society chooses to allocate scarce resources to the production and distribution of goods and services.

2. Macroeconomics studies the way that the national economy works. Microeconomics looks at how individual economic decisions are made. Both approaches examine the same activities, but from different perspectives.

3. Macroeconomics became important during the Great Depression of the 1930s. Crops, banks, and the stock market all failed at once. Nations erected high trade barriers to keep depression out, but these barriers only ended up making the calamity that much worse. Unemployed people who had less spent less, so unemployment rose even more.

4. The Employment Act of 1946 set three national economic goals: full employment, stable prices, and economic growth. The Full-Employment and Balanced Growth Act of 1978 expanded this list of economic goals to include a balanced federal-government budget and a competitive position in international trade. These goals are interrelated and difficult to achieve.

5. The economy's track record has not been good. Recessions have reduced growth rates and caused high unemployment. Inflation has become more, not less, of a problem over the years. Stagflation—the cold combination of inflation plus unemployment—has moved the economy even farther from the goals Congress set in 1946.

6. The Phillips curve shows a historical relationship between inflation and unemployment that held in the 1960s. Unemployment rates were reduced but at the cost of increasing rates of inflation. Many theories exist to explain this inverse relationship.

7. The Phillips curve failed to predict the events of the 1970s and 1980s. Outside forces and changing inflation expectations explain some of the stagflation that prevailed during this period.

DISCUSSION QUESTIONS

1. The major U.S. political parties have developed stereotypes over the years. Many people think that Democrats are most concerned with fighting unemployment, even if this means causing a little inflation, and that Republicans want to keep inflation rates down, even if this means living with higher unemployment rates. Are these stereotypes justified? Use the data supplied in this chapter to explain your reasoning.

2. The Economic Controversy debated the likelihood of another Great Depression. Briefly summarize the arguments on each side of this issue and then state which side you agree with and why. If another Great Depression is coming, are you prepared for it? What should you do now to prepare for a future bust?

3. What is happening to the economy today? What is the inflation rate? What is the unemployment rate? Is RGNP rising or falling? Use the resources of your library to find out.

4. Where can you go to find out what is happening to the economy? Make a list of publications available at your library that discuss economic events and list economic statistics.

5. Who are the "policymakers" that this chapter talks so much about? What offices do they hold? What are their political and economic philosophies?

6. What economic policy does the President support? Are these policies designed to fight inflation or unemployment?

TEST YOURSELF

Choose the best response to each of the following questions. The Answer Key is in the back of the book.

1. Economics is the study of how production and distribution choices are made. Which of the following events would be studied in a class on macroeconomics but not in a class on microeconomics?

(X) an increase in the inflation rate
(Y) an increase in the price of pork and beans
(Z) an increase in the employment of auto mechanics

a. all of the above
b. none of the above
c. only (X) above
d. (Y) and (Z) above
e. only (Z) above

2. People have suggested many possible causes for the Great Depression. Which of the following is NOT listed as a cause of this economic calamity?

a. bank failures
b. hyperinflation in the United States during the 1930s
c. agricultural problems in the United States
d. rapid decrease in the price of stock shares
e. establishment of trade barriers between nations

3. The Phillips curve guided economists during the 1960s. Which of the following statements best describes the policy implications of the Phillips curve?

a. unemployment can only be fought by reducing inflation
b. employment increases as unemployment falls
c. any policy that increases inflation also increases unemployment
d. if you want to put the economy back to work you must first bring down the inflation rate
e. none of these statements describes the Phillips curve relationship

4. The classical economists did not think that mass unemployment was possible. Which of the following statements best summarizes their reasoning on this topic:

a. the government can always step in to solve any problem before it gets too large
b. the economy has many automatic stabilizers that prevent catastrophe
c. unemployed workers can always find work if they are willing to accept a lower wage
d. any of the above statements correctly states the classical view
e. none of the above statements correctly states the classical view.

5. This chapter's Economic Controversy looked at the possibility of another Great Depression. Which of the following statements correctly summarizes an argument in support of the view that another bust is coming?

(X) economic policymakers are reactors, not actors, thus they make boom–bust swings even worse
(Y) inflation is even more of a problem today, so government-induced recessons may bring on a depression
(Z) outside forces like OPEC can easily push an already unstable economy over the brink into depression

a. all of the above are correct
b. none of the above are correct
c. only (X)
d. only (Z)
e. both (X) and (Y)

SUGGESTIONS FOR FURTHER READING

If you are interested in economics you need to begin a daily reading program to keep up with changing events. What should you read? Start with a good daily newspaper. The *New York Times, Washington Post, Chicago Tribune,* and *Wall Street Journal* all provide excellent reports and analyses of economic events. Weekly magazines like *Time, Newsweek,* and the British *The Economist* are good sources, too. Of this list, the author especially recommends *The New York Times, Wall Street Journal,* and *The Economist* for solid analysis of current events.

The periodicals listed above are all good sources. Here are some others. The Council of Economic Advisors' *Economic Report of the President* comes out each year in January. It presents current statistics, the "official" analysis of current problems, and the President's plan for dealing with them. A different view is often presented in the Brookings Institution's *Setting National Priorities.* This thoughtful reaction to the President's plans usually appears in May or June. The Federal Reserve's perspective is published in its monthly *Federal Reserve Bulletin.* Martin Feldstein has edited a good analysis of current conditions: *The American Economy in Transition* (Boston: Houghton Mifflin Company, 1980). Are we heading for another great depression? See Benjamin J. Stein's "A Scenario for a Depression?" *New York Times Magazine* (February 28, 1982).

2

SUPPLY AND DEMAND

Preview

What is a market? What role do markets play in the economy?
What determines the demand for a good?
What determines the supply of a good?
What determines the price of a good?
Why do prices change?
Are price controls a good thing?

THE BEAUTY of economics lies in its simplicity. It is at once simple and sophisticated. How is this possible? Have you ever played with Tinker Toys, Lincoln Logs, Legos, or an Erector Set? All of these toys are built on the principle that complex structures can be formed from simple parts and a few rules of construction. This chapter introduces the building blocks of economics, supply and demand, and shows you how to use them to describe and analyze modern problems.

Supply and demand occupy a central place in economics. This was demonstrated by the Central Intelligence Agency in the early 1970s. Informed sources report that the CIA, in an attempt to gain an advantage in the international espionage game, decided to enlist the forces of economics on their side (the CIA naturally denies this). Economics is so important, they reasoned, that it would be a great advantage to know in advance what would happen to the economics of the world. Toward this end, they bought an extremely powerful electronic computer and set it up, behind a curtain of secrecy, inside the Purdue University football stands.

There, surrounded by security guards, CIA agents fed the computer the economic wisdom of the centuries. Adam Smith, Keynes, Friedman, Samuelson, Laffer—all of their profound thoughts (and some that were not so profound) were carefully programed into the huge electronic memory.

How did the CIA's plan work? We must report that it was a failure. When all of the wisdom of the economics profession had been pumped into the computer, the room was cleared and a single figure typed in the fateful question, "What makes the economy run?" The computer burped, wheezed, and blinked for an hour and then printed out "Demand and Supply always apply." It whizzed for a minute more and then added "On the other hand, it might be Supply and Demand!"

The computer was a true economist. It not only had the economists' knowledge that supply and demand underlie just about everything, it had also picked up the personality quirk of finding more than one answer to each question. (This "on the other hand" comment is so common among economists that President Harry S. Truman once complained that what he needed most was a one-handed economist!) By the end of this chapter you will have both a working knowledge of supply and demand and an understanding of why economists insist on finding hard answers to simple questions.

The Market

market: the general term for institutions where goods and services are exchanged.

A **market** is a place where goods or services are exchanged. We are all actively involved in markets. When you buy, sell, or trade you participate, probably without thinking about it, in market activities. You purchase food, drink, clothing, and the like in markets for goods and services. You find a place to live through participation in the housing market. When you open a bank account or obtain a student loan you enter the credit market.

The term "market" is not meant to suggest some specific place where buyers and sellers meet to make exchanges. This traditional use of the term is derived from the medieval custom of farmers to come to town once a week. The market was the name of the place where buyers and sellers met. Markets still exist as meeting places. Many cities have farmers' markets and the stock market is located on Wall Street in New York. "Market" is used here in a broader sense, however. The market is the collection of all transactions (exchanges) of a particular good, whenever and wherever they take place.

The basic emotions of the market are conflict and competition. Conflict arises because buyers and sellers have different ends in mind. Buyers want to get the most for the least. Their interests are served by low prices and abundant goods. Sellers have just the opposite end in mind. They wish to sell their wares but at the highest possible price. Buyers and sellers battle each other over price, but their conflict is friendly because neither could survive without the other.

Both buyers and sellers also face competition. A seller who asks too high a price finds that customers have all gone elsewhere. Buyers who hold out for too big a bargain find themselves empty-handed as others, who are willing to pay a little more, snap up the goods.

The market makes these forces of conflict and competition work. Price is the market's medium of communication. Falling prices signal producers to shift their efforts to other lines. Rising prices give firms the message that buyers want more, while telling the buyers that supplies are short. The market sends these messages, and thousands of individual buyers and sellers—working with no central plan other than their individual self-interest—somehow manage to match up the goods with the people who want to buy them. The market is magical in its ability to bring buyers and sellers together and the magic is all the more real because people perform this trick without external direction.

The Idea of Demand

Demand is the easiest side of the market for most of us to see because we spend a lot of time buying things. Demand to an economist is a description of how people feel about the things that they buy and how those feelings determine how much of any particular good they want to buy. Your demand for French fries depends on a lot of things including your age, your family background, and the amount of advertising to which you have been exposed. Since demand is such a big idea, it is more digestible if we break it down into smaller bites. Your demand for French fries and other goods depends on many things, but this list of five determinants covers most of the important ideas:

demand: the buyer side of the market: a description of the kinds and amounts of goods people want to buy.

1. PRICE. How you feel about French fries depends a great deal on how

inverse relationship: the relationship between A and B when A and B consistently move in opposite directions.

substitution effect: buying more of a relatively cheaper good due to a price change.

income effect: a change in buying that results from changing purchasing power.

much those greasy potato fingers cost. There is usually an **inverse relationship** between price and the amount of an item demanded. Low prices encourage greater purchases, while higher price drive buyers away.

The inverse relation between price and the quantity demanded is the result of two powerful forces. When the price of one good rises, buyers typically seek out lower priced alternatives. This **substitution effect** is at work all around us. When the price of coffee jumps, smart grocers know that they will sell less coffee but more tea. Rising prices also unleash an **income effect.** If you spend more on coffee, you have less income left over to buy other items. Higher coffee prices end up affecting your whole shopping list. If McDonald's cuts the price of French fries, however, they can count on you spending a little more on burgers, shakes, and fruit pies.

Higher prices both reduce purchasing power (income effect) and drive you to buy cheaper alternatives (substitution effect). Lower prices affect demand in just the opposite ways. The inverse relationship between price and the amount that people want to buy does not always hold, however. Sometimes people desire things because they are expensive and, therefore, are a mark of higher status. Economist and sociologist Thorstein Veblen called this "conspicuous consumption." Purchases of these types of "Veblen goods" (for example, some kinds of designer clothing) might actually fall if the price came down.

direct relationship: the relationship between A and B, when A and B consistently move in the same direction.

negative income effect: purchases of some goods vary inversely with income.

substitutes: goods that perform the same function.

2. INCOME. Demand depends a lot on income. You cannot spend what you do not have (although Visa and Mastercard make this statement less true than it once was). There is usually a **direct relationship** between income and desired purchases. Spending on most goods rises and falls with consumer income.

There are exceptions to every rule, and some goods experience a **negative income effect.** Beans, for example, are purchased less frequently as income rises. Beer sales traditionally rise during recessions as drinkers shift from scotch and bourbon to Miller and Bud. Most goods and services are "normal," however, in that the quantity demanded rises and falls directly with income.

3. PRICES OF OTHER GOODS. We have already noted that the way you feel about one product depends on how much the alternatives cost. The prices of other goods and services are an important part of demand.

Some items can be classified as **substitutes.** Substitutes satisfy the same want, desire, or need. Coffee, tea, milk, and soda can all be considered substitute beverages to a certain extent (although coffee drinkers might not want to substitute Pepsi for milk in their morning coffee!). Fords, Chevrolets,and Toyotas are all substitute forms of transportation.

The demand for a good generally varies directly with the price of its substitute. Demand for Pepsi falls when Coke is on sale, for example, because people switch from one cola to the other. Sales of margarine increase when butter's price goes up. This cross-switching among goods is strongest for items that are the most alike and weakest among imperfect substitutes.

complements: goods that are used together.

Other goods are **complements.** Complements are goods that are used together to satisfy some want or need. The list of complementary items is long: bread and butter, bacon and eggs, beer and pizza, pencils and erasers, economics books and headache remedies. You can fill in your own favorites. Because complements are used together, the desire for them rises and falls together.

Merchants often try to take advantage of complements in pricing decisions. Stores cut the price of one item (like wall paint, for example) in the hope of selling more of the complements (brushes, rollers, and other painting supplies) at their regular prices.

The idea of complements is not difficult, but sometimes we discover complements in unexpected places. Big Macs and gasoline have all the characteristics of complements, for example. Nobody consumes them together ("Give me a burger and a glass of unleaded regular."). But when gasoline prices hit the ceiling in 1979, sales at hamburger stores fell. Why? It turns out that most people jump in the car when they visit fast-food stores. Higher gasoline prices meant that Big Mac Attacks were more costly and Ronald McDonald suffered.

4. TASTES AND PREFERENCES. The idea of demand is closely linked to our needs and desires. Demand changes when tastes and preferences shift. Tastes and preferences often change only gradually. Blue jeans, for example, were once worn mostly by cowboys and workmen who needed their strength and durability. Blue jeans slowly gained acceptance among social and economic groups that had previously shunned them. Jeans finally became a uniform for young people and even appeared in the White House on both Presidents Carter and Reagan. Designer jeans became status symbols—fancy pants covered the bottoms of trendy people who had never worn jeans before.

Tastes sometimes change rapidly, too. "Preppy" clothes used to be worn by east-coast prep-school types who suffered a strange attraction to khaki, Top-Siders, and the colors pink and green. The preppy look suddenly became fashionable on college campuses around the country in the early 1980s. Alligators and ducks were everywhere to be seen.

The sudden popularity of video games also shows how quickly tastes can change. Primitive Pong games were a minor obsession just a few years ago. Since then video games have attracted millions of dollars, one quarter at a time. Demand shifts rapidly from one game to another, too. The once popular Asteroids and Space Invaders games gave way to Pac Man and Donkey Kong, which were themselves soon replaced by other favorites. Keeping up with changing preferences has kept this entire industry on its toes.

Tastes and preferences are so important to demand that businesses spend billions of dollars on advertising and promotion to either change your tastes (so that you will buy their brand instead of some other) or so that your "brand loyalty" will be able to resist the advertising of others. Why do you buy the things that you do? How have you developed your tastes and preferences?

5. EVERYTHING ELSE. Everything else? Sure! There is a whole world of things that affect demand for the products that you buy and not buy. Weather is a big Everything Else, for example. The demands for umbrellas, snow shovels, suntan oil and frisbees all depend on the weather in obvious ways. Your economics professor is another example of an Everything Else. The amounts and kinds of textbooks, tutorial help, midnight oil (for burning while studying for an exam) and No-Doz tablets you demand all depend, in part, on the punishment your professor decides to inflict on you. Everything depends on everything else and this old adage is nowhere more appropriate than when studying the economics of demand.

The Demand Curve

demand curve: a graph showing the relationship between quantity demand and the price of the good.

So far we have taken the simple idea of people wanting to buy things and looked at five different reasons why this behavior could change. Now it is time to put this knowledge to use. But before we use all this information we will have to simplify it again. We can do this with the graphical tool of the **demand curve.**

The demand curve is a map of the way that desired purchases change when the price of an item changes (everything else that could affect demand is temporarily held constant). A hypothetical demand curve for apples is shown in Figure 2-1. Price per apple is measured along the vertical axis and the quantity demanded along the horizontal.

Where does the demand curve come from? You could build one, if you wanted to. Suppose that you asked everyone in your county to list the number of apples that they would be willing to buy this week at ten cents each? At twenty cents? At thirty cents? If you added up all their responses, you would have the same information the demand curve gives. The apple demand curve exists whether such a poll is taken or not because the behavior behind the demand curve is there.

The demand curve in Figure 2-1 shows that 1000 apples are demanded at a price of ten cents. Consumers only want to buy 500 apples if the price rises to twenty cents, holding income, tastes, and everything else constant. Consumers move along the demand curve, asking for a smaller quantity, when the price rises. Only 300 apples are demanded if the price rises again to thirty cents. Substitution and income effects are at work here. Higher apple prices

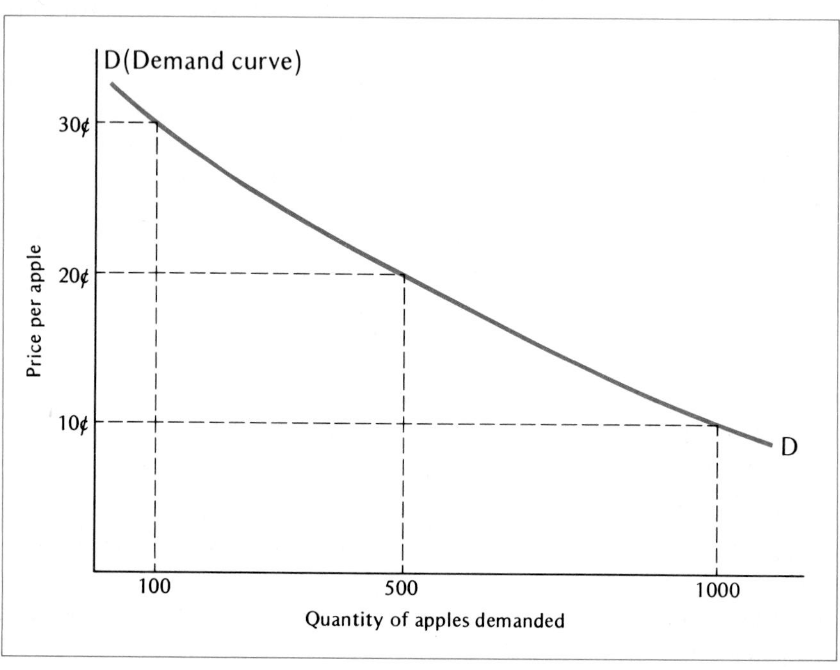

FIGURE 2-1 A DEMAND CURVE FOR APPLES. The amount of apples people want to buy depends on the price of apples. As price rises from 10 cents to 30 cents, a smaller quantity of apples is demanded.

mean that buyers are not able to buy as many apples and that they will buy substitute fruits instead. The quantity demanded, subject to both forces, falls as price goes up.

Shifts in Demand

So far all the demand curve has done is sit there on the page. We have slid up the demand curve by changing prices. In doing this we have held constant the variety of other things that influence the amount of apples people want to buy. What happens when something else—like income or tastes or the price of substitutes and complements—changes? What happens to the demand curve then?

The demand curve only shows one thing: the way that the quantity demanded changes when price changes. A change in price results in a *movement along the curve* to a different amount of desired purchases. A change in anything else *shifts the entire demand curve* because it changes the price versus quantity relationship. You will get this idea quicker through an example.

The only demand curve we have seen so far has been for apples, so let us think about apples for a moment. What sorts of events might alter the way you feel about apples? For the purpose of analysis, divide these nonprice shifters into two categories: those that make you want to buy more apples and those that lead you to buy less of them.

increase in demand: an increase in the quantity demanded at each price; shift to the right in the demand curve.

An **increase in demand** is the economist's term for anything that makes you want to buy more apples even if their price does not fall. Figure 2-2 shows how such a change in buying behavior is graphed. Something has happened here to change the way that buyers feel about apples. Before the change they wanted 500 apples at a price of twenty cents. Price has not changed, but the demand has. Now 700 apples would be needed to satisfy demand at twenty cents. We show this change in behavior by shifting the demand curve out and to the right from D_0 to D_1 until the new curve accurately maps the changed buying patterns. The notations D_0 and D_1 stand for demand at "time zero"—before any changes—and the new demand; D_2 would indicate a second change in demand, and so on.

What causes the demand increase depicted in Figure 2-2? Any event that makes people want to buy more apples at each price would result in an increase in demand. Here are some examples:

- the incomes of apple eaters increase;
- pear prices rise (pears are an apple substitute);
- cheddar cheese cheapens (sharp cheddar is a good complement for a ripe apple);
- medical researchers discover that an apple a day really does keep the doctor away;
- apple growers sponsor a successful "eat more apples" advertising campaign.

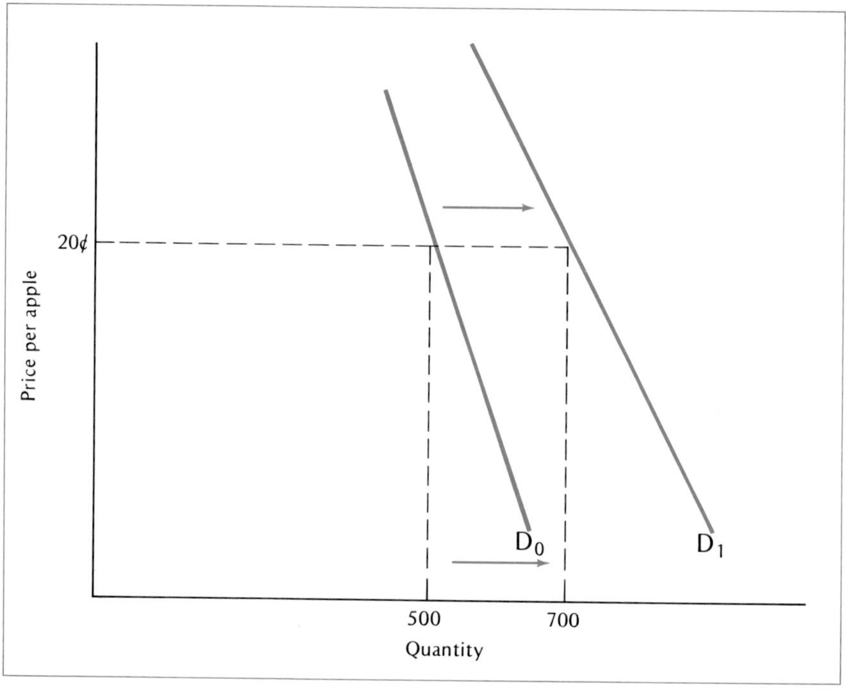

FIGURE 2-2 INCREASE IN DEMAND. Demand increases whenever something other than a change in price causes buyers to desire greater quantities of a good. Demand increases are shown by a shift to the right in the demand curve.

decrease in demand: a decrease in the quantity demanded at each price; shift to the left in the demand curve.

Demand falls when goods become less desirable. A **decrease in demand** is shown in Figure 2-3 as a shift back and to the left in the apple demand curve (the curve shifts from D_0 to D_2). Now only 300 apples are bought at a twenty cent price. Why would demand fall like this? A decrease in apple demand might be caused by the fact that:

- many apple eaters become unemployed;
- oranges and peaches suddenly become cheaper;
- inflation hits the bakery: flour, butter, sugar, and cinnamon (ingredients in apple pie) are more expensive, so fewer apples are needed;
- someone starts a rumor that apples cause constipation;
- a fad that involves eating prunes instead of apples (perhaps inspired by the above rumor) sweeps the country.

The demand curve, as you have just seen, does a good job of illustrating events on the apple market. When people suddenly get a craving for apples, the demand curve shifts out (an increase in demand) to show it. If people find some reason to avoid apples, the demand curve shifts back (a decrease in demand). When the only thing that changes is the price of apples themselves, however, the demand curve does not shift, we simply slide along the curve from one point on it to another. A change in price does not change *demand* (shift the demand curve), it just changes the *quantity demanded* (a movement along the demand curve).

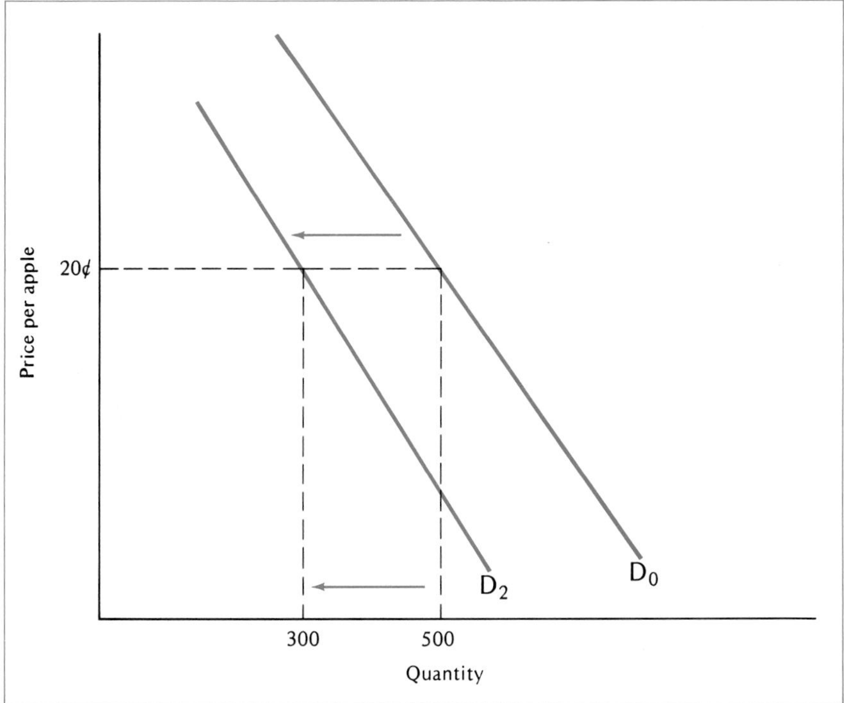

FIGURE 2-3 DECREASE IN DEMAND. Demand falls whenever something besides changes in price causes consumers to be less willing to purchase a good. A shift to the left shows a decrease in demand.

Demand and the demand curve are descriptions of what buyers would like to do. The demand curve shows the amounts of intended purchases at various prices. But it does not guarantee that anyone is willing to sell these quantities. To find this out we need to look at demand's complement: supply.

The Idea of Supply

Supply is a total description of how sellers choose the amounts and kinds of goods and services that they produce and sell. You might think of supply as the other side of the market because you see yourself as a consumer. However, most people are both buyers (of goods and services) and sellers (of time, talent, and experience). We really "live" on both the demand and the supply curves.

supply: the seller side of the market; a description of production and sale choices.

The idea of supply can be complicated or we can choose to make it simple. The easiest way to approach the problem is to look at the economic variables that most influence a typical producer's choice.

1. PRICE. Price has a lot to do with producer choice. There is generally a direct relationship between a good's price and the amount of it offered for sale. Higher prices usually bring larger quantities to the market. Why is there this direct relationship between price and quantity supplied? One reason is easy to understand: greed! The price of pizza rises and makes previously paltry pizza parlors prosper. How do you suppose your local pizza purveyor reacts to the higher price? Chances are that he or she figures that if selling a few pizzas makes a little profit, selling more pizza adds even more profit. Higher prices, all else being equal, increase profits and so make existing sellers increase production and also attract others to the market, further increasing the quantity available. Local junk-food shops are soon selling pizza as well as burgers, fries, and chicken.

A second reason higher prices and greater production go together is more technical. As pizza barons expand production they must hire more workers, pay some of them overtime wages, and purchase new delivery trucks, pizza ovens, and the like. Small kitchens are inefficiently crowded with more workers than they were designed for. Expense and inefficiency mean that the extra pizzas add more to the cost of production than the ones that came before. In the jargon of the economist, **marginal costs** rise when production expands. Since per-pizza costs are going up, pizza peddlers can only afford to expand their operations if they can charge a higher price.

marginal costs: the cost of producing additional units of a product, given the producers' current production rate and facility.

Higher prices give sellers an incentive to produce more. Lower prices, on the other hand, make selling an unprofitable proposition, so fewer goods are offered for sale.

2. COST AND AVAILABILITY OF INPUTS. **Inputs** are just goods and services used to make other goods and services. They are ingredients in the recipe for cars or steel or life insurance. Inputs are used to make **outputs.**

inputs: goods and services used to produce other goods and services; the ingredients of production.

outputs: the items that firms produce.

The cost of inputs has a lot to do with supply because cost, like price, affects seller profits. In general there is an inverse relationship between input costs and quantity supplied. Higher costs chip away at profits, so smart sellers produce less and look around for more lucrative lines. Profits jump when input costs fall, on the other hand, so firms offer larger quantities for sale.

Examples of how input prices affect supply are not hard to find. Labor is a big input for fast food chains that traditionally employ many young people at the minimum wage. When the government raises the minimum wage rate, fast-food firms react to their falling profits by laying off workers and reducing the hours their stores are open. By closing at 10:00 P.M. instead of 11:00 P.M. and opening an hour later in the morning, these firms cut costs during low-profit hours and thus keep profits as high as possible. They also end up selling fewer burgers, fries, and Cokes. The higher input costs force them to reduce supply.

Sometimes the simple availability of inputs is an important production problem. Many inputs are needed to make even simple items. Your professor, for example, does not need many tools to produce education services (and, sometimes, sleep). Yet most professors would be hard-pressed to operate without basic inputs like chalk, lights, chairs, textbooks and . . . oh, yes! . . . students!

Inputs are important, but they are not always available when firms need them. Bottlenecks develop in production lines and output suffers. Stores run out of sale items or cannot get them from the supplier because rail cars and trucking firms are all booked up. Crops go unharvested because workers, machines, or vital fuels are unavailable at the current price or wage. Your favorite professional sports team probably faces a bottleneck making it through the play-offs because the right input—quarterback, center, goalie, or first baseman—is not available.

3. TECHNOLOGY. **Technology**—the way that inputs are combined to make outputs—is at the heart of the idea of supply. Improving technology makes goods cheaper to produce and also improves quality. Much of the growth of American industry stems from innovation and improved technology.

technology: the process by which goods are produced.

You probably own a symbol of the power of technology: a pocket calculator. Just a few years ago such things as electronic calculators did not exist. A room-sized Univac performed the kind of calculations even inexpensive pocket wizards now effortlessly compute. The first small calculators were complicated, expensive to produce, and costly to buy—prices started at $200! Today the march of technology gives us cheap add-subtract-multiply-divide models for under $10. The same technology gives us digital watches that tell the date and time, chime the hour, and "beep" out Beethoven for about $15.

The power of technology to affect supply cannot be denied. It shows up in the unlikeliest of places. Even the humble hamburger benefits from science. Burger emporiums were once slow, greasy places operated by one or two workers. Now McDonald's and similar chains use specialized labor and high-tech machines (like sensors that tell when fries are golden and a soda cup is full) to increase the amounts and kinds of food they sell.

This book is another example of how technology changes production. This edition in *Introductory Macroeconomics* was written on a computer. Computer programs checked the author's spelling and tried to point out common grammatical errors. Another computer was used to set the manuscript in print. And computers controlled the printing process, too. All this gives you a better textbook at a lower price. Ain't technolgy wonderful? (Oops! The computer missed that one!)

4. EVERYTHING ELSE. All sorts of events affect the process of production and sale. You should have no trouble coming up with dozens of examples. Here are two to get you started.

Nature is a basic Everything Else for supply. Weather is important to the supply of agricultural products, for example. Too much rain, not enough rain, too much sun, not enough sun—all these conditions affect the supply of fruits and vegetables. Growers in California know that bugs such as the Medfly are a big little Everything Else. Fruit crops infested by this fruit fly were ordered destroyed. You cannot get a more direct supply change than that!

Another example of Everything Else is government regulation. The government has broad powers to regulate the production and distribution of goods and services. When the government ordered that new cars should use less gasoline, for example, the shape and size of American cars changed. Their prices changed, too—they went up—because the new standards were costly to meet.

The Supply Curve

The **supply curve** simplifies the idea of supply so that we can see it and work with it. The supply curve holds constant the technology, the cost and availability of inputs, and everything else except price. The supply curve maps the way

supply curve: a graph of the relationship between the quantity supplied and the price of a good.

that the quantity supplied (horizontal axis) changes when price alone (vertical axis) varies. A typical apple supply curve is shown in Figure 2-4.

The supply curve for apples is upward-sloping. More apples are offered for sale at thirty cents than at ten cents. Higher prices provide an incentive to greater production, but they also compensate apple-growers for rising marginal costs. It takes extra workers and more time to pick an orchard clean, so these last apples are not offered for sale unless the price rises to, say, thirty cents or more in the figure. When apple prices change, producers slide up or down the supply curve, altering the quantity supplied in response to prices and profits.

Most supply curves that you will run into in the real world and in this book are shaped roughly like this apple supply curve, but not all of them. Supply curves take on different shapes under special conditions. These important exceptions to the "upward-sloping supply" rule are shown in Figures 2-5 and 2-6.

Sometimes supply is physically limited. No matter how high the price goes, no more can be offered for sale because of some roadblock to supply. The supply curve of apples in January is shown in Figure 2-5. The apple crop is already in. No matter how high prices go, no more apples can be produced until next year. This short run limitation gives us the vertical shape shown in the figure. In the long run more apples can be made available, but for now the price can change but quantity is fixed.

Just the opposite case is shown in Figure 2-6. The horizontal supply curve shows that there is an unused surplus of goods for sale. Larger and larger quantities are supplied with no increase in price. How can this be? When does

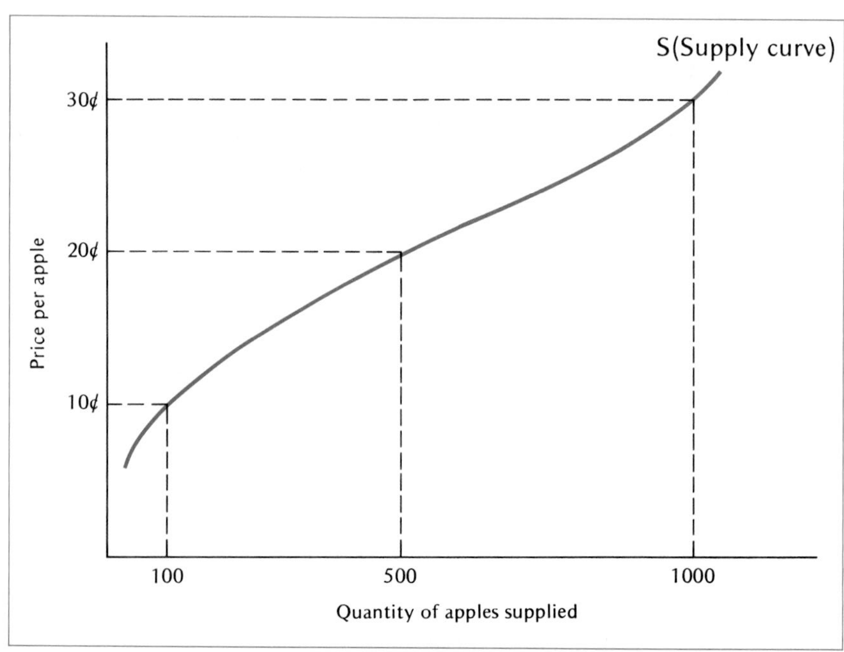

FIGURE 2-4 A SUPPLY CURVE FOR APPLES. The supply curve maps the number of apples offered for sale at each given price. The quantity supplied increases as the price rises.

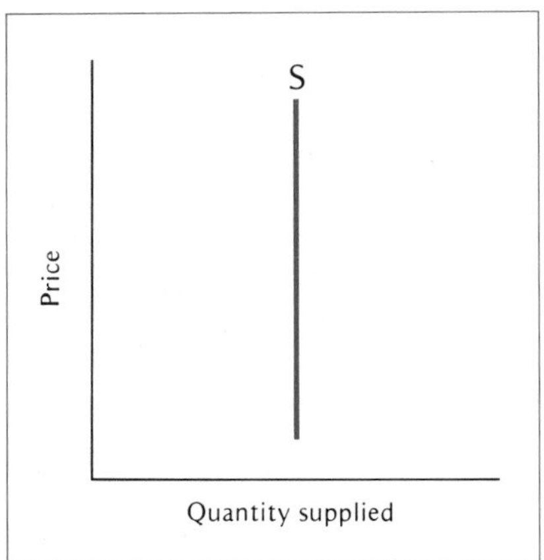

FIGURE 2-5 FIXED SUPPLY. The supply curve takes on this shape when a physical limitation restricts the ability to produce.

the horizontal supply curve apply? Consider the apple merchant with excess capacity. Apple Annie has tons of apples already picked and in storage, but cannot find a buyer. She is willing to sell you as many apples as you want at the going market price. Such supply curves are seldom seen, but they are important when they exist.

Shifts in Supply

A change in the price of apples is a movement along the supply curve. The supply curve itself shifts if something besides price changes to affect desired sales.

Events that make production cheaper, more efficient, and generally increase profits cause an **increase in supply**. The supply curve shifts, as in Figure 2-7, because firms respond to higher prices by increasing production.

increase in supply: an increase in the quantity supplied at each price; shift in the supply curve to the right.

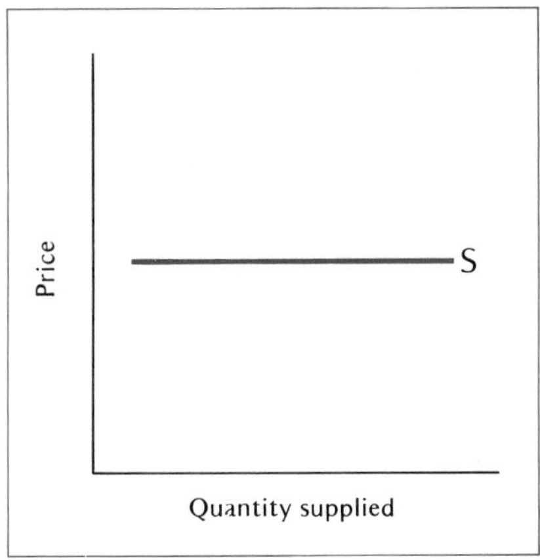

FIGURE 2-6 HORIZONTAL SUPPLY. This supply curve results when more goods can be purchased without higher prices. Excess capacity is often the reason for the horizontal supply curve shape.

FIGURE 2-7 INCREASE IN SUPPLY. Supply increases when profits increase due to falling costs or improved technology. Rising supply is shown by a shift to the right in the supply curve.

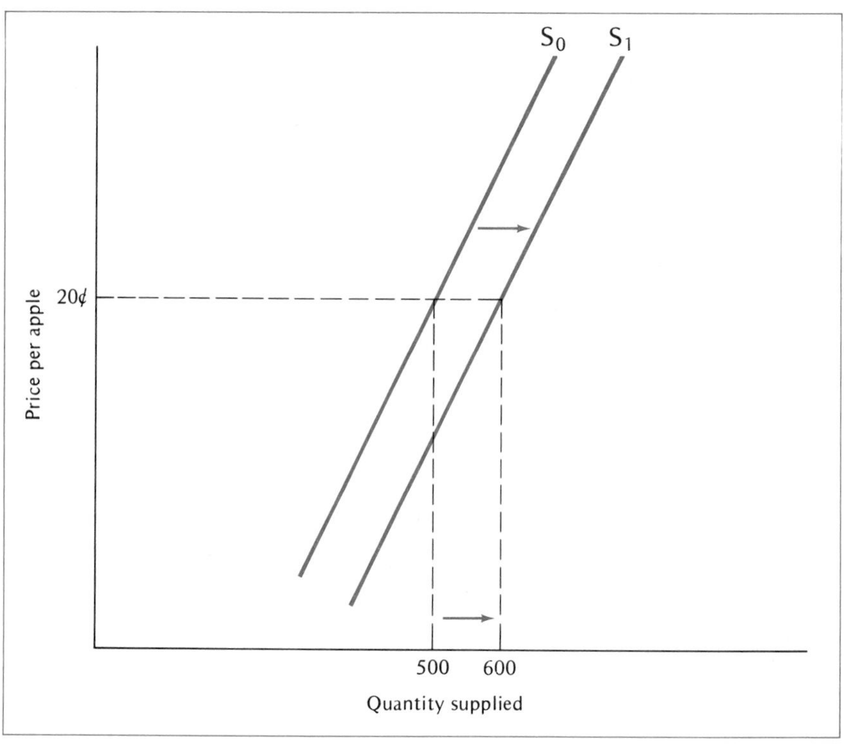

The increase in supply is shown by a shift out and to the right in the supply curve. This increase in apple supply could be caused by the fact that:

- labor costs fall so apples are cheaper to produce;
- raw materials used in apple orchards fall in price;
- inputs become more readily available, reducing bottlenecks that held up production;
- new technology makes production more efficient;
- government regulations change, increasing profits and reducing costs.

decrease in supply: a decrease in the quantity supplied at each price; shift to the right in supply curve.

A **decrease in supply** occurs whenever events increase costs, slow down production, or otherwise reduce profits. Firms offer fewer goods for sale at each possible price, shifting the supply curve back and to the left as in Figure 2-8. This decrease in supply could be caused by the fact that:

- input costs increase;
- labor strikes halt production of some firms;
- Congress imposes higher business taxes;
- local authorities require expensive pollution devices to be installed on equipment.

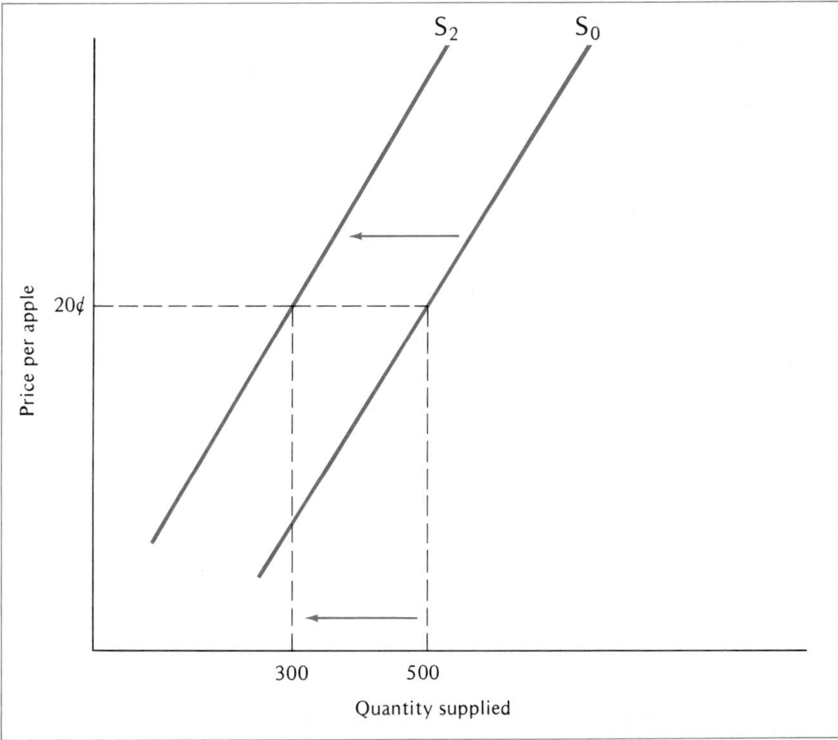

FIGURE 2-8 DECREASE IN SUPPLY. Supply falls when production is less profitable or when inputs are unavailable. Decreases in supply are indicated by a leftward shift in the supply curve.

• IMPORTANT NOTE •

Price changes cause movements *along* supply and demand curves—a change, in the language of economics, in the *quantity* supplied or demanded, but not in the curves themselves. If something besides price changes to affect production, the supply curve shifts and changes supply. Make a point to distinguish between *changes in supply or demand* (shifts in the curves) and *changes in price that just cause a change in the quantity supplied and demanded.* You will find that this distinction makes it easier to tell whether curves shift or if something else is going on.

The supply curve shows the amount that producers offer for sale, but it does not tell us if they can find buyers for all their goods. That decision is made in the market.

The Market at Work

Buyers and sellers exchange their wares in the market. We are all involved in markets; markets for peanut butter, tennis shoes, notebooks, and gasoline. The forces of supply and demand work in all these markets, but the markets are so dispersed that you might have a little trouble at first seeing them. Adam Smith, the father of economics, thought that supply and demand were powerful but transparent so he called them the "invisible hand" of the market.

You can see the invisible hand more clearly when we focus on an imaginary village market in apple country. Pretend that you have been transported to this faraway place. A crowd of apple buyers and apple sellers has gathered in the village square. The show is about to begin.

On one side of the street are the sellers. They are the supply curve. Each producer knows the quantity of apples that he or she is willing to sell at each possible price. Across the square the buyers are arriving. Each wants apples, but each wants different quantities at different prices. Together they are the demand curve.

At the center of the square is the auctioneer, standing on an old apple crate. He is called Leon after the nineteenth century economist Leon Walras who analyzed how markets like this work. The market opens at 10:00 A.M. sharp and the auctioneer calls out the first price, thirty cents. Buyers and sellers scurry to make deals.

The thirty cent price is considered good by apple growers. This relatively high price allows them a tidy profit. They want to supply 1000 apples in total at this price. Buyers are not so pleased, however. They want apples, but they do not want many of them at this price. The quantity demanded at thirty cents is just 100! A **surplus** or **excess supply** of 900 apples exists at this price. You can see this surplus in Figure 2-9.

surplus: the quantity supplied exceeds quantity demanded at a particular price.

excess supply: surplus.

The market does not clear because of the surplus. Many sellers, seeing that they will not find buyers for their goods at this price, tell Leon to call a lower price, to attract more purchases. The auctioneer responds to their request

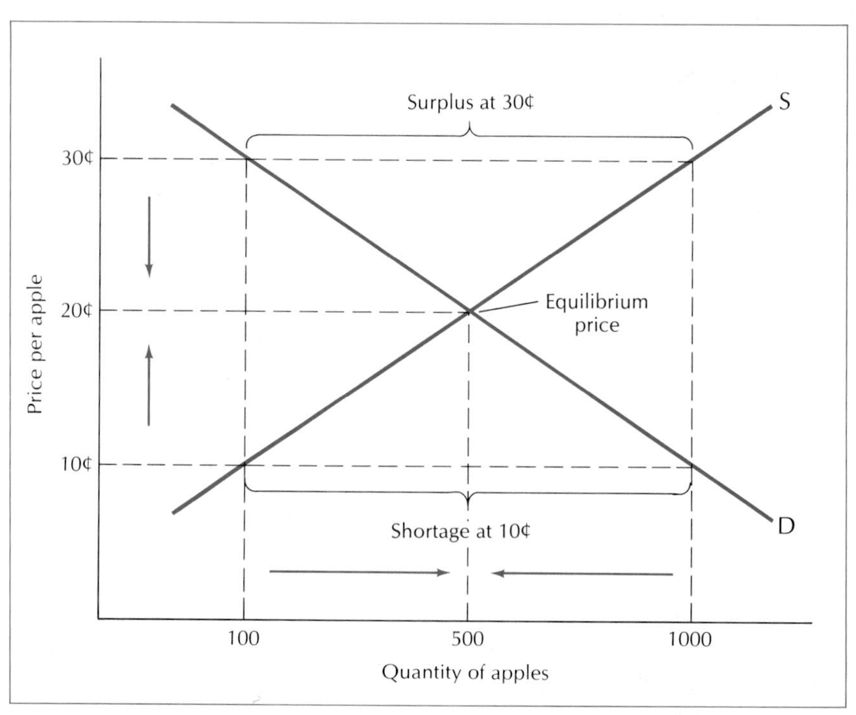

FIGURE 2-9 THE MARKET FOR APPLES. Supply and demand curves tell how many apples are desired and offered for sale at each price. The market clears—quantity demanded equals quantity supplied—at the equilibrium price.

and a price of ten cents is announced. Buyers and sellers huddle again to see what this price means to them.

Ten cents is considered a better price by the buyers. They offer to buy a total of 1000 apples. But ten cents does not leave much profit for the sellers. Only the most efficient apple growers can make money at this price. The quantity of apples supplied here is just 100. The market fails to clear again. In this instance, a **shortage** or **excess demand** of 900 apples exists. Many buyers realize that, at this price, they are not going to be able to buy the apples they want. They are willing to pay a higher price if it means not going home empty-handed. They ask the auctioneer to try a higher price.

shortage: the quantity demanded exceeds quantity supplied at a particular price.

excess demand: shortage.

The auctioneer spends most of the next hour calling out prices between ten cents and thirty cents, but each time he finds a shortage (so a higher price is required) or a surplus (and some call for prices to fall).

Eventually Leon the auctioneer calls out a price of twenty cents (he would have announced it earlier, but he does not have a copy of Figure 2-9 to guide him like you do). Something unique happens at this price. Producers want to supply a quantity of 500 apples—exactly the quantity demanded at that price! No surplus exists and no shortage, either. Every buyer can find a seller at this price. We have reached the market-clearing **equilibrium price.**

equilibrium price: the price at which quantity demanded equals quantity supplied.

The market responds to price and price responds, as we have seen, to shortages and surpluses. A surplus means that some sellers cannot find buyers. They cut price to make sales. Two things happen as price falls. First, people start to buy more goods. The quantity demanded increases as price falls (a movement along the demand curve). Lower prices, however, reduce profits, so less is offered for sale—a movement along the supply curve. As more is purchased but less is offered for sale, the surplus gradually disappears and equilibrium is reached.

The market reacts to a shortage in the same way. A shortage means that some buyers cannot get the goods they want. These buyers offer to pay more—to bid the goods away from other purchasers. As they bid up price, some buyers revise their spending plans (quantity demanded falls as we move along the demand curve), but more goods are offered for sale (the quantity supplied increases—a movement along the supply curve). These dual actions reduce the shortage until equilibrium is achieved.

There is neither shortage nor surplus at equilibrium price, so nothing exists to make the price change. The quantity demanded at this price equals the quantity supplied. The market remains at this equilibrium until something happens to change either demand (like a change in tastes) or supply (like a change in technology).

Applications of Supply and Demand

Supply and demand are at work, changing all around us. We can see how supply and demand work by looking at a market that most people are familiar with: the market for electricity. Unless you are reading this book by candlelight, you are probably active in this market right now.

Electricity is used for heating, air conditioning, and to run machinery. The demand for electricity rises with the snow drifts during cold winters. How does winter weather affect the electricity market? Figure 2-10 shows one possibility.

Cold temperatures change the way that demanders feel about electricity. As temperatures drop, electricity users want more electricity at any given price because they want to stay warm. Figure 2-10 shows what would happen if the supply curve for electricity were horizontal. This supply curve might exist if current facilities could meet the increase in demand without higher marginal costs. This condition exists in many areas at night. Electrical generators operate most efficiently working at set levels 24 hours a day. The excess power at night must be earthed to get rid of it. An increase in demand with a horizontal supply creates no shortage. The larger demand is met without price increases. This happy outcome is possible, but is it likely? Have you looked at your utility bill recently?

A second possible response to increased winter demand for electricity is shown in Figure 2-11. Here the supply curve is vertical. This tells us that the power system has reached its maximum output. No more electricity can be generated no matter how high the price rises. As demand increases beyond this finite limit, shortages appear. Blackouts or brownouts occur. Since no additional power is available in the short run, some way to ration the scarce resource must be found. Voluntary conservation might work, but there are limits to how

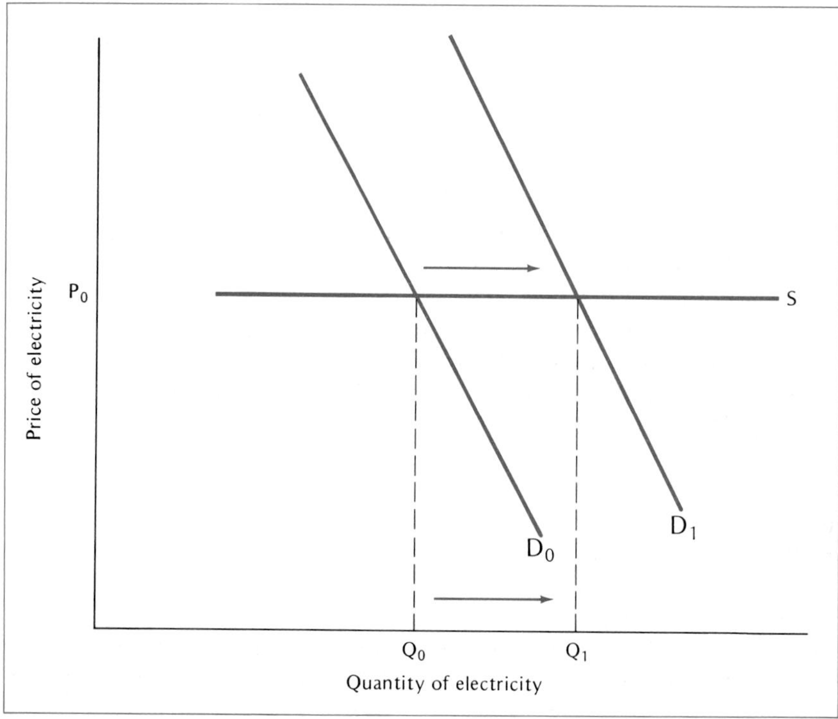

FIGURE 2-10 INCREASING DEMAND WITH HORIZONTAL SUPPLY. Because there is an excess capacity, rising electricity demand can be met without an increase in price.

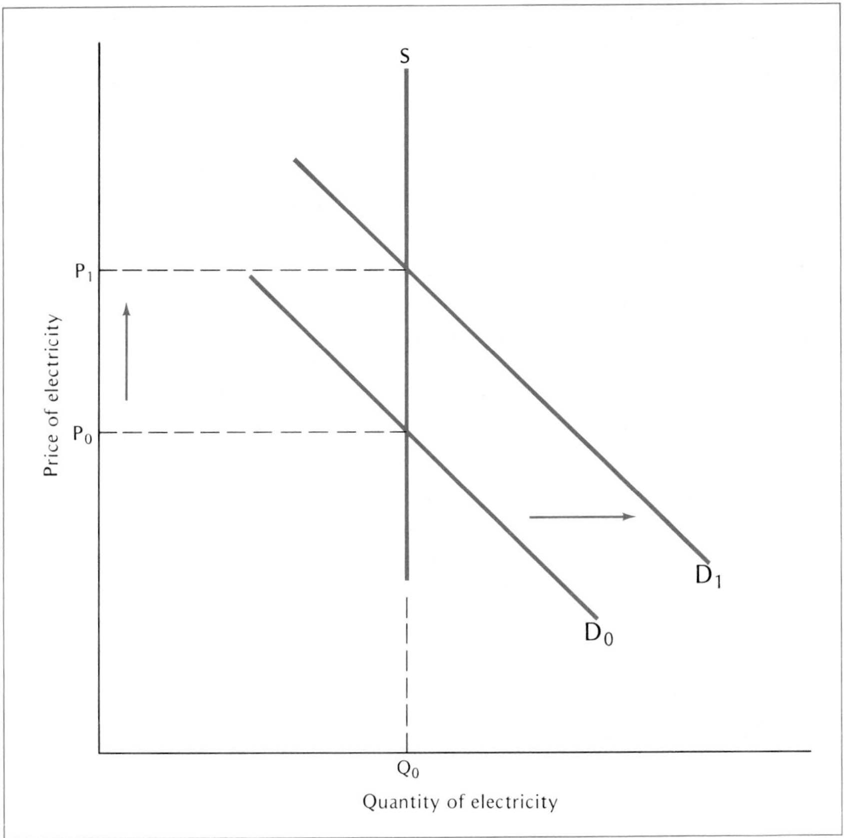

FIGURE 2-11 RISING DEMAND WITH FIXED SUPPLY. In this instance, electricity supplies are limited. The increase in demand brings higher prices but no change in quantity.

cold people—even volunteers—are willing to get. The government might try to allocate electricity, giving priority, for example, to hospitals and schools. Price is another way to ration scarce goods.

No additional electricity is produced when electrical rates increase in the situation shown in Figure 2-11. But households and businesses set back their thermostats when faced with higher utility bills. Price increases reduce the quantity demanded, and the shortage disappears when the equilibrium price is reached. Quantity supplied has not changed, but price has adjusted to the increase in demand.

We have seen how the market responds to higher demand when supply is horizontal (quantity changes, price does not) and when it is fixed (price changes, quantity does not). Neither of these conditions is common in the real world. Supply curves generally slope upward, like the one shown in Figure 2-12. More power can be generated during cold winters, but only at a higher cost. Expensive oil must be fed to inefficient back-up generators. High-cost nuclear power must be purchased from outside suppliers. The extra "juice" is available, all right, but only if you are willing to pay for it!

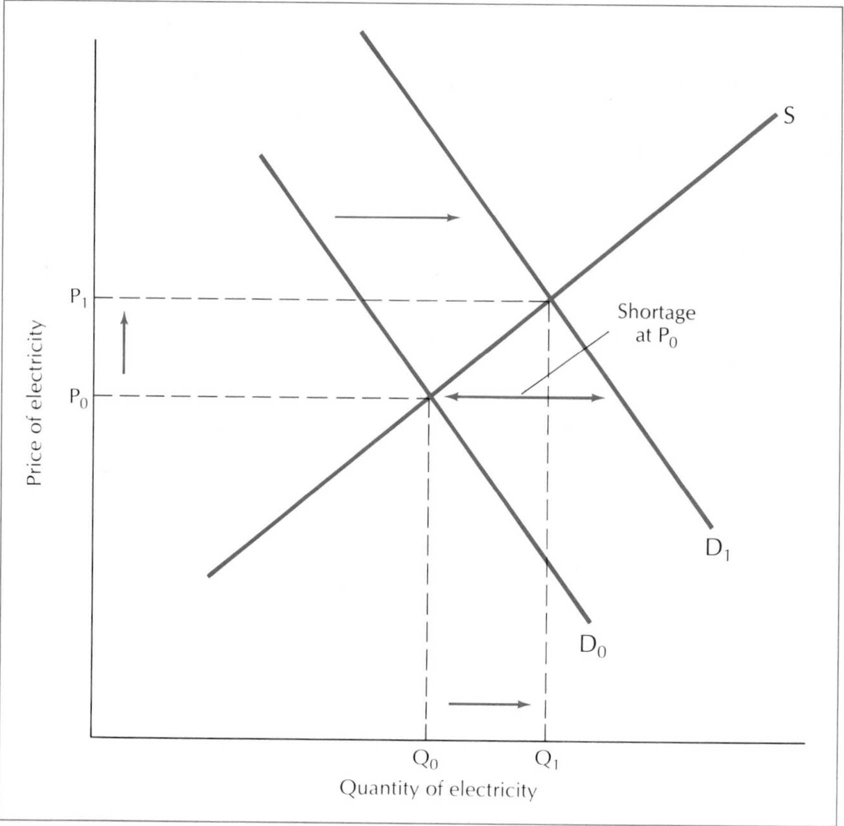

FIGURE 2-12 Rising Demand and Increasing Costs. The upward-sloping supply curve in this figure indicates that larger quantities of electricity can be produced, but only at higher costs. The increase in demand causes both higher prices and increased production.

The rising demand for electricity temporarily outstrips the quantity supplied. A shortage exists. Price rises in response to the shortage and the rising price sets two forces in motion that bring the shortage to an end. Higher price makes possible the expensive additional electrical output—the quantity supplied increases along with price. Higher prices affect consumers, too, who respond by rationing the more expensive resource. The quantity demanded falls as price rises. Shortage vanishes as quantity demanded falls and quantity supplied rises. The new equilibrium finds cold consumers using more electricity, but paying more for it. They have the power they need to be comfortable, but the high price makes it a cold comfort!

Inflation: A Preview

Inflation is going to get a whole chapter of its own (Chapter 4) later in this book. But that does not mean we need to wait that long to talk about it. Inflation is the condition of generally rising prices. We cannot yet tell what might make all prices rise, but we can use the supply and demand tools to see what forces would make one price go up. The ideas we discuss here will come in handy later.

There are two basic ways a price can rise, all things being equal. You have already seen the first one. Price rises when demand goes up because increased buying creates a shortage and the shortage drives up price. Let us call this type of inflation a **demand-pull** price increase.

demand-pull: a price increase caused by increased demand.

Demand-pull price increases, as illustrated in Figure 2-13, make things cost more, but they also give us higher quantities. The higher prices here make possible increased production. More is produced, more jobs are created, and greater profits result.

Compare the results of a demand-pull price increase with those of the **cost-push** price increase in Figure 2-14. Price rises here because of a supply-induced shortage. Higher production costs reduce profits and force a decrease in supply. The supply curve shifts back and to the left. A smaller quantity is supplied at price P_0. A shortage follows since nothing has happened to reduce the quantity that consumers want to buy. The shortage again bids up price. Higher price brings movement along both curves—a larger quantity is supplied, but less is demanded as price rises. A new equilibrium is eventually reached at price P_2. The market clears again, but look at what has happened to quantity. The higher price here brings with it lower quantities. Fewer workers are employed in this market and profits have also fallen. None of us like price increases, but this is a particularly depressing inflation You pay more to get less when prices rise in response to cost-push forces.

cost-push: a price increase caused by decreased supply.

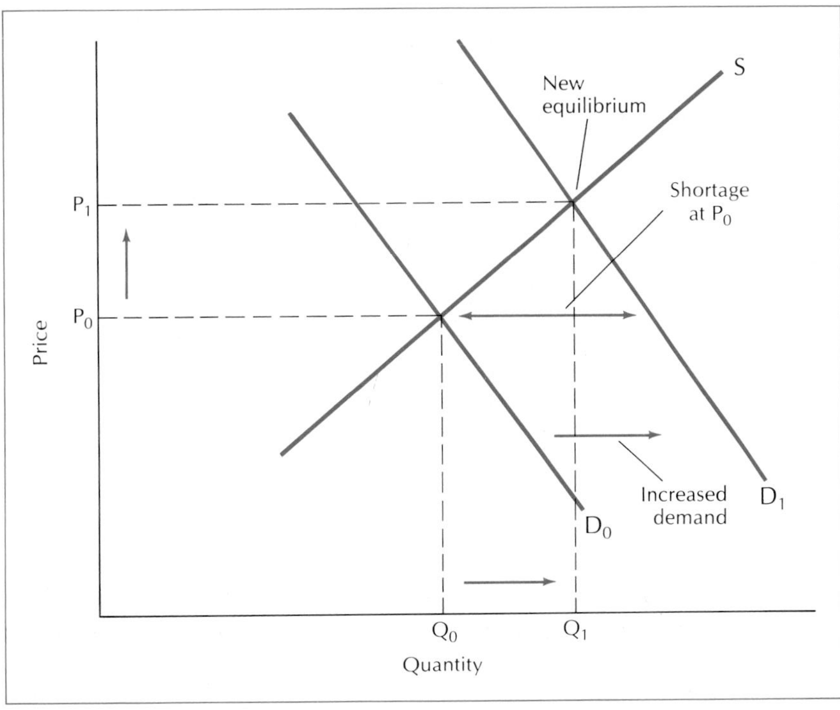

FIGURE 2-13 DEMAND-PULL PRICE INCREASES. Both prices and quantities rise when demand pulls the strings.

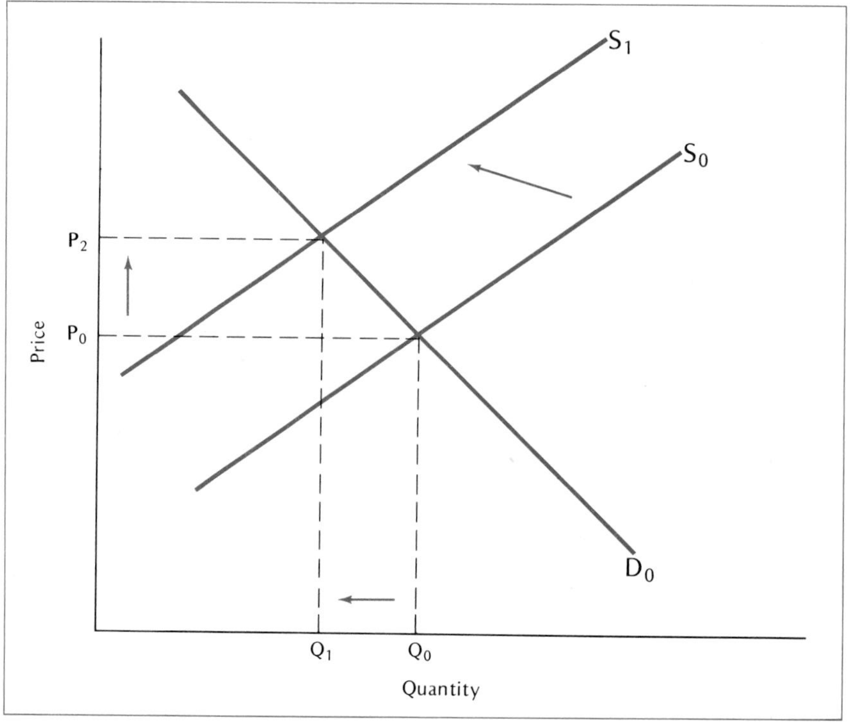

FIGURE 2-14 COST-PUSH PRICE INCREASES. Rising costs push up price, but push down quantity.

Demand for many goods is always rising in the real world as population and income grow. Increasing demand generates demand-pull price increases. Does this mean that we are doomed to a future of rising prices?

The answer to this question is no. If demand increases and all else remains the same, price has to go up. But all else is seldom equal in this complicated world. Increased demand can be met without higher prices if supply and demand grow together, as shown in Figure 2-15.

balanced growth: equal increases in demand and supply.

Rising demand creates no shortage if the ability to produce goods increases at the same time. We call this particular condition the **balanced growth** of the market, and it is a desirable economic state. Since demand frequently grows, markets depend on things like better technology, lower input prices, and more efficient workers to meet buyer needs without increasing price.

Review of Market Actions

You will be using the tools of supply and demand throughout this text, so it is a good idea to get a feel for them now. The following paragraphs describe common market changes. Read along to see that they make sense and check them out by drawing your own demand and supply curves. Be sure you can tell what happens in each case and, more important, why it happens and what

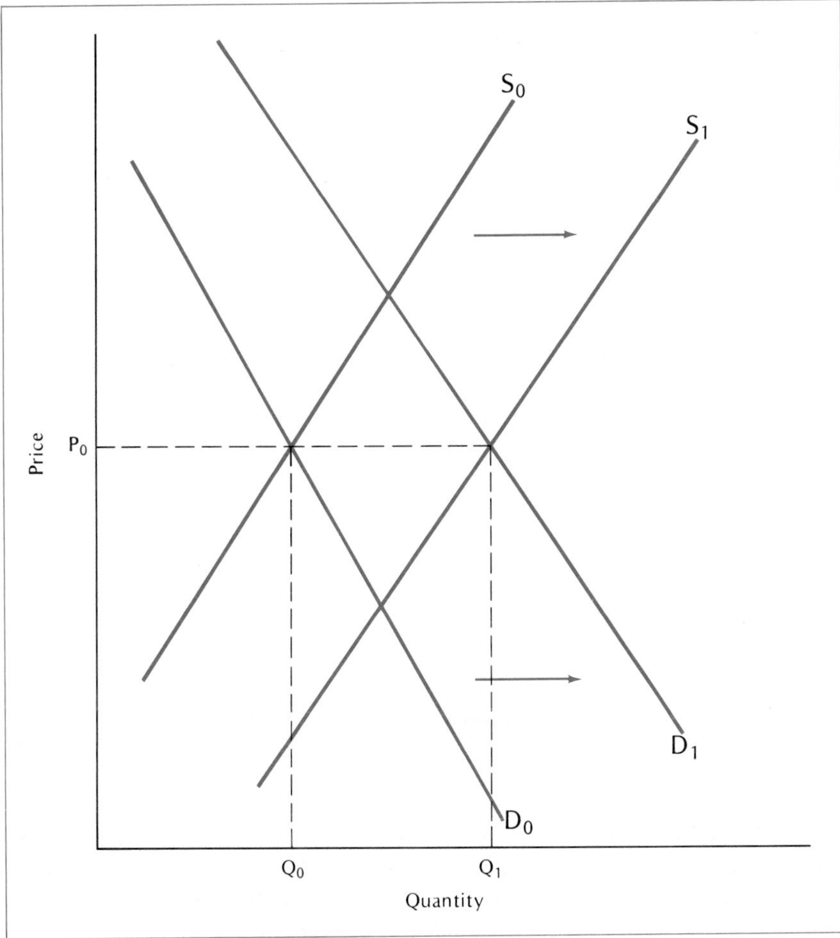

FIGURE 2-15. BALANCED GROWTH IN DEMAND AND SUPPLY. Rising demand is matched by increasing supply. Quantity goes up, but price does not need to rise.

forces are at work in the market. Upward-sloping supply and downward-sloping demand curves are assumed throughout this section.

INCREASE IN DEMAND. An increase in demand creates a shortage since quantity demanded exceeds quantity supplied at the old equilibrium price. The shortage bids up price. The new equilibrium combines higher price with larger quantity.

INCREASE IN SUPPLY. An increase in supply brings forth a surplus of goods. Quantity supplied exceeds quantity demanded at the initial equilibrium price. Price falls in response to the surplus. The new equilibrium occurs at a lower price but larger quantity.

DECREASE IN DEMAND. Falling demand brings a surplus. Producers offer more for sale than buyers desire at the initial equilibrium price. As price falls, however, quantity supplied falls, too. The new equilibrium combines lower price with lower quantity.

DECREASE IN SUPPLY. This is the cost-push problem you have just been reading about. Falling supply causes the shortage that bids up price. Price rises, but quantity falls.

INCREASE IN BOTH DEMAND AND SUPPLY. This is the balanced growth of Figure 2-15. Quantity goes up here, but you cannot be sure about price. Figure 2-15 shows price staying the same because supply and demand increased by the same amount. If supply increases more, equilibrium price falls. If demand has the bigger shift, equilibrium price rises.

DECREASE IN BOTH DEMAND AND SUPPLY. This is the reverse of the last change. If both demand and supply fall, we can be sure that less is produced, but the change in price is ambiguous. The direction of the price change depends on whether demand or supply falls the most.

INCREASE IN DEMAND AND DECREASE IN SUPPLY. This is a perverse set of changes. Consumers want more, but supply falls at the same time. This combination of demand-pull and cost-push forces gives us higher prices, but the change in quantity is ambiguous. Quantity depends on whether supply or demand shifts the most.

DECREASE IN DEMAND AND INCREASE IN SUPPLY. This is the opposite of the last entry. Price unambiguously drops, but the change in quantity cannot be determined unless the size of the supply and demand shifts is known.

ECONOMIC CONTROVERSY:

Are Price Controls Desirable?

You have learned a lot of economics in this chapter. Now you can apply what you have learned to an important economic issue: price controls. Do you remember the comment that began this chapter? Economists love supply and demand and they always find at least two answers to any question. As you read this Economic Controversy you will see why this is true.

price floor: the minimum legal price.

price ceiling: the maximum legal price.

Price controls are laws that prevent the market from seeking its own price. **Price floors** are minimum legal prices. It is illegal to sell an item for less than its price floor. A **price ceiling** is a maximum legal price. The ceiling puts a limit on how much the seller can ask.

Most goods are sold in markets that are free to find their own prices—price floors and ceilings do not apply. But a debate still rages over whether controls should be used in the public interest. The speakers below present two sides of this issue.

Price Ceilings Protect the Poor

We need price ceilings on basic commodities like food, energy, and housing to protect the poor from high prices, prices driven up by the greedy and the rich. Figure 2-16 shows why ceilings are desirable. This is the market for natural

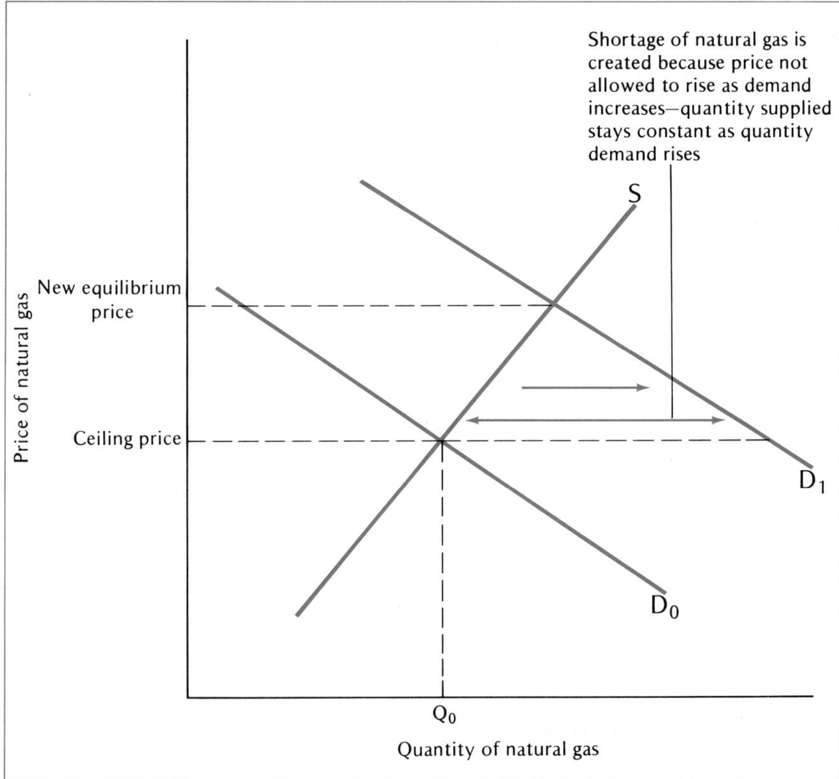

FIGURE 2-16 WINTER AND PRICE CONTROLS. Winter weather increases the demand for natural gas. Should prices be allowed to rise or should a shortage occur?

gas. Many people, including the poor, heat and cook with natural gas. It is among the most important energy sources in the country.

The figure shows what happens in the natural gas market in the winter. The demand for natural gas increases along with the wind-chill factor. Since the supply of natural gas is upward sloping, the increase in demand bids up price and the market, in classic demand-pull form, ends up with higher quantity, too. The figure makes it look like everyone is going to have more gas at a higher price, but is this realistic? Not everyone can afford to pay higher natural gas bills. Look at the large quantity of natural gas demanded at the original ceiling price. Look, in Figure 2-16, how much less is demanded at the new equilibrium price. Rising prices force everyone to be more careful with fuel, but they hit the poor hardest. A price ceiling, on the other hand, would keep prices from rising, even during the coldest winter. The rich might suffer a bit from gas shortages, but the poor would at least be able to keep from freezing to death. Is not this a desirable goal?

Price Controls Create Shortages

The previous speaker did not want the poor to freeze, but does he want them to starve? That might happen if price controls are imposed on markets like this. Look back to Figure 2-16 and you will see what I mean.

Price ceilings keep the market from doing its job of fighting shortages and surpluses. What happens when demand increases in a price-controlled market? People want to buy lots of natural gas because its price is kept artificially low by the price ceiling. Natural gas suppliers cannot afford to provide more gas unless price rises to cover their higher costs. The price ceiling here leads only to a persistent shortage of natural gas.

If natural gas is scarce, who gets it? Who is going to decide whether you freeze or I do? This hard choice is not made necessary by the cold weather, it is the result of the government price ceiling. No politician wants to be responsible for families freezing to death in their own homes, so residential heating generally gets top priority in shortages, and commercial and industrial customers get whatever is left. The poor are warm, but they are also poorer since the price-controlled shortage has forced their employers to shut down.

Poverty is one problem. The price of natural gas is another. Fight poverty directly; do not try to do it through price ceilings that create shortages and reduce market efficiency.

SUMMARY

1. Markets are institutions where goods are bought and sold. Market price is used to signal buyers and sellers about the scarcity and value of items.

2. Demand depends on many variables. The amount of a good demanded is inversely related to its price. A change in price is a movement along a demand curve. Income, tastes and preferences, and the prices of related goods, among other things, also affect demand. These nonprice variables make the demand curve shift.

3. Supply is influenced by many things, too. Price and quantity supplied are usually directly related. Higher prices provide an incentive to produce and also make higher-cost production feasible. A change in price is a movement along the supply curve. The supply curve shifts when nonprice variables like technology, the cost of inputs, or the availability of inputs change.

4. Most supply curves slope upward, but not all. Supply is sometimes vertical if a physical limit on production prevails. A horizontal supply curve shows that larger amounts can be purchased with no increase in price.

5. Equilibrium price is that one price where the market clears. Quantity demanded equals quantity supplied at the equilibrium price. Once at equilibrium, the market stays there until either supply or demand shifts. Shortages push up below-equilibrium prices. Prices above equilibrium fall due to surplus. These shortages and surpluses are the forces that make price move.

6. Prices rise for several reasons. Demand-pull price increases bid up price but also result in a larger equilibrium quantity. Cost-push price increases come from falling supply. Price goes up here, too, but quantities fall.

7. Price ceilings generate controversy because they have more than one effect. They keep prices down, but they also cause shortages. Rising prices are hard on people, but shortages are not good, either. Which ill should we suffer?

DISCUSSION QUESTIONS

1. Consider the supply of beer. What shape would this supply curve have? Why? What effect would each of these events have on the beer supply curve?

a. fall in the price of hops
b. increase in the price of aluminum cans
c. fall in the price of pizza

2. Consider the demand for prunes. What shape would a prune demand curve have? Why? How would each of these events affect the prune demand curve?

a. scientists discover that prunes slow aging
b. the price of Ex-Lax falls
c. good weather reduces the cost of drying prunes
d. the price of prunes falls

3. Now look at the market—both demand and supply—for pizza in your local area. How would each of these events affect demand? Supply? Price? Quantity? Why?

a. decrease in the price of pepperoni
b. decrease in the price of beer
c. increase in local college enrollments
d. increase in the price of hamburgers

4. When would an increase in demand *not* result in higher prices? When would an increase in demand *not* result in higher quantities? (Hint: there is more than one answer to each question.) Explain the reasoning behind your answers.

5. Use supply and demand curves to show how each of the following situations would occur:

a. In the past year the price of Rotgut Lite Beer has increased from \$2.50 to \$3.00 per sixpack. In spite of the price increase a larger quantity of Rotgut Lite was purchased.
b. Badyear Tire Company announced that fewer tires were sold this year than the year before. Badyear's president blames the lower sales on higher prices.
c. The demand for barley increased this year. Barley prices remained constant and the amount of barley offered for sale was also constant. A large, persistent shortage of barley was observed.

TEST YOURSELF

Circle the best response to each question.

1. You are employed as an economist for the Oregon Hazelnut Growers Association. The growers want to know if the demand for hazelnuts is going to increase in the coming year. Which of the following events would cause an increase in hazelnut demand?

(X) increase in the size of hazelnut harvest
(Y) decrease in the price of hazelnuts
(Z) increase in the price of hazelnut substitutes like walnuts and almonds

a. all of the above
b. only (Z)
c. only (Z) and (Y)
d. only (X) and (Z)
e. only (X) and (Y)

2. The growers are also concerned about the supply of hazelnuts. Which of the following events would increase the supply of hazelnuts?

(X) increase in the cost of orchard machinery
(Y) increase in the price of hazelnuts
(Z) increase in the incomes of hazelnut eaters

a. all of the above
b. only (Y) above
c. only (Y) and (Z) above
d. only (X) above
e. none of the above

3. The hazelnut growers want to sell more hazelnuts at a higher price. Which of the following events would have this effect?

a. increase in the wages of hazelnut orchard employees
b. decrease in the cost of transporting hazelnuts to market
c. increase in the price of hazelnut substitutes like walnuts
d. increase in the price of hazelnut complements like honey
e. all of the above would bring higher prices and quantities

4. Hazelnut Toffee is a particularly delicious type of candy. One of Hazelnut Toffee's main ingredients is butter. The price of butter has recently increased. How will this affect the market for Hazelnut Toffee-type candy?

a. the supply of Hazelnut Toffee falls (shift to the left) driving up the equilibrium price
b. since people are buying less Hazelnut Toffee, the price falls; this causes the supply curve to shift to the left since it is less profitable to make Hazelnut Toffee at the lower price
c. the higher Hazelnut Toffee price causes a decrease in demand (the demand curve shifts back to the left) because people do not want to buy as much at the higher price
d. supply increases (shift to the right) because it is more profitable to sell Hazelnut Toffee at the higher price
e. demand and supply both fall (shift to the left); quantity falls, but the change in price is ambiguous

5. Congress has just voted to impose a price floor on hazelnuts. The equilibrium price of hazelnuts is $2 per pound. The new floor price is $3 per pound. How will the price floor affect the hazelnut market?

(W) increase the price of hazelnuts
(X) create a shortage of hazelnuts
(Y) increase the supply of hazelnuts (shift supply curve)
(Z) decrease the demand for hazelnuts (shift demand curve)

a. all of the above
b. none of the above
c. only (W) above
d. (W), (Y) and (Z)
e. (W) and (X)

SUGGESTIONS FOR FURTHER READING

Any good microeconomics text will help you go further in the study of supply and demand. Try the author's *Introductory Microeconomics* (New York: Academic Press, 1981). Want to see the personal side of a market? A particularly interesting view is R. A. Radford's "The Economic Organization of a P.O.W. Camp," *Economica* (1945).

3

THE PROBLEM OF UNEMPLOYMENT

Preview

How serious is the unemployment problem in the United States?
Why do unemployment rates rise?
What does the goal of full employment mean?
Can inflation reduce the unemployment rate?
How does the minimum wage affect the economy?

UNEMPLOYMENT IS a devastating problem. Economists have studied the unemployment problem for years, but their efforts have not produced a final solution. Over 10 million people in the United States were unemployed in 1982—as many as during the Great Depression. The unemployment problem is smaller as a proportion of the population, but it is as big now in absolute terms as it ever has been.

Economists talk about unemployment as statistics and models, charts and graphs. We will see that these are useful methods, but we should not forget that unemployment is a people problem. The unemployed lose income, opportunity, and self-esteem. Unemployment disrupts family lives in ways that might never be resolved.

Unemployment is all the more serious because it affects both those who lose their jobs and those who keep them. Society pays for unemployment in two ways. The first cost is lost production. The ten million people who were unemployed in 1982 did not have a chance to use their talents, skills, and labor. The productive value of time spent in unemployment lines is lost forever. The second cost is more direct. Federal, state, and local governments spend billions of dollars on unemployment benefits, welfare payments, job-search assistance, and other programs to aid the out-of-work. These programs (and the taxes that finance them) would not be necessary in a fully employed economy.

The Unemployment Record

Full employment has not been a frequent visitor to the United States. Figure 3-1 shows the average annual unemployment rates for the United States since 1960. The Humphrey-Hawkins Bill sets a goal of 4 percent unemployment for the United States. Draw a line across Figure 3-1 at the 4 percent level to see how often this target has been hit.

Unemployment rates were low (less than 4 percent) only during the Vietnam War of the late 1960s. Since then, unemployment has averaged 6 percent and higher. The picture that the figure paints is one of increasing joblessness and failure to reach this most basic of macroeconomic goals.

The Unemployment Rate

unemployment rate: a measure of unemployment calculated by dividing the number of people unemployed by the size of the labor force.

How serious is the unemployment problem? Unemployment is usually measured by the government's **unemployment rate.** But what is the unemployment rate? What does it measure? What does it mean?

The unemployment rate, as calculated by the federal government, is the ratio of the number of people who fit the definition of "unemployed" to the number of people who are in the **labor force.** Definitions are important here, so take some time to master them.

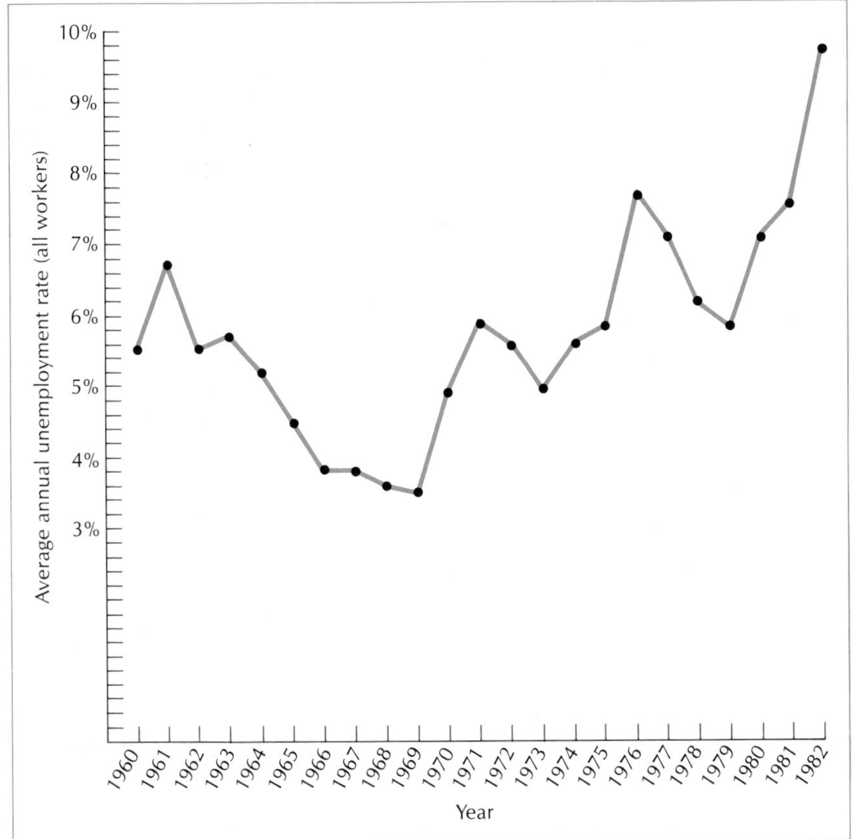

FIGURE 3-1 THE UNEMPLOYMENT RECORD. Unemployment rates have been high in the United States for the past 25 years. The elusive goal of full employment was achieved only briefly in the 1960s during the war years.

The numerator of the unemployment rate is the number of **unemployed workers.** You are considered to be unemployed if you meet the following criteria. You must not have earned any wage or salary income recently. You must be actively seeking work (you are not just sitting the summer out or waiting for a job to come and find you). Finally, you must be unable to find a job in your occupation at the going wage rate. If you have not looked for work or if you have accepted pay or if you have turned down a job in your line of work, you are not "officially" unemployed.

labor force: all those involved in the labor market; people working and those actively seeking work.

unemployed worker: a person willing and able to work, actively seeking work, but unable to find a job at the going wage rate.

The denominator of this statistic is the size of the labor force. The labor force is, roughly speaking, the supply of labor—the number of people actively seeking to supply their time, talent, and effort. Two groups are found here: those who are working and those who are actively seeking work but cannot find any—the unemployed people from the numerator of this fraction.

There were 8.2 million unemployed people in the United States in 1981. Another 100.4 million had jobs, so the labor force summed to 100.4 + 8.2 = 108.6 million men and women. The average unemployment rate for 1981 was equal to 8.2 million (the number unemployed) divided by 108.6 million (the labor force), that is, 7.6 percent. No one goes around and counts all the unemployed people. The Labor Department estimates these figures based on a monthly telephone survey.

Unemployment rates grow in two different ways. The reason most people think of first is people being laid off or fired. The labor force (number of people in the labor market) stays the same, but the number of unemployed workers grows. The unemployment rate increases in this way during recessions like those in 1974–1975 and 1981–1982 in Figure 3-1.

The other way the unemployment rate rises is more subtle. Students, housewives, and others frequently have trouble finding jobs when they enter the labor force. The economy has not grown fast enough to provide them with the work they desire. These **new entrants** to the labor force increase both the numerator (number unemployed) and the denominator (the labor force). The unemployment rate goes up when this happens.

new entrants: individuals who enter the labor force for the first time.

The dilemma of the new entrants is one reason unemployment increased during the 1970s. The workforce grew as "baby boom" students entered the job market and women searched for careers outside the home. Women were encouraged to find jobs by the womens' liberation movement, which said that women should not be bound by traditional roles, and by inflation that eroded paychecks and kept everyone looking for more money. Young people with little work experience and not much experience in looking for work poured out of high schools and colleges. The economy of the 1970s did not grow as fast as the labor force, so many of these new entrants joined the ranks of the unemployed. Today's continued high levels of unemployment attest that growth has not yet caught up to the labor force—a dismal fact facing today's college student and tomorrow's job applicant.

Unemployment and the Unemployment Rate

The unemployment rate is a convenient indicator of the unemployment problem, but it is a flawed one. The unemployment rate might either underestimate or overestimate the unemployment problem. There are four reasons for this uncertainty about the number of employed people:

1. UNDEREMPLOYMENT. The statistics say that you are employed if you have earned any wage or salary income during the past month. Part-time workers (who may be seeking full-time work) and people in low-paid temporary jobs are counted as completely employed. These people are not really unemployed (they have jobs), but some of them are not employed in a broader sense, either. We call them **underemployed workers.**

underemployed workers: part-time workers seeking full-time jobs and people working in occupations that do not use their training or skills.

If you graduated from college with an accounting degree and spent five years working at a truck stop because no one needed an accountant, you might think that you have an unemployment problem. But the statistics would not show it. Unemployment of this sort could be a serious problem in the United States. The unemployment rate understates the problem by counting the gas-pumping accountant as employed, instead of unemployed.

2. **DISCOURAGED WORKERS.** People who are unemployed for a long time get discouraged and stop looking for work. These people suffer the most serious unemployment problem of all. They have the wrong skills or the right skills in the wrong place. But when they stop looking for work and give up, they reduce the unemployment rate—giving the impression that unemployment has gotten better, not worse. Both the number unemployed and the labor force fall when these **discouraged workers** quit actively looking for work. The lower unemployment rate that results should be considered bad news, but economists and politicians are more likely to view it as evidence of an improving economy. The unemployment rate does not tell us of the plight of the discouraged workers, so it tends to understate the real unemployment problem.

discouraged workers: people who leave the labor force when unable to find work.

3. **VOLUNTARY UNEMPLOYMENT.** The first two items on this list were reasons to believe that unemployment is a more serious problem than unemployment statistics imply. The next two suggest that government statistics inadvertently inflate the real unemployment problem. One reason to believe this is that not all unemployment is involuntary (like losing a job you really want or need). Some people are voluntarily unemployed—they choose to be unemployed or to stay unemployed longer than is absolutely necessary.

Why would someone choose to be out of work? Sometimes it is a matter of tastes and preferences. People who prefer low income and leisure to higher income and work are frequently jobless. They may work just often enough to qualify for unemployment benefits or other government assistance. Some of these people pretend to look for work so they can continue to receive government cash, but they are really on a taxpayer-financed vacation. The government counts them as unemployed, but they are not out of work in the same sense as others.

Other people choose to remain unemployed to search for even better jobs. It takes a long time to find the "perfect" job. You might be out of work for weeks or months as you search out the best match of your talents against the available job openings. Higher unemployment in recent years is due in part to people remaining unemployed longer as they search for ever better positions. The economy might benefit in the long run from higher job productivity, but it suffers in the short run from higher rates of joblessness.

People who prefer leisure or who avoid taking one job as they search for a better one are not unemployed in the same sense as others. To the extent that **voluntary unemployment** exists, it tends to inflate the unemployment rate, making us spend too much time worrying about unemployment.

voluntary unemployment: unemployment that is by choice; the opposite of forced unemployment.

4. **THE UNDERGROUND ECONOMY.** There is a whole economic world that exists "off the books." The **underground economy** is a collection of illegal markets. People hide their activities from the eyes of the law because they deal in illegal goods like drugs or because they want to avoid paying taxes on income from otherwise legal acts. How big is the underground economy? Economists cannot tell for sure because it is difficult to measure what you cannot see. The subterranean system could involve $500 billion per year. The underground economy, in other words, is big enough to employ all of 1982's 10 million jobless workers at a wage of $50,000 each!

underground economy: illegal markets; the part of the economy that sells illegal goods or acts to hide activity from taxation.

Many people who are officially counted as unemployed really have underground occupations. They work as plumbers or sell firewood or deal in drugs—all under the table to deceive the police or the Internal Revenue Service. They are counted as unemployed, but they are not. We cannot tell how many unemployed people are earning substantial incomes in the underground economy, but we can be sure that some of them are. The unemployment rate overestimates the number of unemployed workers because of the subterranean economy's existence.

Unemployment is a difficult problem made worse because economists and politicians cannot even agree on the number of people who are unemployed. Is the unemployment problem worse than the numbers show, or do underground activities and voluntary unemployment mean that the social harm of unemployment is less severe?

Types of Unemployment

Understanding unemployment is difficult because joblessness has many causes. The people you meet in an unemployment line share an idled state, but they suffer it for different reasons. Economists sometimes divide the unemployed into three groups:

cyclical unemployment: unemployment resulting from falling aggregate demand.

structural unemployment: unemployment caused by poor matching of worker skills and job needs.

1. **CYCLICAL UNEMPLOYMENT.** We can find the cause for some unemployment in the economy's broad spending swings—the bust and boom of recession and good times. Consumers do not buy new cars during a recession, so auto workers face layoffs. Jobs will not open up for these workers until the economy accelerates and spending habits resume speed. **Cyclical unemployment** is the unemployment of the Great Depression and the recessions of 1974–1975 and the early 1980s. Fighting cyclical unemployment means getting the whole economy moving. This is no simple feat, as you might guess from looking at the high peak unemployment rates shown in Figure 3-1. But the next two types of unemployment might be even more difficult to reduce.

2. **STRUCTURAL UNEMPLOYMENT. Structural unemployment** is the problem faced by people who lack the skills needed to compete for a job in today's labor market. Maybe they are untrained teenagers who have few skills at all. Maybe they are skilled workers in their fifties who find themselves replaced by computers. They have skills, but the wrong ones.

Rapid technological advance is a good thing for the economy as a whole—it gives us better products and lower prices. But it is no sweet deal to its structurally unemployed victims. They need new skills if they are to find new jobs. But training is expensive and risky—you might obtain new skills that are quickly made obsolete. Training might simply make you unemployed at a better class of jobs.

You can fight cyclic unemployment by stimulating the economy using taxes or government spending or other tools discussed in this book. But there is no guarantee that increased spending alone will solve the structural unemployment problem. The ex-auto worker does not care if you buy more cars. His welding job has been taken away by a robot.

3. **FRICTIONAL UNEMPLOYMENT** Even during periods of pros-

perity, **frictional unemployment** persists among workers with needed skills. Frictional unemployment is a failure of the labor market to match up willing workers with unfilled jobs. It has many causes, including:

frictional unemployment: unemployment resulting from imperfections in the labor market such as poor information about jobs and lack of mobility.

IMPERFECT INFORMATION. Information is scarce and expensive. Who is hiring? Where are jobs opening up? What industries are expanding or moving into town? Information is important, but systems for matching idled workers with unfilled jobs are primitive.

Where would you go to find a job? Unemployment offices often list mostly blue-collar jobs, and even then their lists do not show all the jobs available. Private employment agencies can help, too, but they are expensive and specialize in particular occupational areas. Union hiring halls and newspaper classified advertisements are also important sources of information. But the most effective source of information on jobs is word of mouth—friends and relatives pass information along, often before the job is listed in the newspaper, employment bureau, or anywhere else. It pays to have many friends if you are unemployed!

But word of mouth is not a very scientific way to bring jobs and the jobless together. Poor channels of communication mean that an unemployed janitor can stay jobless for months while a corresponding job remains unfilled in the same city or county. Finding a job is difficult and poor information makes the task even harder and the unemployment rate higher.

Students face a different information gap. College students often train for specific careers, not knowing what jobs will be available when they graduate. Poor job information results in structural unemployment. Students of the early 1970s heard that teachers were needed, so millions of education majors entered the labor force. These highly trained teachers acted on the wrong information and ended up unemployed, underemployed, and discouraged. There is a surplus of unemployed school teachers in many areas of the country even today.

Information about the labor market is expensive and often incorrect. College students are therefore forced to gamble when choosing a major and a career. Students who select specific training get a high return on their tuition investment if their occupation happens to be in high demand. But they bear a great risk, too. Demand for their skill could disappear soon after graduation, leaving them structurally unemployed. This gamble explains the current emphasis on many campuses of "education for a lifetime." Education that teaches students to think, speak, and write is one way to hedge your bets. Chances are that these talents will always be in demand even when more specific skills are not. This type of education prepares students for a variety of interesting occupations, not all of which are likely to disappear at once.

Economics is such a useful, universal field of study. Economists learn how to think and how to analyze problems. Economists work in a variety of interesting occupations and are readily adaptable to changing labor-market conditions. If you can think, write, and speak and you enjoy this sort of analysis, you should consider an economics major. End of commercial.

BARRIERS TO ENTRY. Sometimes a person has all the talents, skill, and experience necessary for a job, but cannot get one because of **barriers to**

barriers to occupational entry: institutional factors that limit one's ability to enter a job market.

occupational entry. Unions' rules sometimes make it difficult for nonmembers to get a job and difficult for them to join the union, too. Barbers, embalmers, pharmacists, dentists, architects, and many others must pass state licensing examinations before they can practice their trades. Lawyers must do well on the bar examination or their employment opportunities are restricted. Some good college teachers find opportunities limited by their lack of a doctoral degree.

Many of these barriers to occupational entry are erected to protect the public interest. You might find it comforting to know that the doctor who is removing your appendix has graduated from an approved medical school. But other barriers exist simply to keep competition out. These barriers keep the prices that consumer pay high—boosting the income of those who already have jobs, but creating unemployment for those who are kept out of the market.

DISCRIMINATION. A rational employer hires workers based on their skills and ability to do the job. But this rule is not always applied. Many employers consciously or unconsciously discriminate against women, blacks, the young, the old, or others, causing higher unemployment in these groups. Overt discrimination ("I don't want to hire women") is difficult to combat, but the more subtle forms are just as damaging. Over the years an employer might have developed a mental image of a "successful employee." This is a worker who shows up every day, does not cause trouble, and gives good value for the wage dollar. Job applicants who do not fit the image might be just as good or better on the job. But they end up back in the unemployment line because their color, sex, or hair length does not fit the pattern the employer is looking for.

LACK OF MOBILITY. Jobs remain unfilled and workers idle because they are separated by long (and sometimes not-so-long) distances. Moving to a different city or state is costly and disruptive to family life. Unemployed people who are unwilling or unable to pay this price end up jobless for longer periods. Americans are, in general, a mobile lot, but lack of mobility is still an important part of the unemployment problem.

Economic conditions in the late 1970s and early 1980s made this problem worse. High interest rates made buying or selling homes a difficult and expensive proposition. Unemployed people could not move to take new jobs because they could not sell their homes. This increased frictional unemployment and was part of the reason for the higher average unemployment rates of this period.

A variety of labor market problems result in frictional unemployment. Jobs and the jobless do not match up because of problems with information, discrimination, mobility, and entry barriers. The quantity of labor supplied and the quantity demanded can be equal at the going wage, but frictional unemployment still results.

The Goal of Full Employment

full employment: a goal of macroeconomic policy; the minimum normal unemployment rate in a healthy economy.

Economists and policymakers like to talk about achieving **full employment.** What does full employment mean? One hundred percent employment? Zero percent unemployment?

A zero percent unemployment rate is a practical impossibility. Some people always quit good jobs to search for better ones. Students spend time unemployed, waiting for the right job to open up. Declining industries lay off workers while other firms expand. It takes time for people and jobs to match up. Some unemployment always exists and a little unemployment is a sign of a normal healthy economy.

If full employment does not mean that everyone is employed, what does it mean? The Humphrey-Hawkins Act sets a full employment goal of 4 percent unemployment for workers aged 16 and over, but even at 4 percent over four million workers would be jobless. How bitter to be unemployed in a "fully employed" world!

The idea of full employment keeps changing because the nature of the unemployment problem will not stand still. The growth of the underground economy and of voluntary unemployment now means that full employment might come at a 5 or 6 percent unemployment rate. The full employment level seems to increase, too, as more women and more young people enter the labor force. These less experienced workers are without work for longer periods as they search for a niche in the job market.

Economists will not be pinned down to an exact full employment figure. One of President Gerald Ford's economic advisors even went so far as to tell Congress that full employment was whatever the unemployment rate was at election time (Ford did not win, so maybe this economist was wrong). The most accurate statement might be that full employment exists whenever the cyclical rate of unemployment is zero. Unemployment in a fully employed world would be caused by structural and frictional problems alone.

You can chide economists for refusing to set a specific numerical full-employment goal, but it is just as well that they do not. Unemployment is more than just the numbers of the unemployment rate. Many jobless people are not even counted in the unemployment rate. And structural and frictional problems would prevail even if the unemployment rate fell to half.

How Serious Is the Unemployment Problem?

The unemployment rate is an important indicator of joblessness, but it does not tell the whole story. Unemployment is not one problem, it is really a group of problems called "unemployment" for convenience. How serious is the unemployment problem today? To answer this important question economists must really answer four separate questions:

1. HOW MANY ARE UNEMPLOYED? This is the only question where the unemployment rate published in the newspaper is much help. The unemployment rate tells us the number of people who meet the official definition of unemployment. It is, as we have seen, a flawed measure of joblessness, but it is still a good indicator since overall unemployment rises and falls with this statistic, even if the exact numbers are not always meaningful.

The unemployment rate for 1981 was 7.6 percent. This tells us that over eight million people were without jobs. Eight million is a lot of people, but the figure might understate the degree of hardship that unemployment causes. Jobless workers have spouses and families that also suffer when paychecks stop. An unemployment rate of 7.6 percent might impose hardship on as many as twenty million people.

The unemployment rate is the easiest way to look at the unemployment problem, but it does not tell the whole story. The remaining three questions are seldom answered (or even asked!) in the news; nevertheless, they are every bit as important.

2. WHO ARE THE UNEMPLOYED? What is the difference between a recession and a depression? It is a recession, the old joke goes, when my neighbor loses his job. If I'm unemployed, that's a depression! Who the unemployed are is as important at times as how many people are unemployed.

Unemployment does not strike all groups evenly. Like a cancer, unemployment destroys some parts of the economic body and leaves others healthy. Figure 3-2 shows how the 1981 unemployment rate varied within the labor force.

The overall unemployment rate in 1981 was 7.6 percent, but unemployment was more likely to strike the young and the black than adult white men and women. Adults suffered proportionately less unemployment than the population as a whole (although unemployment among females was higher than unemployment among males). Nonwhites had unemployment rates twice those of whites. Teenaged workers (just entering the labor force and searching for the experience that all employers seek) were hit the hardest. White teenagers

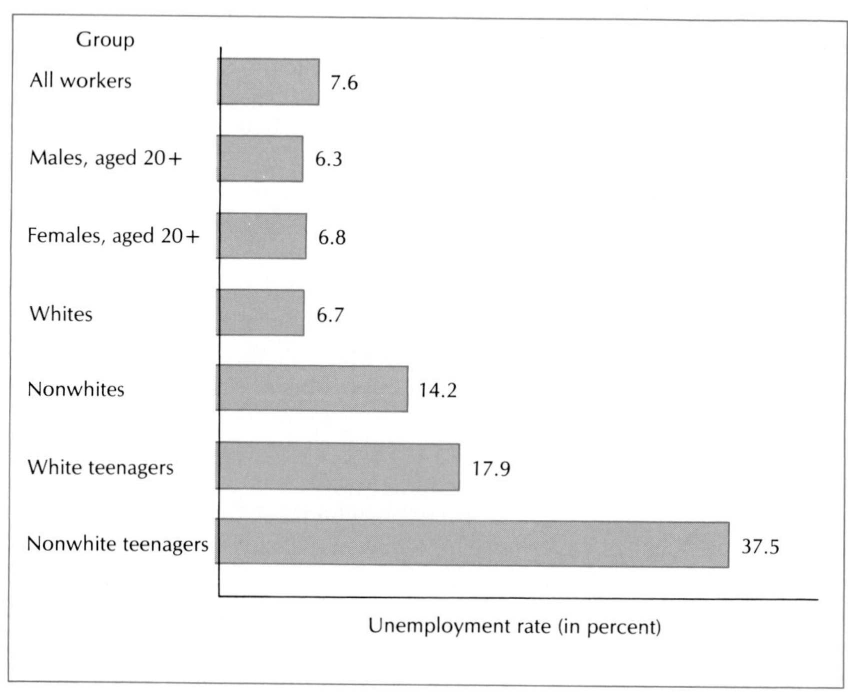

FIGURE 3-2 WHO ARE THE UNEMPLOYED, 1981? Unemployment does not strike all groups equally. Young and nonwhite workers are hit the hardest.

endured almost 18 percent unemployment; unemployment rates for nonwhite teenagers were more than twice as high.

The vast variation in unemployment rates among these groups shows how many unemployment problems there are. Unemployment difficulties of adults are different from those of teenagers. The adults work in depressed industries or have obsolete skills. The young have few skills at all and experience prejudice in a job market, as well. Nonwhite unemployment is a different problem from white unemployment. Policies that try to address the problem of, say, adult white males are likely to have little effect on other groups.

Unemployment also varies considerably from one part of the country to another. Figures for November 1981 show that Oklahoma had a modest problem—the unemployment rate was just 3.8 percent (the lowest state average in the nation at that time). Kansas, Nebraska, Wyoming, and the Dakotas had low unemployment rates, too. But Ohio, Indiana, Washington, and Oregon all had more than 10 percent unemployment, and the figures were over 11 percent in Michigan and Alabama. While 2.3 percent of the labor force was jobless in Lincoln, Nebraska, Flint, Michigan had a 20.7 percent unemployment rate. The industrial regions of Ohio, Michigan, and Indiana were idled by one set of economic problems, the lumber mills of Washington and Oregon were shut down for different reasons. And work was plentiful in Oklahoma and North Dakota.

The incidence of unemployment also varies by industry. Unemployment was high among construction and agricultural employees in 1981. Workers in government or transportation occupations had unemployment rates of less than 5 percent.

3. HOW LONG HAVE THEY BEEN UNEMPLOYED? Unemployment is a minor inconvenience or life-shattering trauma depending, in part, on how long unemployment hangs on. Figure 3-3 shows statistics on the length of unemployment for 1981.

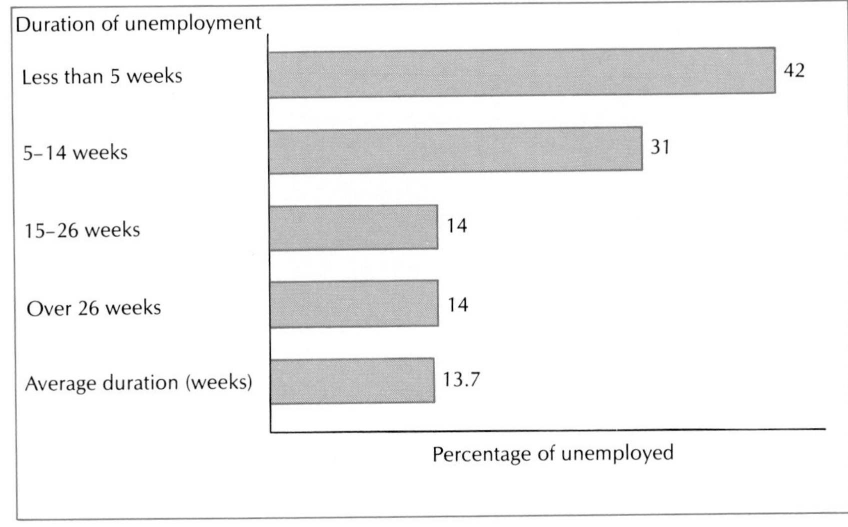

FIGURE 3-3 HOW LONG ARE THEY UNEMPLOYED, 1981? Many workers were jobless for long periods in 1981, an indicator of a severe unemployment problem.

Most people are unemployed for a relatively short time—less than five weeks. Workers with valuable skills move from one job to the next quickly, although poor communication and mobility problems prolong unemployment even here. Savings and unemployment compensation can often finance short job-search periods. Forty-two percent of those unemployed in 1981 had been jobless for five weeks or less. More worrisome about the 1981 figures are the numbers of people in the next few groups. Nearly one-third of the unemployed population had been jobless for between five and fourteen weeks. These people were having more than a little trouble finding a job—their unemployment was not purely frictional. Many, as the figure shows, had been without work for more than six months—this indicates a serious problem. These hard-core unemployed risk becoming discouraged workers, their skills and talents lost forever because they cannot find a job.

Unemployment in a healthy economy should be short term. The high proportion of the population that was out of work for more than a few weeks in 1981 was an indication of difficult economic times. Many of these people remained unemployed through 1982, leading to the even higher jobless rates observed then.

4. WHY ARE THEY UNEMPLOYED? We can gain another view of the unemployment problem by asking why people are jobless. Is their unemployment structural, frictional, or cyclic? Figure 3-4 helps us answer this question.

Unemployment in a prosperous economy would include many "job leavers"—people who leave one job to look for another. This group made up only 11 percent of the unemployed in 1981, however, indicating that job opportunities were limited. Over half of all the jobless were "job losers"—people who were fired because they had the wrong skills or laid off because the goods they produced could not be sold. The high level of job losers indicates substantial cyclical unemployment and also suggests structural unemployment problems. Over one-third of the unemployed were stymied in attempts to enter the working world. This is an indication of a stagnant economy, unable to expand to meet the needs of a growing working-age population.

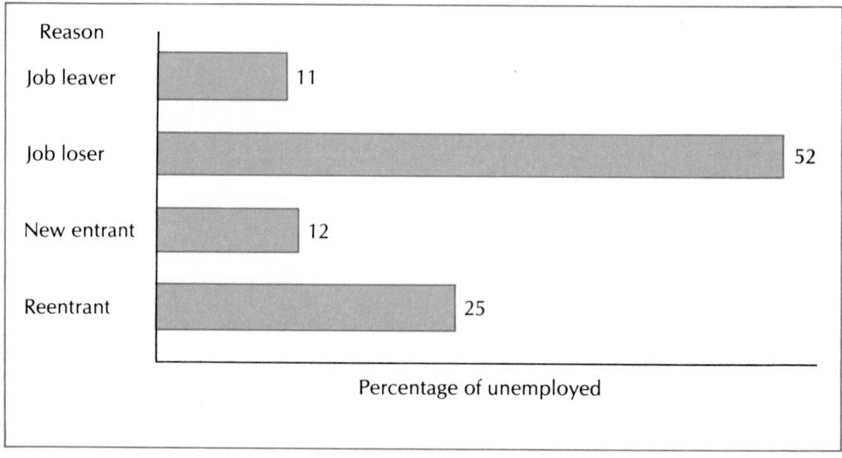

FIGURE 3-4 WHY ARE THEY UNEMPLOYED, 1981? The high percentage of job losers coupled with the low percentage of job leavers indicates falling labor demand. In addition, many of the unemployed have just entered the labor market.

Unemployment was a serious set of problems in 1981. Understanding these problems involves knowing more than numbers, however. Real understanding of unemployment forces us to learn something about the market where employment and unemployment are created. We turn next to an analysis of the labor market.

The Labor Market

The labor market is really a set of markets where workers and employers meet to exchange wages for work. There are different markets for engineers, teachers, computer specialists, and unskilled laborers, just to name a few. All these are markets, however, in the sense that we can look at them as modeled by demand and supply.

LABOR SUPPLY. Workers are the supply side of the labor market shown in Figure 3-5. The labor supply curve shows the number of workers who offer their time and talents to employers at each wage rate. The curve shows

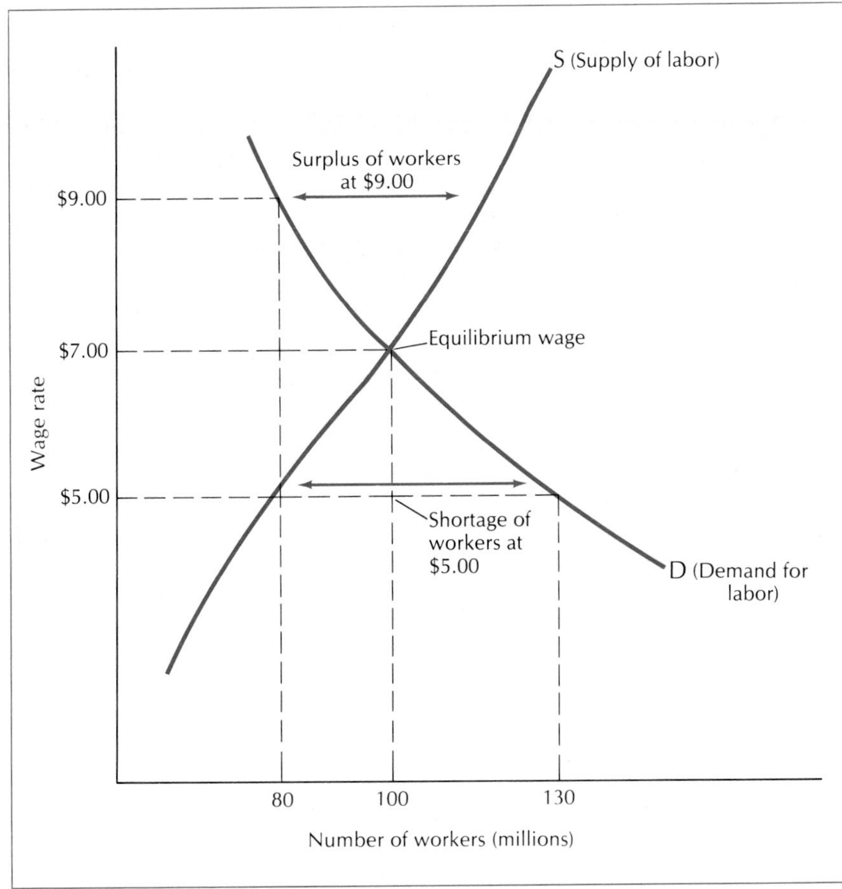

FIGURE 3-5 THE LABOR MARKET. Employers (labor demand) and workers (labor supply) come together in the labor market. Together they set the equilibrium wage rate. Frictional unemployment still occurs, even at this supply-demand equilibrium.

a positive wage response—more workers enter the market as the wage rate rises.

The supply of labor depends on many variables. Labor supply rises as new workers enter the labor force. Union rules and other barriers to occupational entry can restrict the supply of labor in a given market through artificial means. Inflation also affects the supply of labor. Higher prices mean that today's wages buy fewer goods and services. Inflation, therefore, tends to decrease labor supply for the same reason that a cut in wages reduces the quantity of labor supplied. Government tax policies affect workers' desires, too.

LABOR DEMAND. The labor demand curve is made up of businesses who hire workers to produce and sell their goods. What determines the number of workers a firm wants to hire? The wage rate is one thing, as the figure shows. The quantity of labor demanded falls as wage rates increase. But changes in wages are not the only thing involved in the hiring decision.

productivity: the ability of a resource to produce goods and services.

Productivity is an important part of labor demand. Employers base hiring decisions on a comparison of the amount that a worker can add to output against the cost of employment. An employee who generates $15 more goods per hour is profitable at a wage cost of $10 per hour. Another worker who adds only $7 per hour to output, however, will not find work at the same wage. Employers can profitably hire more workers (and even pay them higher wages, if necessary) if their productivity has increased.

aggregate demand: desired total spending in the economy; the combined demand for all goods and services.

Michigan's unemployed auto workers are productive: they suffer from a lack in **aggregate demand.** How many workers a firm needs depends on the number of goods it expects to sell. When the demand for an industry's output declines, the demand for labor in that industry falls, too. Cyclical unemployment is caused by falling aggregate demand.

Expectations and technology play an important part in labor demand. Firms adjust their workforce based on expectations of future production and prices. Employers alter the way they use labor when the technology of the production process changes. Foreign trade is also an important determinant of labor demand. Many workers in the United States produce goods for export—goods that are sold to buyers in other lands. Their jobs depend, in part, on economic conditions abroad. Other U.S. workers compete with imported goods for a job. One reason for unemployment in the auto industry is the popularity of cars produced in Japan and Germany.

Supply and demand search for equilibrium in the labor market, as Figure 3-5 shows. An equilibrium wage rate does not guarantee full employment, however. At equilibrium the number of people seeking work and the number of jobs available are equal. But the frictional problems of information, mobility, and discrimination, among others, keep some jobs unfilled and willing workers unemployed.

Causes of Unemployment

The labor market shows why unemployment increases. The first and most obvious cause of unemployment is a fall in labor demand. The demand for labor might fall in a particular industry because of changing buyer behavior, foreign competition, or other problems. For the economy as a whole, falling labor demand is associated with falling aggregate demand.

Falling aggregate demand shifts the labor demand curve from D_0 to D_1 in Figure 3-6. The least productive or least experienced workers in each industry are given pink slips (unemployment notices). The market adjusts to a new equilibrium with lower employment and lower wages, too.

This cyclical unemployment is made worse by wage rigidities—the **sticky wages** shown in the figure. Wages in many markets are not as flexible as the supply-demand model normally assumes. Union contracts, government wage rules, or an employer's unwillingness to risk driving away long-term employees are all reasons wages sometimes refuse to drop even in the face of a surplus of workers. Sticky wages make the unemployment problem even worse and create substantial involuntary unemployment. Employers must cut costs in the face of falling aggregate demand. If they cannot reduce wages, they resort to cutting the work force. Even more workers get the axe when demand falls because of the sticky wages. John Maynard Keynes believed that wage rigidities were part of the cause of the Great Depression.

sticky wages: inflexible wages; wage rates that do not fall in response to labor surplus.

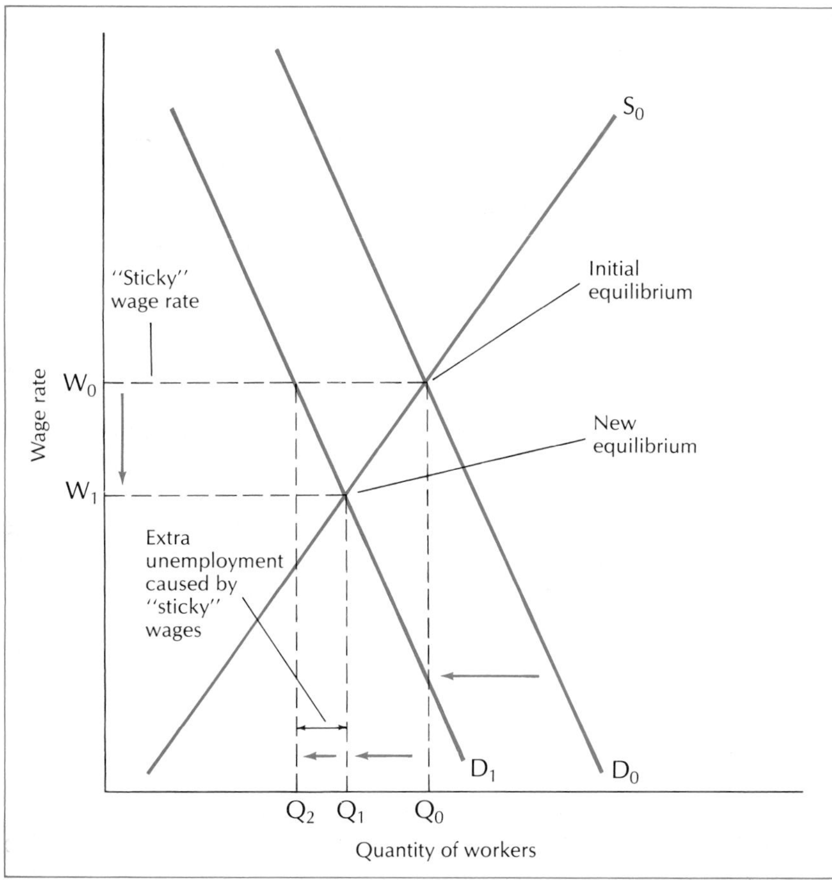

FIGURE 3-6 CAUSES OF UNEMPLOYMENT. Falling labor demand causes unemployment. Sticky wages in this labor market force employers to fire workers instead of cutting wages. Consequently, employment falls even more.

Sticky wages cause another kind of unemployment, as Figure 3-7 shows. The labor force expanded rapidly in the 1970s—the labor supply curve shifted out and to the right. This increase in labor supply normally results in higher employment at lower wages. New workers bid down the wage rate until firms can profitably hire them. But sticky wages keep this from happening. Since wages cannot fall, there is no reason for firms to hire additional employees (unless aggregate demand, productivity, or expectations change, too). The result? Many of these new workers enter the labor market only to find no job awaiting them. They make up an increasing proportion of the jobless, as we saw in Figure 3-4, and boost the overall unemployment rate. The kind of unemployment shown in Figure 3-7 was one reason for higher average unemployment rates in the 1970s and the 1980s.

minimum wage laws: laws that specify a minimum legal wage rate for workers in many job markets.

The **minimum wage law** is one important sticky wage. You will read about minimum wages in this chapter's Economic Controversy.

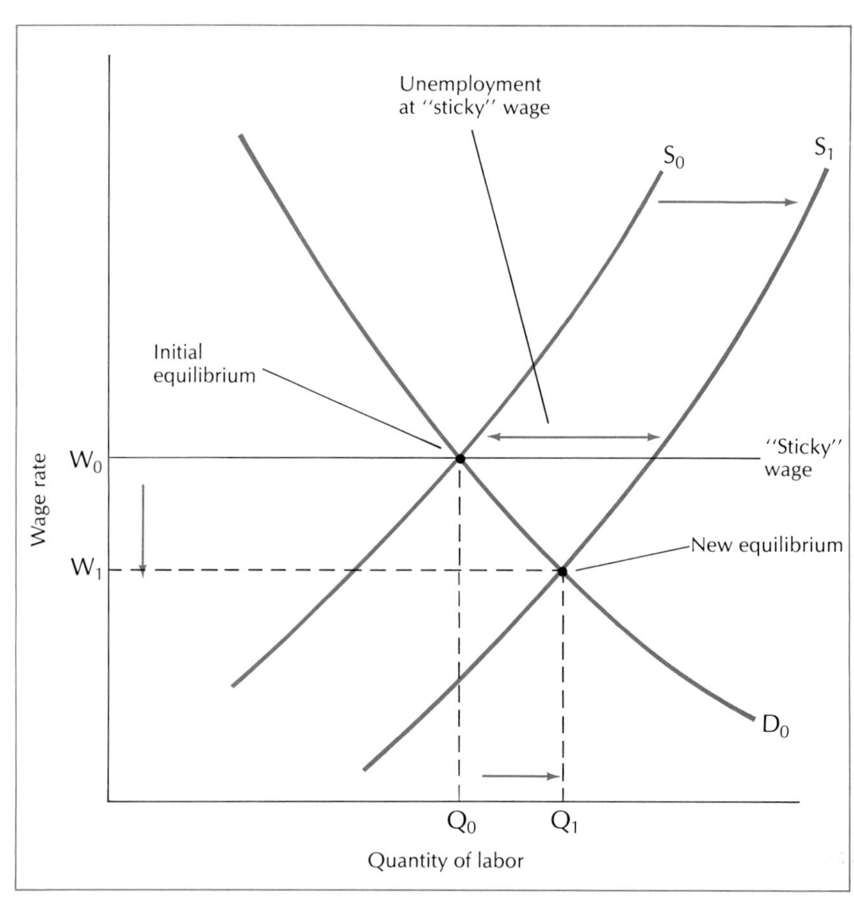

FIGURE 3-7 RISING LABOR SUPPLY CAUSES UNEMPLOYMENT. Rising labor supply, combined with inflexible wages, results in unemployment. Wages do not fall, so employers cannot hire more workers. As a result, the new entrants to the labor force are unemployed.

Inflation and Unemployment

Prices are important to firms who sell their goods and to workers who buy them. Inflation has important effects on the labor market. Figure 3-8 tells part of the story of inflation and unemployment.

Inflation—especially if it is caused by rising aggregate demand—increases the demand for labor. Firms that sell more goods or sell the same goods for higher prices can profitably employ more workers. Rising demand for labor boosts wages and employment. These demand-pull forces result in a Phillips curve–like combination of higher inflation and lower unemployment. If the supply of labor is unaffected by the higher prices, the employment gains are permanent.

But many economists believe that workers do not suffer from a **money illusion.** They see that having more money means little if each dollar buys less because of the inflation. Workers demand higher wages and fewer workers supply their labor at the current inflation-shrunk wage. The supply of labor falls due to inflation if workers think that higher prices have cut their purchasing power. Employment falls and wages are further bid up when the labor supply curve shifts from S_0 to S_1.

money illusion: the illusion that workers can buy more because they have more dollars (workers ignore inflation's effects).

How has inflation affected the labor market? A glance at Figure 3-8 shows that prices and wages have been bid up, but the number of workers with

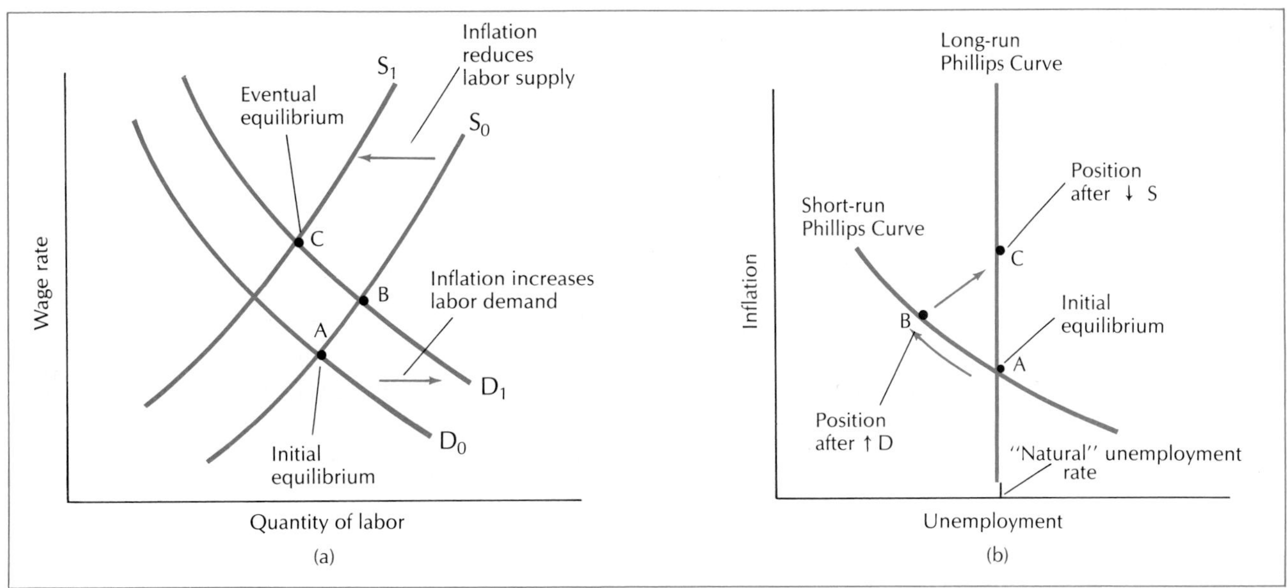

FIGURE 3-8 INFLATION AND THE NATURAL RATE OF UNEMPLOYMENT. As shown in the first half of the figure (a), inflation increases the demand for labor. In the long run, however, workers reduce the labor supply because inflation cuts the purchasing power of their wages. Increased inflation gives no relief to unemployment. This behavior creates the vertical Phillips curve shown in the second half of the figure (b).

jobs has remained about the same after all shifts are accounted for. No Phillips curve trade-off shows up here. Inflation has not reduced unemployment. Many economists think that in the short run inflation shifts out labor demand. But in the long run workers recognize the effect of inflation on their pocketbooks and reduce labor supply.

In the long run, therefore, the Phillips curve might be vertical, as the second part of Figure 3-8 shows. Government policies might increase inflation but do little in the long term to reduce the unemployment rate. This idea is termed the **natural unemployment rate** hypothesis because it suggests that the government can do little to alter the market rate of unemployment by creating artificially high inflation rates.

natural unemployment rate: the level of unemployment that occurs in an economy without government action.

Macroeconomists hotly debate the shape of the Phillips curve. Look back at the pictures in Chapter I and see if you "see" a traditional Phillips curve or if you see the vertical relationship discussed here. Economists sometimes see both shapes.

ECONOMIC CONTROVERSY:

Minimum Wage Legislation

Sticky wages are one reason for higher unemployment rates and one of these sticky wages is set by the government. Minimum wage laws apply in many markets for unskilled labor. Government sets the minimum wage that employers can pay and workers receive (the federal minimum wage is adjusted each year to account for inflation). Should such laws exist? Let us hear from both sides of the issue:

We Need Minimum Wage Laws

The first speaker is in favor of the minimum wage: Minimum wage laws are an important part of government economic policy. They are desirable and should be retained. Minimum wages are good for several reasons.

Minimum wage laws are an important tool in the fight against poverty. The minimum wage assures that all workers (except those in certain industries not covered by these laws) receive a living wage for their labor. Without minimum wages, workers might take home $2 an hour or less. Can you imagine paying rent, buying food and gasoline, and supporting a family in the 1980s on less than $100 per week? Impossible! Yet this is the world that minimum wage opponents would lead us to! Minimum wages give dignity to even unskilled workers.

Minimum wages are desirable, too, because they put workers on equal footing with their employers in the market place. Unskilled workers have little clout by themselves. They may be poorly trained and poorly informed about job opportunities. It would be easy for mighty employers to exploit these disadvantaged folks—paying them wages far below the so-called equilibrium wage.

Supply and demand works just fine when suppliers and demanders carry equal weight. In the off-balance world of labor markets, the government must throw its weight behind the workers. The minimum wage, by assuring balance in the labor market, prevents this exploitation.

If you believe that people should be protected from unscrupulous employers and should receive a living wage in exchange for their labor, then you support the minimum wage.

Minimum Wages Cause Poverty

The second speaker opposes minimum wage laws: Minimum wage laws are no cure for poverty and exploitation—they are an important cause of both of these problems. Figure 3-9 shows how minimum wage laws cause unemployment. The quantity of unskilled workers demanded falls when the minimum wage is raised each year. Young and poorly trained workers get laid off. The problem is made worse because the government's announcement of a higher minimum wage encourages even more unskilled workers to enter the labor force, resulting in an increase in the quantity of labor supplied. But these "fooled" workers will not find jobs—there are not any. They have been fooled by the minimum

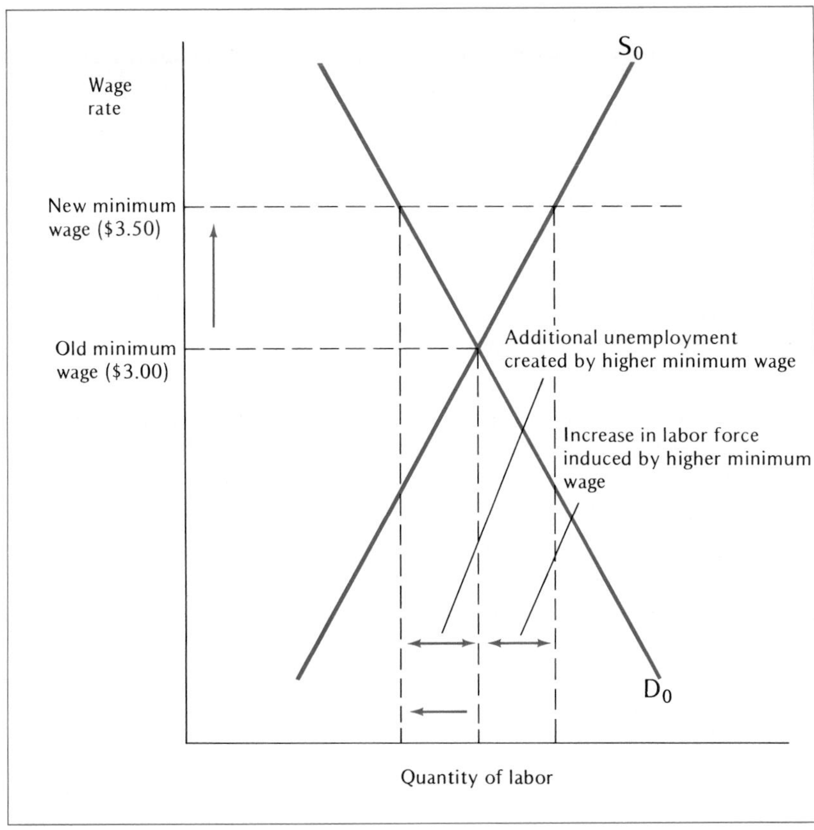

FIGURE 3-9 MINIMUM WAGES AT WORK. Minimum wage laws increase wages above the market equilibrium. More workers seek jobs, but fewer jobs exist at this higher wage. Unemployment is the result.

wage rate into entering a labor market where even fewer jobs exist. The unemployment rate necessarily grows.

Is this analysis correct? Do minimum wages cause unemployment? You have only to look at the astronomical jobless rate for teenagers to see that minimum wage laws create a serious unemployment problem among less skilled workers.

Do minimum wage laws prevent employers from exploiting workers? Exploitation is unlikely without a minimum wage. Competition prevents exploitation. If one firm sees that another has hired productive workers for too little, he or she tries to bid them away. This competition for workers keeps wages from dropping too low.

Minimum wage laws, on the other hand, probably create exploitation and sweat shop conditions. Illegal firms (in the underground economy) are free to pay whatever wage they want. Workers who cannot find jobs in the legal economy because of high minimum wages are forced into the clutches of criminals. They not only receive slave wages, they are also deprived of unemployment benefits and government health and safety protection.

Why do people favor minimum wage laws when they create poverty and force workers into sweat shops? It is all politics. Many workers keep their jobs and get paid more when minimum wages rise—they win. Unions support minimum wages, too, because higher wages for unskilled workers mean greater demand for the substitute—trained union workers. The poor and uneducated who endure the ravages of unemployment and illegal sweat shops are not equipped to protest. People who favor minimum wages do not care about the poor—they care about themselves. If they cared about the poor they would eliminate minimum wage laws.

SUMMARY

1. Unemployment is a serious problem in the United States. Unemployment has remained above the Humphrey-Hawkins Bill's 4 percent goal for many years.

2. The unemployment rate is the ratio of the number of jobless people actively seeking work to the number of people in the labor force. The unemployment rate rises when people lose their jobs or if new workers fail to find jobs on entering the labor force.

3. The unemployment rate is not a perfect measure of the unemployment problem. It does not count the underemployed and discouraged workers. But it also overstates involuntary unemployment because of voluntary joblessness and employment in the underground economy. The unemployment rate alone also fails to tell who is unemployed, why they are jobless, and how long unemployment lasts. These additional questions must be answered to understand the unemployment problem.

4. Full employment is an economic goal, but the definition of full employment is uncertain. The unemployment rate corresponding to full employment

has probably increased in recent years. Even at full employment, however, some unemployment problems would remain.

5. Employers (labor demand) and workers (labor supply) meet in the labor market. Rising unemployment rates are observed in a variety of situations. Falling aggregate demand is one cause. Unemployment is made worse when wages are sticky and refuse to fall. Sticky wages create unemployment even when demand is stable—if the supply of labor increases.

6. Does inflation reduce unemployment? The answer to this question depends on how workers react to the higher prices. If they do not have money illusion, inflation might succeed in driving up wages but not increasing the number of workers employed. The natural unemployment rate could remain constant in the long run.

7. Are minimum wage laws good? They succeed in raising wages, but they also cause unemployment. The speakers disagreed about whether minimum wages increased or decreased exploitation of unskilled workers.

DISCUSSION QUESTIONS

1. Congress is considering a bill to provide a lower minimum wage rate for teenagers than for adult workers. How would this law affect the market for teenaged workers? For unskilled adult workers? Would you favor such a change? Explain.

2. How can government act to fight cyclical unemployment? Structural unemployment? Frictional unemployment? Explain how each policy would work. Do you know someone who is unemployed? Would the policies you suggest solve his or her problem?

3. How would an increase in the minimum wage rate affect the demand for union workers? Should union workers favor or oppose minimum wage laws? Explain.

4. How serious is unemployment today? Answer the four questions posed in this chapter. (Hint: you will find the numbers you need in the periodicals, *Economic Indicators* or *Monthly Labor Review*, or in the annual *Economic Report of the President.*)

TEST YOURSELF

Circle the best response to each question

1. The total population of Academia is 200 million. Of this total, 10 million are unemployed and another 90 million have jobs. The unemployment rate in Academia is:

a. 10 percent
b. 11 percent
c. 20 percent
d. 5 percent
e. none of the above is correct

2. Rapid technological change is most likely to cause:

a. cyclical unemployment
b. structural unemployment
c. underemployment
d. frictional unemployment
e. underground unemployment

3. Sticky wages are an important cause of unemployment. Sticky wages tend to increase the unemployment rate whenever:

(W) labor demand falls
(X) labor supply falls
(Y) labor supply rises
(Z) wage rates fall

a. all of the above
b. only (W) and (Y) above
c. only (X) and (Z) above
d. (W), (X) and (Y) above
e. none of the above is correct

4. Which of the following statements is *true?*

(X) the unemployment rate can fall even if fewer workers have jobs
(Y) discouraged workers are not included in the labor force
(Z) the unemployment rate underestimates joblessness because of the existence of the underground economy

a. all of the above are true
b. only (X) and (Y) are true
c. only (Y) and (Z) are true
d. only (Y) is true
e. none of these statements is true

5. Minimum wage laws tend to:

(X) increase wage rates paid to unskilled workers
(Y) reduce the number of jobs available to unskilled workers
(Z) increase the number of unskilled workers seeking employment

a. all of the above
b. only (X) above
c. (X) and (Y) above
d. only (Z)
e. none of the above are true

SUGGESTIONS FOR FURTHER READING

The current unemployment problem is analyzed in the Labor Department's *Monthly Labor Review.* Harvard economist Martin Feldstein has written an interesting article analyzing the changing nature of unemployment in America: "The Economics of the New Unemployment," *Public Interest* (Fall, 1973). The *New York Times* reviewed the changing face of unemployment in a series titled "Out of Work" that appeared beginning with the January 10, 1982 issue. Where does unemployment come from? A theory of inflation and unemployment based on search costs is presented in Arthur Okun's influential *Prices and Quantities* (Washington, D.C.: Brookings Institution, 1981).

4

UNDERSTANDING INFLATION

Preview

What is inflation? How do today's inflation rates compare with those of the past? How does inflation in the United States compare with inflation in other countries?

How are people affected by inflation? Who loses? Does anyone win?

How can you protect yourself from inflation?

How is inflation measured? What do these price indexes mean?

What is the difference between real and nominal values?

inflation: a substantial, sustained increase in the general level of prices.

money value: value expressed as the number of dollars, not purchasing power or real value.

real value: statement of value adjusted for inflation.

INFLATION IS like the caterpillar's magic mushroom in *Alice in Wonderland.* "One side will make you grow taller and the other side will make you grow shorter," the caterpillar told Alice. Inflation has the same double effect on the economy as the magic mushroom had on Alice. One side of inflation increases wages and makes the things that we own worth more and more dollars. **Money value** grows in inflationary times. But at the same time inflation shrinks the **real value** of the dollar—each dollar buys fewer goods and services than before.

Inflation makes us both richer (in the number of dollars we hold) and poorer (in the value of those dollars). We are left wondering, like Alice, "Now which is which?"

What Is Inflation?

price index: mathematical measure of price increases.

inflation rate: rate of increase in inflation index.

deflation: falling price levels.

disinflation: falling inflation rate.

price stability: zero inflation rate.

Inflation is a substantial, sustained increase in the general level of prices. All price increases should not be called inflation, however. Many prices rise—and fall!—through perfectly normal movements of supply and demand. Individual price movements are not inflation. Economists reserve this label for periods when many prices rise simultaneously, possibly for related reasons. These rising prices increase the average cost (measured by a **price index** of the things we buy. The **inflation rate** is a measure of the speed at which average prices increase.

Deflation is the opposite of inflation. Deflation is a substantial, sustained decrease in the general level of prices. Deflation is historically tied to recession and depression, so the silver lining of lower prices comes wrapped in the dark cloud of unemployment. **Disinflation** is a period of falling inflation rates; prices still rise during deflationary periods but by smaller and smaller amounts. Disinflation and, eventually, **price stability** is one goal of modern macroeconomic policy.

Price stability is a foreign concept to today's student. It is easier to imagine life on Mars than to think of stable prices, but give it a try. Close your eyes and try to imagine stable prices. Tuition next year and the year after is the same (not more!) as tuition today. Tomorrow's grocery bill is no larger than today's. Candy bars neither rise in price nor shrink in size. Weird, huh?

This chapter doesn't explain what causes inflation—there is plenty of time for that later. This chapter tells you what inflation is and how it affects your daily life and the economic life of the nation. You will come away from this discussion with an understanding of inflation and an appreciation of its dreadful consequences.

The Inflation Record

How have we done in achieving price stability? The inflation record has been dismal in recent years. Figure 4-1 tells the story.

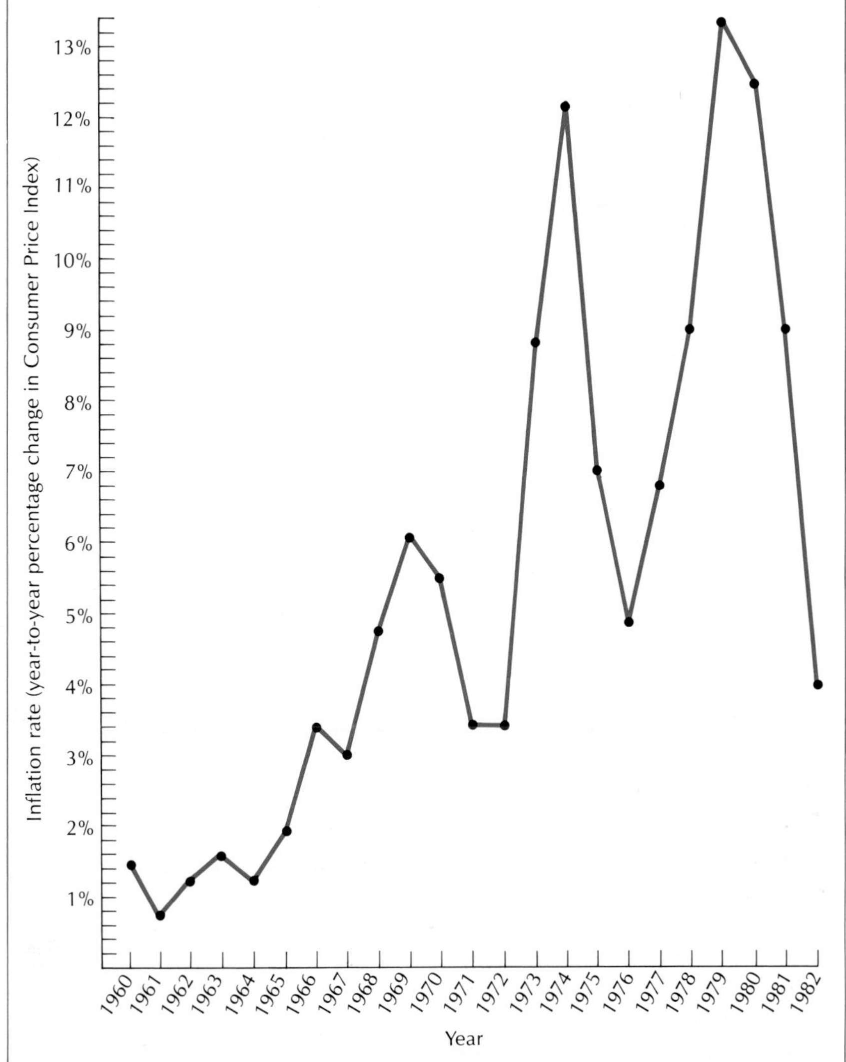

FIGURE 4-1 INFLATION RATES, 1960–1982. Inflation seems to get increasingly worse during the period from 1960 through the end of the 1970s. The low inflation rates of the early 1960s give way to the double-digit figures of the late 1970s.

Inflation rates were low in the early 1960s, but people did not think they were so low then. The *Wall Street Journal* reported "runaway" inflation of 1 or 2 percent. Inflation rates rose as the U.S. economy slid up the Phillips curve in the latter part of the decade. Oil shocks and other problems pushed inflation above 10 percent several times in the 1970s. Inflation was lower, but still a problem, in the early 1980s. Have we ever had price stability? The inflation rate averaged zero for the period 1954–1955. Prices have not remained stable for more than a month or two since.

Inflation problems have increased in the United States since the early 1960s. But even the high U.S. inflation rates of the late 1970s are modest compared to those experienced by other countries. Figure 4-2 shows an inter-

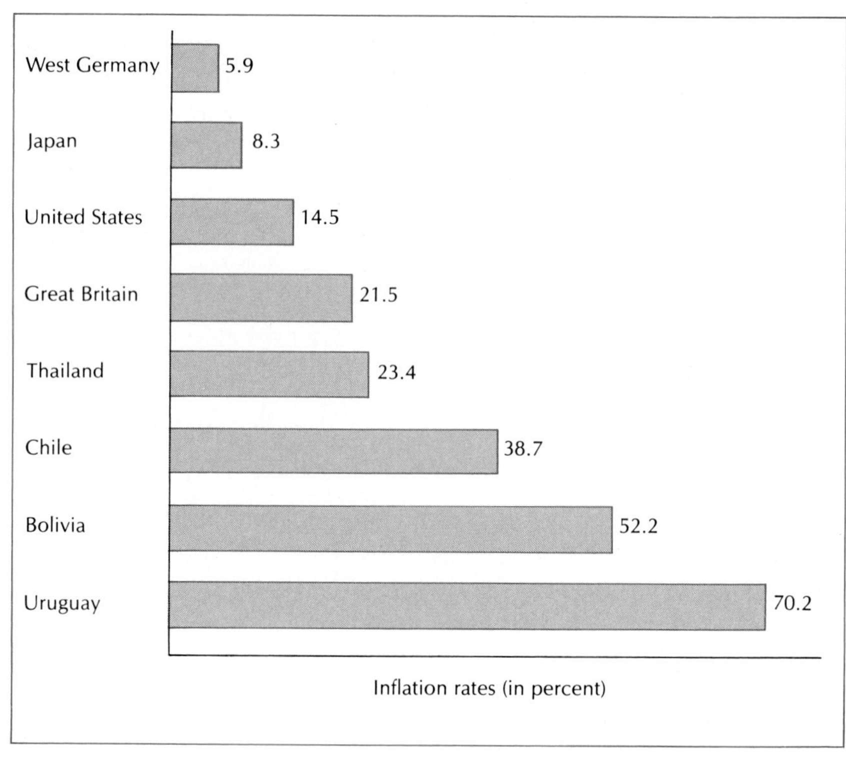

FIGURE 4-2 INTERNATIONAL INFLATION RATE COMPARISON, MID-1979 TO MID-1980. Inflation rates were high in the U.S. in the 1979–1980 period, at least compared to West Germany and Japan. Nevertheless, U.S. inflation rates were modest compared to those found in some other countries.

national inflation comparison for 1980. The United States' inflation rate was high compared to Japan or West Germany but low compared to Britain, Chile, or Uruguay.

hyperinflation: very high rates of inflation.

Even the high inflation rates of these other countries are modest, however, compared to the **hyperinflation** that history tells us is possible. Post-World War I German inflation rates were astronomical. Prices doubled and tripled in just weeks or days. Whole wheelbarrows full of paper money bought just a few groceries. Workers demanded to be paid several times a day so that they could rush out and spend their pay before its real value shrank. Economic collapse followed this period of monetary chaos.

Economic Effects of Inflation

purchasing power: the value of money measured in the amount of goods and services that it purchases.

Inflation means that your money has less **purchasing power.** We use money like a scale or a yardstick to measure value. You can compare the cost or value of two goods by comparing their price measured in money terms. This useful yardstick suddenly shrinks when inflation hits. It takes more money to measure the same value. The incredible shrinking dollar is a complex set of problems. Any list of inflation's economic effects would include the following items:

1. INFLATION HURTS PEOPLE LIVING ON FIXED INCOMES. Retired people living on fixed-dollar pensions and others who receive payments that do not vary with the price level know inflation shrinks their dollars and shatters their standard of living. The fixed amount of money buys fewer goods and services than before.

Inflation's effect on fixed incomes is important. Consider elderly pensioners who cannot pay rent or doctor bills and end up eating catfood in cold, dark rooms. Inflation's effect on fixed incomes is smaller now that many of these payments are indexed. **Indexation** is a link to a price index; income rises along with the inflation rate. Social Security checks have been indexed for many years, reducing the burden of higher prices on retired people. Not all such payments are linked to the price index, however, so indexation has only reduced, not solved, this problem.

indexation: linking money payments to a price index.

2. INFLATION DISTORTS RELATIVE PRICES. Inflation would not be such a problem if it hit everyone in the same way. Some prices skyrocket during inflationary times, but other prices stay constant or even fall. **Relative prices** are distorted by inflation. People gain or lose depending on how higher prices hit the goods they buy and sell. Housing seems particularly susceptible to inflation's effects. A little inflation means a lot higher housing costs. The following example shows why.

relative prices: price of goods compared to one another.

The *Wall Street Journal* reports that the price of an average new home increased from $87,000 to $100,600 in the period between February 1981 and February 1982. This increase of about 15 percent was higher than the national inflation average during this period. It is not hard to understand why home prices rise quickly in inflationary times. Higher construction costs reduce the supply of new housing—a cost-push price rise. Demand for housing rises at the same time. Homes were among the best inflation hedges during the 1970s—money invested in a house did better than cash in stocks or bonds. Price can only rise if demand increases while supply falls.

But higher home selling prices do not tell the whole story. People do not generally pay cash for a new house—they borrow (a mortgage loan) to make purchases as large as this. If your bank requires a 20 percent down payment, this one year's inflation means that the required sum increased from $17,400 to $20,120 between 1981 and 1982; in other words, you would have to save almost $3,000 more during the year. Do you think you could save the extra $3,000? (Do not even think about the problem of finding the first $17,000!)

But the tale gets even scarier. Interest rates also increased during the year, boosted by inflation. The monthly mortgage payment is based on both the house's price and the interest rate you pay. The average mortgage interest rate in Febrary 1981 was 15.38 percent, so the monthly payment for an average new home was $892 (excluding insurance and property taxes that might add another $100 to $400 per month to this sum). One year later the interest rate had risen to 17.33 percent. This higher interest rate, in combination with higher prices, meant that the monthly payments on the same house increased to the princely sum of $1162 per month!

One year's inflation raised average prices in the United States by approximately 10 percent, but the price of a new home (measured in monthly payments) went up by over 30 percent! Thus, assuming the requirement of 20 percent down, young people were only eligible for a home loan if they had saved an extra $3,000 during the year for the higher down payment.

Older families who already own homes escape the direct effect of higher housing prices and might even benefit if they sell their homes at a profit. Younger people, on the other hand, find that inflation pushes home costs out of reach. This dramatic example shows how inflation, hitting some markets harder than others, distorts economic life.

3. INFLATION AND INTEREST RATES. The interest rate is an important price in the U.S. economy. Interest is the income savers receive on their nest eggs and the cost consumer and business borrowers pay for funds they spend and invest. Inflation reduces the purchasing power of interest income, so lenders demand higher payments to compensate for lower real values. Inflation, then, tends to drive up money or **nominal interest rates.**

nominal interest rate: interest rate expressed in money terms.

The economist Irving Fisher studied interest rates and suggested that, all else being equal, an increase in the expected inflation rate brings an equal increase in interest rates. As the housing example has just shown, the prices of goods financed by borrowing can be doubly affected by inflation. However, the next section will show that the link between inflation and interest rates is more complex than this.

4. INFLATION AND BORROWERS AND LENDERS. Assume that there is no inflation. Would you be willing to lend $100 today in return for $110 a year from today? If this deal appeals to you, then you find a **real interest rate** of 10 percent appealing. Would you make the same deal if an inflation rate of 10 percent is expected? Probably not. If prices rise by 10 percent, the $110 you would receive at the end of the year would have the same real value as the $100 you lent in the first place. You would make no profit to compensate you for risk and patience during the year. You would be smarter to demand an additional $10 payment to compensate for higher prices. A repayment of $120 (20 percent interest) makes sense in this situation.

real interest rate: interest rate adjusted for inflation rate.

Suppose that you and I strike the bargain just described. You lend me $100 now and I agree to repay $120 in a year. We both expect prices to be 10 percent higher, so my repayment has three parts: $100 principal that I borrowed, $10 to compensate you for the lost purchasing power of this $100 loan, and another $10 interest on the loan. If the inflation rate actually is 10 percent over the coming year we both come out even—paying and receiving just what we expected in real terms. But inflation is seldom what we expect, so two possibilities need to be explored.

What if inflation is unexpectedly low? I (the borrower) find that the $120 loan repayment has greater real value than I expected. Borrowers lose when inflation is unexpectedly low because they give up more purchasing power than they anticipated. Lenders gain because their interest income is worth more than they guessed.

Borrowers win and lenders lose when inflation is unexpectedly high. If the actual inflation rate for the year is 30 percent, for example, the $120 I repay you is worth less than the $100 I originally borrowed. Borrowers gain when inflation is unexpectedly high because they give up less real value than they bargained for. Lenders are hurt by unexpectedly high inflation because they receive lower real interest income.

Inflation was an unexpected surprise in the 1970s—borrowers and lenders were generally amazed at how high inflation was. Borrowers gained at the lenders' expense for most of the decade. The disinflation of the early 1980s turned the tables, at least for awhile. Unexpectedly low inflation put borrowers in a bind. Mortgage foreclosures were at an all-time high in 1982. Borrowers who figured high inflation rates would protect them from high mortgage payments were hit by two surprises—inflation slowed way down and a recession hit, increasing unemployment. These borrowers lost in the interest rate lottery.

5. INFLATION DISCOURAGES AND DESTROYS SAVINGS. Saving is important to economic growth. Savings cushion unemployment and give the economy funds needed for major spending and investment projects. Inflation discourages saving and encourages spending to the long run detriment of the economy.

Inflation encourages people to spend because their money might be worth less in the future. "Buy now and save" is the consumers' motto in high-inflation times. High spending reduces the money left over for savings accounts.

This spendthrift behavior might be wise, given the interest rates that many people receive on their savings. If you put $1,000 in a 5½ percent passbook savings account in 1970, through the miracle of compound interest, it would have grown to over $1,700 in ten years. But the inflation rate in the 1970s was much higher than 5½ percent. It took $2,122 in 1980 to buy the goods that $1,000 purchased in 1970. The $1,700 savings account balance in 1980 bought fewer goods than the $1,000 originally deposited in 1970, despite 10 years of interest! If you were saving for a car or house or college tuition, you would have been farther from your goal at the end of the decade than you were at the start.

It makes individual sense to spend instead of save when inflation outstrips interest rates. But the economy suffers when everyone spends and no one saves.

6. INFLATION AND TAXES. Riddle: what do you get when you cross inflation with the U.S. tax system? Give up? The answer is: an inflation tax.

Suppose that prices rise 10 percent in the next year, but that your wages are indexed. You have a cost-of-living clause in your pay agreement so your wages rise by 10 percent, too. Have you been protected from inflation? No. The 10 percent "raise" that you received just balanced the lost purchasing power, but in the eyes of the Internal Revenue Service the extra funds are an increase in income, subject to the highest rate that applies. As much as half of the extra income can fall to income taxes. Result? You keep only 5 percent of the 10 percent cost-of-living adjustment and your purchasing power declines.

The inflation tax is an important part of the U.S. tax system. This "bracket-creep" shoves people into higher and higher tax rates. Congress is able to increase tax receipts without increasing tax rates—inflation does the work for them. Taxes—the price of government—were among the most rapidly rising prices Americans paid in the 1970s. Congress voted in 1981 to index the income-tax system—remove the inflation tax—in 1985. It remains to be seen if indexation will really take place. Congress may be too deeply addicted to the tax "high" that inflation brings.

7. INFLATION DISTORTS BUSINESS PROFITS. The inflation tax is bad enough for wage earners, but it is worse for businesses and people who make investments. Inflation artificially increases profits. Firms and investors make "paper profits" that do not really exist—and then they have to pay taxes on them. Accountants figure profits by looking at the money cost of doing business against the money revenues from sales. Accounting profits give a false picture during inflationary times. An example should help you see this invisible profit.

Suppose that you bought $1,000 worth of General Nuisance Corporation stock five years ago. You have been fortunate—the stock's value has increased by 50 percent to $1,500. You sell the stock and take the profit. The IRS taxes the $500 gain. But have you really profited? Suppose that the inflation rate over this period was also 50 percent. In real terms you have made no profit—your $1,000 initial investment has the same real value as the $1,500 you received for the stock. In fact, you lose because the government taxes the paper profit, not the real value. Investors experience this tax problem during inflationary times and business firms that buy inputs and then sell them at inflated prices also earn—and pay taxes on—imaginary paper profits.

8. INFLATION'S DEADWEIGHT LOSS. Inflation makes winners and losers, so rational people spend time trying to minimize their loss and maximize their gain. This is sensible behavior, but the time and money they spend trying to get around inflation's effect are wasted—they do not add to the stock of goods and services available. Economists call this a **deadweight loss.**

deadweight loss: loss due to wasted effort and resources.

People put a lot of effort into coping with inflation. Consumers spend time, labor, and gasoline shopping for bargains. Investors hedge their bets by buying gold and silver—investments that might protect them from higher prices but do not build a factory or harvest a crop. People run back and forth between savings banks and commercial banks, trying to get the last ounce of interest on their savings before writing a check.

Inflation's deadweight loss is most visible in the grocery store. More and more time is spent marking and remarking goods with higher prices during inflationary times. The rising pile of price stickers on a can of peas shows both how fast costs go up and how much labor is wasted in changing prices. Some stores have installed computerized check-out counters simply because the deadweight loss of changing prices was too high!

9. INFLATION IS A SELF-FULFILLING PROPHESY. Inflation feeds on itself. A little inflation gives rise to more and more. Suppose, for example, that you expect inflation to be higher next year. What should you do about it? If you are smart, you will try to buy things now, before prices and interest rates rise. You will pull your money out of savings and use it while it still has high value. You will also ask for higher wages at work.

All of these actions make sense for you as an individual, but if everyone takes the same course only more inflation will result. If everyone spends, demand-pull price increases prevail. If wages and business interest costs go up, you can expect cost-push price increases. When demand-pull and cost-push forces join hands, inflation really goes through the roof.

The Power of Compound Inflation

Inflation is disruptive if it lasts for only a year or two, but long-term inflation is really disastrous. Inflation generates compound price increases over a period of years. Figure 4-3 gives you an idea of what you might have to look forward to if the inflation problem is not controlled.

Textbooks like this one often cost about $20. What will this book cost in 5, 10, or 20 years? The answer depends in part on the inflation rate. Figure 4-3 shows that textbook prices rise to about $53 in 20 years if inflation averages 5 percent per year (like the inflation experienced in the 1960s). Can you imagine

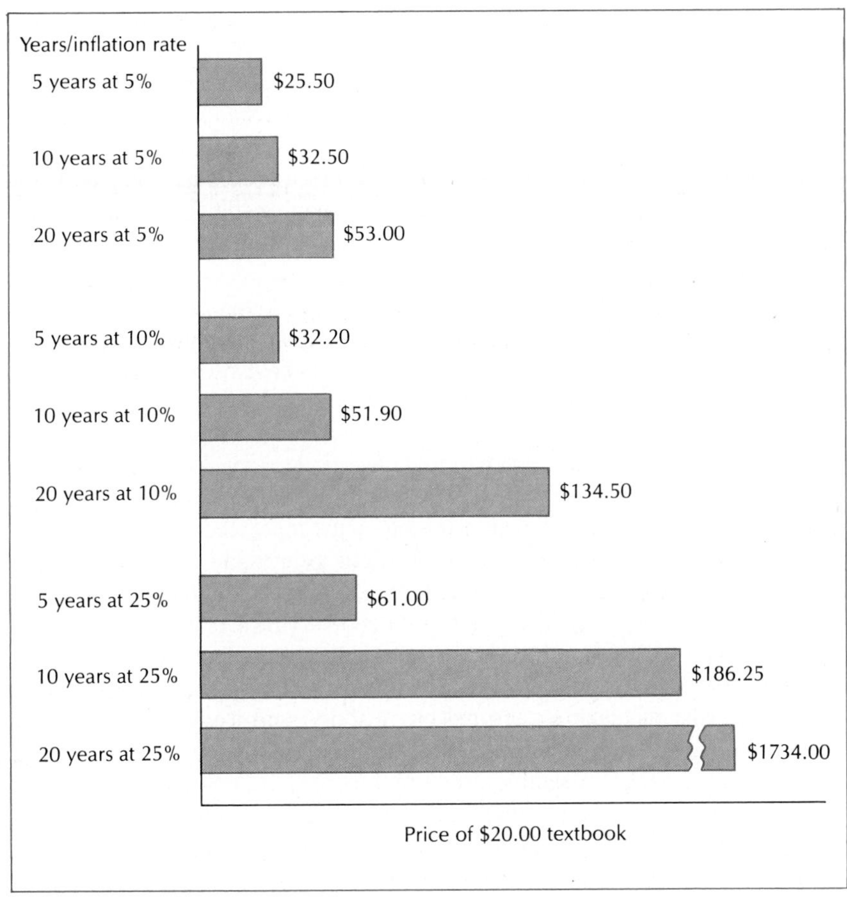

FIGURE 4-3 THE POWER OF COMPOUND INFLATION. What will this book cost in the future? If the inflation rate averages 5 percent per year, a $20 item's cost will rise to $53 in 20 years. But if 25 percent annual inflation prevails, the same good will cost over $1700!

paying $53 for this book? The "sticker shock" gets worse as the inflation rate increases. If inflation averages 10 percent (about the level of the 1970s) over the next 20 years, the book's price might be over $130! Worse yet (but mathematically true), a 25 percent average inflation rate means that students a generation from now would pay $1,734 for each textbook they need! Wow!

It is important to put these prices in perspective. If prices rise this fast, income would probably go up too. But do you think that your income will rise so that you can afford a $1,700 textbook?

This story has two morals. First, you have a personal stake in fighting inflation. Second, save this book—it might be worth something someday!

Coping with Inflation

If inflation is here to stay, we had better learn how to cope with it on both national and individual levels. For the nation, indexation seems the most logical way to shield ourselves from inflation's effects. Many countries, like Brazil, indexed in the face of persistent high inflation rates in the 1970s. Wages, prices, interest rates, and tax payments were all linked to a measure of the inflation rate.

Indexation reduces inflation's effect on the economy, but it has two important flaws. First, indexation cannot level all inflation's distortions. Indexation does not end winning and losing so much as it changes the names of the winners and losers. Second, inflation would still be a problem. And the problem might be worse because indexation makes it more difficult for the government to fight inflation. Thus, we might end up with even higher prices than would otherwise be the case.

We can cope with inflation on an individual level, too. Recent history suggests three rules to follow to reduce inflation's burden on you and your family (these rules would have worked in the past, but there is no guarantee that they are also right for tomorrow's world). The rules are:

1. BE SMART. Be smart and try to avoid inflation wherever you see it. Get the highest interest rate you can find. Keep your checking account money in the kind of bank account that pays interest, if you can. Take advantage of bargains. Invest your money in sale-priced items instead of the stock market. A cut-price can of beans in the cupboard might gain value faster than a share of IBM during inflationary times. You might even try to develop tastes for low-inflation goods. Wine prices have shot up in recent years: if inflation has not hit Kool-Aid as hard try to develop a taste for this beverage instead. Try shopping at discount grocery stores that are able to pass on savings to you because they eliminate the cost of marking the prices on individual items or bagging your groceries. Learn to enjoy shopping for bargains. Haunt garage sales and flea markets. Find out where discount stores and factory outlets are. You are smart if you shop in ways that keep inflation from hitting you as hard as others.

2. BE LUCKY. Being smart may not be enough. You probably need to be lucky, too. Pick the right career—one that generates pay raises that beat the cost of living and the inflation tax. Live in a region that does not suffer inflation at the national average. Buy goods just before the merchant raises the price. Being lucky really pays off during high inflation years.

3. BE DEEPLY AND SINCERELY IN DEBT. In the past, most bouts of inflation have been surprises—unexpectedly high inflation rates that benefited borrowers and hurt lenders. If you are smart—and you think that history repeats itself—then being in debt makes you a winner. You can borrow money to buy goods now, before their prices rise, and then pay off the loan with inflation-shrunk dollars. Go to school with borrowed tuition—investment in education gives high real returns. If you are lucky, inflation might outstrip expectations and your strategy will pay off. You should be aware that this plan could backfire, however. You might be unlucky enough to end up saddled with high interest payments while inflation rates fall. Then you would be on the loser's end of the stick.

Thus, on an individual level, the answer to inflation is to be smart and buy now, be lucky so that your purchasing power rises in spite of inflation, and be deeply and sincerely in debt so that you get the borrower's share of unexpected inflation's winnings. But if everyone follows this advice, the combination of their actions gives us the self-fulfilling inflation discussed a few pages back. Prices rise because of our actions, and the economy's problems get even worse.

What *is* the best way to cope with inflation? The best way is, ultimately, not to have any. Until price stability arrives, however, the best advice is simply to know what inflation is and what it does.

Measuring Inflation

It is bad enough to know that inflation rates are high. Why do we need to measure inflation? What good is it to know how much prices rise?

We need to know the exact inflation rate for several reasons. First, Congress and the President cannot make sound judgments on inflation versus unemployment issues unless they know the facts. Second, it is important to know how fast prices are rising so that individuals can develop realistic expectations. Inflation can make you a winner or a loser depending on how well you anticipate price increases. Finally, billions of dollars ride on the inflation rate. Pay contracts, social security checks, and many other payments are indexed. A percentage point change in the measured inflation rate means hundreds of dollars difference to individual workers and pensioners and billions of dollars to employers and the government. It is important to all these people that inflation be accurately measured.

How can you measure inflation in the prices that you pay? There are several possibilities. You could go to the grocery store today and make a list of all the prices there. You could then go back in a year and compare the prices, making a list of those that went up and those that went down. If more prices rise than fall, you might conclude that there was inflation during the year. This method is quick and easy, but it would not give you a numerical inflation rate.

Another way to measure inflation would be to add up the prices of everything in the store at the start and the end of the year and then divide by the number of items to compute the average price. This provides a number, but not a very useful one. This inflation index suffers several problems. First, it mismeasures inflation because you do not buy everything in the grocery store. You might never buy calf's liver, for example, and seldom buy paper towels, but both of these items would get equal weight in your price index with the popcorn and soda that you regularly buy. Furthermore, this grocery price index does not include many items—like rent and transportation costs—that soak up most of your budget. Thus, this price index misses many things that affect your life and includes much that is not important to you.

base year: arbitrarily chosen year, used to construct the price index market basket.

market basket: list of types and quantities of goods and services purchased in the base year.

The best measure of inflation is a price index like those used by the United States government. The Commerce Department begins by picking a **base year.** Consumers are surveyed in the base year to see what types and amounts of goods they purchase. This information is used to construct a **market basket** that weights the goods and services that are purchased regularly by consumers more heavily than those that are infrequently purchased. The inflation rate is calculated by comparing the cost of the market basket in the base year with the bill for buying the same market basket in other years.

All this is easier to see if you build your own inflation index. The Class of 1982 was surveyed about their spending habits when they entered college in September 1978. The result of this consumer survey is shown in the first half of Table 4-1. The average freshman bought two pizzas per week and washed this down with two bottles of reasonably good wine (this was a particularly intemperate group of freshmen). Two tickets to the campus movie were included in the budget and four quarters were lost each week in Pong-type video games (a true market basket for this or any group would include hundreds of items—this list is limited to four for ease of discussion). These goods and amounts are the Student Price Index market basket.

Four years later the Class of 1982 was ready to graduate. How much inflation did these seniors experience during four years in school? We can compute the inflation rate from the information given in the table. The cost of the 1978 market basket at that time was \$29. Students spent \$16 on pizzas (two at \$8 each), \$8 on wine (two bottles at \$4 each), a total of \$4 on movie tickets, and \$1 on video games.

TABLE 4-1 A Hypothetical Student Price Index

	September 1978[a]		June 1982[b]	
Item	Price	Quantity	Price	Quantity
Pizza (delivered to dorm)	\$8.00	2	\$16.00	1
Wine	4.00	2	1.50	12
Campus movie ticket	2.00	2	3.00	2
Video game	.25	4	.25	12

$$\text{Inflation rate 1978–1982} = \left(\frac{\$42}{\$29} - 1\right) \times 100 = 44.8\%$$

[a]Cost of 1978 goods (in 1978 prices) = \$29.
[b]Cost of 1978 goods (in 1982 prices) = \$42.

What would the same goods cost the graduating seniors? Pizza (delivered to the dorm) went up a lot over the years—its price increased from $8 to $16. Two pizzas (the amount purchased in 1978) would total $32. The wine that the students drink actually went down in price. The quality of the wine is changed, and much of the price decrease is due to a change in state tax laws. The two bottles in the 1978 market basket would cost $3. Tickets to the campus movie increased from $2 to $3. Two tickets add $6 to the total. Video games still cost just a quarter, so four tries still cost $1 in 1982.

If you add up the total cost of the 1978 market basket at 1982 prices you will get $42. The inflation rate for this four year period is calculated using the following formula:

$$\text{Inflation rate} = \left(\frac{\text{Cost of 1978 market basket at 1982 prices}}{\text{Cost of 1978 market basket at 1978 prices}} - 1\right) \times 100$$

Table 4-1 makes the calculation. The inflation rate is ($42/$29 − 1) × 100 = 44.8 percent. (Multiplying by 100 converts the decimal fraction to a percent.)

Does this seem like high inflation for just a four year period? The Class of 1982 thought so—they were convinced that they were hit harder than anyone else by inflation. Alas, they were wrong. The inflation rate for the U.S. economy between September 1979 and June 1982 was also about 44 percent. Inflation was a serious problem for these students and for the economy as a whole.

Price Index Problems

The inflation index just discussed has several practical advantages. It is easy to calculate the inflation rate once the market basket is constructed—all you have to do is find current prices for the items on the list. The Commerce Department employs people to check these prices monthly in every region of the country. They publish the national inflation averages and separate price indexes for major metropolitan areas. But a glance at Table 4-1 shows some problems with measuring inflation in this way.

One big problem is that many students have different buying habits than the "average" market basket. Students who spend less money on wine and more money on orange juice will not suffer exactly the same inflation rate as the one calculated here. Average price indexes cannot measure the true inflation rate for any individual because no one buys the average market basket.

A second problem is that the senior students did not actually buy the goods in their freshman market basket. A glance at the table shows that students bought fewer pizzas and more wine and video games (all useful items in studying for final exams). The price index has to hold the market basket constant if it is to measure changes in price only (if you change both price and quantity, neither is accurately measured). But students buy different things at the end of college than they do at the start—they even buy things that are not on this list. But the inflation index cannot adjust for this and still measure just inflation.

The third problem with this price index is that it does not adjust for differences in the quality of goods. You can argue about movies in 1982 versus movies in 1978—there probably is some difference in quality. But more to the point are the differences in wine ($1.50 wine—yuk!) and the video games. A twenty-five cent investment in 1982 buys a more colorful and entertaining game than it did in 1978. But the price index cannot adjust for this quality change.

A fourth problem is that student buying habits have changed. The pizza that was delivered to the dorm in 1978 has gone up in price so much that 1982 students go out to eat or buy other, less costly, delights. Students do not buy the same things at the same prices as before, but the price index must keep measuring the same things or else it will not have any meaning at all.

A final flaw is that the index does not include an important item—government—that everyone buys. The state sales tax went up over this period, but this price was not even included in the price index.

The Student Price Index shown here is full of holes—you would not want to put much faith in it. Yet all these faults apply to the government's price measures, too. Picking an average market basket means that people who use different shopping lists have different individual inflation rates. Buying habits change over time, too; but the government can only update the official market basket every few years, so it is always a little out-of-date. Taxes and changes in where people buy goods are flaws in the official price index just as they were in the Student Price Index. Quality changes also cause problems.

What does this mean to you? First, it means that official inflation measures are only general indicators of how fast prices rise—they should not be taken as precise statements of how much prices paid by any individual or group go up. Second, you should conclude from this discussion that the inflation index does not measure the cost of living, as many people think. Look at the students in Table 4-1. They buy different goods at different prices with different qualities, and some frequently purchased goods are not even included in the market basket. While the inflation calculation that uses this data can give a general idea of how fast the prices of these particular goods have gone up, how can it tell us how fast the cost of living has increased? It cannot.

Three Inflation Measures

Three general measures of inflation are used in the United States. Many other indexes are available—look at the figures in the annual *Economic Report of the President* to see inflation measures for specific industries and groups. Each measure of inflation is useful—if it is used correctly.

consumer price index (CPI): a measure of inflation based on goods purchased by consumers.

1. CONSUMER PRICE INDEX. The **Consumer Price Index (CPI)** is the most widely used measure of inflation. It is designed, as its name suggests, to gauge inflation's effect on consumers. The index is calculated with the 1967 base year set equal to 100. The index has increased every year since 1967 showing inflation in each year. The CPI is shown in Figure 4-4.

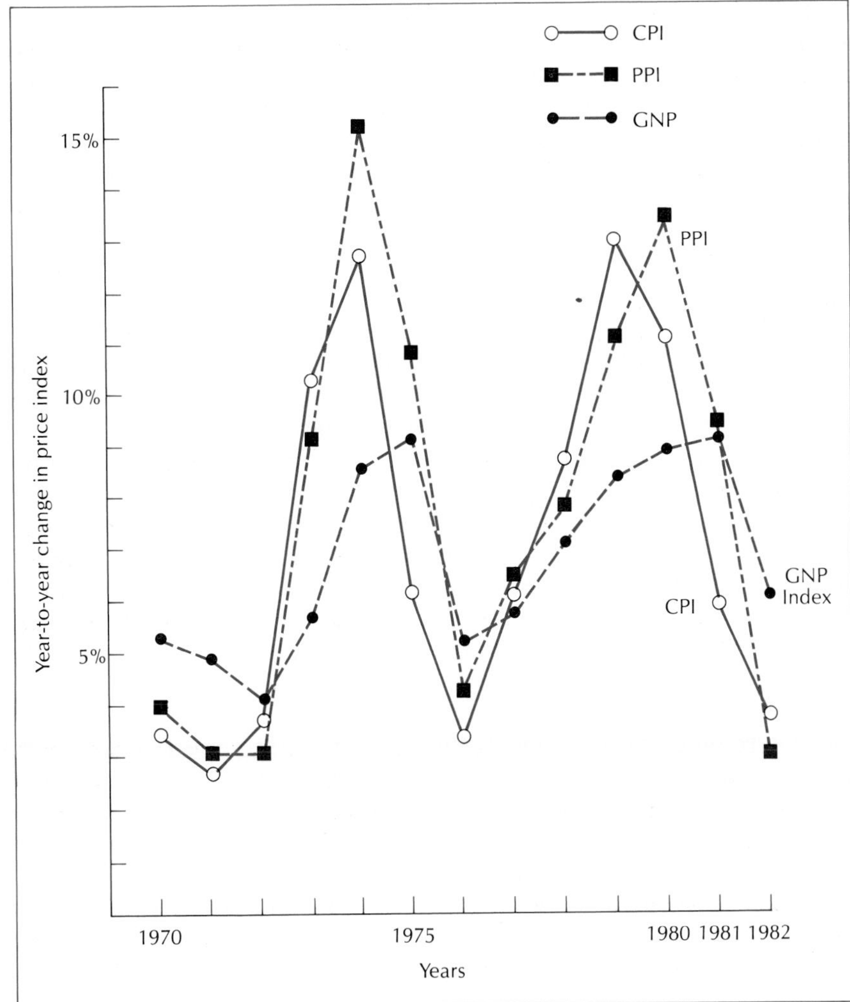

FIGURE 4-4 THREE PRICE INDEXES. The GNP index shows the underlying inflation rates. The CPI and PPI show how inflation hit consumers and producers, respectively.

The Consumer Price Index was revised in 1978 to bring the 1967 market basket up to date. The revision also expanded the market basket to look at a wider range of shoppers. The CPI looks at the buying habits of urban families. If your shopping list is much different from theirs, the CPI does not accurately reflect your inflation burden.

The CPI has become controversial. The *Wall Street Journal* (p. 22) called it the "Confounded Price Index" in a May 13, 1981 editorial. The CPI overstates inflation some of the time and understates it in other periods. Inflation in the late 1970s and early 1980s hit housing particularly hard. If you bought a new house you found costs rising rapidly. But people who did not exchange homes did not suffer similar price increases. A family that bought their home in 1975 would have experienced only modestly increased housing costs despite the huge rise in monthly costs that new purchasers felt. The CPI, many argue, overestimates the burden of higher housing costs on consumers in general.

So what? Why does it matter if the CPI is biased when housing prices and interest rates rise? It matters because the CPI is used to calculate inflation increases in Social Security checks, military pensions, and the like. If the CPI overstates inflation, the government pays out billions of dollars too much and your taxes rise to make up the difference!

The CPI was put on a "rental equivalent" basis starting in 1983 to end the overestimation of inflation noted above. But the practical significance of this change was called into question in early 1982. Interest rates fell a little (reducing housing costs measured the old way) while average rental costs increased (raising the CPI measured the new way). If the new CPI had been in use in early 1982 it would have shown a larger increase in the CPI than would have the old index, thereby resulting in bigger social security indexation payments.

Should the CPI be modified to compensate for the special buying habits of specific groups? The answer to this political question probably depends on whether you are a young worker (paying high social-security taxes) or an elderly retiree (receiving modest social security benefits). The technical problems of measuring inflation have become a practical problem to Presidents, Congressmen and voters.

producer price index (PPI): measure of inflation based on goods used by business firms.

2. PRODUCER PRICE INDEX. The **Producer Price Index (PPI)** is sometimes referred to by its old name, the Wholesale Price Index. The PPI measures inflation experienced by business firms. Since it looks at the average purchases of a wide range of businesses, it cannot really indicate the inflation rate suffered by any particular firm or industry. It is, however, a good general indicator of the price increases firms experience.

leading indicator: a statistic that foretells future changes.

The PPI is particularly useful to economists because it is a **leading indicator** of consumer prices. Changes in producer prices tend to foreshadow changes in consumer prices. Firms that bear higher costs today raise their prices tomorrow. If we see a 10 percent increase in the PPI in January, we can expect big increases in the CPI in February, March, or April. If you want to get an idea of where consumer prices are going in the future, keep your eye on the PPI today!

GNP index: a measure of inflation for the entire economy.

3. GNP IMPLICIT PRICE DEFLATOR INDEX. The **GNP index** is the broadest measure of inflation for the economy. The GNP index takes as its market basket all goods and services produced in the United States—everything is included somewhere in the GNP index. The GNP index cannot tell us much about the inflation rate of any group or individual, but it does give us a good idea of how overall prices change.

Figure 4-4 shows how the CPI, PPI, and the GNP index have moved from year to year since 1970. The GNP index effectively measures the underlying inflation rate. It does not jump when specific products suddenly rise in price. The CPI and PPI indexes are more volatile. The overall trend of all three indexes has been up since 1970.

Calculating Real Values

Someday you are going to be asked a question like, "What was the inflation rate last year? Did our pay increase to keep up with inflation?" As a student of economics you ought to be able to answer questions like these. This section shows you how.

The first problem is to calculate the inflation rate between two years using the CPI. The easiest way to do this is to use the formula

$$\text{Inflation} = \left(\frac{\text{CPI this year}}{\text{CPI comparison year}} - 1\right) \times 100$$

The inflation rate between 1978 and 1979, for example, is found by first looking up the CPI numbers in Figure 4-5 and then plugging the values into the formula to get

$$\text{Inflation} = \left(\frac{217.4}{195.4} - 1\right) \times 100 = 11.1 \text{ percent}$$

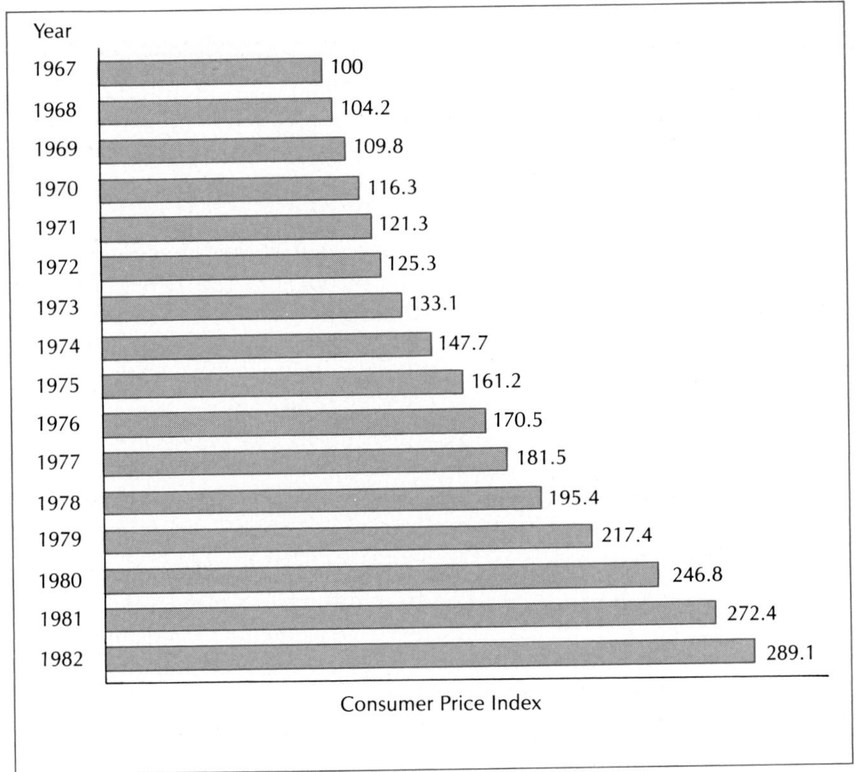

FIGURE 4-5 CONSUMER PRICE INDEX, 1967–1982.

As an exercise, calculate the inflation rate between 1980 and 1981. The answer is provided at the end of the Summary section of this chapter.

Now suppose that your pay increased from $20,000 to $25,000 during 1978. Did you beat inflation? One way to tell is to compare the increase in income to the increase in prices. Your wages went up by

$$\left(\frac{25{,}000}{20{,}000} - 1\right) \times 100 = 25 \text{ percent}$$

Prices went up an average of 11 percent over this period, so income increased faster than prices. Thus, your real income increased.

nominal value: value expressed in money terms.

A more exact way to look at real values is to convert everything from **nominal values** to dollars of the same "size." Suppose, for example, that you want to compare your pay in 1978 and 1979 in dollars of the same value. You can compute this real value using the formula

$$\text{Value in 1978 dollars} = \text{value in 1979 dollars} \times \frac{\text{CPI in 1978}}{\text{CPI in 1979}}$$

Your $25,000 pay in 1979 is equivalent to

$$\$25{,}000 \times \frac{195.4}{217.4} = \$22{,}470 \text{ in 1978 dollars}$$

In real terms, then, your pay increased from $20,000 in 1978 to $22,470 in 1979. Of your $5,000 raise, $2,470 of the increase represented higher purchasing power, the rest of the raise went to pay higher prices. You can use this formula to make calculations for other time periods by changing the years consistently throughout the formula.

You are lucky, by the way, if your pay went up as the example shows. Real incomes declined for most Americans throughout the 1970s. Wages and salaries rose, but not as fast as the inflation rate!

ECONOMIC CONTROVERSY:

Inflation or Unemployment?

Economists often disagree about basic social, political, and economic issues. These arguments stem as often from differences in personal values as from divisions of economic theory. Differences in values and philosophy account for the sometimes maddening propensity of respected economists to draw different conclusions from the same set of facts.

The question of inflation versus unemployment has stirred much debate within the economics profession. If there is a Phillips curve trade-off between these two ills, then one goal must be sacrificed to achieve the other. Even if the Phillips curve does not hold, it is still true that economic policies often choose to fight either inflation or unemployment but seldom both. A choice must be made: which problem is more demanding, inflation or unemployment?

This question is particularly interesting because it has a political as well as an economic side. Republicans are stereotyped as inflation fighters, willing to suffer high unemployment rates if necessary. Democrats are often viewed as willing to bear inflation to reduce the unemployment rate. These labels are oversimplifications, to be sure, but voters may still cast ballots on the basis of this view.

Winners and Losers

One problem that we face in weighing inflation against unemployment is that both problems create losers (and winners), but they affect different groups to different degrees. In choosing between the two ills we must make an uncomfortable judgment. Mr. A and Ms. B are both sick. Which is the sicker? Should A's illness be prolonged if it helps B? Or is it the other way around?

In making judgments like these we leave the realm of **positive economics.** We cannot prove that either inflation or unemployment hurts people the most. We must make a normative decision, thus we enter the realm of **normative economics.**

positive economics: economic analysis that can be proved right or wrong.

normative economics: economic analysis based on value, judgment, or philosophy; statements that are a matter of opinion, not fact.

Unemployment brings two sorts of loss. The private burden of unemployment falls on those who lose their jobs. This burden takes the form of lower income, reduced opportunity, and lower self-esteem. The social costs of unemployment are many. The government (and therefore taxpayers) pays out more for unemployment benefits and social programs. Tax collections go down when people lose their jobs, putting a second social burden on the economy.

Lost production is another social cost. When workers remain unemployed their talents and skills are unused. Less is produced to satisfy society's wants, needs, and desires. Finally, crime and conflict often stem from unemployment. This is particularly likely if unemployment is heavily concentrated in one ethnic, social, or geographic group.

Inflation imposes a different set of losses. Inflation strikes throughout the economy. Money holders, taxpayers, investors, and people on fixed incomes are particularly hard hit. Inflation benefits some people, however. Borrowers gain during periods of unexpectedly high inflation, for example. This chapter discussed inflation's effects in detail.

How do we weigh these gains and losses? Let us allow the two speakers to present their views.

Unemployment Is More Important

Unemployment rates should be reduced, even if it means higher inflation rates. The unemployment burden falls directly on people, lowering their standard of living and increasing the gap between the rich and the poor in an economy already known for its unequal distribution of income. How can we justify poverty and unemployment in a nation as rich as ours?

Unemployment is a more serious problem than inflation because the principal effects of joblessness are heavily concentrated. No individual suffers as much from inflation as some people do from unemployment. That unemployment strikes already disadvantaged groups in our society—like blacks and young people—with more force than others only adds to the problem.

The people who are hurt by inflation are those who have the most to begin with: people with money, investments, and savings. Unemployment strikes those who are the least able to bear the burden: low-income families who often possess few job skills. The unemployed desperately need help. Those harmed by inflation are able to help themselves.

Finally, people are able to protect themselves from inflation. It is more difficult to hedge against unemployment. Unemployment is the more serious problem.

Fight Inflation First

Inflation is a bigger problem than unemployment. It affects everyone and distorts all sorts of economic decisions. The severity of unemployment is overstated. The unemployed bear a lower private cost than the last speaker suggests. Unemployment benefits, social welfare programs, and food-stamp subsidies all reduce the burden of unemployment. Much unemployment is voluntary, anyway. We should not get too upset if someone chooses to take a vacation, should we? People use their unemployed time to search for ever better jobs. This is not always true, but it occurs often enough to make the idea of devastating unemployment largely invalid. The suffering from unemployment is, in general, overrated.

The unemployment rates overstate the magnitude of the problem. When voluntary unemployment and the underground economy are considered, unemployment rates today are not much above the full-employment level. Inflation rates, however, do not lie. Inflation is a more serious problem today than it has ever been.

Inflation hurts the elderly poor, robs us all through higher taxes, and forces a deadweight loss on society. Should not the harm to everyone in the economy be more important than the modest discomfort of unemployment?

A final argument is perhaps the most important. History teaches us that unemployment eventually goes away. Governments do not fall because of high unemployment rates. Inflation, however, feeds on itself. It grows and grows and becomes hyperinflation that destroys the economic system. Inflation threatens political and economic unrest. At its worst, inflation is a fatal disease. Inflation is the Plague of the modern world. If we do not want to enter another Dark Age, we have to deal with this contagious disease now.

SUMMARY

1. Inflation is a substantial, sustained increase in the general level of prices. Inflation rates have varied widely over the past 20 years, but there has been a general upward trend.

2. Inflation affects the economy in many ways. Inflation affects people living on fixed incomes and those who borrow or lend money. Inflation distorts relative prices, boosts taxes and profits, and discourages saving. Inflation, at its worst, can become a self-fulfilling prophecy.

3. Most inflations in recent years have been unexpected. This surprise inflation benefits borrowers and hurts savers and lenders. If history repeats itself the best way to cope with inflation is to be smart, be lucky, and be deep in debt. There is no guarantee that past is prologue, however.

4. Indexation is one way for the economy to cope with inflation. Indexation cushions inflation's blows but also encourages inflation by making it easier to live with. Many countries that have suffered high inflation have resorted to indexation.

5. Inflation is measured using a price index. The price index compares the cost of a market basket in a base year with its cost in the current year. The inflation index gives a general measure of price increase but does not perfectly measure inflation's burden on any individual.

6. The Consumer Price Index, the Producer Price Index, and the GNP Index are the main inflation measures in the United States. The PPI is a leading indicator of changes in the CPI.

7. The inflation rate is calculated from the CPI (or any other inflation index) using the formulas given in this chapter. You can compute the inflation rate and convert values from nominal to real terms using the CPI. In the suggested problem in this chapter, the inflation rate between 1980 and 1981 is 10.4 percent.

DISCUSSION QUESTIONS

1. Using 1970 as the base year, calculate the inflation rate based on the hypothetical market basket shown below. If a worker made $100 per week in 1970 and $125 per week in 1977, would he or she have gained or lost to inflation?

	1970		1977	
Item	Price	Quantity	Price	Quantity
Beer	$1.25	10	$1.50	7
Pizza	$3.50	8	$4.00	6
Tums	$ .25	6	$ .20	6

2. There is another way to calculate inflation. Suppose that you used the more recent (1977) year's purchases as the market basket instead of the 1970 one you used in Problem 1. Is the inflation rate you calculate any different? Which one is correct? Why does the government not compute inflation both ways? Explain.

3. Suppose that you expected a 20 percent inflation rate over the next year. How would this expectation alter your behavior? What would you do differently? Explain.

4. Deflation is the opposite of inflation. Is deflation good or bad? List the winners and losers from an unexpected deflation. Why would each group gain or lose?

5. Use the CPI values in Figure 4-4 to calculate the inflation rate between 1970 and 1980. If your wages went from $4 per hour to $6 per hour over this period, would the real wage have increased, decreased, or remained constant? Explain.

TEST YOURSELF

Circle the best response to each question.

1. Which of the following events would likely *not* result from rapid inflation?

a. rising interest rates
b. rising tax burdens
c. rising real incomes of fixed-income recipients
d. rising business profits
e. falling savings rates

2. Which of the following events represents inflation?

(X) rising prices of hamburgers and french fries
(Y) increased prices for theatre tickets
(Z) tuition increases for college students

a. all of these are inflation
b. none of these represent inflation
c. only (X) and (Z) are inflation
d. only (Y) and (Z) are inflation
e. only (X) is inflation

3. You have been assigned by the Commerce Department to measure the inflation rate in a small isolated town. Last year a market basket of goods and services bought there cost $200. This year the same types and quantities of goods cost $240. Based on this comparison the inflation rate is:

a. 40 percent
b. 20 percent
c. 120 percent
d. 10 percent
e. it is not possible to tell from information given

4. Last year Joe College spent $500 on food and clothes during the fall semester. This fall Joe bought different items (he is now buying preppy clothes to replace his jeans and cowboy boots) and he ended up spending $750. Joe's inflation rate, based on this data, is:

a. 25 percent
b. 50 percent
c. 150 percent
d. 125 percent
e. it is not possible to tell from information given

5. You think that prices are going to increase in the future. Which of the following would be rational actions for you to take given this expectation?

(X) buy a new car now instead of waiting
(Y) borrow money to purchase real estate
(Z) deposit money in a passbook savings account

a. all of these are rational actions
b. none of these are rational actions
c. only (X) and (Y) are rational
d. only (Z) is rational
e. only (Y) and (Z) are rational

SUGGESTIONS FOR FURTHER READING

Robert Solow's "The Intelligent Citizen's Guide to Inflation," *Public Interest* (Winter, 1975) remains one of the best discussions of inflation's effects. *Wall Street Journal* writer Lindley H. Clark's *The Secret Tax* (Homewood, Illinois: Dow Jones Books, 1976) also provides a good discussion of inflation. What happens when inflation slows down? See "Some People, Firms Feeling the Pain that Goes with Declining Inflation" by Ralph E. Winter in the January 22, 1982 *Wall Street Journal*.

II

A SIMPLE MODEL OF THE ECONOMY

5

MEASURING ECONOMIC ACTIVITY

Preview

Are we better off today than in years past?

Why do economists measure economic activity?

What is the best measure of the economy's health?

What is the difference between GNP and RGNP?

Are people in the United States better off than people in other countries?

What is the value-added tax and why do some people think a VAT should be part of the U.S. tax system?

THE 1980 presidential election might have been decided by the public's answer to a basic economic question. Ronald Reagan, in a televised debate with incumbent Jimmy Carter, asked the voters, "Are you better off today than you were four years ago?" It was a telling question, and Carter was soundly defeated at the polls as people answered, "No!"

There was certainly more to the 1980 election than just this question—the Iranian hostages, defense strategies, and tax issues all played important roles. Still the simple question, "Are you better off?" seemed to help some people decide how to vote.

Are we better off today than in years past? This chapter presents the economist's response to this question. You will learn how economists measure economic health, you will be exposed to three measures of economic activity and see how they are used. More important, you will learn the limitations of economic statistics in answering questions like the one that Reagan posed in 1980.

Why Measure Economic Activity?

Why bother with measurement? Who cares if we know exactly how fast or slow the economy expands and contracts? Certainly the consequences of the economy's behavior are the same whether they are measured or not.

There are three important reasons to accurately measure the size and growth of the economy: theory, policy, and business application.

1. **THEORY.** Economics, like any science, is based on measurement. Have you ever thought about how important measurement is to physics, chemistry, and biology? All sciences develop hypotheses and theories. Testing these theories requires accurate observations and measurements that disprove invalid beliefs. Economic science is less exact than physics or chemistry, for example, because economists cannot set up control economies to better test their theories. Measurement in economics is less accurate, too, because many important variables (like expectations) cannot be observed directly or are subject to substantial measurement errors.

Economic policy is built on what are considered the valid economic theories of the day. It is impossible to prove a theory wrong without accurate data on which to base the judgment. Is this important? Many economic policies of the Great Depression were based on the mistaken beliefs of the classical economists. If better data had supported a valid alternative theory, much of the suffering of the depression might have been avoided through improved national economic policies.

2. **POLICY.** Congress, the President, and the Federal Reserve directors all face important policy decisions that can only be answered if they know the true state of the economy. Imagine what could happen if economic statistics lied. Congress might vote a tax cut to stimulate spending at a time when spending was already growing. Demand-pull price increases would spread

throughout the economy. Alternatively, Congress might increase taxes to cool off a rapidly growing economy. If the economy is really slumping, however, the result would be a major recession. So long as government is involved with economic policy decisions, it is important that these choices be based on accurate and detailed knowledge of the economy.

3. BUSINESS APPLICATIONS. Any firm that expects to make a profit needs to know a lot about its market. Is income growing? Are consumers spending more? Are buying habits changing? Firms invest a great deal of money in market research. Economic statistics like those discussed in this chapter provide much of the information that businesses need to make intelligent production and marketing choices. Good data results in higher incomes and profits for producers and a lower bankruptcy burden for the economy.

This chapter tells you about three of the most useful measures of economic activity, gross national product, real GNP, and per capita real GNP. Many other measures and submeasures are also compiled for special uses. You can find a complete listing in any issue of the monthly *Survey of Current Business* (found in most libraries).

Gross National Product

Gross national product (GNP) is the basic measure of national economic activity used by economists, policymakers, and business firms to gauge changes in economic performance. The GNP is oft-quoted, but little understood.

gross national product (GNP): the total market value (in current dollars) of all final goods and services produced in an economy in a year.

Gross national product is the total market value (measured in current prices) of all final goods and services produced in a nation in a year. This is a long definition, and all the words are important. GNP is, first, a measure of national production. It tries to count all the cars, boats, houses, insurance commissions, and other items that are produced anywhere in the economy during a one-year period.

How are all these things added together? The definition says that the total market value (measured in current prices) is used to sum them. GNP is much like the cash-register receipt you get at grocery check-out counters. The sales clerk adds up the number of items you buy multiplied by the price per unit to get your final bill. The GNP looks at the items the economy produces and weights each by its market value. The resulting GNP is like the economy's sales slip—it shows the value (in dollars) of everything that has been produced (since everything is "bought" by someone, it also shows the total amount spent on these goods—just like the grocery receipt).

There is one more important similarity between the GNP and the cash register tape that you are handed at the supermarket counter. When you buy a can of tuna, for example, you expect to pay for the tuna just once. You would feel double-charged if the clerk asked you to pay for the canned fish and then to pay for the can by itself and for the raw tuna that the processor bought and for the oil used in packing and for the bait used to catch the fish. You know that you pay for these things indirectly when you buy the canned tuna, but it would be too much to pay for the tuna and for all of these things in addition.

double-counting: a potential GNP error; counting production more than once.

final good: a good purchased by its ultimate user.

intermediate good: an item used as an input; not counted in GNP.

GNP gets around this **double-counting** problem in much the same way the supermarket does. The GNP counts only **final goods**—goods, like your tuna, that are sold to their ultimate consumers. **Intermediate goods,** like the can, the tuna oil, the bait, and everything else that went into getting the tuna in a can and into your shopping basket, are not added separately into GNP. The value of intermediate goods is reflected in the price of the final good; consequently, this output would be double-counted if both intermediate and final goods were added to GNP.

What sorts of transactions are part of GNP? All activities that result in the production of final goods and services. Examples include:

- Joe Malibu buys a new American car for $10,000 (the $10,000 price of the final good is part of GNP).
- Joe Sassoon pays $10 for a haircut (the $10 enters GNP as the value of the haircutting service).
- Uncle Sam (the federal government) pays $5 million for a new computer.
- Bakery owner Joe Croissant spends $10,000 for a new oven (his bakery is the final user of this investment good). Since the oven is expected to last for more than a year it is treated as a final good while the quickly used-up flour that the bakery buys is tallied as an intermediate good.
- Yukon Joe (the president of a Canadian firm) pays $5000 for computer software sold by a U.S. business. The software leaves the country, but the production took place here, so it is counted in GNP.

Many purchases are not included in GNP. These important exceptions include:

financial investment: purchase of stocks, bonds, or other financial instruments that do not directly increase production.

investment spending: purchase of long-lasting inputs like factories, machinery, and structures.

- Jill College (a college purchasing agent) buys chalk for professors' use. This is an intermediate good—the value of the chalk is included in GNP as part of tuition.
- Jill Investor buys 100 shares of Mobil Oil stock. No goods are produced by the stock sale—paper money is just traded for paper stock certificates. Any increase in GNP occurs if Mobil itself uses funds to buy goods for investment purposes. The **financial investment** does not directly add to national output, so it is not part of GNP; but the economic **investment spending** of buying new equipment or factories is. One part of Jill's transaction does enter the GNP, though. Jill's payment to her stock broker is a currently produced service and thus adds to the GNP total.
- Auto dealer Jill Studebaker still has a $12,000 1983 Belchfire on her car lot in 1984. The $12,000 sticker price does not enter GNP in either year. The wholesale price that Jill paid for the car entered the 1983 GNP because Jill was the final purchaser for that year. The profit she makes when (if!) she eventually sells it will show up the following year.
- Jill Hotrod buys a 1964 Pontiac GTO from Flybynight Motors for $300. Since the car was built back in 1964, its value has already been counted

before. To add this total to the GNP this year would be double-counting. Flybynight Motor's profit on the deal is part of GNP, however; it represents the value of their marketing service.

- Jill Fix-it buys $100 worth of paint and paints her own house instead of paying $1000 for a professional to do the job. The $100 paint is a final good and enters GNP, but the $900 value of Jill's labor is not counted because Jill did not actually pay for the labor. GNP understates national output because it does not include production of this sort.
- Jill Dee Minus buys a term paper from another student for $50. Her purchase does not enter the GNP because this underground activity cannot be measured. GNP understates production because this type of illegal activity is not included in the official statistic.

Three Views of GNP

GNP is a measure of production, but we can view that production in different ways because there are really three sides to production. Figure 5-1 shows the circular flow between spending, income, and production.

The economy can be simply viewed as a circular flow of money between households (who supply labor and savings) and business firms (who sell goods and services and purchase labor and savings). Households buy the output of firms and firms purchase the production (labor, and so forth) of households. Spending creates income through this circular flow. Money flows smoothly, in a healthy economy, from one sector of the economy to the other and back again.

The goal of GNP is to measure the amount of money pumped through this system in a given period of time. Think of GNP as a meter that measures the circular flow of funds. If you put the GNP meter between households and firms, the measurement shows the amount of final goods and services produced and purchased—the view of GNP as production that we have used up to this point. But GNP takes on a different meaning if we move the meter.

Suppose that the GNP measurement is taken between the firms and the households. The number that we get for GNP here is the same as in the first place over the long run. What can firms do with the money they receive, other than pay it out to workers as wages, to savers as interest and rent, or to investors as dividends and profits? But, measured at this point, GNP is better termed a measure of income.

All production eventually results in income for workers, lenders, and the owners of business. The second view of GNP, then, is that GNP measures the total income of the economy. When $1 worth of goods are produced (the first view of GNP), $1 of income is earned by various economic actors (the second view of GNP). Production and income are linked in the GNP, just as they are in the real world.

The third view of the GNP is more complex. The GNP also measures the **value-added** in the production process. Value-added is the difference between the value of intermediate goods and the value of the final goods that result

value-added: increase in value of inputs in production.

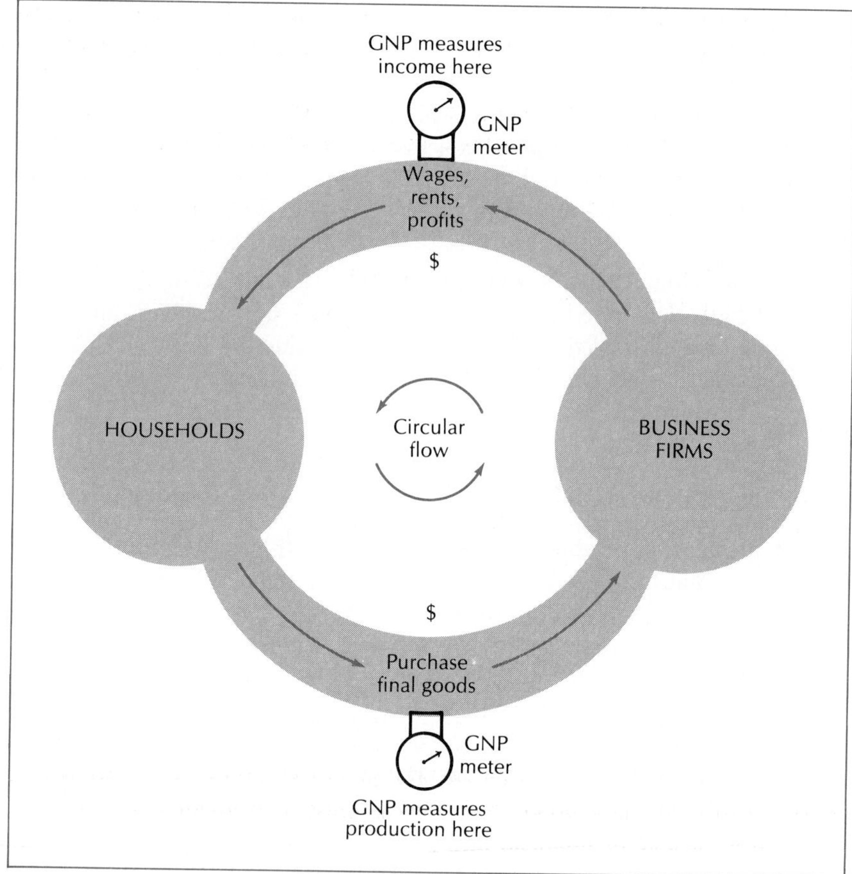

FIGURE 5-1 CIRCULAR FLOW OF INCOME AND GNP. Spending creates income as money flows from households to firms and back to households. If we measure GNP as the amount households buy, it is a measure of production. If we measure GNP as money paid from firms to households, it is a measure of income. GNP is both a measure of income and production.

from the production process. The idea of value-added is easier to see in an example like the one provided in Table 5-1.

The farmer starts with nothing and grows wheat worth twenty cents (suppose, for the sake of simplicity, that the seeds, fertilizer, and other intermediate goods the farmer needs are provided free by God). The farmer adds twenty cents value in growing the wheat. The twenty cents worth of wheat is used to make thirty cents worth of flour. The miller therefore adds ten cents value to the total. The baker buys thirty cents worth of wheat and sells bread

TABLE 5-1 GNP AND VALUE-ADDED

Firm	Input price	Output price	Value-added	Total value-added
Farmer	$.00	$ .20	$.20	$ .20
Miller	.20	.30	.10	.30
Baker	.30	.80	.50	.30
Merchant	.80	1.00	.20	1.00

for eighty cents. The baker adds fifty cents of value-added. Finally, the merchant buys bread for eighty cents and sells it for $1, adding twenty cents value in the process.

A few points are worth noting here. First, the value-added at each step in production is roughly equal to the income received at that level. If we add up all of the value-added, therefore, we will get the combined income of the farmer, miller, baker, and merchant. Since income and value-added are the same, GNP measures both of these items.

The table shows that if we add up all the value-added in this example the total is equal to twenty cents plus ten cents plus fifty cents plus twenty cents or one dollar; that is, to the value of the final good, bread. Total value-added is the same as the market value of final production: GNP. This shows that value-added equals GNP and value-added equals income, thus income is identical with GNP.

The concept of value-added shows up again in this chapter's Economic Controversy. For now you might note that it is easier to add up GNP by looking at value-added (easily extracted from firms' tax returns) than by trying to sum either income or sales of final goods.

Take This with a Grain of Salt

Who counts the GNP each year? Who adds up all of the transactions that take place? Have you not seen the GNP Police at the supermarket? Have they not asked you whether that typing paper you bought should be counted as a final good or an intermediate good? No. This is silly. The government estimates GNP from a variety of financial and production data, using the value added method, among others. No one really counts everything that was produced or sold in a given year.

The GNP and other economic statistics are estimates and they are subject to a variety of errors. It is important, therefore, to take the exact figures with a grain of salt. They are not as exact as they appear to be on the surface.

In his book, *On the Accuracy of Economic Observations* (Princeton, New Jersey: Princeton University Press, 1963, second edition), Oskar Morgenstern tells the story of one particularly silly statistical error. Pig production is an important part of Bulgaria's GNP. Bulgaria used to take a pig census on the first of January of each year to gauge the health of the pig industry. The pig count on the first of January 1910 was given as 527,311 pigs in total (imagine counting every one of these porkers!). The same count on the first of January 1920 was 1,089,699 pigs —an increase of over 100 percent in just 10 years! The Bulgarian economy (at least the pig farmer part of it) must have been prosperous. Or was it?

Lots of pigs lived and died between 1910 and 1920, but another change was made that altered the meaning of this statistic. Bulgaria officially moved from the old Gregorian calendar to the modern Julian calendar—the difference amounted to 13 days. This bookkeeping change meant that January 1, which had previously fallen several days after Christmas, was now a few days before the Christmas feast (still observed according to the old calendar). And what do you suppose people in Bulgaria ate at Christmas? Right—roast pig.

The statistical error is clear. The 1920 pig census counted hundreds of thousands of doomed pigs—a few days later they would be reduced to leftovers. The massive measured increase in pork production was more apparent than real. Did pig farming improve during the 10-year period? It is impossible to tell from these figures because the simple calendar change made the data meaningless.

Gross national product figures for the United States are not as silly as Bulgaria's Gross National Pig count, but the lesson is well taken. You need to question statistics to see what they say, and do not say, about the economy.

GNP errs in measuring economic activity in two important ways. First, it fails to count the growing underground economy discussed in Chapter 3. Gross national product, already over three trillion dollars (that is $3000 billion!), could be up to 20 percent larger if the underground economy were included. This makes conclusions based on GNP less reliable. People who go underground reduce measured GNP while possibly increasing both output and income. This could lead Congress to fight unemployment when employment, above and below the surface, has really increased. The second error in GNP is discussed next.

Real Gross National Product

GNP measures income, production and value-added in current prices. GNP rises, then, if production goes up (people produce more goods and services and have higher real income) or if prices rise (people produce and buy the same goods but pay more for them). In fact, GNP sometimes rises when production falls, if prices go up faster than output goes down. This fact is illustrated in Figure 5-2.

The GNP can be adjusted for the effects of changing prices using the GNP Implicit Price Deflator Index you read about in Chapter 4. The result of this calculation is **real gross national product (RGNP).** A much different picture of economic performance is painted once inflation's effects are removed.

real gross national product (RGNP): GNP adjusted for changing price level; a good indicator of national production.

The GNP has steadily increased since 1960 as Figure 5-2 indicates. Gross national production in 1981 was 477 percent higher than it was in 1960. The GNP over this period is a picture of steady, consistent economic growth. You can hardly imagine a more prosperous growth in income. Or can you?

Adjust GNP for inflation and you get the less cheery chart labeled RGNP. Most of the increase in GNP over this period was the result of higher prices (the area between the two curves in the figure). The RGNP doubled over this period—a good performance for the economy but nothing like the triumph that GNP shows. The RGNP also shows that the economy had its ups and downs. The economy has not grown steadily as GNP suggests; recessions pulled down RGNP in 1970, 1974–1975, 1980, and 1982. Falling RGNP means less production of goods and services and shrinking real income (changes in the size of the underground economy might have accounted for some of the decreasing RGNP shown here).

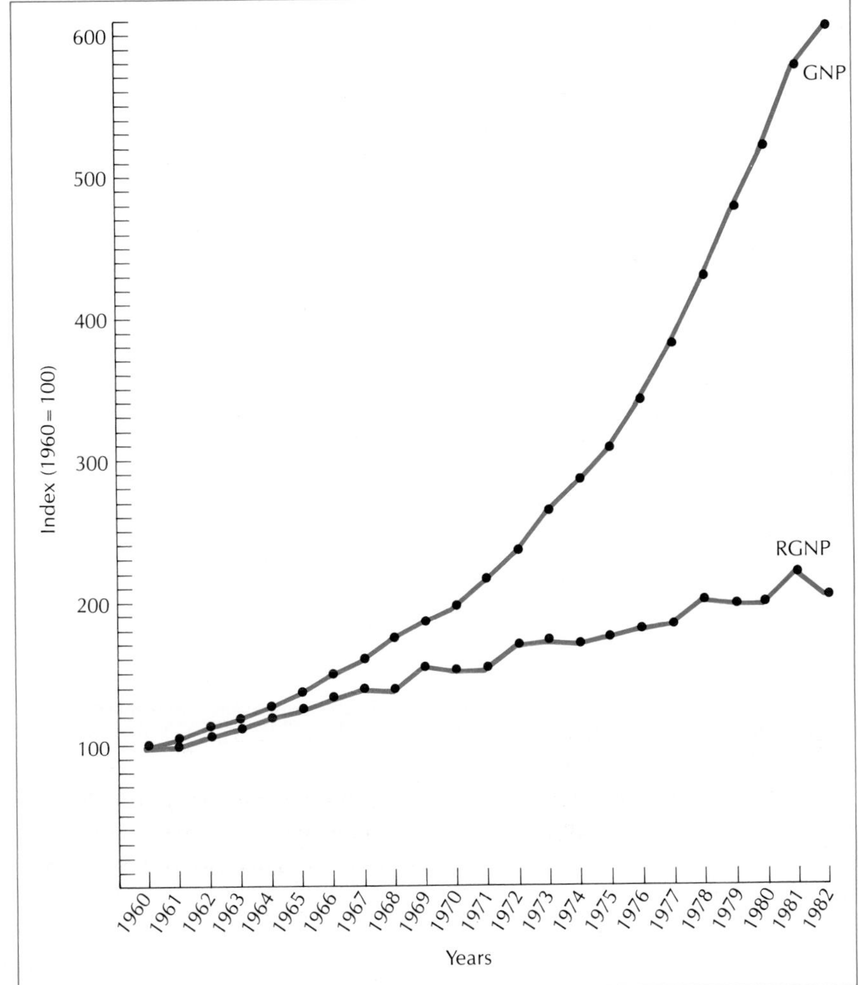

FIGURE 5-2 GNP VERSUS RGNP. According to the GNP, the U.S. economy grew steadily from the 1960s through 1982. However, when the RGNP is plotted for these years, a different picture emerges. Production grew slowly, with several recessions.

Gross national product is a good measure of short-term changes in the economy when price effects are likely to be small. If you want to gauge economic performance over a period longer than a few months, however, RGNP is the right tool to use. An increase in RGNP indicates more production, higher real income, lower unemployment rates, and economic growth. Falling RGNP suggests falling real incomes and production and higher unemployment and recession.

Are We Better Off Today than in Years Past?

Let us return to Ronald Reagan's question. Are you better off now than a few years ago? What was the answer to this question in the year it was posed, 1980?

If you choose to measure the economy using GNP, the answer is yes—there is more production and income. The GNP rose from $1,918 billion in 1977 (when Jimmy Carter took office) to over $2,600 billion in 1980. The GNP went up; but, as we have just seen, GNP cannot be trusted over this long a period because rising prices mask real changes.

If you choose to measure the economy using RGNP, the answer is the same. RGNP (measured in 1972 dollars) increased from $1,371 billion in 1977 to almost $1,500 billion in 1980. Production and real income, as measured by RGNP, increased during Jimmy Carter's presidency.

There seems to be a problem here. Ronald Reagan asked America if it was better off. The public said "No" at the polls. The GNP and RGNP give a different answer. Who is wrong here? The public or the numbers?

The error here falls on the person who interprets the statistics. The GNP and RGNP are measures of income and production; they are *not* measures of well-being. They cannot, therefore, tell us whether people are better off (in whatever sense) now than they were in past years. They only tell us if they have produced more goods now than before. This is an important distinction, as the following examples make clear.

Suppose that a big thunderstorm came through your town. Lightning hits every television antenna in town and all the sets blow up. Would this make the people in your town better off? Television critics might argue that it does—the townsfolk might discover conversation, literature, and each other. But they are likely to feel that they have been hurt by this freak accident. Would GNP go down to reflect their lost welfare? Not a chance. The GNP would balloon as new television sets were produced and sold to replace the wrecked ones. Higher GNP here would reflect reduced individual well-being. The GNP and RGNP both typically increase the fastest during war periods.

Now suppose that the famous inventor, Marvin Lungrot, discovers that people can be cured of their addiction to smoking with vitamin C. Would this make people better off? You bet! Would GNP increase to reflect this? Not a chance. If people quit smoking you would find unemployment in the tobacco and health-care industries. People would even live longer, reducing output at funeral homes in the short run. The economy's citizens would be better off because of a discovery like this one, but GNP would fall. The moral to this story is that many things determine whether you are better or worse off. You cannot draw any conclusions by just looking at GNP or RGNP.

Per Capita RGNP

per capita RGNP: RGNP adjusted for change in population.

RGNP is an improvement on GNP because it adjusts for changes in prices; this makes it a good indicator of changing production and real income over long periods of time. We further refine RGNP by dividing it by the size of the population. The result of this exercise is called **per capita RGNP.** Per capita RGNP is roughly equal to the amount of real income or production per person in the economy. This puts the economy's output on a human scale—we see production changes on a per-person basis. Per capita RGNP increased more slowly than RGNP during the 1960s and 1970s—more goods were produced, but they had to be shared by larger numbers of people.

Per capita RGNP is a convenient measure of production per person, but it should not be pushed much beyond this interpretation. It cannot, for example, be used to chart economic well-being for the same reasons that GNP and RGNP fail this test. Whether you are better or worse off simply cannot be measured by GNP-type statistics.

Per capita RGNP cannot tell if the population is richer or poorer in any meaningful sense, either. Per capita RGNP is just an average—it tells whether average production has gone up, but nothing more. One important thing that per capita RGNP cannot account for is a changing distribution of income. Per capita RGNP might rise, for example, if the King of a country were to take all the wealth of his subjects and invest it in a profitable toll road. Income per person, on average, might rise in this example, but 99 percent of the population would be poorer because of the King's RGNP-raising activities.

International Comparisons

Per capita RGNP figures are available for most countries, so it is tempting to use them to compare the standard of living in different lands. Differences in per capita RGNP are dramatic, as Figure 5-3 indicates.

Per capita RGNP in the United States was over $10,000 in 1979—higher than in oil rich Saudi Arabia. The Saudis earn many dollars from oil sales, but they have a large, relatively poor population to divide it among. Most of the oil

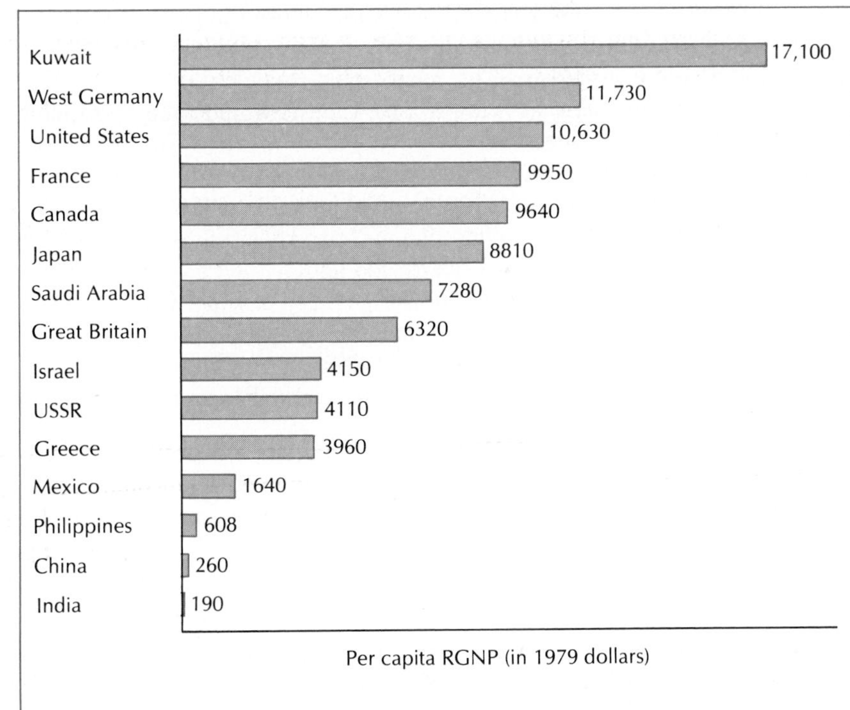

FIGURE 5-3 PER CAPITA RGNP IN SELECTED COUNTRIES. Per capita RGNP varies widely around the world. These 1979 figures are provided by the World Bank.

income goes directly to the Saudi government, which uses the funds to provide the population with free medical care, education, and the like. Most income in the United States goes directly to workers who use it to buy the things they want. Kuwait's per capita RGNP tops this chart—over $17,000 in 1979 dollars per person. This high per capita RGNP results from billions of oil dollars meeting a relatively small Kuwaiti population.

The world is full of haves, like Kuwait, and have-nots. Per capita RGNP was only $260 in China and $190 in India in 1979. Why so low? Large populations in both of these countries convert relatively high RGNP figures to low per-person amounts. Much of the world's population has low real income, as measured here.

What conclusions can we draw from this example? One correct conclusion is that there is great disparity in production and income between richer and poorer lands. Germany and Japan must have a higher standard of living than China and India, for example. The differences in per capita RGNP are too great to supply any other conclusion. But can we say more than this?

Can we say, for example, that people in Kuwait are about 50 times better off than people in China? No. The large gap in average income does not support this conclusion. First, GNP-type figures cannot be used for welfare comparisons. Second, errors in GNP accounting make a big difference in comparisons like this. Recall that goods produced for own-use (like the house painting example) are not included in GNP. Do you think that many Kuwaitis grow their own vegetables or make their own bread? Probably not. Do you think that many people in China and India do? Probably so. The difference in nonmarket production (not counted in the GNP) can substantially close the gap between these two groups. Cultural differences are also important to this comparison. Hindu people in India, for example, eat no meat. They may be able to support a vegetarian standard of living at a lower cost than it would take to support a meat-eating standard of living.

If we cannot conclude that Kuwait is 50 times better off than China, can we at least say that China ($260) is better off than India ($190)? Or that West Germans ($11,730) are better off than people in the United States ($10,630)? Absolutely not, for the same reasons discussed above.

All this is not meant to downplay the poverty of third-world countries like India and China nor to ignore the immense wealth of western lands. But there are limits to what GNP-type figures tell us. They illustrate the great difference in income around the world, but they should not be stretched to accommodate a broader use than this.

ECONOMIC CONTROVERSY:

A Value-Added Tax?

Taxes are always an important issue in economics—particularly among people who think they are overtaxed. The biggest tax in the United States is the federal income tax. Economists in recent years have called for a change in the emphasis of the U.S. tax system—away from taxing income and toward taxing value-added. This Economic Controversy debates the **value-added tax (VAT).**

value-added tax (VAT): a tax on value-added at each stage of production.

Value-added taxes are widely used in European countries. We can see how a VAT might work by going back to the bread example of value-added shown in Table 5-1. Suppose that a 10 percent VAT is levied. Each producer would pay a 10 percent gross tax on his or her sales but would then receive a credit equal to the VAT already paid by suppliers. Thus, for example, the baker would pay a 10 percent tax on her eighty cent sales (the gross tax would equal eight cents) but would get a credit for the three cents tax already paid by the miller (the miller paid 10 percent of thirty cents, or three cents). The net tax on the baker is therefore eight cents minus three cents, or five cents (in other words 10 percent of her fifty cents value-added). This sounds kind of complicated (and it is), so read it through again, glancing at Table 5-1 when necessary.

The result of all this maneuvering is that 10 percent of value-added is collected at each stage of production, so that the tax ends up being 10 percent of the total value-added. The price of the bread would end up ten cents higher when the VAT is included. In other words, the VAT is a 10 percent tax on production and income (since they are the same as value-added).

Why should this particularly complicated tax be proposed? Let us allow both sides to speak their piece.

VAT: An Idea Whose Time Has Come!

There are many reasons for switching to value-added taxation; the two most important are the effects of VAT on economic growth and the underground economy.

A tax on value-added, on the face of it, is the same as an income tax. This chapter made a big deal of the identity between value-added and income, right? But there is a difference between income and value-added taxation. People pay the income tax whenever they receive income. The tax falls with equal weight on money spent and money saved. Consumers pay VAT in the form of higher prices (much like state sales taxes). They could avoid or delay the VAT bill by saving their money instead of spending it.

Many of the United States' economic problems exist because we spend too much and save too little. Our low saving rates have slowed investment and innovation. This is why the United States has fallen behind foreign competitors who saved and invested and now reap the fruits of frugality. The VAT, by encouraging saving in the United States, would put us on the road to prosperity.

The second reason for favoring a VAT is that it would tax the underground economy. If the baker in the example above purchased flour from an undergound miller, she would be liable for the full eight cent VAT bill (since the underground supplier, by definition, did not pay his taxes, the above ground buyer would be stuck with the entire bill). This is really the reason that they have VAT in Europe—it forces people to be honest and pay their taxes. The VAT, by forcing the subterranean economy to the surface, would improve the accuracy of GNP statistics, reduce the unemployment rate, and probably lower tax rates on legal individuals and firms. Right now you and I (honest taxpayers) end up paying the underground's share of the national tax burden.

VAT would improve economic growth and bring the economy above ground. These are good reasons for supporting the value-added tax.

VAT: Just Another Tax!

There is nothing to get excited about here. The VAT is just another tax. If you like taxes, you will like the VAT. That is why people who are tired of paying taxes oppose the VAT. There are several things wrong with the argument presented by the first speaker.

First, a tax on value-added really is nothing more than a tax on income with a difference: it would be unfair. The current income tax includes special provisions that keep the tax from hitting the poor. The VAT would hit the poor harder than any other group. The VAT taxes your income only when you spend it and gives a tax break to savers. Who saves money these days? The rich? You bet. They would benefit from this tax break, just like they do from all the others. Can the poor save? Not a chance; thus they would have to pay heavy and unfair taxes. If you favor taxing the poor and giving the rich a break (Robin Hood in reverse) you favor a VAT. If you think taxes should be fair, you oppose the VAT.

The VAT would make problems worse in another way. The VAT would boost the prices of all goods—it would cause inflation at a time when we are trying to reduce this problem. Higher inflation rates reduce real incomes. Smart consumers spend more and save less when they realize inflation is on the way. Saving rates would fall, not increase, with a VAT.

The opposing speaker argues that the VAT would bring the underground economy to light. Hogwash! Do you think that drug dealers will turn themselves in because the tax laws have changed? If underground plumbers went legal with the VAT change they would have to explain to the income tax auditors what they were doing in previous years. The risks of surfacing are too great for those already underground. Once a person or firm goes underground they stay there. A tax law is not going to change this.

The VAT would be an additional, unfair tax. Worse, VAT record-keeping costs would be astronomical. All this payment and credit nonsense would inflate the cost of doing business. Many firms would go out of business. Others would raise prices to cover this governmental cost-push problem. Prices go up and production goes down under cost-push forces. It is hard to believe anyone could favor a tax like the VAT.

SUMMARY

1. It is important to be able to measure rational economic activity. Economists need this data to test and refute their theories. Government policymakers need it to guide wise policy decisions. Business firms need this information to make smart production and marketing plans.

2. This chapter looked at three measures of economic activity. Gross national product measures market production in current dollars. The GNP can be viewed as income, production, or value-added. The GNP has several flaws, however, and must be used with care.

3. Real gross national product adjusts GNP for changes in the price level. The RGNP is a good measure of production for the economy as a whole (although growth in the underground economy is not reflected in either GNP or RGNP).

4. Neither GNP nor RGNP should be interpreted as a measure of economic welfare or well-being. These statistics measure production and income, but they cannot tell us whether people are better or worse off.

5. Per capita RGNP puts RGNP on a human scale. Be careful not to use this statistic to make international comparisons of well-being, however.

6. Income and value-added are the same (both equal GNP) but income and value-added taxes are different. In any case, the VAT is certainly an economic controversy.

DISCUSSION QUESTIONS

1. Which of the following transactions would enter GNP? Why?

a. Joel Smith buys a stamp from the Post Office.
b. Joe L. Smith buys a birthday present to be given to Joel.
c. Jo Lee Smith buys paper to use in her computer programming firm.
d. Jim Smith pays for a motel room while on vacation.
e. Jack Smith buys a Victorian house.
f. John Smith pays his electric bill.

2. Here are some facts concerning a less-developed country:

Year	GNP	Population	GNP Price Index
1970	$100 billion	10 million	100
1975	$120 billion	15 million	110
1980	$150 billion	20 million	130

a. Describe how GNP changed between 1970 and 1975 and between 1975 and 1980.
b. What happened to RGNP over these periods? Did it increase, decrease, or stay the same? Explain.
c. What happened to per capita RGNP over these periods? Did it increase, decrease, or stay the same? Explain.
d. Were the residents of this country better off in 1980 than in 1970? Explain.

3. Where do you stand on the value-added tax? What are the main arguments in favor of a VAT? What are the counterarguments? Evaluate both sides and state your position.

TEST YOURSELF

Circle the best response to each question.

1. The people who calculate GNP try to avoid ________ by counting only ________ goods (fill in the blanks).

a. error, market
b. error, underground
c. inflation, real
d. double-counting, final
e. error, value-added

2. In GNP terms, which of the following transactions would be considered an investment?

(W) a university buys a certificate of deposit at a bank
(X) a firm hires more workers
(Y) a delivery firm buys a new truck
(Z) a trucking firm buys diesel fuel

a. all of these are investments
b. none of these are investments
c. only (Y) is an investment
d. (Y) and (Z) are investments
e. (X), (Y) and (Z) are investments

3. Puget Sound Herring Corporation issued stock and used the money to build a new herring-packing plant. How was this transaction entered into GNP?

(X) the sale of the stock went into GNP
(Y) the purchase of the stock by investors went into GNP
(Z) the purchase of the herring-packing plant went into GNP

a. all of the above
b. none of the above
c. (Z) only
d. (X) and (Z)
e. (Y) and (Z)

4. Which of the following changes (all else being equal) would increase GNP but would not necessarily increase RGNP?

(X) increase in the price level
(Y) increase in production
(Z) increase in population

a. all of the above
b. none of the above
c. (X) only
d. (X) and (Z)
e. (Y) and (Z)

5. Which of the following events would indicate that people in France are better off than they were before?

(X) increase in France's GNP
(Y) increase in France's RGNP
(Z) increase in France's per capita RGNP

a. all of the above
b. none of the above
c. (Z) only
d. (Y) only
e. either (Y) or (Z)

SUGGESTIONS FOR FURTHER READING

The details of GNP accounting are provided in the monthly *Survey of Current Business*. How big is the underground economy? See Peter M. Gutmann's "Statistical Illusions, Mistaken Policies" in *Challenge* (November–December, 1979). What is happening to RGNP around the world? The September–October *World Bank Report* analyzes this question. Many other World Bank publications look at poverty and income around the world. Are you interested in the debate over the Value-Added Tax? See the discussion in the author's *Public Finance* (Reston, Virginia: Reston Publishers, 1984).

6

KEYNESIAN AGGREGATE DEMAND

Preview

Why do we have recessions and depressions?

Can government stabilize the economy? How?

Why is spending important? What are the main spending categories? What determines the amount of total spending?

Is the economy inherently unstable or does it tend toward equilibrium? Is equilibrium good?

Is government economic policy necessary? What is the role of government in the economy?

aggregate demand (AD): desired total spending in the economy (measured in RGNP).

MACROECONOMICS IS an invention of the Great Depression. The depression problem, according to John Maynard Keynes, was insufficient **aggregate demand (AD).** Economic policies since Keynes have been built around the idea that government's job is to manipulate aggregate demand toward full employment.

This chapter begins analysis of aggregate demand and macroeconomic theory; it builds the first story of the macroeconomics temple. Past chapters poured the foundation of supply and demand, an understanding of inflation and unemployment, and the workings of the GNP. Following chapters add to this framework and complete the structure.

Depression Economics

The Great Depression was a real surprise to many economists. Up until then, they had assumed that markets work to balance supply and demand. Equilibrium price provides every buyer a willing seller and all goods offered for sale find buyers. Markets that work efficiently always clear. But the Great Depression, viewed in microeconomic terms, is the failure of markets to clear. The labor market, in particular, persists in surplus during depression and recession—willing and able workers stand in unemployment lines (these days) and soup lines (in the 1930s), not on production lines. How can this happen in a market economy like the United States?

Say's Law of Markets: Jean Baptiste Say's statement that supply creates its own demand.

The economist Jean Baptiste Say is responsible for a simple idea that convinced many economists that continuing depression was impossible. **Say's Law of Markets** holds that "supply creates its own demand." Production of $1 worth of bread (as in Chapter 5's value-added example) necessarily creates $1 of income (the value-added income of the producers). In theory, then, there is always sufficient income to purchase everything industry produces. How can massive surplus and unemployment persist if supply creates its own demand?

The answer to the 1930s depression was suggested by British economist John Maynard Keynes. Keynes' new view of macroeconomics was controversial in the 1930s and 1940s and still is today. Keynes' basic theory is presented in this chapter and debated in the Economic Controversy. The Appendix to this chapter outlines an alternative graphical method for expressing Keynes' views.

sectors: parts of the economy that respond to different economic events.

circular-flow model: a description of the flow of spending and income between the business and household sectors.

Spending Creates Income

Keynes chose to view the economy as groups of people and firms or **sectors.** Economic progress depends on how these sectors interact. We have already seen a simple model of how two sectors are related: the circular flow diagram of Chapter 5. This **circular-flow model** is shown again in Figure 6-1.

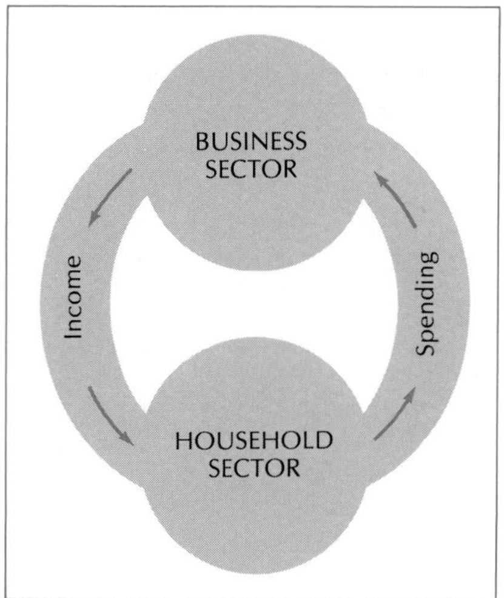

FIGURE 6-1 THE CIRCULAR-FLOW MODEL. Spending creates income in a circular flow around the economy. Household spending provides funds that businesses use to pay workers, lenders, and the firms' owners.

The circular flow shows the basic relationship between the household sector and the business sector. Households' spending provides funds for business production. Production creates income—wages, rents, interest, and profits—for households. Spending creates income in the circular flow diagram. Income rises and falls with total spending.

How can spending rise or fall in Figure 6-1? It cannot. Figure 6-1 shows an economy where Say's Law works perfectly and full employment must prevail. Since households have nothing to do but spend and business has nothing to do but pay wages, spending and income must be the same. This is an economy of permanent equilibrium.

This picture of the economy looks unrealistic, and it is. We must add to this simple economic model to understand the Great Depression. Figure 6-2 adds new sectors to the circular flow picture.

What can people do with their income other than spend it on goods and services? Three **leakages** from the circular flow correspond to the three new sectors introduced in this figure. The first leakage is saving. Money not spent can be sent to the **financial sector** and saved. Saving is important; it provides funds needed for investment. But saving has a dark side, too; it cuts spending and increases unemployment. Consider the **paradox of thrift.** Saving makes us wealthy, right? If you saved all your income, you would be wealthier. But what would happen if we all saved all of our income for several years? With all saving and no spending we would all be out of work—laid off for lack of demand. Saving here is listed as a leakage from the circular flow because saving, by itself, cuts spending and so reduces national income.

The next leakage is taxes. Taxes are money the government takes. Higher taxes reduce the **disposable income** consumers have left to spend.

The final leakage is **imports.** Imports give us the valuable goods and services that other lands produce, but spending leaks to their economies, increasing income abroad.

leakages: uses of income that reduce spending.

financial sector: the part of the economy that deals with borrowing, lending, and the exchange of assets like stocks and bonds.

paradox of thrift: saving makes any individual better off, but everyone suffers if everyone saves.

disposable income: income available for spending; income after direct taxes have been paid.

imports: purchases of goods produced in other countries.

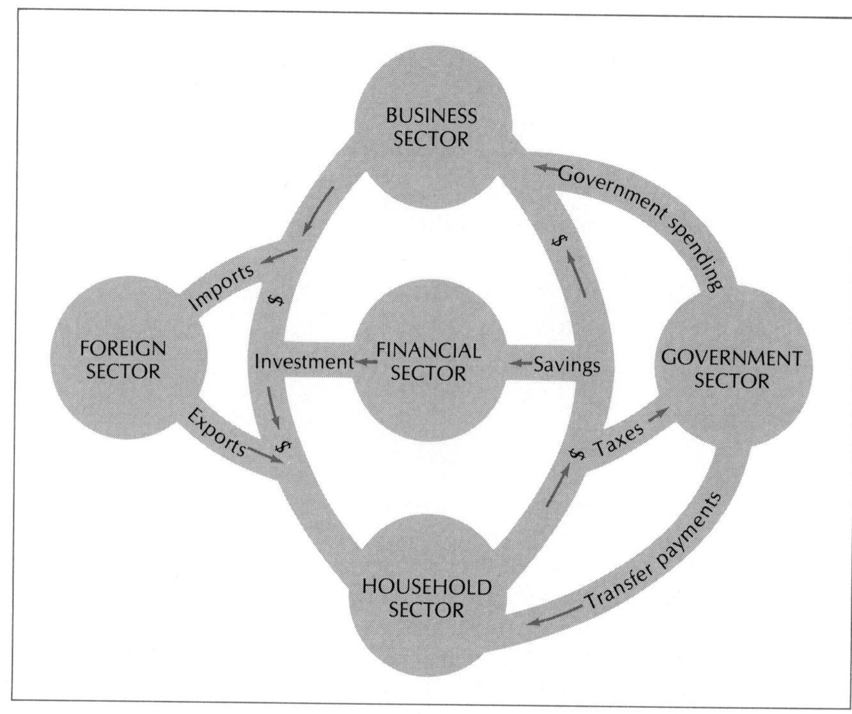

FIGURE 6-2 LEAKAGES AND INJECTIONS. The circular flow is complicated by a variety of leakages and injections. Money leaves the circular flow as savings, taxes, and imports. Exports, investment, and government spending increase the circular-flow level. Transfer payments from government to the household sector indirectly increase spending and income.

injections: sources of spending that increase income.

The leakages from the circular flow are matched by **injections**—economic activities that increase spending and so swell a country's income. The first injection is investment spending. The financial sector channels saving funds to investors (and consumers) who spend them. Investment spending is an injection because increased investment spending brings higher total spending and income.

transfer payments: payments from one group to another with no payment of goods or services in return.

Two injections flow from the government sector. Government spending directly increases the circular flow. Government purchases of bombs, bullets, bridges, and books increase total spending and income. **Transfer payments,** like social security benefits and unemployment payments, are an indirect injection. Transfer payments increase disposable income and thus indirectly produce more consumer and business spending.

exports: sales of items to the residents of other countries.

The foreign sector's injection is **exports.** Aggregate demand in the United States rises when American producers sell wheat or computers or other items to foreign buyers. Consumers in other lands get the goods; workers and producers in the United States get the income this spending creates.

It is useful to think of aggregate demand as a big bathtub, like the one shown in Figure 6-3. The level of water in the bathtub at any time measures the flow of spending and income. The injections are faucets pouring water into the tub, increasing spending and income. The leakages from the circular flow are drains, letting spending and income decrease. This silly picture, combined with the circular flow diagram of Figure 6-2, says much about macroeconomics and the causes of the Great Depression.

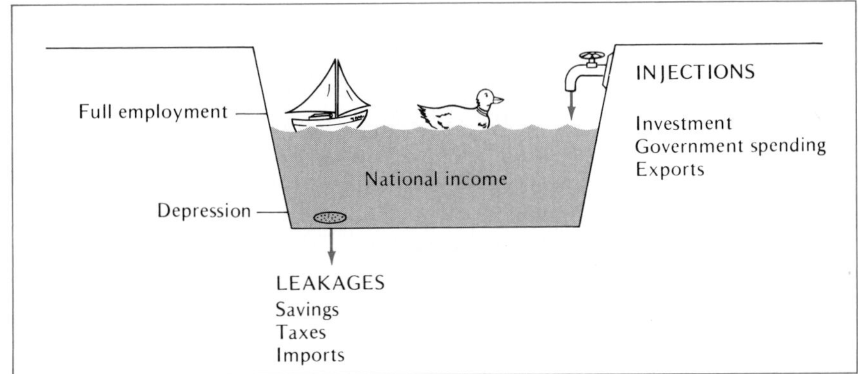

FIGURE 6-3 THE BATHTUB MODEL OF THE CIRCULAR FLOW. Injections increase income in the economy in the same way that injections increase the level of water in this bathtub. Leakages that reduce spending also decrease income. The macroeconomic equilibrium occurs when total injections are equal to total leakages.

Macroeconomic Equilibrium

The economy is at **macroeconomic equilibrium** when total leakages (the sum of saving, taxes, and imports) equal total direct injections (investment, government spending, and exports)—transfer payments only indirectly increase spending and so are not included in this list. This corresponds to a "bathtub" equilibrium with total injections (entering the tub) balanced by total leakages (down the drain).

macroeconomic equilibrium: level of income where desired total spending equals income; leakages equal injections.

Does the economy ever reach such an equilibrium? Keynes' answer was yes. Spending and income, leakages and injections are all interrelated in ways that guarantee some level of equilibrium is finally reached. The economy is not inherently unstable (good news to people in depression unemployment lines). If income rises for some reason, government tax collections rise, consumer saving increases, and more money goes for imported goods. These higher leakages balance out whatever injection pushed income higher. Falling income gives rise to similar equilibrium-seeking forces.

Is Equilibrium Good?

It is comforting to know that the economy is not unstable, but is the macroeconomic equilibrium necessarily a good thing? Keynes' answer here was no. Equilibrium occurs wherever current leakages and injections dictate. Equilibrium might happen at full employment, but this happy end is not assured. Equally likely is a Great Depression equilibrium, with spending and income equal but unemployment rates through the roof.

If equilibrium can be either good or bad, are we doomed to busts and booms? No, said Keynes. Leakages and injections are not pure random events. Government can adjust the macroeconomic equilibrium by manipulating taxes, government spending, and transfer payments. These government actions are called **fiscal policy.**

fiscal policy: government policies that infuence aggregate demand.

What Caused the Great Depression?

What makes income fall, as it did in the Great Depression? Income cannot fall if leakages and injections are equal, so falling income is a sign that leakages exceed injections. Figures 6-2 and 6-3 suggest three reasons for falling income.

The financial sector is the first place to look. Suppose that people save (not spend), but that the financial sector is unable to route their money to investment spending. Why should firms fail to invest? Business investment decisions are complex—they depend on the interest rate on borrowed money, profit prospects, and projections for future demand. There is no guarantee, therefore, that firms want to invest all the funds that households save. Spending and income fall when the saving leakage exceeds the investment injection (all else being equal).

surplus: the condition where money received by a sector exceeds money paid out.

The government sector provides a second reason for falling income. If the government's budget shows a **surplus**, the tax leakage exceeds the spending injection. Governments that show a profit by taking in more than they spend draw down spending and national income.

The foreign sector is our last stop. Income falls here if spending on imports is greater than export sales. The net contribution of the foreign sector is negative when imports exceed exports.

Why did income fall during the Great Depression? All three sectors of the economy were involved. Savings surpassed investment in the financial sector. Interest rates tumbled to less than 2 percent in the early 1930s, but even these low interest rates could not convince investors to build factories or modernize existing plants.

deficit: the condition where money paid out by a sector is more than money received.

The government sector was also part of the problem. A federal government budget surplus in 1929 and 1930 reduced aggregate demand and contributed to falling income (budget **deficits** prevailed in 1931 and for the rest of the 1930s).

The foreign sector was involved, too. The United States erected high trade barriers in an attempt to reduce imports. But other nations followed our lead, and U.S. exports also fell. Jobs were destroyed at both ends of the trade trail.

Growing leakages and shrinking injections reduced spending and drove down income. Unemployment was made worse by sticky wages in labor markets. Wages fell, but not far enough—given falling price levels—to balance labor demand and labor supply. Falling aggregate demand results in unemployment, but even more workers are idled (as Chapter 3 made clear) when wages stick instead of fall.

Depression Economic Policies

What government policies are appropriate for recessions and depressions? If the problem is insufficient aggregate demand, the leakage and injection solutions are suggested by Figures 6-2 and 6-3.

Government economic policies during a depression, in Keynes' view, should create budget deficits. Government spending and transfer payments should exceed tax revenues. Where does the extra money come from? Government borrows to finance the deficit. Borrowing was especially appropriate during the Great Depression when low investment spending left surplus funds in the financial sector.

What should government buy? It really does not matter; all spending creates income. Government can act as an investor and build highways or port facilities, for example, that add to the economy's ability to produce. Or it can pay people to dig ditches or paint murals. All such actions increase spending and income.

The second problem area is the financial sector. Saving can only be used for investment if saved dollars actually enter the financial sector—if they are saved through banks, insurance companies, or other **financial intermediaries.** Bank failures in the 1930s convinced many people that all banks were unsafe. Families that saved money often kept it in a sock under the mattress or buried in a coffee can in the backyard. This saving reduced consumer spending (a leakage) but could not possibly produce the investment spending injection. Government's role here was to create confidence in the banks.

financial intermediaries: firms that act as go-betweens for savers and borrowers; banks, insurance companies, and credit unions are examples.

Many people who lived through the Great Depression still mistrust banks. United States savings bonds and savings stamps (once sold in small denominations by the Post Office) were used to channel funds from cautious savers to the government spenders. If people did not trust banks, at least they would trust Uncle Sam.

The foreign sector is the final stop for government policies, but Congress' actions during the 1930s did little to improve the leakage–injection imbalance. The Smoot-Hawley tariffs tried to deal with depression by taxing imported goods. Foreign retaliation, however, made a mess of the matter. Exports that might have stimulated the economy were slashed as foreign buyers reacted to the U.S. trade barriers against their goods.

Inflation and Unemployment

Economic policies during the 1940s and 1950s were based on the leakage–injection ideas just discussed. Spending and income were manipulated through leakages and injections, with taxes and government spending playing an important part. War bonds were offered as a saving incentive during World War II, when income was high. Wage and price controls followed as high spending led to higher rates of inflation.

The Phillips curve added a new wrinkle to policy in the 1960s. The Phillips curve, combined with the circular flow relationship between spending and income, gave government a tasty policy menu. Is unemployment too high? Increase injections like government spending or transfer payments and cut tax leakages. Spending and income rise; unemployment rates decline as inflation increases along the Phillips curve. Is inflation too high? The solution is to increase unemployment. More leakages (encourage saving or enact a tax increase) or fewer injections (cut back government spending and transfer payments and discourage new investment) accomplish this goal.

Four Components of Aggregate Demand

This leakage and injections analysis is a good way to see how spending and income work. Another way to view aggregate demand is to break total spending into four components: consumption, investment, government, and net export spending. This division is useful because each spending part responds to different economic events. We can learn more about what makes aggregate demand change by examining its four pieces.

consumption spending: household spending on consumer goods.

1. **CONSUMPTION SPENDING. Consumption spending** is the largest component of aggregate demand, as Figure 6-4 shows. Over 60 percent of total spending was by consumers in 1982. What variables influence total consumption spending? Think about your own spending habits and a short list should come to mind. Your list probably includes:

INCOME. Consumer spending rises and falls with the level of income. Unemployed people cut back purchases when income falls, and college students go on spending binges when their first post-graduation paycheck arrives. A direct relationship between income and consumer spending makes intuitive sense.

Economists have taken the income-consumption spending link one step beyond intuition. When disposable income rises, consumers tend to spend a fraction (fixed in the short run) of that increase on greater purchases of goods

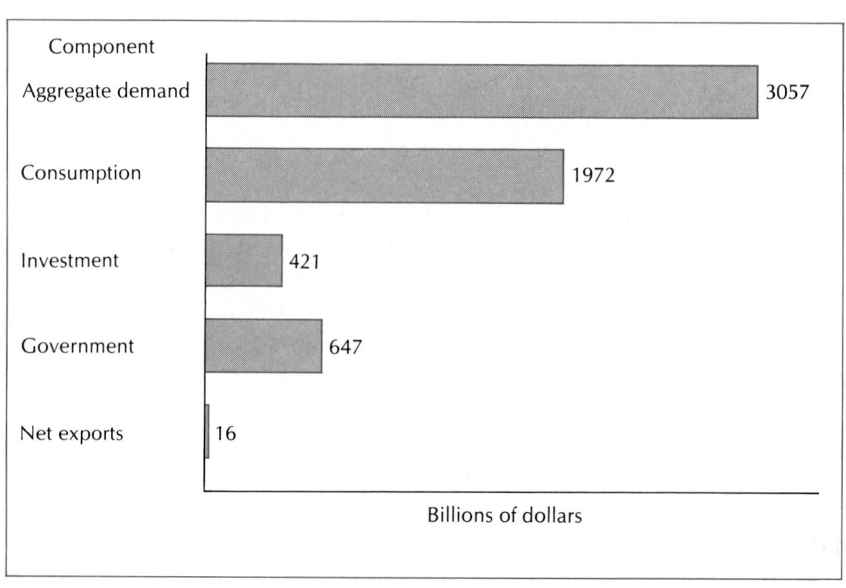

FIGURE 6-4 COMPONENTS OF AGGREGATE DEMAND, 1982.

and services. If income falls, however, consumption spending falls by a fixed fraction of the pay cut. Keynes gave the name **marginal propensity to consume (MPC)** to the relationship between changes in disposable income and changes in spending. The MPC refers only to how spending responds to changes in income. The **average propensity to consume (APC)** describes the relationship between total consumption spending and disposable income.

marginal propensity to consume (MPC): fraction of any change in disposable income spent on consumption.

average propensity to consume (APC): the fraction of total income spent on consumption.

Suppose that your income is $1000 per month (you spend $900 of it for a 90 percent APC) and you get a $100 raise. If your MPC is 80 percent, then consumption spending should increase by 80 percent of the increased income ($80) with the other 20 percent going to saving. Consumption spending rises to a total of $980 ($900 plus $80) or 89 percent APC. The MPC is assumed to stay constant as income changes (you behave the same way concerning pay increases and decreases), but the APC changes as consumers in the economy spend different fractions of total income on consumer goods. A $100 pay cut would force an $80 reduction in consumption spending and reduce saving by $20 per month.

No individual acts exactly this way, but the relationship between changes in income and changes in spending for a group as large as the whole economy is constant (in the short run) and predictable.

TAXES AND TRANSFER PAYMENTS. Consumption spending also depends on changes in disposable income due to taxes and transfer payments. Spending by retired people increases, for example, when social security benefits grow. Spending by workers falls when social security taxes go up, thereby reducing their disposable income. Taxes and transfer payments are two important ways government influences consumption spending decisions.

EXPECTATIONS. Spending decisions are based on both current and projected future events. Expectations play a big role in the choices consumers make. People who think that their jobs are secure and pay increases likely spend readily and buy big ticket items like cars and new homes. People who think unemployment is a possibility cut back spending in anticipation of hard times.

Inflationary expectations are important, too. People who think prices are going to jump in the future hedge by spending money now. People who expect stable prices spread their purchases out over a longer period. People also anticipate government acts and the consequences of those actions, making spending choices consistent with their expectations. The power of expectations is immense.

CREDIT COST AND AVAILABILITY. Big consumer purchases are financed with loans. The availability and cost of credit helps determine how much consumers buy. High interest rates in the early 1980s, for example, kept consumers away from new car showrooms and real estate offices. High interest costs discouraged consumer spending.

2. INVESTMENT SPENDING. Investment spending is crucial to the economy. Spending on factories, machines, and technology adds to aggregate demand and improves the economy's ability to supply goods. Investment spending is a large and volatile component of aggregate demand. Investment spending rises and falls subject to:

INTEREST RATES. Most investments use borrowed funds. Business firms weigh interest costs against expected profits from a new store or factory. Higher interest costs reduce the list of profitable investments. There is, therefore, usually an inverse relationship between interest rates and investment spending.

EXPECTATIONS. Investment choices are difficult because firms spend now (on the new machines or other investment goods), but the pay-off comes months or years in the future when production finally begins. Economic events move quickly these days, so a lot can happen in a few months or years. Will consumer spending increase? Will interest rates drop further? What about government policy? A simple investment choice hinges on all these uncertain matters.

GOVERNMENT POLICIES. Government policies affect investment decisions in many ways. Zoning rules can either encourage or discourage investment at the local level. The federal government frequently uses tax policy to regulate investment. Special tax breaks are given to encourage specific business investments.

3. GOVERNMENT SPENDING. Government spending was the second largest category of aggregate demand in 1982. What makes government spending go up and down? This is a complicated question because there is no one government in the United States. The federal government is the king of Capitol Hill, but 50 states and over 25,000 local governments taken together have as much spending clout as Congress and the President.

Government spending choices depend on many variables, including voter moods and the length of time to the next election. Important determinants of government spending are:

NATIONAL EMERGENCY. Government spending rises fastest in times of stress like war or deep recession. This follows, at least in part, Keynes' view of government as "spender of last resort" during hard times.

POLITICAL PHILOSOPHY. Ideas are important. The conservative political philosophy of Ronald Reagan held back growth in government spending just as the more liberal views of Lyndon Johnson expanded both the role of government and the size of the government budget.

automatic stabilizers: government programs that automatically react to changes in income and unemployment.

AUTOMATIC STABILIZERS. Many government policies automatically respond to changing economic conditions. These policies are termed **automatic stabilizers.** Antipoverty programs, for example, start up by themselves when unemployment grows and reduce spending automatically when jobless lines shorten.

net exports: exports minus imports; a component of aggregate demand.

4. NET EXPORTS. **Net exports** are the smallest piece of aggregate demand—they hardly make the chart in Figure 6-4. Do not let the numbers fool you, however. Net exports are important. The United States exported $349 billion worth of goods and services in 1982 (that is 12 percent of GNP) and imported goods costing $333 billion (one dollar out of nine went for imports). The net effect of all this international trade was a $16 billion boost in aggregate demand.

How much would it cost us to produce the oil and other goods we buy from abroad? We gain from imports by buying goods for less than it would cost us to produce them ourselves. Trade serves as a market for U.S. goods—many U.S. workers have jobs because of international trade. What variables influence net exports? The list includes:

EXCHANGE RATES. Import prices and the ability of U.S. firms to compete abroad depend on the exchange rate. Imports cost more and U.S. goods sell better, for example, when the dollar falls against foreign currencies.

BARRIERS TO TRADE. Tariffs and quotas keep out foreign goods, increasing aggregate demand at home. But they also reduce export jobs if foreigners retaliate. Most economists favor free trade that increases both imports and exports.

POLITICS. Political actions affect international trade, too. Richard Nixon's "Ping-Pong" diplomacy opened up China to U.S. traders. Senator Henry Jackson succeeded in linking United States–Soviet trade to human rights policies. United States exports of military equipment, like the proposed sale of surveillance airplanes to Saudi Arabia in 1981, depend on Congressional approval.

International trade is complex and important. Part IV of this text takes an in-depth look at exchange rates and international economics.

The Aggregate Demand Curve

The aggregate demand (AD) curve summarizes total spending just as the apple demand curve in Chapter 2 described buying habits for that product. An aggregate demand curve is shown in Figure 6-5.

What does the aggregate demand curve show? The AD curve looks like a demand curve for a specific good, but its meaning is much different. The vertical axis measures the average price of *all* goods—the price level—not the price of any *particular* good. An increase in the price level indicates inflation; a constant price level signifies price stability. Total desired purchases (the horizontal axis) are measured by RGNP. An increase in RGNP means more total goods and services purchased, higher real income, and lower unemployment rates. Falling RGNP signifies lower real incomes and higher unemployment.

WHY DOES AGGREGATE DEMAND SLOPE DOWNWARD? The AD curve slopes downward in Figure 6-5—showing fewer goods and services (RGNP) demanded as the price level rises. What accounts for this behavior? The AD curve has the same shape as the demand curve for an individual good, but it takes this shape for completely different reasons. The slope of the AD curve depends on how consumption, investment, government, and net export spending react to changes in the price level. There is good reason to believe that these four groups demand fewer goods and services at higher price levels. Two examples illustrate why this is so.

An increase in the price level—inflation—quickly boosts interest rates. Higher interest rates discourage investment spending for the reasons outlined before. Lower investment spending means falling incomes for workers in construction and other industries. Their consumption spending falls by the MPC fraction of the income change. Lower investment spending sets in motion a

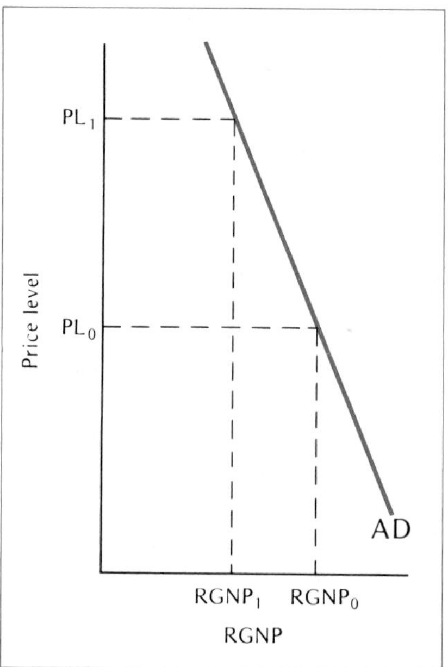

FIGURE 6-5 The Aggregate Demand Curve. The AD curve shows the relationship between the desired total purchases by consumers, investors, the government, and the foreign sector (measured by RGNP) and the price level. The AD curve is downward sloping, as the figure indicates. The amount of aggregate demand falls as the price level increases—a movement along (not a shift in) the AD curve.

chain reaction of reduced purchases by other groups. The quantity of RGNP demanded falls.

Inflation also affects net export spending. Higher price levels in the United States, all else being equal, make foreign goods look cheaper and U.S. products more expensive. Imports tend to rise and exports fall, reducing this component of aggregate demand.

The slope of the AD curve depends on the size of effects like these on investment and net exports and the magnitude of the indirect effect on consumption spending.

SHIFTS IN AGGREGATE DEMAND. A change in the price level brings a movement along the AD curve like the one shown in Figure 6-5. But the price level is only one of many things that change spending patterns. When spending changes because of anything other than the price level, the result is a shift in aggregate demand like those illustrated in Figures 6-6 and 6-7.

Aggregate demand rises, as Figure 6-6 shows, if consumption, investment, government, or net export spending increases for any reason besides a change in the price level. Examples of rising aggregate demand are:

- Consumers increase spending in anticipation of a tax cut.
- Investment spending rises because of the invention of more profitable computer technology.
- Government increases spending on highway construction.
- Wheat exports rise because of crop failures in the USSR.

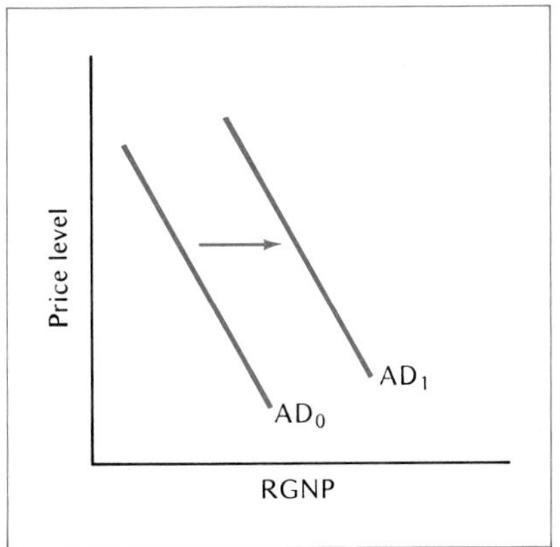

FIGURE 6-6 INCREASE IN AGGREGATE DEMAND. Aggregate demand rises when consumption, investment, government, or net export spending increases for any reason other than a change in the price level.

Aggregate demand falls whenever intended purchases contract due to something other than a change in the price level. Examples of falling aggregate demand include:

- Consumers spend less because they expect a recession soon.
- Investment spending falls because of a change in the tax laws that reduces investment profits.
- Government signs a nuclear arms reduction treaty with the USSR and is able to cut back defense spending.
- Imports of Japanese cars increase.

The aggregate demand curve is a convenient tool because it summarizes all of the spending activity described in this chapter. What good is demand by itself, however? Aggregate demand is united with its mate, aggregate supply, in the next chapter.

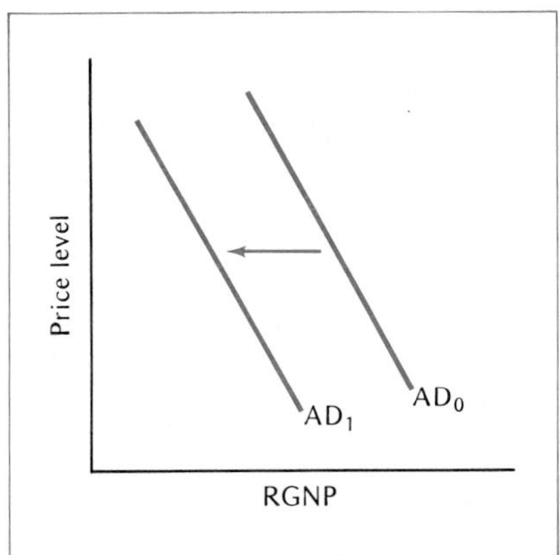

FIGURE 6-7 DECREASE IN AGGREGATE DEMAND. Aggregate demand falls when any spending component decreases for any reason other than a change in the price level.

Note: Students who plan to go on in economics should be sure to explore the appendix to this chapter. This appendix presents a graphical representation of the circular flow model of Keynesian aggregate demand.

ECONOMIC CONTROVERSY:

Keynes versus the Classics

Keynesian economics, with its focus on aggregate demand and government intervention, was controversial in the 1930s and is no less so today. Frustrated modern economists question Keynes' theory more closely than ever. This Economic Controversy looks at Keynes versus the classical economists and asks you to question both economic theories.

Simplified Classical Economics

It is a shame to oversimplify the complex economic theories of Adam Smith, David Ricardo, Thomas Malthus, and Alfred Marshall. Still, in the interest of this discussion, we can collapse the classical view of the macroeconomy into two simple propositions:

laissez faire: a policy of minimum government interference in market actions.

1. Markets Clear. Wages and prices are sufficiently flexible for markets to clear—if they are left alone! A **laissez faire** economic policy is required. Government should stay out of markets and let wages and prices be free to signal consumers and producers.

2. Say's Law Holds. Macroeconomic problems do not exist when markets are allowed to do their job. Production creates income sufficient to purchase all goods made. Say's Law guarantees that no persistent surplus of goods exists, just as the first proposition assures us that no persistent surplus of any individual good is possible. The appropriate government policy, given these two propositions, is hands off!

The Keynesian Response

The fact of the Great Depression refutes the propositions presented above. Markets clearly do not clear. Are the long unemployment lines of 1932 (and 1982!) indicators of labor market equilibrium?

The classic view is flawed in two ways. First, wages and prices are not as flexible as economists might like to think. Wages and prices are sticky and do not fall far enough to eliminate surpluses. Since supply does not adjust to surpluses by cutting price, the demand side of the market must be helped by government.

Say's Law of Markets does not apply, either. Production of $1 worth of bread does make $1 income for bread workers and bakery owners, but there is no guarantee that anyone wants to spend that dollar. Workers might save it and investors refuse to use it for new projects. Falling spending and income eventually drive down income and saving until a new macroeconomic equilibrium is reached. But that new equilibrium comes with higher unemployment rates like those of the Depression years.

Classical economics is flawed in its simple belief that microeconomics is all there is to know. Markets do not work as well as classical supply–demand analysis. Laissez faire means letting the economy drift in a stormy economic sea. Government must take hold of the tiller and guide us to prosperity.

The Classical Rebuttal

There are at least two things wrong with the Keynesian argument. The first is that Keynes' theories are built out of thin air—what individual microeconomic behavior gives rise to the MPC and other constructs of the Keynesian model? Keynesians complain that we look too closely at microeconomics, but they fail to look at individual actions at all, focusing their analysis only on faceless aggregates.

The second flaw with Keynesian analysis—the Keynesian claim that the classical economy does not work and so needs more government interference—is more important. Why does the classical economy fail to find full employment? Why are wages and prices sticky? These problems exist precisely because of a failure to follow classical policy prescriptions. The failure is that laissez faire has been abandoned for government interference.

Why do wages not fall when unemployment lines grow? Because of government policies like sticky wages and government-supported groups like labor unions that get in the way of market forces. Transfer payment programs and unemployment benefits also set an indirect floor on how far wages can fall. Why should someone work for $100-per-week wages if they can get $100 from the government just by standing in line? Transfer payments keep wages from seeking their own level in hard times.

The government uses subsidies and price floors to keep prices artificially high. Laws governing the financial sector make it impossible for savings to always find their way to where they are needed. Trade barriers like tariffs also keep international markets from clearing.

There is a failure here, but it is not a failure of classical economics. The problem is that the classical policies of laissez faire have been ignored. Keynesian economics succeeded not because it is better theory—it is not—but because it is a theory that tells politicians what they want to hear: spend more and get even more deeply involved in the economy. Keynesian economics must eventually fall apart, and the classical medicine will be waiting when that day arrives.

SUMMARY

1. Keynesian aggregate-demand analysis was a reaction to classical economic theories that failed to adequately deal with events like the Great Depression. The Economic Controversy indicates that the debate between Keynesian and classical economists is not through yet.

2. The circular-flow diagram illustrates the Keynesian view of spending and income. Spending creates income; consequently, income and employment can be regulated through policies that affect spending decisions.

3. Saving, taxes, and imports are leakages from the circular flow. Investment, government, and net-export spending are all injections. Macroeconomic equilibrium occurs when total leakages equal total injections. The economy always seeks an equilibrium, but there is no guarantee that equilibrium and full employment coincide.

4. Economic policies affect national income by altering aggregate demand. Income rises when injections exceed leakages. Falling incomes are the result of lower injections or greater leakages. The economy reponds to leakage and injection changes by moving to a new equilibrium income level.

5. The four components of aggregate demand are consumption, investment, government, and net-export spending. Consumption spending depends on the MPC relationship between changes in income and changes in spending, among other things. Interest rates are an important part of investment choices. Politics and philosophy influence government spending. Exchange rates and trade barriers are two of net exports' variables.

6. The aggregate demand (AD) curve shows how total purchases (measured by RNGP) and the price level are related. The slope of the AD curve depends on how much investment spending is affected by changing interest rates, among other things. The AD curve shifts when consumption, investment, government, or net-export spending change for some reason other than price level movements.

DISCUSSION QUESTIONS

1. Economic policies in the 1960s were based on the combination of the circular flow model of the economy and the Phillips curve relationship between inflation and unemployment. Given only these two ideas, answer the questions below:

a. Name two government policies that would reduce the unemployment rate.
b. Name two government policies that would reduce the inflation rate.
c. Government spending increased rapidly during the 1960s, but taxes were not raised to finance the deficit. How would this affect inflation and unemployment? Why? Explain in terms of the two models used for this question.
d. What government policies would fight both inflation and unemployment? Explain.

2. The Johnson family's income is $2000 per month. They typically spend $1800 on consumer goods and save the remaining $200. Mrs. Johnson just received a $200-per-month raise.

a. Assume that the Johnsons' MPC is 80 percent. What effect does this raise have on their monthly spending and saving totals?
b. What was the Johnsons' APC before the raise? Did it change? Explain why or why not.
c. Mr. Johnson now loses his job—the family's income falls by $1000 per month. Explain how this event affects spending, saving, MPC, and APC.

3. What are the main issues in the debate between the Keynesians and the classical economists? What is your opinion? Do government policies create economic problems or correct them? Explain.

TEST YOURSELF

Circle the best response to each question.

1. Macroeconomic equilibrium in the circular flow model is best described as:

(X) saving equals investment, taxes equal government spending, and imports equal exports
(Y) full employment with stable prices
(Z) total leakages equals total investments

a. all of the above
b. none of the above
c. (X) above
d. (Z) above
e. (X) and (Z)

2. Say's Law holds that ________ creates its own ________ . The Keynesian circular flow model is based on the idea that ________ creates ________ . (choose the response that best fills in the blanks)

a. spending/income, demand/supply
b. supply/demand, spending/income
c. demand/supply, income/spending
d. none of the above is correct

3. Suppose that the MPC is 80 percent and that national income rises by $100 billion. According to the theory presented in this chapter, consumption spending would ________ and the MPC would ________ . (choose the response that best fills in the blanks)

a. rise/fall
b. rise by $100 billion/fall
c. rise by $80 billion/remain constant
d. rise by $80 billion/fall
e. fall by $100 billion/remain constant

4. Which of the following policies would increase national income according to the circular flow model?

(X) increase taxes by $20 billion
(Y) increase imports by $20 billion
(Z) increase saving by $20 billion

a. all of the above
b. none of the above
c. only (Z)
d. only (Y)
e. (Y) and (Z)

5. Which of the following events would increase aggregate demand (shift the AD curve to the right)?

(X) fall in the price level
(Y) higher business investment purchases
(Z) increased consumer spending on imports

a. all of the above
b. (X) and (Z)
c. (X)
d. (Y)
e. (Z)

SUGGESTIONS FOR FURTHER READING

It is tough reading, but John Maynard Keynes' *General Theory of Employment, Interest, and Money* (London: Macmillan, 1946) is a classic! Not ready for that yet? Try a good intermediate macroeconomics text. One of the best is *Macroeconomics* by Rudiger Dornbusch and Stanley Fisher (New York: McGraw-Hill). Also useful is Alvin Hansen's *A Guide to Keynes* (New York: McGraw-Hill, 1953).

APPENDIX:

The 45-Degree Model of Circular Flow

The Keynesian aggregate demand model is often presented using the graphical device developed in this appendix. Students who plan to go on in economics should read this section because they will see these graphs in later courses. Students who do not plan to take advanced courses can read this or not, depending on their own or their professors' preferences.

The 45-Degree Line. The graphical analysis of aggregate demand begins with a different-looking graph, like the one shown in Figure 6-8. The axes of this graph carry new meanings. The horizontal axis measures income. The vertical axis measures total spending (aggregate demand). A **45-degree line** is drawn between these two axes—the 45-degree line shows all the points where spending equals income. Since "spending equals income" is the equilibrium condition for the circular-flow model, the 45-degree line shows all possible points of macroeconomic equilibrium. Equilibrium can prevail at any level of income, high or low. When spending equals income (when spending crosses the 45-degree line), macroeconomic equilibrium is achieved.

45-degree line: a line showing all the possible income levels where macroeconomic equilibrium can occur; points where spending equals income.

The Consumption Function. Figure 6-8 shows a second line labeled "C" for consumption. This line shows how consumption spending varies with income when everything other than income is held constant. The slope of the C line is the "rise over the run"—the change in consumption spending divided by the change in income. The slope of C is therefore the MPC.

Look at the point where the C line crosses the 45-degree line in Figure 6-8. Consumption spending at this point equals income—this point gives us the level of income at which consumers spend all their income. Consumers *dis-*

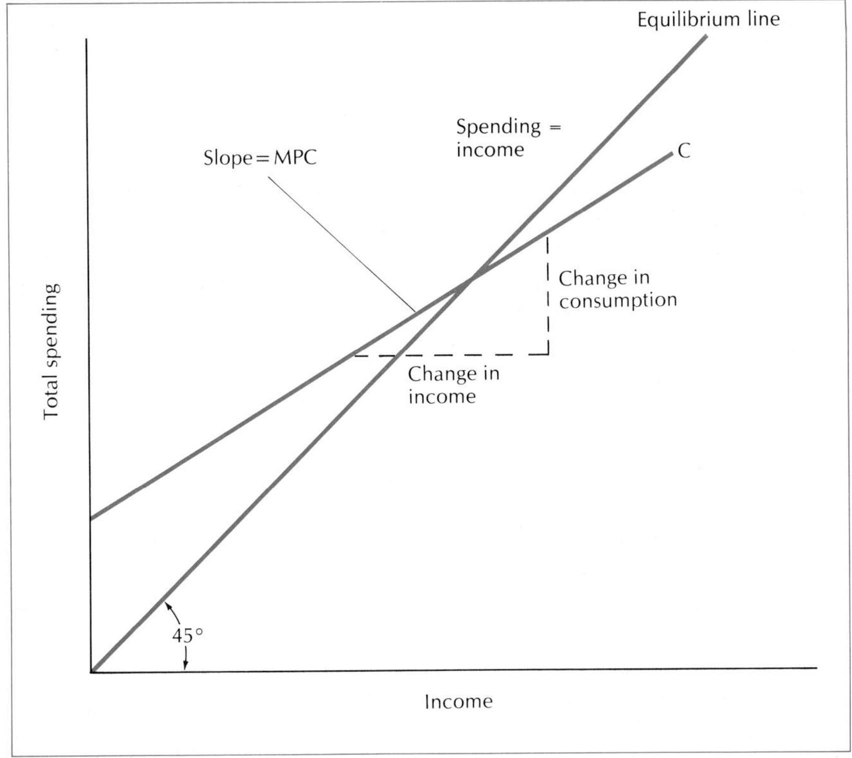

FIGURE 6-8 45-DEGREE LINE AND CONSUMPTION FUNCTION. The 45-degree line shows all points where spending equals income—that is, where macroeconomic equilibrium is possible. The C line plots how consumption spending varies with income. The slope of the C line is the MPC.

save—spend more than they take in—at income levels below this and *save*—spend less than their income—at income levels above this. The amount of saving or dissaving is given by the vertical difference between the C and 45-degree lines.

Aggregate Demand. Consumption spending is just one of four components of aggregate demand. What about investment, government, and net-export spending? Suppose that these three do not change with the level of income. We can treat them as constants and add them vertically to the C line, as shown in Figure 6-9.

The line labeled C + I +G + X is appropriately called an aggregate demand curve because it shows how total spending (given the assumptions already listed) varies with income. Macroeconomic equilibrium occurs when C + I + G + X crosses the 45-degree line. At this point, total spending equals total income. The level of income, listed as Y* in the figure, is the macroeconomic equilibrium. Spending (C + I + G + X) exceeds income (the 45-degree line) at income levels below this, pushing income up toward the equilibrium. If

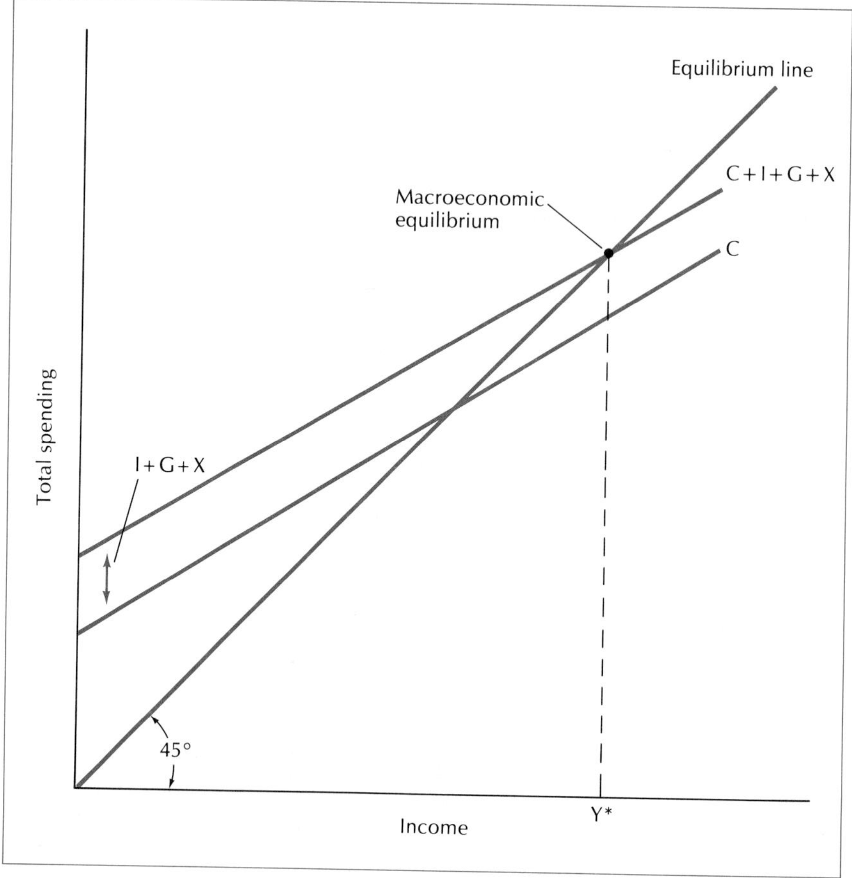

FIGURE 6-9 MACROECONOMIC EQUILIBRIUM. Total spending is given by the C+I+G+X line in this figure. Macroeconomic equilibrium occurs at the income level where the C + I + G + X line crosses the 45-degree line. Spending equals income and leakages equal injections at Y*.

income were already above Y*, spending would be less than income (the C + I + G + X curve lies below the 45-degree line). Income must fall.

There is another way to view the macroeconomic equilibrium in this figure. If the 45-degree line is income and the C line is consumption, then the distance between these two lines must represent saving (the only leakage in this figure). The difference between the C line and the C + I + G + X (total spending) line is I + G + X—the injections into this system. Leakages (saving) equal injections (I + G + X) at the macroeconomic equilibrium Y* in the figure. Injections exceed leakages when income is below Y*, moving the economy toward equilibrium. Leakages are greater than injections, however, if income exceeds equilibrium. The net leakage forces income down to the macroeconomic equilibrium level.

Changes in Aggregate Demand and Income. If income is greater or less than the equilibrium level, the forces of spending and income—leakage and injection—move it toward Y*. What makes the equilibrium change? Equilibrium income changes only if aggregate demand (C + I + G + X) changes for some reason. One possibility is illustrated in Figure 6-10.

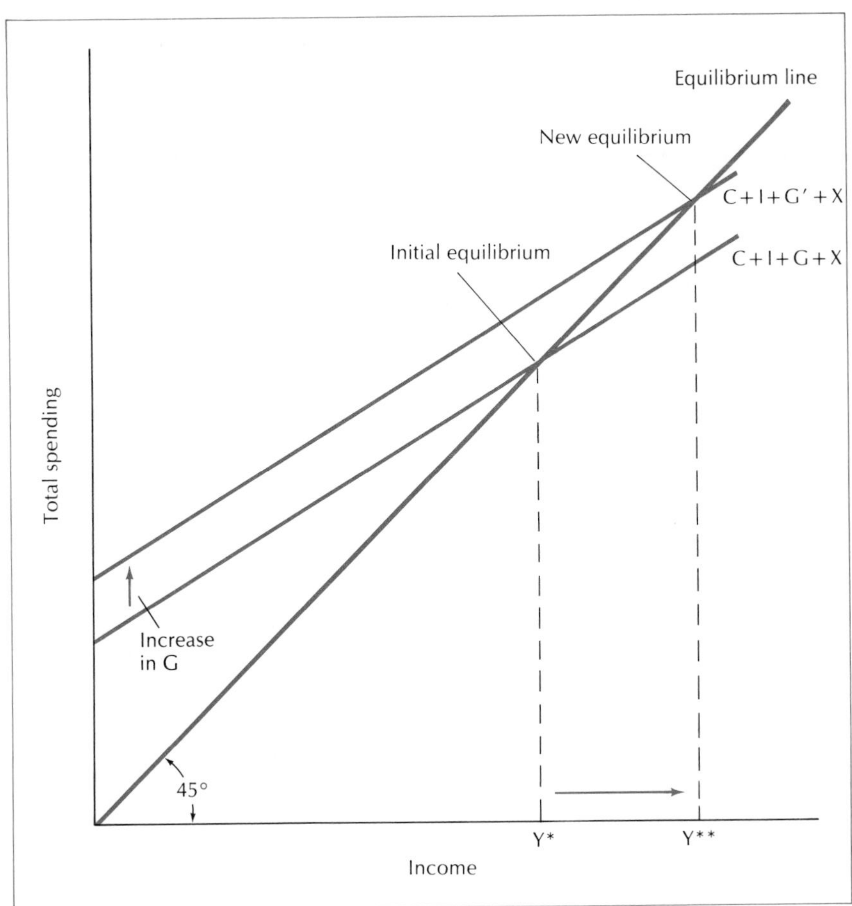

FIGURE 6-10 Impact of Increased Government Spending. Government spending increases from G to G′ in this figure. Total spending rises to C + I + G′ + X. A new macroeconomic equilibrium level is reached at Y**, where spending and income are again equal.

Congress has decided that Y* has too high an unemployment rate. Increased government spending shifts the aggregate demand curve up—the total spending line shifts to C + I + G′ + X (the ′ next to G indicates a change in this spending component). The economy moves from the initial equilibrium to the new, higher one at Y**. The government spending injection increases total spending and so pushes total income up until the leakage-injecton equilibrium is restored at Y**. Government policy in this 45-degree line model means choosing a target level of income (one with a low enough unemployment rate) and then manipulating total spending so that the new equilibrium occurs at the target level of income.

The 45-degree line model discussed in this section is based on the ideas of the circular flow and bathtub models of the main chapter. The advantage to this presentation is that you can actually plot out the changes in spending and see how large the resulting change in income is. You can also see where equilibrium is on the graph, rather than simply noting the income would increase or decrease in a given situation.

AGGREGATE SUPPLY AND THE ECONOMY

Preview

What causes inflation and unemployment?
What is the best way to fight inflation and unemployment?
Are demand-management policies as effective at full employment as they are during recessions?
How can we increase aggregate supply?
Are wage and price controls a good way to fight inflation?
What do leading indicators like inventories tell us about the economy?

WHY DID economic policies in the 1970s fail in fighting inflation and unemployment? At least part of the problem was that these policies were based on the successful experience of the 1960s, when aggregate demand policies traded off inflation and unemployment. But the economic problems of the 1970s (and 1980s) are not exclusively problems of demand. Economists of the 1970s rediscovered the economics of aggregate supply and learned that a complete analysis of the economy includes both demand and supply.

Is aggregate supply a new idea? No. Keynes's demand-based economic theory best describes an economy in recession where insufficient spending is the most important problem. Keynes realized, however, that depression economics are not always appropriate. Therefore, in *The General Theory of Employment, Interest, and Money* (London: Macmillan, 1964), he suggested that a complete description of the economy must include **aggregate supply.** This chapter follows in Keynes' footsteps, using aggregate demand and aggregate supply to analyze inflation and unemployment in a modern economy.

aggregate supply: total intended production of goods and services.

This chapter looks at the determinants of supply in the economy and then goes on to explore economic policies that fight inflation and unemployment. The Economic Controversy debates wage and price controls.

Aggregate Supply

Aggregate supply describes total desired production measured, like aggregate demand, by the level of real gross national product (RGNP). Aggregate supply is to the supply of goods in an individual market as aggregate demand is to market demand. Aggregate supply is the sum of supplies in all individual markets and is influenced by economic events that affect market supplies around the economy.

What determines the supply of apples or oranges? You ought to be able to make a quick list of things that affect any particular supply curve; things like weather, labor costs, and the like. What determines the level of aggregate supply in the economy? The list here contains many of the same items. Aggregate supply depends on variables that influence production choices, not in just one market, but in many markets throughout the economy. Aggregate supply hinges on problems common to most business decisions. A list of determinants of aggregate supply includes:

1. PRICE LEVEL. Producers in individual markets respond directly to changes in market price. Aggregate supply depends on the price level. The reasoning is similar between market and economy-wide supply. Why does an individual firm produce more only if market price rises? Chapter 2 suggested that the direct relationship between price and quantity supplied was based on two ideas. First, price acts as an incentive. Higher prices (and price levels) at least temporarily increase profits. These profits give firms an incentive to produce more and induce new firms to enter markets and add to output.

The second reason is cost. Firms experience rising marginal costs as output expands. Additional production costs more and so cannot be profitably sold unless prices go up, too. Thus, higher prices are needed for increased production. The combination of incentive and cost explains aggregate supply as well.

2. CAPACITY AND INVESTMENT. The physical ability to produce constrains production. The economy is limited by its **capacity**—the existing stock of machines, factories, trained workers, farms, and the like—in the short run.

capacity: the physical ability of the economy to produce, limited by the stock of factories, machines, tools, and so on.

Investment spending increases capacity in the long run. Investment replaces worn-out factories and machines and expands the economy's ability to produce. Investment spending takes awhile to be felt, however. In the short run, investment spending adds to aggregate demand, as spending on training and tools increases total spending and income. In the long run, however, investment spending brings increased capacity and greater aggregate supply. Investment spending stimulates both aggregate demand and aggregate supply and promotes the balanced growth of the economy.

When you think of investment you probably think of spending by business firms, but government is an investor, too. Government spending on roads, port facilities, and power projects expands capacity in the same way as similar private ventures.

Low investment spending in the Great Depression had a double effect on the economy. First, the low investment spending contributed to low incomes, as you saw in Chapter 6. But the tiny flow of new investment was not even enough to make up for **depreciation**—the wearing out of existing capacity. Negative **net investment** meant that capacity was actually less at the end of the depression than at the start. The demand problem became one of supply, too.

depreciation: the wearing out of machines and other productive resources.

net investment: investment over and above that necessary to compensate for depreciation.

3. TECHNOLOGY. Technological change reduces cost and increases aggregate supply. New inventions and improved processes make existing resources go farther and improve the quality of output.

Technology and investment go hand in hand. First, implementation of new technology requires business investment. The American auto industry found that it had to spend money to make money in the 1980s. High-technology-automated factories that produce cars most profitably cost billions of dollars to construct. Technology creates jobs in investment industries as it expands capacity.

Technology is a consequence as well as a cause of investment. Breakthroughs come only after years of research and development. Cost-cutting inventions are costly to invent and expensive to put in place. Many economists blame low research investment for many of the problems U.S. firms have on international markets.

The U.S. government is a big spender on research and technology. Government grants support scientific and agricultural research at many colleges and universities, for example. Breakthroughs made in these laboratories and in government programs like NASA have helped U.S. producers stay competitive.

4. PRODUCTIVITY. Labor's ability to produce determines workers' real incomes and aggregate supply. **Productivity** is important to economic growth.

productivity: the relative ability of a resource to produce goods and services; often measured by the amount of production per man-hour.

investment in human capital: investments in training and education that increase worker productivity.

Productivity depends on many things. Training and **investment in human capital** increase worker skills and aggregate supply. Government is responsible for much of this investment in people. Public high schools, colleges, and technical schools (and similar private institutions that receive public support) all improve productivity. The skills these programs provide help both the individuals who receive the training and those who consume the lower-cost goods they produce.

Productivity has not increased as fast in the United States as it has in many other countries. What is the reason for poor U.S. productivity? Part of the productivity problem goes back to seriously low rates of investment in capacity and research. Worker productivity depends both on human skills and on technological factors. Trained workers using modern tools produce more and better goods than other workers. Highly trained U.S. workers in outdated plants have little chance against more modern foreign competitors.

5. AVAILABILITY AND COST OF RESOURCES. A printing firm is out of business if paper and ink are unavailable or cost more than customers are willing to pay. Aggregate supply rides on the cost and supply of basic production goods like oil, steel, energy, labor, and natural resources. Price increases or general shortage of these goods reduce aggregate supply. Three examples show how important some items are to the economy.

Prices and shortages of oil brought on the recessions of 1974–1975 and 1979–1980. The Arab oil embargo of 1974 and the Iranian oil cutoff of 1979, combined with price increases in each case, reduced aggregate supply and hurt the economy. Oil is so important to the economy that even small changes in its cost or availability have big effects on aggregate supply.

A shortage of a different kind brought on a recession in 1958–1959. A steel strike robbed the economy of one of its most widely used inputs. Steel prices skyrocketed and factory after factory shut down for lack of raw materials.

The transportation sector is also important to the economy. A threatened train strike during Harry Truman's administration might have brought on a recession by disrupting transportation of people and goods. Jobs disappear when no one delivers parts and raw materials. Farmer incomes rot along with crops if their oranges and tomatoes cannot be shipped to market. Truman threatened to call out the troops to man railroad engines and thus prevented the economy-shattering strike.

Investments and new technology take a long time to work—they increase aggregate supply in the long run. Rising producer costs and input shortages hit in the short run, however, reducing aggregate supply and eliminating jobs.

6. EXPECTATIONS. Producers, workers, and investors all base supply decisions on their view of the future. Expectations influence intended production in many ways. Firms that expect higher input prices in the future, for example, stock up now or produce for inventory so that they have lower cost items to sell later. Investment and production decisions depend on projected future consumer buying and expected government policies. Action is based on anticipation, so changing expectations alter aggregate supply.

7. GOVERNMENT POLICIES. Government policies affect aggregate supply in ways both obvious and subtle. Government investments in dams, highways, and in education and training have already been discussed. The government also owns many resources like timber and mineral deposits. Government decisions concerning the use of these inputs affect aggregate supply now and in the future.

Taxes are another variable in the supply decision. Taxes affect worker and employer incentives. High tax rates reduce the return on extra work or investment. High taxes discourage workers and firms from expanding aggregate supply. But taxes also help channel investment funds to specific purposes when tax breaks are allowed for spending in particular areas of the economy.

Government regulations affect aggregate supply, too. Many economists think that environmental regulations are a reason for reduced productivity in the United States. Many workers now spend their time producing cleaner air and water, not toasters and refrigerators. This might be good for the country, but productivity falls because the better environment that results is not counted in RGNP.

8. **EVERYTHING ELSE.** You can add "everything else" to this list, if you like, because there are many other variables that influence production. The weather and politics are two important everything-else items. Low economic capacity during the Great Depression was in part the result of bad weather in the farm belt. Political uncertainty translates into economic uncertainty. Managers and corporate heads are loathe to commit investment funds when political skies are cloudy. A stable political system is a prerequisite for a stable economic system (and vice versa).

The Aggregate Supply Curve

The aggregate supply (AS) curve maps the relationship between RGNP produced and the price level. The AS curve takes on different shapes depending on the state of the economy. The three aggregate supply curves are:

1. **DEPRESSION AGGREGATE SUPPLY CURVE.** An economy in a depression or deep recession is plagued with idle resources. Such an economy has high capacity, but this potential is not realized because of deficient demand. Surplus resources—machines, factories, trucks, and workers—stand ready to answer the call to produce. Output can be expanded in the depression economy by drawing on the ranks of unemployed resources—higher prices are not a requirement here.

The **depression aggregate supply curve** is horizontal as shown in Figure 7-1. Higher levels of RGNP are possible without rising prices because the economy is well below the point at which rising marginal costs become a problem. Increased demand can often be met from unused **inventories** accumulated before production lines shut down and workers were laid off.

depression aggregate supply curve: aggregate supply in an economy with many unemployed resources.

inventories: stocks of goods that firms hold for future production or sale.

2. **FULL CAPACITY AGGREGATE SUPPLY CURVE.** The AS curve changes shape when capacity limits are reached. Production cannot expand further if all machines or all workers are already in use. Full capacity can coincide with full employment, but the roadblock to further production might result from full use of machines, factories, or other nonhuman capital.

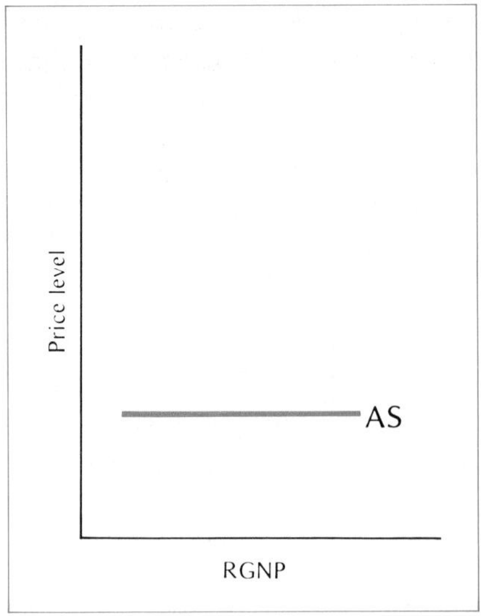

FIGURE 7-1 THE DEPRESSION AGGREGATE SUPPLY CURVE. The aggregate supply curve is horizontal in periods of depression or recession since many resources are not utilized. In this instance, higher output does not require higher price levels.

full capacity aggregate supply curve: aggregate supply in an economy that has reached production limits determined by finite capacity.

The **full capacity aggregate supply curve** is vertical. Aggregate supply can be increased in the long run through investment, innovation, or training. In the short run, however, total output is limited. Expanded production in one part of the economy comes at the cost of reduced output elsewhere. The government can produce more airplanes and bombs, for example, but only by bidding workers and inputs away from other uses. The RGNP remains about the same, but price levels rise as government and private firms compete for

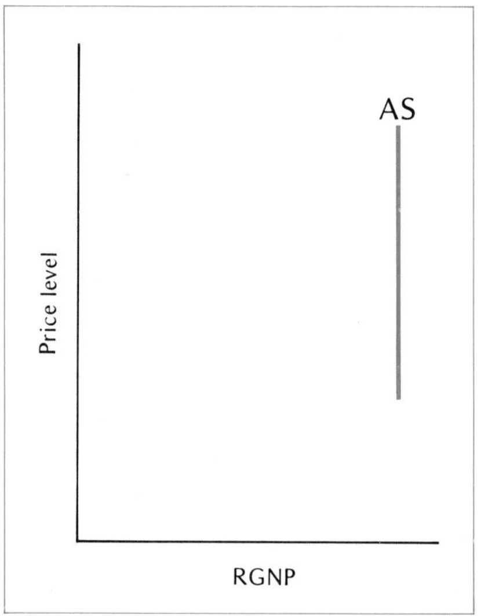

FIGURE 7-2 THE FULL CAPACITY AGGREGATE SUPPLY CURVE. The aggregate supply curve is vertical when resource limits appear. Total production cannot rise in the short run even if the price level increases.

scarce resources. The message is clear: any attempt to expand production brings only higher prices in the short run, once capacity is reached.

Many economists believe the AS curve is vertical for a different reason than capacity limits. Expectations, they think, determine the shape of the aggregate supply curve. Firms and individuals adapt to changes in the price level and return to their original production plans. They end up producing no more or less than before. These **adaptive expectations** are important to the economy today. We will look at this economic theory in more depth in Chapter 12.

adaptive expectations: expectations that change in light of new information.

3. BOTTLENECK AGGREGATE SUPPLY CURVE. Depressions and full capacity are exceptions, not the rule, in modern economies. Resources like oil and skilled workers are scarce, but still available. Marginal costs rise in the short run as producers expand. This "normal" condition is described by the **bottleneck aggregate supply curve** of Figure 7-3. The RGNP grows in the short run only if the price level increases—inflation goes with expanded output.

bottleneck aggregate supply curve: aggregate supply in an economy with rising marginal costs and production bottlenecks.

Why does the AS curve slope up as this figure shows? Rising marginal costs and the incentive function of price are part of the reason. Keynes suggested that production bottlenecks are important, too.

Bottlenecks are temporary tie-ups and shortages that get in the way of production. Have you ever seen a traffic bottleneck? Speed plummets when highway construction forces two lanes to merge into one. Individual drivers get in one another's way, congesting the flow of traffic.

Producers do the same thing as these drivers in the bottleneck economy. Suppose, for example, that defense spending increases in a world like this one. Are the resources available for expanded production? Yes—eventually—but not immediately. In the short run, firms compete for available steel, workers, and factory space. This competition bids up price until temporary shortages (the bottlenecks) are eased. Output increases, but prices are bid up, too.

Each of these three AS shapes are really part of a bigger AS curve shown in Figure 7-4. The AS curve is flat when RGNP is at low depression

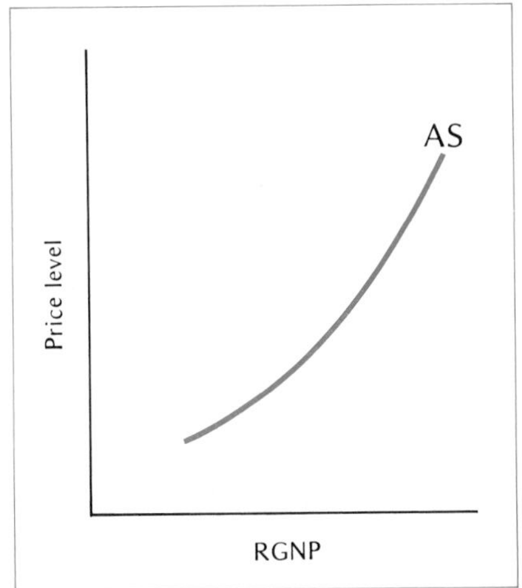

FIGURE 7-3 THE BOTTLENECK AGGREGATE SUPPLY CURVE. Rising marginal costs and production bottlenecks bid up prices as production grows. Inflation accompanies higher RGNP in the short run.

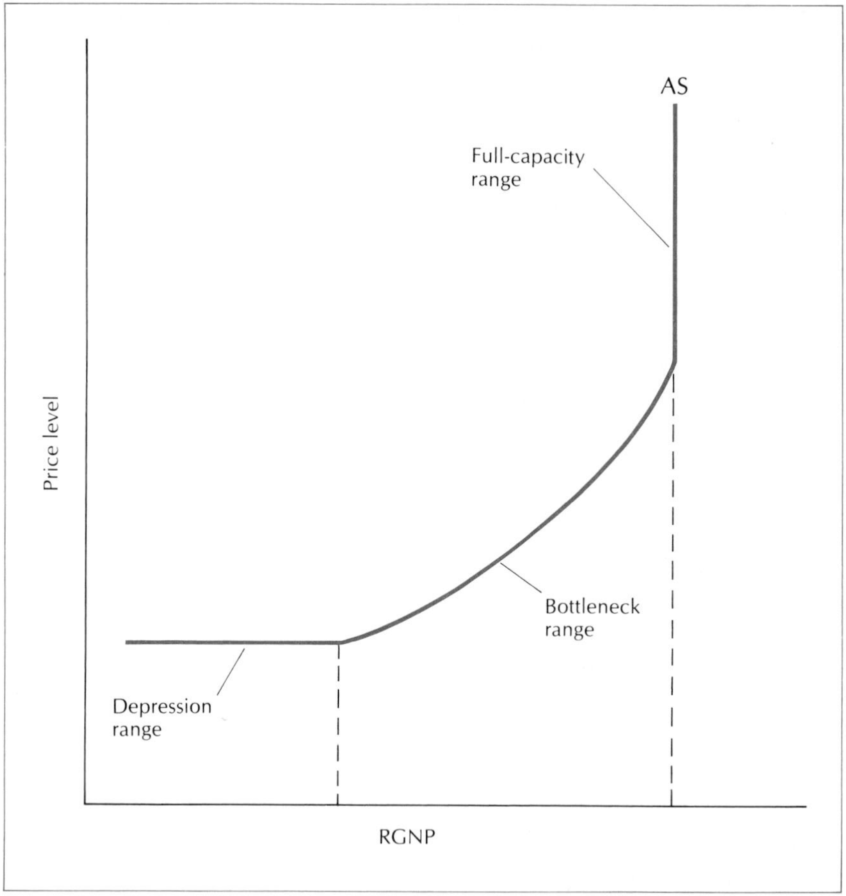

FIGURE 7-4 THE LONG-RUN AGGREGATE SUPPLY CURVE. The slope of the aggregate supply curve depends on the state of the economy. The AS curve is flat at low RGNP levels, then becomes upward sloping as bottlenecks appear, and finally becomes vertical when resource limits are reached.

levels. The AS curve slopes up as surplus resources are used up and bottlenecks begin to appear. The AS curve finally finds its vertical part when capacity roadblocks appear.

Shifts in the Aggregate Supply Curve

Aggregate supply shifts in the short and long run in response to the variables already listed. A change in just the price level brings a movement along the AS curve, from one level of RGNP to another. A change in any determinant other than the price level shifts the AS curve, as Figures 7-5 and 7-6 show.

Aggregate supply increases when something happens to make firms want to expand production at the current price level. In the short run aggregate supply could increase because:

- OPEC cuts the price of oil, an important production input, or
- Costly government regulations are modified to make production cheaper than before.

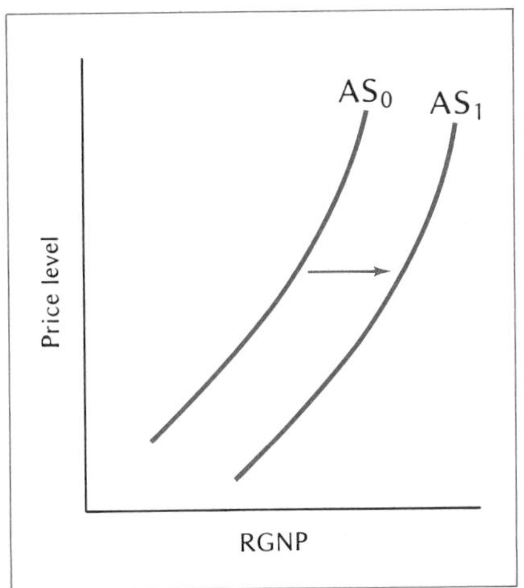

FIGURE 7-5 INCREASED AGGREGATE SUPPLY. Aggregate supply increases when capacity, productivity, production costs, or other events increase desired output at the current price level.

Changing expectations could also increase aggregate supply in the short run. Aggregate supply increases in the long run if:

- Education and training programs improve productivity;
- Investments in new plants and factories increase economic capacity;
- Engineering advances improve technology.

A decrease in aggregate supply, as Figure 7-6 illustrates, results from any change in the economy that reduces overall production. Examples of changes that might lead to falling aggregate supply include more costly government regulations, labor strikes or other input limitations, falling economic capacity (due to low levels of investment), or deteriorating productivity.

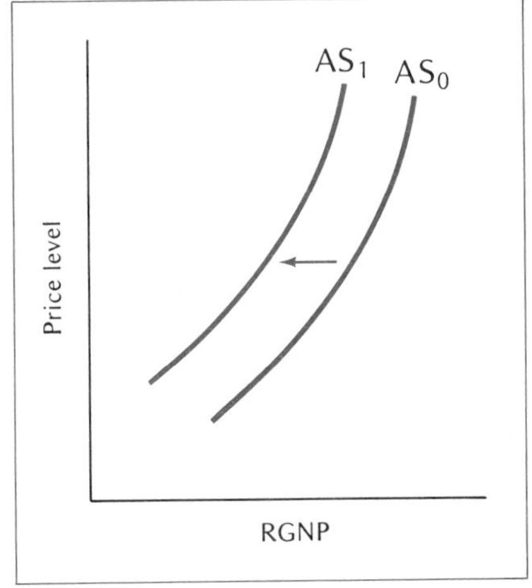

7-6 DECREASED AGGREGATE SUPPLY. Aggregate supply falls when government regulations, higher input costs, or other events reduce desired production levels.

Macroeconomic Equilibrium

A macroeconomic equilibrium occurs when the quantity of goods and services people want to buy at a particular price level equals the quantity firms want to produce at that price level. Macroeconomic equilibrium takes place where aggregate demand crosses aggregate supply in Figure 7-7. Aggregate demand equals aggregate supply at a price level of 100 and a RGNP of $1500 billion. Neither surplus nor shortage force price level changes.

The macroeconomic equilibrium shown in this figure is stable in the sense that the economy moves toward the equilibrium and, once there, remains in equilibrium until either aggregate demand or aggregate supply changes to upset the balance.

Suppose that, for some reason, the price level is above equilibrium (like price level 110 in the figure). The quantity of aggregate supply exceeds aggregate demand at this price level—there is a general surplus of goods. Firms find

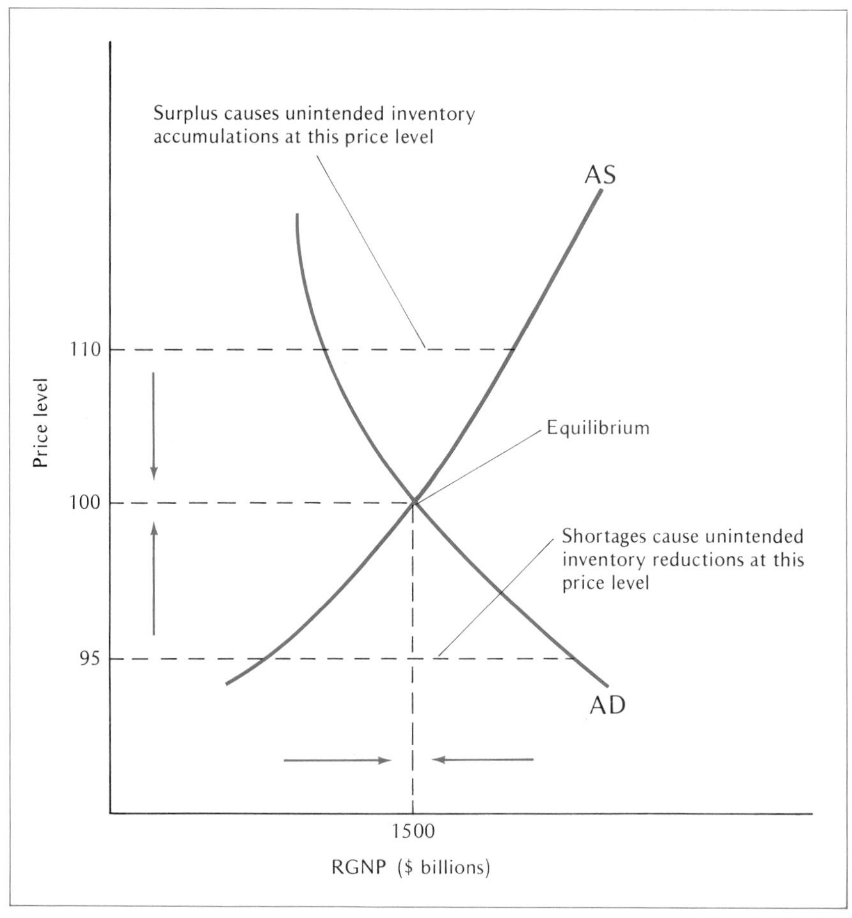

FIGURE 7-7 THE MACROECONOMIC EQUILIBRIUM. The forces of shortage and surplus bring the economy into a price level-RGNP equilibrium at the intersection of the aggregate supply and aggregate demand curves.

that they have **unintended inventory accumulations**—overproduction fills their shelves. Merchants reduce inventories by cutting price and ordering fewer new goods. More goods are purchased and fewer are produced as the price level falls until the AD-AS equilibrium is reached.

Goods are scarce if the price level is below equilibrium, like the 95 price level in the figure. Businesses experience **unintended inventory reductions**—goods disappear from their shelves faster than anticipated. Consumers bid up price and merchants increase orders for new goods. Higher prices reduce purchases and increase production until equilibrium is reached.

unintended inventory accumulations: increases in inventory levels that occur when demand falls behind production.

unintended inventory reductions: decreases in inventory levels that occur when demand rises above supply.

Adjusting to Equilibrium

The economy adjusts to changing aggregate demand and aggregate supply in much the same way as individual markets react to supply-demand shifts. Two examples illustrate the adjustment process.

Tax cuts stimulated increased consumer spending in the Kennedy years of the early 1960s. Increased aggregate demand led to higher prices and increased RGNP, as Figure 7-8 shows.

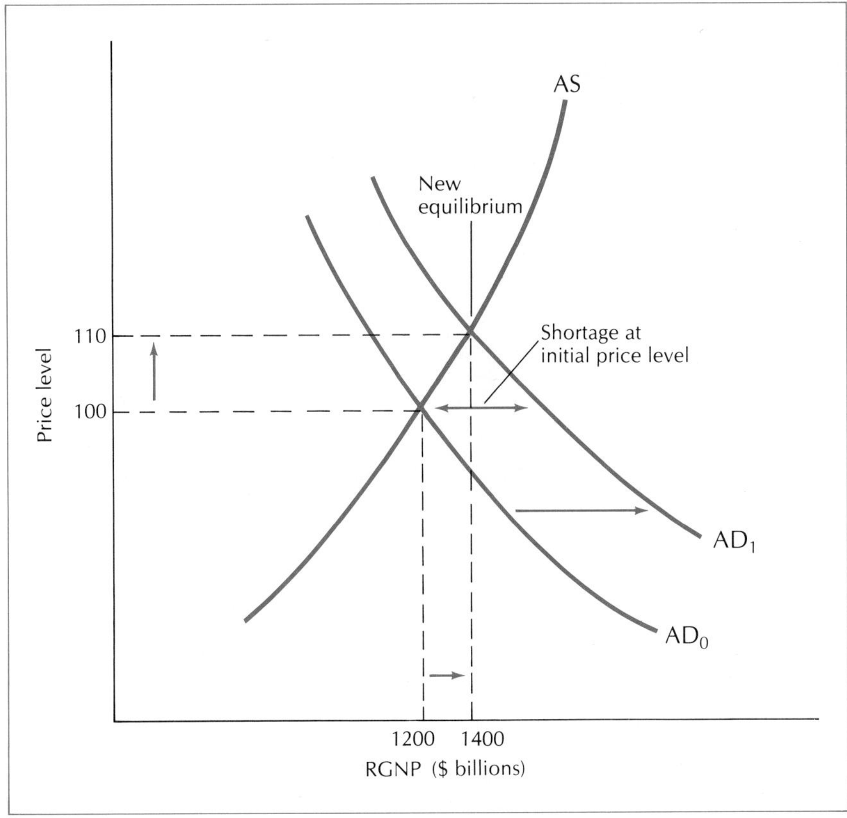

FIGURE 7-8 DEMAND-PULL INFLATION. Rising aggregate demand pulls the economy to a new equilibrium with a higher price level and RGNP. Unintended inventory reductions are a key part of this adjustment process.

Businesses saw extra spending first as an inventory adjustment. The shortage of goods and services drew down inventories. Consumers bid up the price level. Merchants put in new orders to fill their shelves and the wheels of industry went round. The economy adjusted to the new equilibrium shown in the figure. Higher RGNP indicates more production, more jobs, and lower unemployment rates. The higher price level shows inflation.

High interest costs and government spending cuts reduced aggregate demand in the early 1980s. Let us see how the economy adjusted to falling aggregate demand. The economy's condition is illustrated in Figure 7-9.

Producers and retailers see falling aggregate demand as an inventory problem. Consumers buy fewer goods than expected; the surplus of goods is initially felt as an unintended inventory surplus. Firms adjust to excess inventories by cutting new orders and production. They let consumer spending gradually draw down the too-high stocks of goods. Prices fall, too. Merchants discount goods to quantity buyers, print "cents-off coupons" in local newspapers, or simply reduce price on the shelves (only this last action would show up as a

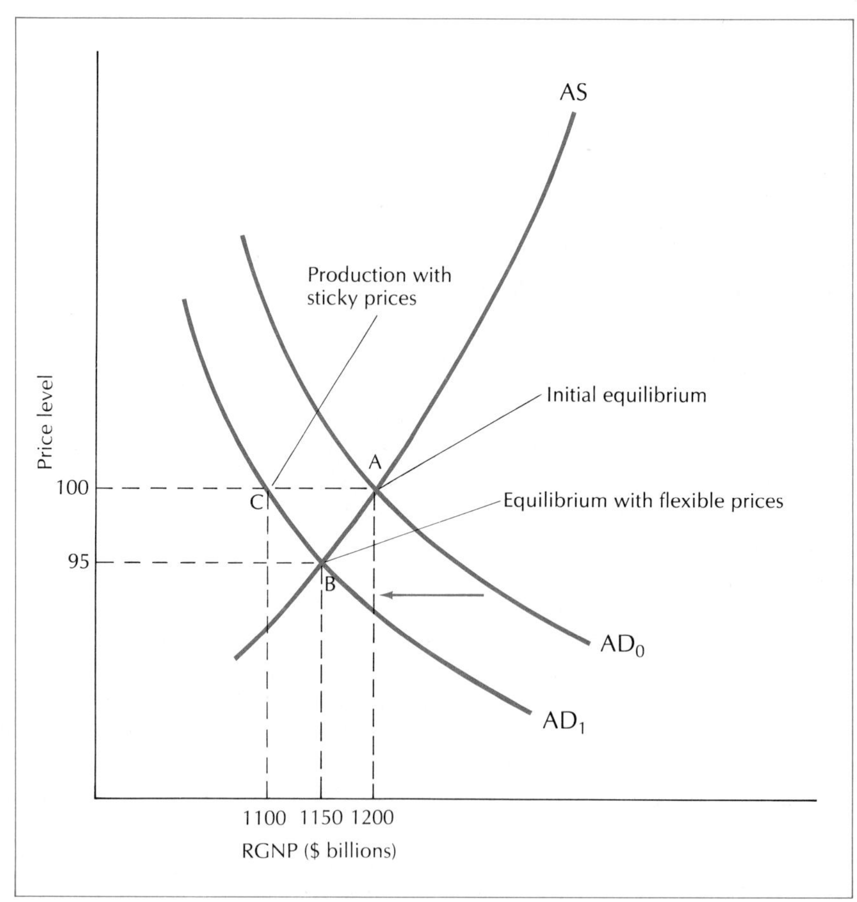

FIGURE 7-9 FALLING AGGREGATE DEMAND. Falling aggregate demand causes unemployment. The unemployment problem is worse if the price level is "sticky," as is the case in this figure. The economy begins at A and moves to B if prices are flexible. If, on the other hand, prices are sticky, the economy moves to C, resulting in a lower RGNP and higher unemployment.

price cut in the Consumer Price Index, however). Inventories fall faster as prices drop until the economy finds the new equilibrium with a lower price level and lower RGNP. Less production means fewer jobs and so more unemployment.

The unemployment problem we see here is worse if sticky prices prevail in the economy. Prices in some markets are inflexible—set by contract or government regulation or kept from falling by high production costs. The RGNP falls even more—from $1200 billion to $1100 billion in the figure—when prices are sticky. Production falls to whatever level consumers want to buy at the going price level (the AS curve shifts back to this level in the long run if firms adjust expectations to the lower RGNP).

Falling aggregate demand is always a source of unemployment, but sticky wages and prices make unemployment worse than it would otherwise be. Prices may be stickier today than in years past (this is difficult to prove either way). Years of inflation make producers and sellers loathe to cut prices they are used to raising. Prices of many goods fell in 1982, however. The price level even decreased for one month. Semi-sticky prices mean that the economy probably adjusted to RGNP somewhere between the frozen price ($1100) and the flexible price ($1150) levels of the figure.

Leading Indicators

Inventories are a leading indicator of RGNP changes. Unintended inventory accumulations, for example, are a clue that merchants will reduce new orders and that production and RGNP will fall in the future. The inventory condition does not tell us what might have caused the problem, just which direction RGNP is likely to go.

An unintended inventory reduction sends the opposite signal to economic observers. Merchants and others increase new orders to rebuild stocks. The new orders eventually translate into increased output and higher RGNP. Again, we cannot tell what caused the inventory reduction, only its consequences.

Inventories are the second leading indicator covered in this text; the first (discussed in Chapter 4) was the Producer Price Index (PPI). Changes in the PPI foretell movements of consumer prices in the same way that inventory changes signal future RGNP movements.

These two widely reported statistics are handy tools for amateur economic prognosticators. Inventories often foretell changes in unemployment and the PPI signals changes in inflation as measured by the Consumer Price Index. Thus inventory accumulations and rising PPI, for example, hint at a future combination of higher inflation and rising unemployment rates. The movements signaled by inventories and the PPI do not always occur—government policies or changing expectations, for example, might get in the way—but predictions made using these tools are often accurate.

What are some other leading indicators? The idea behind leading indicators is to look for early signs of actions that generate future economic behav-

housing starts: number of new homes begun in a given period; a leading indicator of production.

Dow Jones average: an index that measures prices of major stocks on the New York Stock Exchange.

index of leading indicators: an index that foretells future changes in the RGNP.

ior. The number of new homes constructed (called **housing starts**) is such an early warning device. A builder pours the foundation for a new house today. In coming months carpenters, plumbers, and electricians are going to be employed to build this structure and wood, wire, and plumbing fixtures will be purchased. When the house is sold, carpets, major kitchen appliances, paint, and new furniture will be sold to furnish the new house. The start of the house is the first step in a long chain of economic activity. Rising housing starts are, therefore, a sign of future RGNP growth and falling housing starts signal rising unemployment rates.

The stock market is often cited as another leading indicator. People buy and sell stocks based on how they think companies will profit from the future. A rising **Dow Jones average** therefore means that people think production, profits, and income will grow. A falling stock market signals expectations of recession. Be careful not to draw too many conclusions from the stock market's behavior, however. Louis Ruckeyser has noted that the stock market has predicted something like 10 out of the last 5 recessions—it fell many times when the economy did not.

These leading indicators and several more go into the government's **index of leading indicators.** Take care not to jump to conclusions about the economy based on a single month's index. It takes several months to build a reliable picture of future activity.

Some good leading indicators of future economic activity are not included in any index. Sales of brooms turn out to be a good predictor of consumer spending. Brooms? You bet. Brooms are the ultimate delayable expenditure—you can always make an old broom last a little longer. People stop buying brooms when they think a recession is coming. Falling broom sales foretell falling sales in general and falling RGNP. Sales of brooms pick up quickly when people see the economy booming. They buy brooms and many other things. Keep your eyes open for new brooms that foretell sweeping changes in the economy.

The football Super Bowl is another good, but not necessarily reliable, leading indicator. Good economic times seem to follow Super Bowl victories by teams from the old American Football League. Recessions seem to strike when teams originally from the National League win this game.

Inflation and Unemployment

What do aggregate demand and aggregate supply tell us about the causes of inflation and unemployment? We have seen one reason for higher unemployment rates in Figure 7-9: falling aggregate demand. Unemployment rates increase when aggregate demand falls. Jobless lines grow even faster if sticky wages and prices accompany falling aggregate demand.

A different reason for unemployment is shown in Figure 7-10. Energy prices went up and available supplies shrank during the oil embargo of 1973–1974 and the Iranian oil cutoff of 1979. Aggregate supply in the United States fell due to the double forces of scarcity and higher production cost. Firms raised

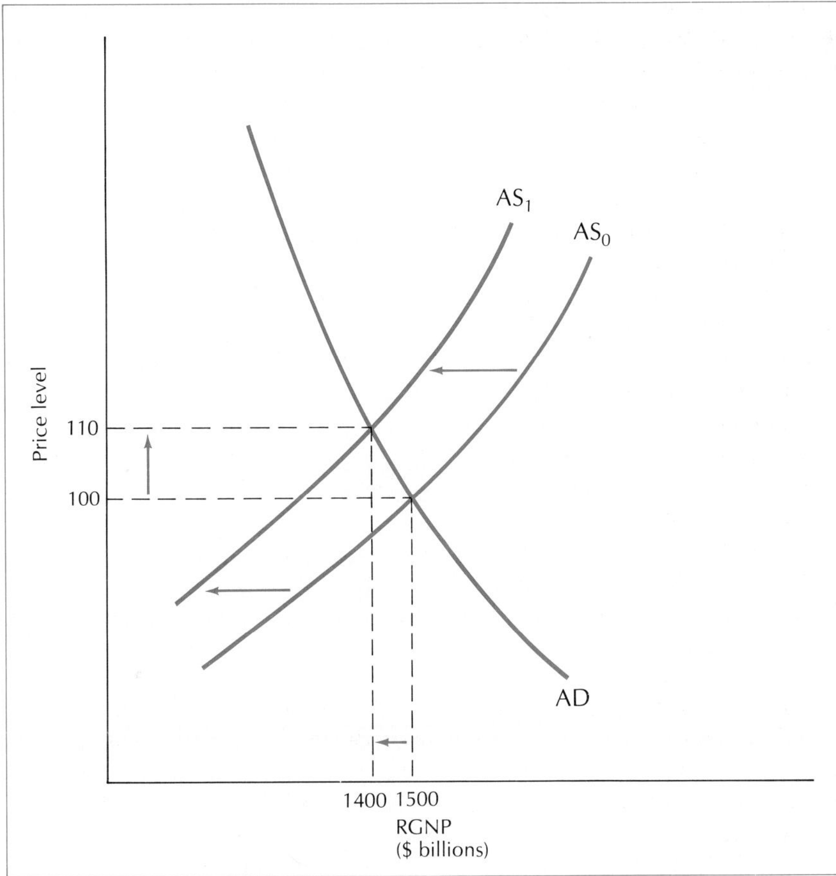

FIGURE 7-10 COST-PUSH INFLATION. Falling aggregate supply pushes up prices and pushes down the RGNP. Unemployment is accompanied by higher inflation when this happens.

prices, but unsold goods accumulated. Production orders fell. The RGNP went down and unemployment lines went up.

Falling aggregate supply reduces RGNP and creates unemployment, but that is not the only problem it brings. Price levels rise due to cost-push forces, as the figure shows. Falling aggregate supply brings both unemployment and inflation.

Look back at the inflation and unemployment figures given for the 1950s, 1960s, 1970s, and 1980s in Chapter 1 of this book. Was the unemployment of the 1950s the result of falling aggregate demand or falling aggregate supply? See if you can tell which force made unemployment rise in each period.

Cost-push inflation is a horrible fate. Goods cost more and falling RGNP leaves us less able to purchase them. A different type of inflation was illustrated in Figure 7-8. Prices rise here in response to increased aggregate demand. Demand-pull inflation gives us the problem of inflation but compensates for higher prices with increased RGNP and shorter unemployment lines.

What kinds of inflation did the United States experience in years past? Go back to the inflation and unemployment figures in Chapter 1 and determine when demand-pull and cost-push forces prevailed. (Hint: the economy moves *along* the Phillips curve when demand pulls the strings and moves *off*—or shifts—the Phillips curve in cost-push conditions.)

That Old-Time Religion

Which economic policy best fights inflation and unemployment? Traditional economic policies—that Old Time Religion—use aggregate demand to move along the Phillips curve. Is unemployment too high? Increase aggregate demand and RGNP rises. Is inflation too high? Reduce aggregate demand and the price level falls or at least stops rising.

Demand-management policies were appropriate in the 1930s and 1960s when demand-pull inflation dominated the scene. Demand-based policies work fine when aggregate supply is either constant (not shifting) or growing. These policies fail, however, when cost-push forces prevail. What is the best way to fight cost-push inflation and unemployment? Figures 7-11 and 7-12 show the pitfalls that await policies based on aggregate demand alone.

If cost-push inflation is viewed as an unemployment problem the dogma of the Old-Time Religion says to increase aggregate demand. Does this policy work? Figure 7-11 tells the story. The combination of falling aggregate supply and rising aggregate demand brings RGNP back to its original level but sends

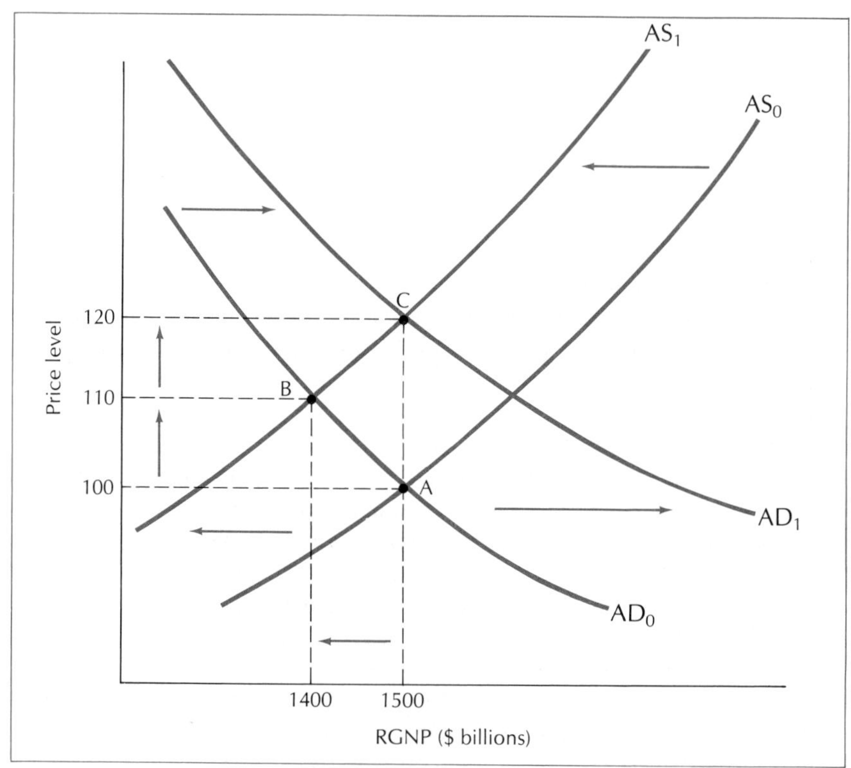

FIGURE 7-11 FIGHTING SUPPLY WITH DEMAND. Falling aggregate supply would normally move the economy from A to B in this figure. If the government fights unemployment by increasing aggregate demand, the economy ends up at C instead. The RGNP no longer falls and the price level goes up even more.

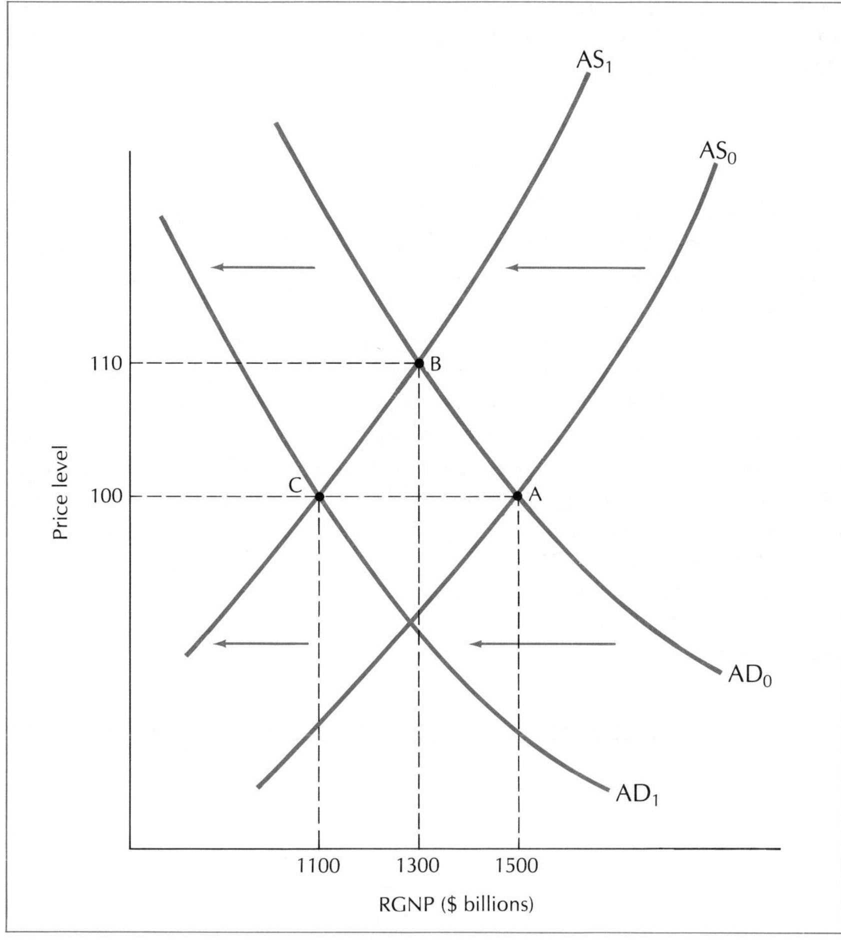

FIGURE 7-12 FIGHT INFLATION, GET UNEMPLOYMENT. Falling aggregate supply normally causes inflation, moving the economy from A to B. If the government fights the inflation by reducing aggregate demand, the economy ends up at C instead. The price level does not change, but the RGNP falls even more than before.

the price level through the roof. Inflation rates jump as they did in 1978 and 1979 (look back to Chapter 1 for historical evidence). Fighting cost-push unemployment with demand-based policies only makes the inflation problem much worse.

What is the alternative to high inflation? The traditional policy choice is to reduce aggregate demand to fight the inflation. This policy is effective when the inflation is demand-pull, but it is the wrong policy when cost-push forces prevail, as Figure 7-12 shows. Price stabilizes when aggregate demand cuts are applied, but unemployment lines grow longer. The inflation problem is licked, at least temporarily but an even worse unemployment problem appears. The high unemployment rates of 1975 and 1982 are at least partially the result of policies like this.

Neither of these aggregate demand policies successfully deals with cost-push inflation. How should government react to cost-push problems? Wage and price controls, indexation, and increasing aggregate supply are frequently discussed alternatives.

Wage and Price Controls

wage and price controls: laws that freeze or control most wages and prices in an economy.

If you cannot fight both inflation and unemployment with aggregate demand, perhaps we need **wage and price controls** like the ones that President Nixon put in place in 1971. Controls hold prices down by law and so artificially solve the inflation problem. Government sets maximum prices in many markets. Firms and workers who seek higher prices and wages must appeal to a government board for permission. The question of wage and price controls is the subject of this chapter's Economic Controversy debate, so we will save most of the discussion for there.

How do wage and price controls affect inflation and unemployment? Price controls hold down prices, but that does not necessarily solve the nation's economic problems. Figures 7-13 and 7-14 show two price control puzzles.

What happens when prices are frozen in a period of demand-pull inflation? Price controls keep the price level stable, but production cannot expand precisely because prices cannot rise. The RGNP produced remains constant and the quantity of goods demanded increases with the rising aggregate demand.

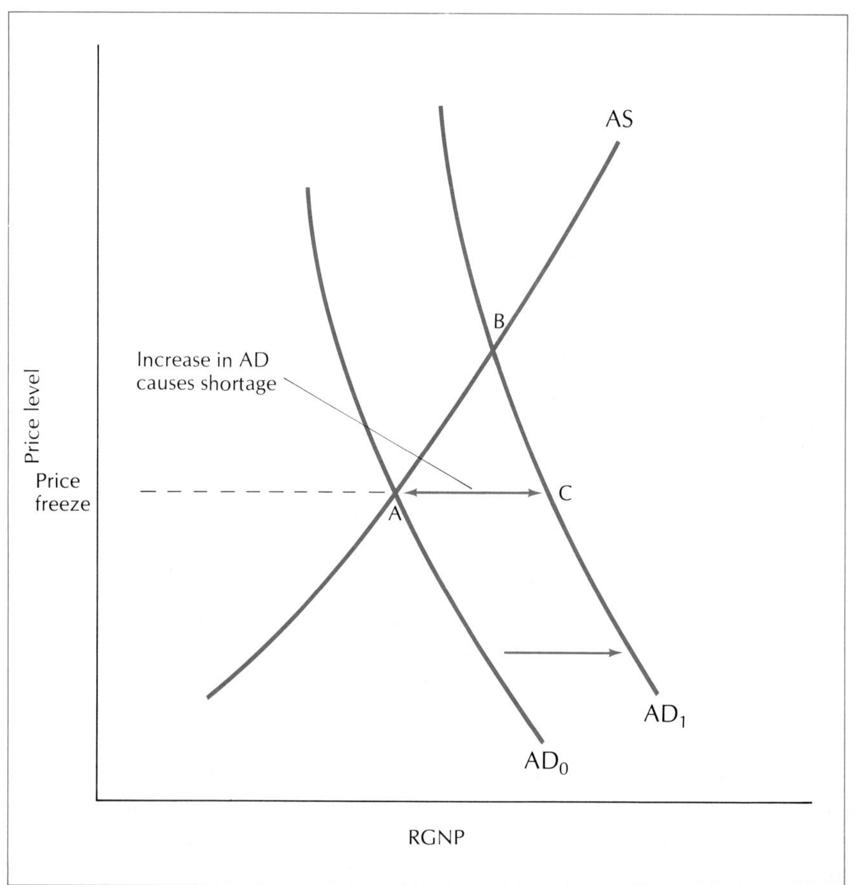

FIGURE 7-13 WAGE AND PRICE CONTROLS. The demand-pull inflation shown in this figure would have moved the economy from A to B. Wage and price controls keep prices from rising but lead consumers to demand the quantity represented by point C. The RGNP stays constant and a physical shortage results.

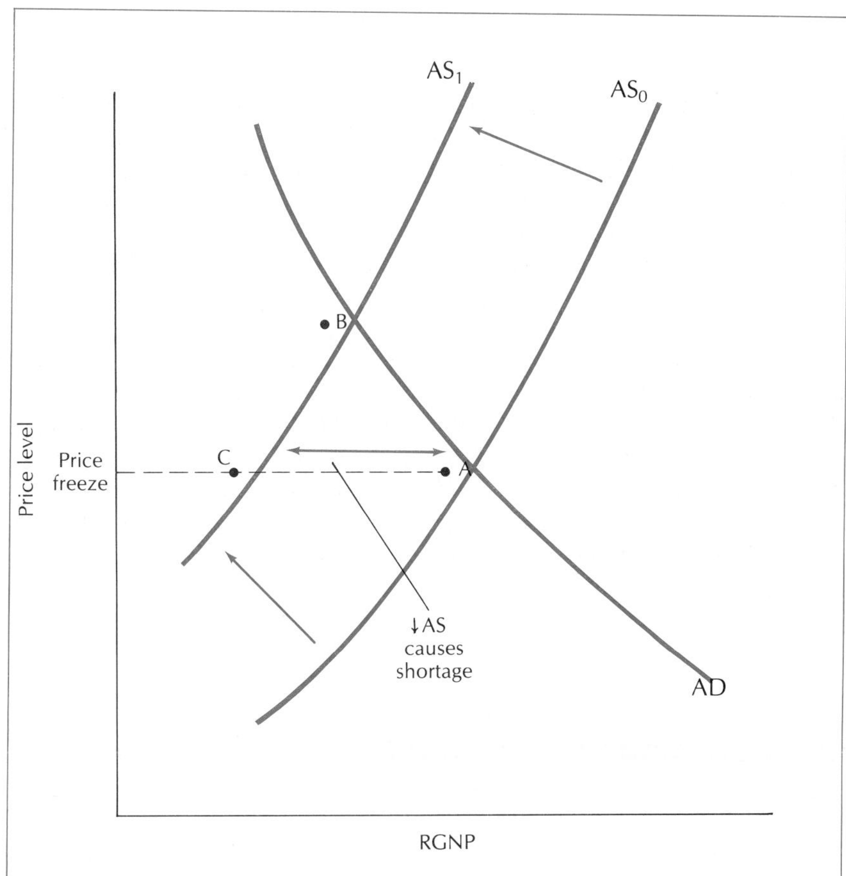

FIGURE 7-14 PRICE CONTROLS WITH COST-PUSH. Cost-push inflation would normally result in a movement from A to B. Wage and price controls force producers to cut output to the level depicted by C. The RGNP falls more than before and another physical shortage occurs.

The result? There appears a physical shortage of goods like the one shown in Figure 7-13. Inventories are drawn down and not restocked because firms cannot expand production unless the price level rises. In this instance, wage and price controls create shortages and keep RGNP from growing.

As can be seen in Figure 7-14, price controls make more mischief in cost-push inflation. Laws keep the price level frozen, as before. Firms that cannot raise prices to meet higher costs are forced to lay off workers and cut production even more. The result? The RGNP falls more than it otherwise would. Shortage and deep recession are the cost of stable prices here.

Indexation

If wage and price controls are not the answer to cost-push inflation, perhaps indexation can fill the bill. Indexation schemes do not try to hold down inflation, their goal is to hold down inflation's damage. Indexation plans like those adopted in Brazil and other high-inflation lands, tie wages, prices, interest rates, and taxes to a price index. Prices still rise, but inflation's gains and losses are reduced.

Indexation reduces inflation's burden, but several problems remain. First, indexation would not prevent high inflation in the United States from hurting U.S. producers through international trade. Firms with built-in wage increases cannot compete with sellers from low-inflation countries. Second, indexation cannot adjust all payments and prices for inflation. Different winners and losers show up, depending on how price indexes change.

A third indexation failure is that it could perpetuate inflation, making it even harder to solve through other policies. Higher indexed wages unleash cost-push forces that increase prices and lengthen unemployment lines. Inflation would be easier to live with, but higher unemployment rates would be the painful price.

The final indexation problem is technical. Which price index should be used? How should the indexation factor be calculated? These technical questions become political problems if the government adopts indexation. Labor and management, savers and borrowers, all these groups and more would lobby Congress to get an indexation scheme that favors their interests. Indexation helps reduce inflation's burden and is useful in a limited role. It is not, however, a final solution to the inflation problem.

Increasing Aggregate Supply

The logical way to reverse the cost-push inflation is to stimulate growth in aggregate supply. Increasing aggregate supply lowers the price level and increases RGNP—fighting inflation and unemployment at the same time. Why has this logical policy not been used?

Aggregate supply depends on many variables—investment, regulations, productivity, and more. How can government increase aggregate supply? Lower interest rates and increased investment spending are two ways, but they take time to work. Investment spending increases aggregate demand in the short run, as Figure 7-15 shows, and aggregate supply rises in the long run with increased capacity. The result? Balanced growth of aggregate demand and aggregate supply that stimulates RGNP without high inflation rates.

Long-term economic policies frequently encounter short-term political troubles. Presidents and members of Congress face election regularly and they may not be willing to wait for the "long run" for economic success. Keynes realized that short-term policies are often required, saying that "In the long run we are all dead." In the long run, politicians can be turned out of office. Policymakers search for ways to increase aggregate supply in the short run. One proposal is Ronald Reagan's **supply-side economics.**

supply-side economics: policies that try to increase aggregate supply by cutting tax rates.

Reagan's plan uses tax cuts to stimulate production. With lower tax rates, the plan goes, individuals and firms keep more of what they earn and have a powerful incentive to produce and earn more than before. Production

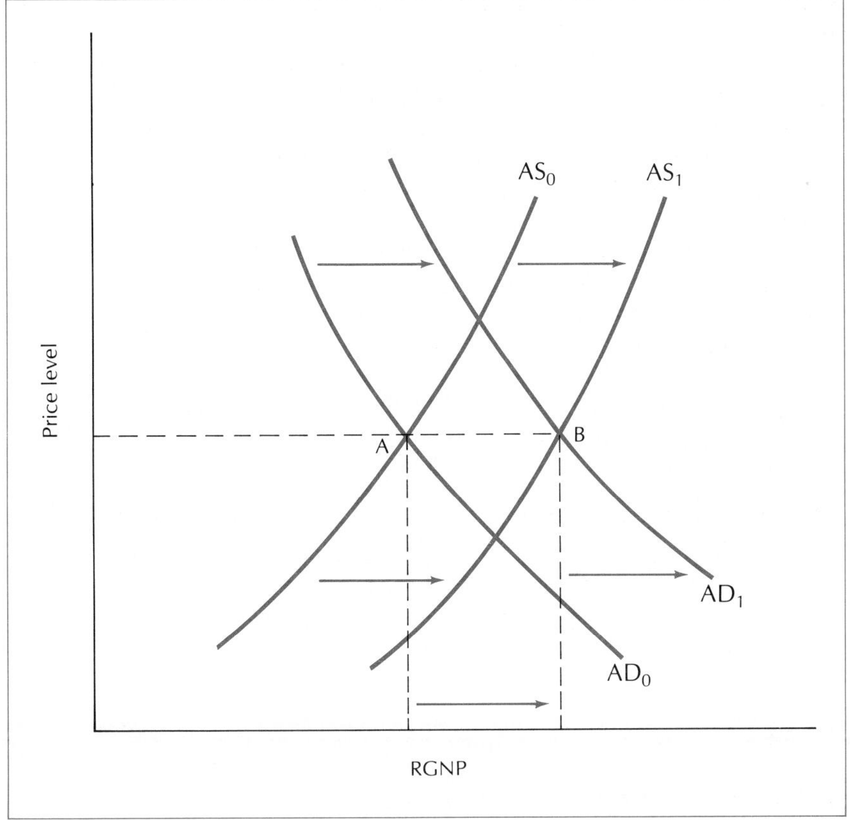

FIGURE 7-15 BALANCED GROWTH OF AGGREGATE DEMAND AND AGGREGATE SUPPLY. The economy moves from A to B as aggregate demand and aggregate supply both grow. The RGNP increases with little inflation in this instance.

and aggregate supply are supposed to rise so much that the lower tax rates collect more tax revenues.

The economics of supply-side policies like this are debated in the next chapter. The politics of supply side make these programs unpopular. Policies that stimulate saving, investment, and production must give incentives to savers, investors, and producers—people who are relatively well off already. The benefits of higher income **trickle down** to poorer groups only when and if aggregate supply rises. In the long run, rising aggregate supply is good for both rich and poor. In the short run, however, supply-side policies look suspiciously like "welfare" for the rich, since high-income groups get the initial benefits of these programs.

trickle down: the idea that benefits given to high income groups eventually help poorer groups.

Economic policies that stimulate aggregate supply make sense in a world of stagflation. Economists ranging from the conservative Martin Feldstein to the liberal Lester Thurow support plans to increase aggregate supply. But supply-based policies start the game with two strikes against them: they are unlikely to work in the short run and they seem to favor the rich in their initial distribution of benefits.

Winners and Losers from Economic Policies

Economic policies are popular or detested depending, in part, on the type of aggregate supply curve they face. President Franklin Roosevelt increased aggregate demand during the Great Depression and his actions were applauded. Why was this policy popular? Part of the reason is that it created more winners than losers.

An increase in aggregate demand in a depression economy, as Figure 7-16 shows, increases RGNP with little effect on the price level. Unemployment lines fall, but no inflation appears to sacrifice the real incomes of those already at work. Rising AD has its greatest effect on RGNP in this depression world.

President Lyndon Johnson followed in Roosevelt's footsteps in the 1960s, but LBJ did not gain FDR's popular acclaim. Figure 7-17 suggests why: Johnson faced a full-capacity economy in the 1960s. Government spending to fight poverty in the United States and a war in Vietnam made winners and losers. Higher aggregate demand made inflation rates rise, taxing worker income by reducing its purchasing power. Higher government production at full capacity meant fewer goods for consumers—government's gain was the private economy's loss. A policy that makes many losers and few winners is sure to be unpopular. Increased aggregate demand at full capacity generated inflation with no increase in RGNP in the short run.

An increase in aggregate demand in today's bottleneck economy makes some people losers while others gain. Rising aggregate demand here, as illustrated in Figure 7-18, brings both inflation and rising RGNP. Is this a politically wise government program? The answer depends in part on whether people want rising real incomes more than they dislike more inflation.

Economics and politics are necessarily interrelated, as this chapter has

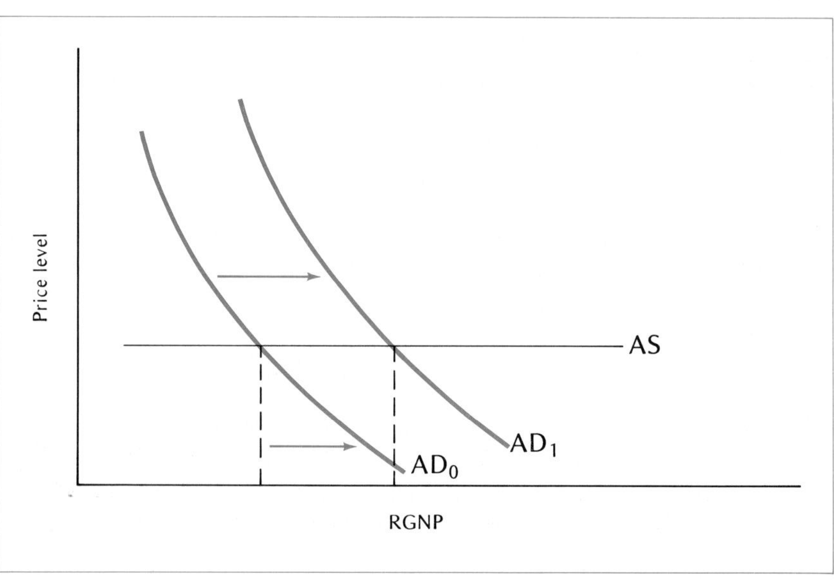

FIGURE 7-16 INCREASING AGGREGATE DEMAND—1932. Rising aggregate demand increases RGNP without inflation in a depression.

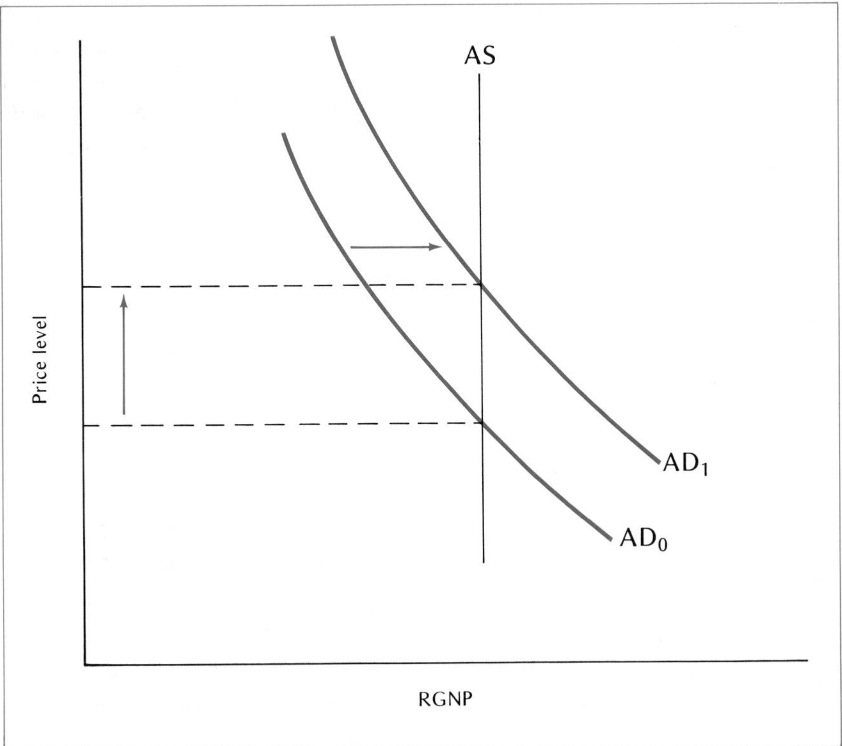

FIGURE 7-17 INCREASING AGGREGATE DEMAND—1967. Rising aggregate demand causes nothing but inflation in a full-capacity economy.

shown. The disciplines of economics and political science claim common roots. The accepted name for economics a hundred years ago was 'political economy.' We call economics by a different name now, but its political side cannot be denied.

ECONOMIC CONTROVERSY:

Wage and Price Controls

Long-run policies to increase aggregate supply may be the best solution to today's inflation, but practical politicians and economists look for short-term answers, too. Many call for wage and price controls when inflation rates begin to soar.

Wage and price controls have been around for centuries. The Roman emperor Diocletian used a brutal form: he cut off the hands of those who increased price! Price controls in this century have been less severe. Wages and prices were put under government control in the United States during the Second World War and the Korean War. Richard Nixon froze wages and prices in 1971 and some of the controls that followed lasted for a decade. Let us hear both sides of this issue.

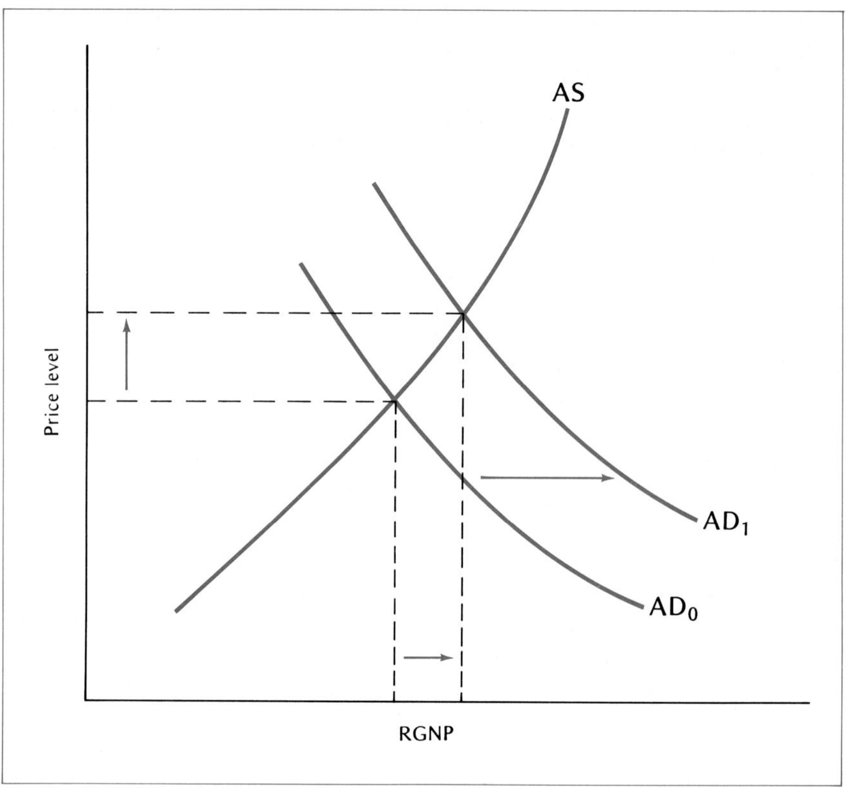

FIGURE 7-18 Increasing Aggregate Demand Today. Rising aggregate demand in a bottleneck economy causes higher inflation while boosting the RGNP.

We Need Price Controls

Price controls should be part of the United States' economic policy. Price controls are an important tool for three reasons:

1. Expectations. The inflation problem is made worse by inflationary expectations. Workers and producers who lived through the 1970s have come to expect higher and higher inflation rates each year. They demand higher wage increases that lead to cost-push price rises and strategically spend money now causing demand-pull problems. Government policies do not affect expectations and so cannot really solve the inflation problem.

What would make people stop expecting inflation? Price controls that promise to truly keep prices frozen for a long period! No other policy can bring expectations into line.

2. Aggregate Supply. Wage and price controls would solve the long-run problems of the economy by stimulating aggregate supply. Why has supply fallen in recent years? High inflation rates have pushed up interest rates and have discouraged investment spending. Government price controls would keep both inflation and interest rates low. This would give business the climate it needs to invest for the future and increase capacity.

3. Unemployment Is More Important. Inflation is not the most important problem the economy faces—unemployment is. But we will never be able to focus on unemployment while inflation threatens. Wage and price controls take away the distraction of higher prices and let Congress focus its attention on the more serious problems of the unemployed.

Wage and price controls are not perfect. They cause shortages, but shortages are a small price to pay for the short- and long-run benefits the economy receives from stable prices.

Oppose Price Controls!

Arguments in favor of wage and price controls sound good, but they do not hold up under close scrutiny. Wage and price controls have four fatal flaws:

1. They Do Not Stop Inflation. Wage and price controls, even the brutal types, always fail to keep prices down. Look at what happened during the Nixon years—"frozen" prices still rose by 4 percent! No one has ever been able to halt inflation through executive order. Even if they did work, their effect is only temporary because price controls treat the symptoms of high inflation but do not get to the real causes. Using wage and price controls to fight inflation is like sticking a thermometer in ice water to cure a patient's fever. Why pay a high price for a medicine that never has worked?

2. They Cause Shortages. Wage and price controls lead to the shortages discussed in this chapter. Frozen prices take away incentives to produce—they reduce aggregate supply because firms cannot afford to invest while prices and profits are frozen. Who gets the scarce goods when price controls create shortages? People who have connections or who line up early. Goods go to the quick and the well connected, not to those who really need them.

3. They Are Expensive. Price controls are costly to administer and enforce. A huge bureaucracy must be created to handle all the paperwork needed to monitor wages and prices. Price police patrol grocery aisles. Who pays for these extra costs? You do. You pay higher taxes, reduced profits, and higher prices when controls are lifted. Price controls do not hold prices down, they increase costs to the economy and cause higher prices.

4. They Never Last. Price controls do not change inflationary expectations because no one expects them to last more than a few months. Wage and price controls are used as a temporary policy. They are so disruptive that they are only used for longer periods during wartime emergencies. Wages and prices are held down during the control period, but people try to catch up when the laws are repealed. Expectations never change and so the high costs of price controls are all paid for nothing.

SUMMARY

1. Aggregate supply describes the production side of the economy. Many things affect aggregate supply including investment and capacity, technology, productivity, expectations, and government policies.

2. The shape of the aggregate supply curve depends on the condition of the economy. A horizontal AS curve appears during depressions when many

resources are unemployed. The AS curve becomes vertical when full capacity is reached or adaptive expectations prevent an increase in RGNP when the price level rises. An upward-sloping AS curve shows that bottlenecks in production link higher RGNP with higher prices.

3. Aggregate demand and aggregate supply determine the equilibrium price level and RGNP. The economy adjusts to equilibrium through price, inventory, and production changes.

4. Inventories are a leading indicator of RGNP. Unintended inventory reductions foretell rising RGNP. Unexpected inventory accumulations are linked with future RGNP decline.

5. Cyclical unemployment is caused by falling aggregate demand or falling aggregate supply. Unemployment caused by falling aggregate demand is worse when prices are sticky.

6. Inflation can be based on either cost-push or demand-pull forces: both cause inflation but have different effects on RGNP. How do you fight inflation? The text showed that the choice of tools depends on the cause of the inflation.

7. Demand policies, wage and price controls, indexation, and supply-side policies have all been proposed as inflation cures. Each policy has pros and cons; both economic and political factors have to be considered.

8. Aggregate demand policies produce different winners and losers depending on the shape of the AS curve. Rising aggregate demand increases RGNP in a depression but does nothing but boost the price level at full capacity.

9. Are wage and price controls a good policy? One side says that they control expectations and promote economic growth. The other side maintains that they only add to costs and fail to keep prices down.

DISCUSSION QUESTIONS

1. How would an increase in government spending for missile bases affect the economy in the short run (look at aggregate demand, aggregate supply, RGNP, and inflation)? In the long run? Explain.

2. How would an increase in investment spending affect the economy (aggregate supply, aggregate demand, RGNP, and inflation) in the short run? In the long run? Explain.

3. Which is more inflationary in the short run, investment spending or government spending? Which is more inflationary in the long run, investment spending or government spending? Explain.

4. Use inventory analysis to explain how the economy would adjust to an increase in aggregate supply and to a decrease in aggregate supply. Do inventories act as a leading indicator of RGNP here? Explain.

5. The price level was roughly constant in 1954–1955, but the unemployment rate fell. Use AD-AS analysis to explain what must have occurred during this period.

6. What are the arguments in favor of wage and price controls? Is the argument for wage and price controls stronger when inflation is caused by cost-push forces? Explain your reasoning.

TEST YOURSELF

Circle the best response to each question.

1. Which of the following events would directly increase aggregate demand in either the short or long run?

(X) increase in the price level
(Y) increased investment spending
(Z) increase in average wage rate

a. all of the above
b. none of the above
c. only (X)
d. only (Y)
e. only (Z)

2. Inventories and the Producer Price Index are leading indicators of the economy. Inventory changes foretell the direction of RGNP and the PPI predicts CPI changes. Suppose that you observe an unintended inventory accumulation at the same time that the PPI rises. Which of the following events is the most likely cause of these changes?

a. increase in aggregate demand
b. decrease in aggregate demand
c. increase in aggregate supply
d. decrease in aggregate supply
e. increase in both aggregate demand and aggregate supply

3. The economy is operating at full capacity. An increase in government spending in this situation results in:

(X) higher RGNP
(Y) higher price level
(Z) higher unemployment rates

a. all of the above
b. none of the above
c. only (X)
d. only (Y)
e. both (X) and (Y)

4. The economy is experiencing cost-push inflation. Suppose that this inflation is fought by reducing aggregate demand. Which of the following statements best describes the result of this policy?

a. unemployment will fall, but inflation will be even higher
b. inflation will fall, but unemployment will be even higher
c. both inflation and unemployment will increase
d. both inflation and unemployment will fall
e. the economy will enter the full-capacity part of the AS curve

5. Congressman Snort is debating Senator Gotrocks; the subject is wage and price controls. Both agree that wage and price controls cause shortages. Gotrocks says that RGNP should remain constant if Congress enacts a price freeze. Snort says that RGNP will fall even further than it otherwise would under price controls. Snort is correct if:

a. inflation is caused by rising aggregate demand
b. Congress increases aggregate demand at the same time it freezes prices
c. inflation is caused by falling aggregate supply
d. prices are frozen at the current equilibrium level
e. Snort is incorrect in all cases

SUGGESTIONS FOR FURTHER READING

Nobel Prize winner Lawrence Klein talks about the importance of aggregate supply in "The Supply Side," *American Economic Review* (March, 1978). Walter Heller and Charles Schultz debate wage and price controls in an exchange published by the *Wall Street Journal* (February 27, 1980) and reprinted in the author's *Coursebook for Introductory Economics* (New York: Academic Press, 1981). Leading indicators are discussed in Alfred L. Malabre, Jr.'s, "Tracking a Trend" in the December 22, 1981, *Wall Street Journal*. Francis Bator's solutions to current macroeconomics problems are presented in "The Sins of Wages," *The Economist* (March 21, 1981).

8

FISCAL POLICY

Preview

What tools can government use to alter the course of economic events? Which one is best?

How does multiplier analysis predict the effect of fiscal policies on aggregate demand?

Are all taxes the same in the way they affect taxpayers and the economy?

How do tax expenditures affect the economy?

Should we worry about deficit spending and the national debt?

Are supply-side tax cuts a good idea? Why is the Laffer curve important?

THIS CHAPTER looks at the government's arsenal of weapons in the fight against inflation and unemployment. What ammunition works best? Money—if names mean anything. The term "fiscal" policy derives from a Latin word for basket or purse. Fiscal policy is all tied up in the government's purse strings.

The Economics Role of Government

Governments play many roles in mixed economies like the United States and Canada. It is important to use the plural form for government because the federal system includes many partners. There are over 38,000 separate units of state, local, and county governments in the United States—and over 500,000 elected public officials!

This discussion of fiscal policy focuses on the federal (not state and local) government because it is this level of government that is assigned the macroeconomic **stabilization function.** A big part of the federal government's job is to fight inflation and unemployment and promote economic growth. But government does much more than this.

stabilization function: the role of government in fighting inflation and unemployment.

Government is also responsible for an **allocation function.** Keynes said there is no guarantee of full employment. Other economists point out that the market economy does not automatically assure that scarce resources always go to their best use. Market failures like **externalities** and **public goods** get in the way of efficient production. **Monopolies** send the wrong price signals and reduce economic well-being. One government role is to correct for misallocations by regulating pollution, encouraging training and education, building parks, and stimulating business competition, for example.

allocation function: the role of government in allocating scarce resources to their best use.

externalities: actions by one person or group that affect others.

public goods: goods that, once produced, yield benefits that can be shared by all.

monopolies: firms that are able to control market price.

The **distribution function** of government charges Congress and state legislatures with improving the distribution of income and wealth. Programs like social security, welfare, and unemployment benefits all move income from rich to poor, young to old.

distribution function: the role of government in improving the distribution of income and wealth.

A final part government plays is its **public-choice function.** Decisions in a democratic society are made by "the people." But how are varied individual desires assembled into one government policy? Part of government's job is to listen to voter voices and translate the babble of many separate songs into a harmonious melody of public policy.

public-choice function: the role of government in making social choices.

Each individual government function is challenging; playing all four roles at once is sometimes impossible. The four government jobs are frequently contradictory. Suppose, for example, that government wants to fight inflation by cutting government spending. This stabilization policy might result in too little national-defense spending (an allocation function) or a less satisfactory distribution of income, in addition to posing problems of public choice.

An increase in social-security benefits to equalize the distribution of income between the young and the old might be a desirable distribution policy. But higher social security taxes might tend to misallocate resources if young taxpayers and old retirees buy different things. Lower saving by young and old alike and higher business tax costs reduce aggregate supply and hurt the stabilization function. Young voters might vote against the change—a public-choice question.

Tools of Fiscal Policy

Government policies affect the economy in many ways. This chapter concentrates on the three most-used fiscal policy tools: government spending, taxes, and transfer payments.

Congress influences the economy directly through government spending. Defense gear, public highways, new schools, and many other goods are bought by the government. Government spending is a powerful and direct tool for stabilization policy.

Taxes work indirectly by changing the disposable incomes of businesses and consumers. Tax increases and cuts alter overall buying plans. Special tax breaks, called **tax expenditures**, can even change spending patterns for particular goods.

tax expenditures: special tax reductions given for individual spending on approved items.

Transfer payments also work indirectly on consumer spending. Increased transfer payments add to disposable income and stimulate consumption spending and aggregate demand. The government also pays some transfer payments as **subsidies** to individuals or firms. These subsidies encourage production and consumption of selected items.

subsidies: government payments to individuals or firms to encourage specific activities.

Government spending, taxes, and transfer payments are the main tools of government but not the only ones. Price regulations, like minimum-wage laws, are used to alter income distribution and change spending patterns. Tariff and quota trade barriers are government tools to shift buying away from imports and toward home-produced merchandise. Government borrowing and lending actions affect individual behavior, too. Many students pay tuition with government-guaranteed loans. The government's borrowing power helps some home buyers make mortgage payments and helps exporting firms sell goods abroad. Government's involvement in the economy is ubiquitous.

Multiplier Analysis

How do government tools affect the economy? The most direct effect is felt on aggregate demand. Changes in government spending, taxing, and transfer payments all end up as changes in aggregate demand. Keynes recognized this fact and added two surprising observations: (1) a change in government spending results in a much larger change in aggregate demand, and (2) we can predict how big the AD change will be. Keynes' insights are based on the analysis of multipliers.

An increase of government spending does not just buy missiles or school books or freeway markers. This initial spending sets in motion a chain of consumer purchases that raise aggregate demand by far more than the original government purchase. You can see how this works in the Multiplier Game of Figure 8-1.

Suppose government spends $100,000 on red tape (they really use it!). This initial increase in aggregate demand creates $100,000 more income for workers and firms in the red-tape business. What do these folks do with $100,000 more income? The Marginal Propensity to Consume (introduced in Chapter 6) describes how consumption spending changes when income is altered. If the MPC is 60 percent, for example, $60,000 of the additional $100,000 goes to consumption spending (the other $40,000 is saved).

induced-consumption spending: changes in consumption spending resulting from fiscal policy.

Government spending of $100,000 generates **induced-consumption expenditures** of $60,000. Does the chain end here? No! The $60,000 spent by red-tape workers creates $60,000 more income for people who produce the cars, furniture, and clothing they buy. These folks use the extra $60,000 to spend

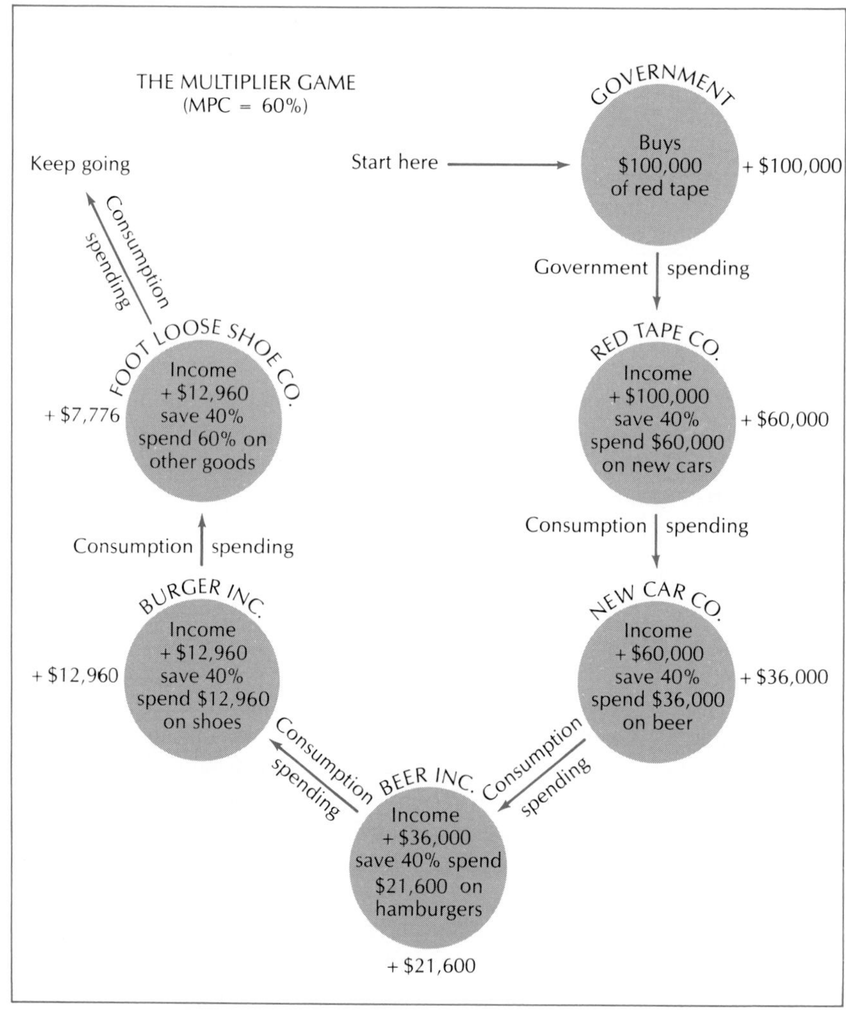

FIGURE 8-1 THE MULTIPLIER GAME. Government spending starts the multiplier game. Government spending leads to higher consumption spending as money moves through the economy. The spending multiplier gives the total effect.

(60 percent or \$36,000) and save, too. Aggregate demand continues to grow as spending creates income that leads to still more spending.

A small ripple of government spending makes big waves in consumer spending. How much does aggregate demand change altogether? You can find out by playing the multiplier game through to the finish (do not pass Go, do not collect \$200). The numbers you would get are shown in Table 8-1. The \$100,000 increase in government spending induces a total of \$150,000 extra consumption spending (assuming MPC is equal to 60 percent). Aggregate demand rises by the sum of these two spending parts or by a total of \$250,000.

Is there an easier way to find the total change in aggregate demand (Table 8-1's calculations wear down calculator batteries)? Yes. The figures shown in Table 8-1 are a geometric progression that can be summarized by the formula

TABLE 8-1 THE MULTIPLIER GAME: GOVERNMENT SPENDING (MPC = 60%)

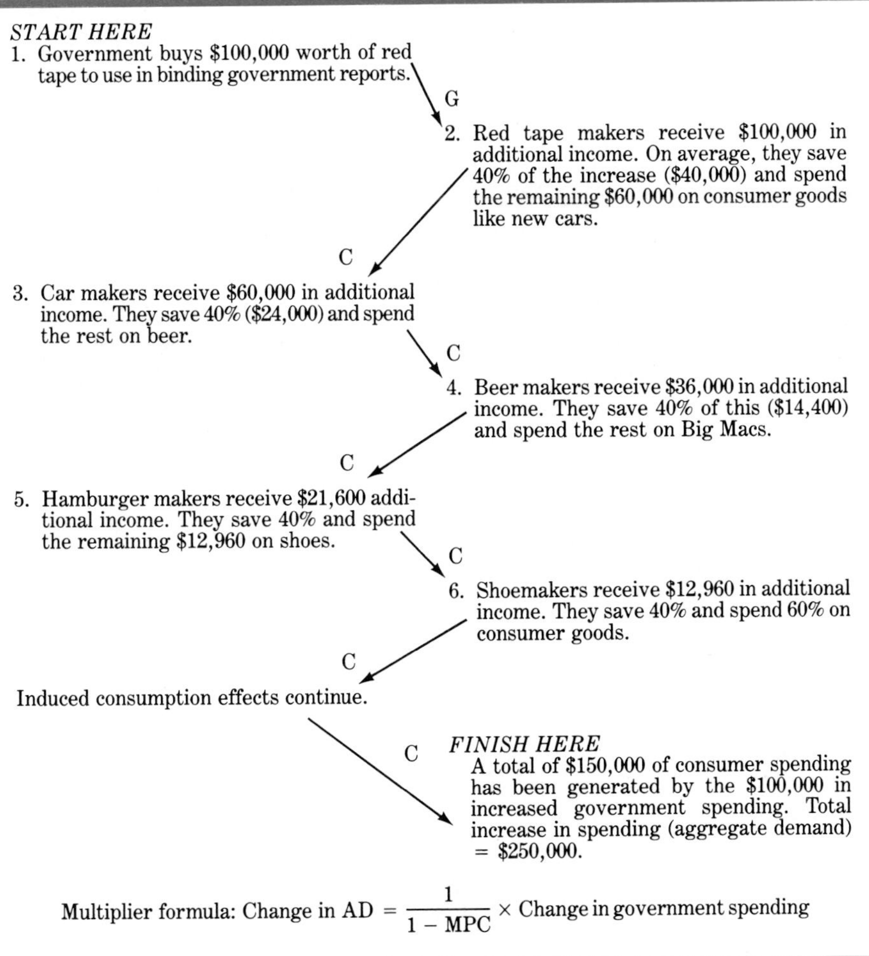

Multiplier formula: Change in AD $= \frac{1}{1 - \text{MPC}} \times$ Change in government spending

$$\text{change in AD} = \frac{1}{1 - \text{MPC}} \times \text{change in government spending}$$

spending multiplier: the total effect of a change in spending; change in aggregate demand equals 1/1 − MPC × change in spending.

The term 1/1 − MPC is called the **spending multiplier** because it shows the relationship between a change in spending and the resulting change in aggregate demand. The example here is an increase in government spending, but this multiplier works just as well for increases or decreases in investment, net export, or consumer spending. To get the right answer, just plug the appropriate numbers into the equation. The change in government spending is +$100,000 and the MPC is 60 percent or 0.6 in this example. The change in aggregate demand is therefore

$$\begin{aligned}\text{change in AD} &= \frac{1}{1 - .6} \times \$100{,}000\\ &= \frac{1}{0.4} \times \$100{,}000\\ &= 2.5 \times \$100{,}000\\ &= \$250{,}000\end{aligned}$$

The government's direct contribution amounted to $100,000 of this total; the remaining $150,000 is induced consumption spending.

Tax and Transfer Multipliers

Taxes and transfers have multiplier effects, too, but smaller ones than for spending changes. An increase in government or investment spending directly increases aggregate demand. Changes in taxes and transfer payments affect spending only indirectly when they change disposable income. The Taxation Multiplier Game shows what happens.

Consumers get a $100,000 tax cut. Does aggregate demand rise by the full amount of the tax cut? Not according to the MPC theory discussed in Chapter 6. Disposable income rises by $100,000, but part of this increase goes to savings. Consumption spending rises by just $60,000 if the MPC is 60 percent. A $100,000 tax cut has a smaller effect on aggregate demand than a $100,000 increase in government spending because part of the tax cut is initially saved, not spent.

Follow the tax cut through the economy. At each stage spending creates income that leads to still more spending. The total change in aggregate demand is $150,000. You can find this total the hard way with your pocket calculator, or you can use the formula

$$\text{change in AD} = \frac{-\text{MPC}}{1 - \text{MPC}} \times \text{change in taxes}$$

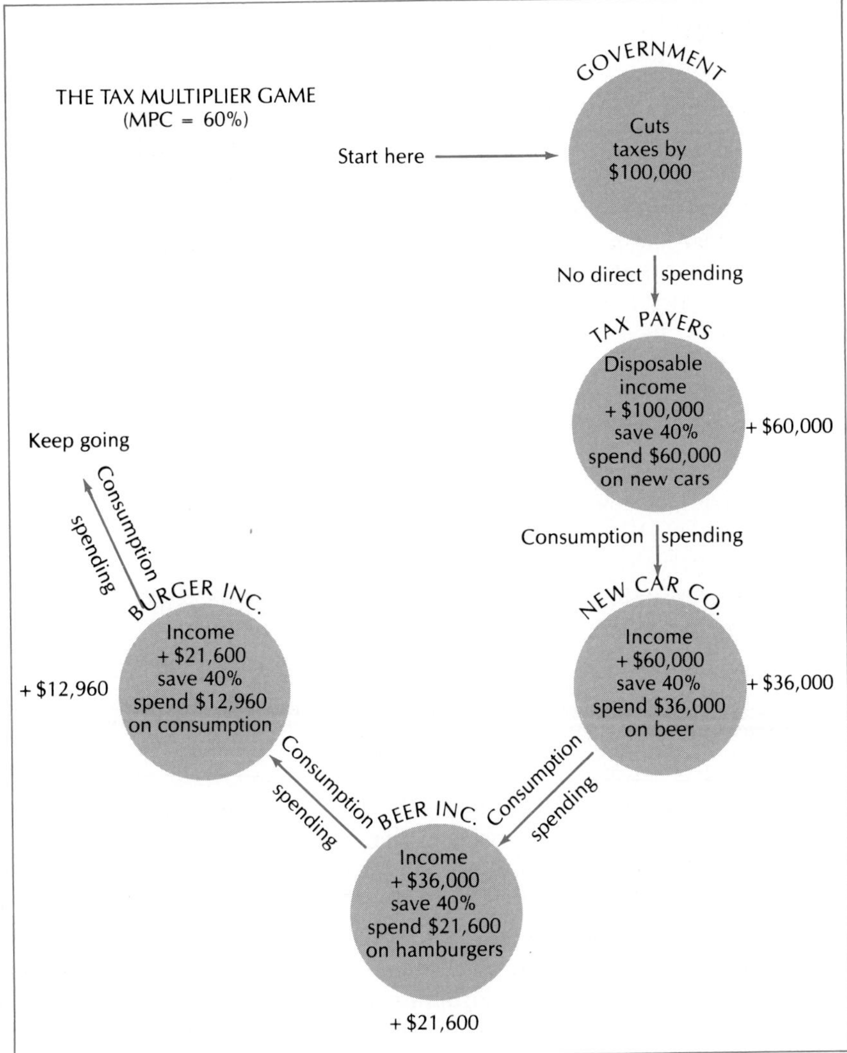

FIGURE 8-2 THE TAX MULTIPLIER GAME. Tax cuts do not directly increase spending. Part of the tax cut is saved and the rest spent, starting the multiplier process. Multipliers for taxes and transfer payments are less than the spending multiplier because of this initial saving.

This multiplier has a minus sign because there is an inverse relationship between taxes and aggregate demand—aggregate demand goes down (minus) if taxes rise (plus). Plug the numbers from this example into the multiplier formula and see if you get the correct answer.

Transfer payments are much like negative taxes because they first hit disposable income and so indirectly lead to more aggregate demand. A $100,000 increase in social-security payments, for example, increases the disposable incomes of retired people by $100,000. If they spend and save with a 60 percent MPC, then consumption spending rises by $60,000 and the rest of the action is the same as in the Taxation Multiplier game.

The multiplier formula for transfer payments looks much like that for taxation

$$\text{change in AD} = \frac{+\text{MPC}}{1 - \text{MPC}} \times \text{change in transfer payments}$$

The only difference between tax and transfer multipliers is that the transfer formula has a plus (+) because of the direct relationship between changes in transfer payments and aggregate demand.

Multipliers and Government Policy

The government spending, tax, and transfer payment multipliers tell us much about how fiscal policies work. First, they imply that government's ability to shift the AD curve depends on three things

(1) whether spending, taxes, or transfers are used (the shift is bigger with government spending);
(2) the size of the fiscal policy—the greater the size of the increase in fiscal policy, the greater the shift in aggregate demand (a $200,000 tax cut has more clout than a smaller one);
(3) the value of the MPC; a $100,000 increase in government spending shifts aggregate demand by $250,000 if the MPC is 60 percent, but aggregate demand rises by $500,000 with an 80 percent MPC (plug in the numbers and check this out).

Fiscal policies have little power if consumers save most of their higher disposable incomes. Government spending and the like are powerful tools, however, if the MPC is high. What determines what people will do with increased disposable income? Tax cuts in the early 1960s successfully increased aggregate demand in part because they were aimed at low-income groups who quickly spent them. Gerald Ford's 1975 tax-rebate program had little effect on aggregate demand, however. Consumers decided to save this one-time-only increase in disposable income.

Multiplier analysis tells how combinations of government programs work. What happens if Congress votes to spend $100,000 more on defense and raises taxes by $100,000 to pay for it? How does this change aggregate demand? Do these two policies cancel out, with no change in aggregate demand? The multipliers tell us that the government spending plan increases aggregate demand by a total of $250,000 (assuming MPC is equal to 60 percent) and the tax increase makes aggregate demand fall by a total of $150,000. The net effect of the two changes is to increase aggregate demand by $100,000 ($250,000 minus $150,000).

Aggregate demand changes by the amount of the initial spending increase when taxes and government spending change in the same direction by the same amount. The **balanced-budget multiplier** equals one (1) multiplied by the change in government spending.

Here is an exercise for you. What happens to aggregate demand if Congress reduces transfer payments by $100,000 and uses the money to give $100,000 in tax cuts? Work it out. The answer is in the Summary section at the end of this chapter.

balanced-budget multiplier: change in aggregate demand when government spending and taxes change in the same direction by the same amount; the balanced budget multiplier equals one (1) multiplied by the change in government spending.

Government and the Economy

Multiplier formulas tell us how fiscal policies alter aggregate demand, but how do they affect inflation and unemployment? The answer to this question depends on the shape of the aggregate supply curve.

What if government spends $100,000 on new highways during a depression, as Figure 8-3 shows? The $100,000 increase in government spending starts the multiplier process—the AD curve shifts to the left by $250,000 when the multiplier has run its course. All this spending produces additional goods and services in the depression economy—none goes for higher prices. The result?

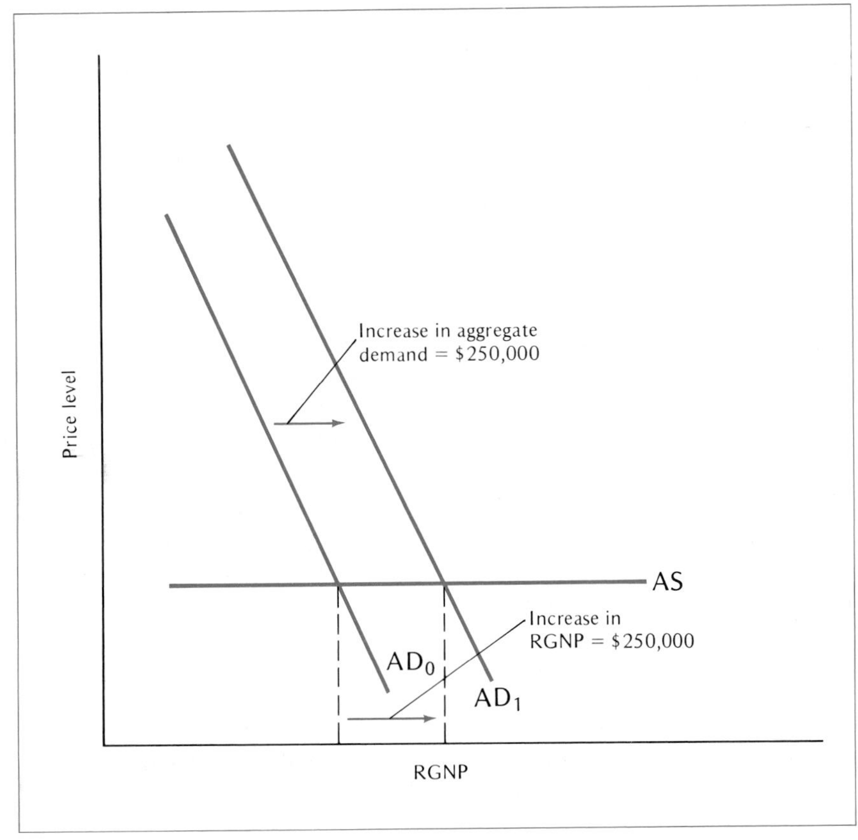

FIGURE 8-3 THE MULTIPLIER IN A DEPRESSION. Government spending in the amount of $100,000 shifts the aggregate demand curve by $250,000 (assuming MPC = 60 percent). The RGNP rises by the full multiplier amount in a depression economy.

The RGNP feels the full multiplier effect and rises by \$250,000. Government spending is a powerful tool in a depression.

Fiscal policy's effect is much different when the economy is at full capacity, as in Figure 8-4. Aggregate demand still shifts by \$250,000 in response to the \$100,000 increase in government spending, but all the extra spending goes to bid up prices. The RGNP cannot rise because of capacity roadblocks. Government spending brings only high inflation rates.

Higher government spending increases both the price level and the RGNP in the bottleneck economy shown in Figure 8-5. The \$100,000 in new government buying still shifts the AD curve by the \$250,000 multiplier total, but increased spending is divided between price and quantity effects. The price level goes up and RGNP rises by just part of the AD shift. The size of RGNP's rise depends on the slope of the AS curve.

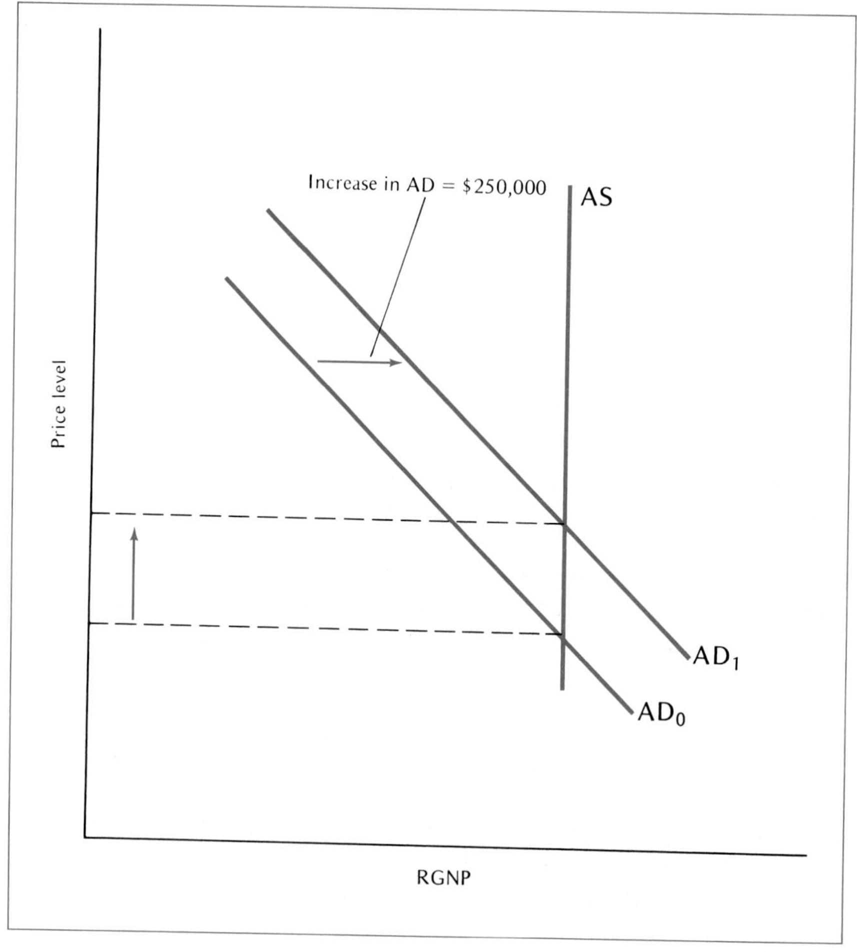

FIGURE 8-4 THE MULTIPLIER WITH FULL CAPACITY AGGREGATE SUPPLY. The same spending multiplier is at work in this figure, but the change in the RGNP is much different. All of the \$250,000 increase in aggregate demand goes to pay higher prices. The RGNP does not change because the economy is at full capacity.

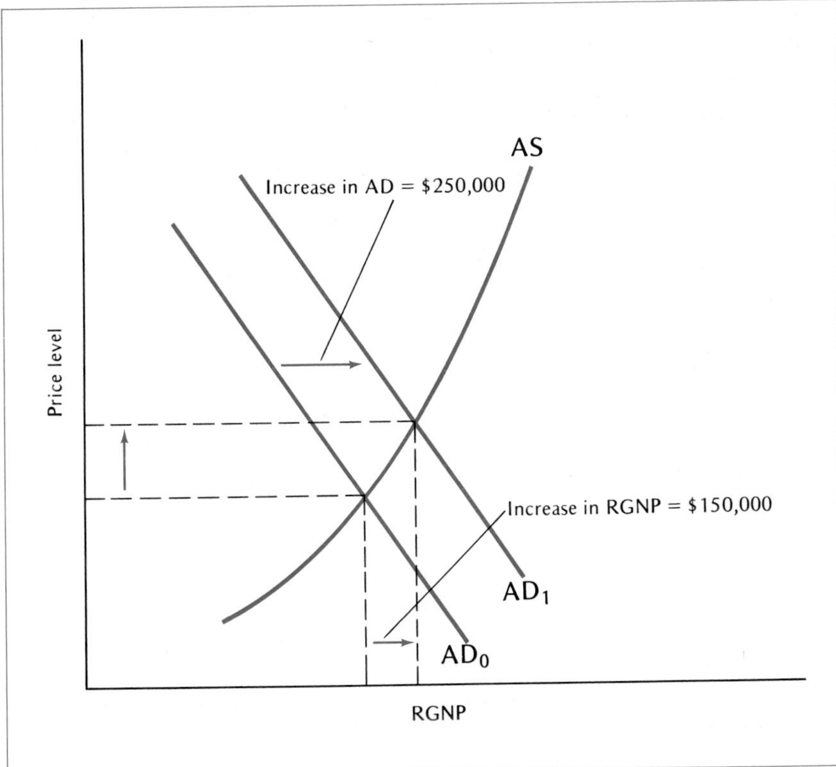

FIGURE 8-5 THE MULTIPLIER WITH BOTTLENECK AGGREGATE SUPPLY. Government spending in the amount of $100,000 again shifts the aggregate demand curve by $250,000. Part of the increase goes to higher prices; the rest becomes increased RGNP.

Multipliers in the Real World

Fiscal policy in the real world is more complex than the simple multiplier analysis presented here (but these multipliers do give you a feel for how policy works). Multiplier formulas need to be more complicated because people do more than just spend and save. Part of any increase in income goes to federal, state, and local taxes, for example. These tax leakages reduce consumption spending and so diminish the multiplier effect. Some income buys imports; spending for imports leaves the country, thereby reducing the multiplier effect. A realistic analysis of fiscal policy would have to take these added leakages into account. The multiplier formulas in this book give only a rough approximation of multiplier effects.

The multipliers summarize fiscal policy's effect on aggregate demand, but aggregate demand is not all we need to know. Government policies also alter aggregate supply. Taxes can either encourage saving (providing funds for investment in aggregate supply) or promote additional consumer spending. Part of the value-added tax debate in Chapter 5 centered on this difference. There are no AS multipliers, however, so multiplier analysis of aggregate demand tells only part of the story.

Government Spending Policies

The multiplier analysis of government spending focused on spending's impact on aggregate demand. Since all government spending has the same multiplier, it does not matter what the government buys. A million dollars spent on red tape has the same multiplier effect as a million dollars spent on highways or education.

Multipliers aside, what government buys does make a difference in two respects. First, government programs with the same AD effects can have different aggregate supply effects. Some government spending is really government investment that increases capacity or productivity. Government-financed education increases aggregate supply in the long run by improving the quality and quantity of labor supply. Government grants to research and development bring new inventions and improved processes. Government spending on power plants and postal equipment, for example, increase capacity in the same way as do corresponding private investments. The aggregate supply effects of government spending cannot be ignored.

economic efficiency: the best use of scarce resources.

Another important distinction between government projects concerns **economic efficiency**. Some government purchases improve the way resources are distributed among competing uses. No individual or firm could profitably build and operate the efficient interstate highway system, for example. Government spending here fills an important gap in private economic activity and improves economic efficiency by improving transportation and reducing production costs.

Not all government plans aid economic efficiency, however. Many economists think government price supports in the dairy industry, for example, keep inefficient farmers in business because the government buys up excess milk at high floor prices. Government purchases like this lead to a less efficient, higher-cost economy.

Different Types of Taxes

Multiplier analysis treats all taxes the same because all taxes have the same effect on aggregate demand. All taxes are not the same, however, and the differences are important. Taxes differ in their effect on aggregate supply and in the distribution of the tax burden.

Congress wants to cut taxes by $10 billion. Which taxes should they cut? Reducing consumer taxes increases aggregate demand, but cutting business taxes might add to both aggregate demand and aggregate supply, bringing balanced economic growth in the long run. It is difficult to know in advance exactly how tax changes will change private behavior. Will businesses really buy additional equipment if an investment tax break is enacted or will they simply pocket the tax break and keep investment at current levels? The difference between taxes that affect aggregate demand alone and those with supply-side effects too is important, but not always predictable.

A second difference among taxes is the distribution of the **tax burden.** Some taxes hit high-income groups the hardest, while others fall heaviest on the poor. Economists classify taxes as progressive, proportional, or regressive depending on how the tax burden varies with income.

tax burden: the fraction of total income going to a tax; tax divided by income.

1. **PROGRESSIVE TAXES.** A **progressive tax** is one that imposes higher tax burdens on families with more income. Suppose, for example, that the Johnsons' income is $20,000 per year and the Smith family earns $40,000. A tax that takes $2000 (10 percent) from the Johnsons and $6000 (15 percent) from the Smiths would be progressive.

progressive tax: a tax whose burden increases with income; the rich bear a higher tax burden than the poor.

2. **PROPORTIONAL TAXES.** A **proportional tax** imposes the same tax burden on all families. A proportional tax would take $2000 (10 percent) from the Johnsons and $4000 (10 percent) from the Smiths. Higher-income families pay more dollars to tax collectors but bear the same burden in this example.

proportional tax: a tax that imposes the same burden on all income levels.

3. **REGRESSIVE TAXES.** A **regressive tax** falls heaviest on the poor. A tax that takes $2000 (10 percent) from the low-income Johnsons and $3000 (5 percent) from the upper-crust Smiths is regressive. The Smiths still pay more dollars to this regressive tax, but their tax burden is lower.

regressive tax: a tax whose burden increases as income falls; the poor bear a higher tax burden than the rich.

Which tax is best? All three tax types are used in government today. Taxes can be fair or inequitable depending on how they are administered (uniformly or with error or bias) and depending on which government services they finance. The social security tax, for example, is regressive, but viewed as fair by many people because people who pay the tax now receive social-security benefits in the future.

Major United States Taxes

Four taxes dominate the fiscal scene. They differ significantly in their economic effects and distributional burden. These four are the federal income tax, the social-security tax, general sales taxes, and property taxes.

1. **FEDERAL INCOME TAX.** The federal income tax is the biggest tree in the fiscal forest; millions of Americans curse the 1040 form every April 15. To understand what the income tax does, you first need to know how the income tax is calculated. This brief discussion will not qualify you for a job at H&R Block, but it will give you an idea of how the tax works.

Your family earned $20,000 last year. How much income tax do you owe? The answer to this important question depends on where the income came from and where it went. Certain sources of income are not taxed. Interest from state or local bonds is not subject to federal taxation, for example. Social-security benefits are tax free, too. Only 40 percent of income from **long-term capital gains** is taxed (all figures in this example are based on 1983 tax laws—check current income-tax forms for recent changes). Many other sources of income receive special tax treatment.

long-term capital gains: profits from investment owned for one year or more.

Suppose that all $20,000 came from wage and salary income (so it is all taxable). What next? Each dependent in the family is worth a $1000 deduction.

If there are four people in your family you can subtract $4000 from the total. Do you pay taxes on the $16,000 that is left? Not so fast. If you are filing as a married couple, you get your choice of a standard deduction of $3400 (this amount is only $2300 if you are single) or itemized deductions. If you take the itemized route you can subtract the money you paid in state and local taxes, charitable contributions, interest payments, certain medical and business expenses, and more. These uses of income reduce taxable income.

Let us suppose that your family opts for the standard-deduction route. You would then subtract the $3400 from $16,000 and pay taxes on the $12,700 that is left.

The tax rates are progressive. The first bracket taxes income at a low rate. As income increases, each additional chunk falls into a higher bracket. The highest tax rate is 50 percent.

The income tax is generally progressive. The combination of deductions for dependents, the standard deduction, and a progressive tax rate schedule means that low-income people bear a zero or low income-tax burden. Taxes rise with income. The income tax becomes proportional at high income levels as people take advantage of tax-free bonds and the like.

social security tax: tax on wages and salary income used to finance the social-security system.

payroll tax: a tax deducted directly from paychecks.

2. THE SOCIAL SECURITY TAX. The **social security tax** is a **payroll tax.** It is a tax on wage and salary income only (it does not tax investment or interest income, for example) that comes right out of your paycheck.

Many people have the wrong idea of how the social security tax works. The government takes social-security contributions out of your paycheck and invests them in high-grade securities that are cashed in when you retire. Right? Wrong. Nothing about this description is accurate. The social security "contribution" is really a tax, not an insurance or pension payment. The money that comes out of your paycheck goes to Washington, D.C., where it is almost immediately sent to retired social security beneficiaries. Your taxes pay for your parents' and grandparents' retirements. Who will contribute to your retirement social security check? Your children and others who work in the future.

The social security system is financed on a pay-as-you-go plan, which means that taxes have to be raised whenever social security transfer payments increase. Both the employee and the employer paid taxes of 6.7 percent of the worker's first $32,400 wage income in 1982 (economists think that some of the employers' tax is really paid by workers as reduced wage income). The tax ceiling of $32,400 rises every year, and the combined tax rate of 13.4 percent increases when more money is required for social security benefits.

The social security tax is regressive for two reasons. First, the tax ceiling means that high income people escape taxes on that part of their income above the ceiling. A worker who made $32,400 and another who made $324,000 (all wage income) both paid the same social security taxes in 1982. The second reason for regressivity is that the social security tax falls on wage and salary only. Poor people who pay no income tax at all often end up with high social security tax burdens. Richer folks who earn all of their income from investments or business profits pay no social security tax.

The social security program is in fiscal distress these days. Social-security benefits went up rapidly in the 1970s to compensate for rising prices. High unemployment rates meant that there were fewer and fewer workers paying taxes for each retired beneficiary. Social security began to run out of money.

This problem is going to get worse in the future. The post–World War II baby-boom generation is getting older. They will start retiring in a few years and the economy will be faced with tens of millions more people collecting social-security checks with even fewer workers to pay taxes. When an irresistible force (the aging population) meets the undeniable fact of fewer workers, something has got to give, but what?

We could raise taxes, but social-security taxes are already high. They might total 25 percent of income by 2010 if benefits formulas do not change. Are you willing to pay 25 percent social security tax (plus all the other taxes)? The social security tax could be expanded to include nonwage income, which would even out the tax burden somewhat, but the money still has to come from somewhere.

A second solution is to cut back social-security benefits or to limit social-security checks to only the truly needy. Social security benefits are not extravagant now, however, so reducing them could inflict real hardship on the elderly. Baby-boom workers who paid social security taxes all of their working lives are not likely to support proposals that deny them retirement benefits. Another proposal would have the retirement age raised from 65 to 67 or 70 so that workers would pay taxes longer and collect benefits for fewer years.

What is the solution to the social security crisis? No single action can solve this problem. Chances are that several of the ideas discussed above will be combined to bail out the system. You have a real stake in whatever policy Congress adopts.

3. GENERAL SALES TAXES. State and local governments get money from four main sources: income taxes, general sales taxes, property taxes, and grants from the federal government. The sales tax is an important part of state finances.

The **sales tax** looks like a proportional tax—everyone pays the same sales-tax rate, right? But everyone does not bear the same burden. Nancy works at a print shop and earns $20,000 per year. She spends $16,000 of this total and thus pays $800 in sales tax (assuming that there is a 5 percent sales-tax rate). Her tax burden is

sales tax: a tax based on the value of purchased goods.

$$\frac{\$800}{\$20{,}000} = 4 \text{ percent}$$

Michael is a physician and makes $50,000 per year. He saves a relatively high fraction of his income, spending only $30,000 on consumer goods. The 5 percent tax he pays on the $30,000 spent generates $1500 in taxes, for a tax burden of

$$\frac{\$1500}{\$50{,}000} = 3 \text{ percent}$$

They both pay the same sales-tax rate, but saving is not taxed, so people who are cheap or who save a larger fraction of their income bear lower tax burdens.

Michael and Nancy's spending habits are not unusual; sales-tax burdens fall heavier on the poor than on the rich.

The sales tax is less regressive in practice than this example shows. Food, drugs, and housing costs are tax free in most states, reducing the tax bite felt by the poor. The sales tax moves toward proportionality when these items are excluded from the tax base.

property tax: a tax based on the value of land and structures.

4. PROPERTY TAXES. The **property tax** is a tax on the value of land and structures. Many people consider the property tax to be the least fair tax they pay because it is based on their home's value, not their income or ability to pay the tax. Here is how the property tax works. Your home's market value is $100,000. The property-tax assessor tries to estimate its market value—not an easy trick—for tax purposes. Suppose the assessor guesses right and your property is put down at $100,000 on the tax roll. Your property tax bill now depends on the local property-tax rate. If the tax rate is 2 percent, for example, your annual tax bill is 2 percent of $100,000 or $2000 (that is about $165 per month!).

Who sets the 2 percent tax rate? The tax rate is determined by the relationship between total property value and local government services. Suppose, for example, that all the property in your town has a combined value of $100 million (it is probably much more than this). If the school board votes to spend $2 million of property-tax revenues, then the tax rate is

$$\frac{\$2\text{ million}}{\$100\text{ million}} = 2\text{ percent}$$

The property tax rate goes up when you vote for better schools or other services funded by property-tax revenues. Tax rates go down when property values rise or local-government spending falls.

The property tax is controversial. High inflation in the 1970s boosted both property values and the cost of schools, police, and other local services. The result? Taxpayers found their real incomes shrinking while home values and property-tax bills shot through the roof. Were they upset? You bet! Voters in Massachusetts, California, and other states enacted legal limits to property-tax bills.

Who pays the property tax? Is it regressive, progressive, or proportional? Economists are not in agreement on these questions. Property ownership is more prevalent among people with high incomes. If land owners pay the property tax, its distribution is progressive. But the *incidence* of the property tax is not so easily determined. The tax may be partially shifted to consumers or other groups. Differences in local property-tax rates and errors in assessing property value make the analysis even more difficult. The prevailing view today is that the tax is progressive, but some low-income people still bear heavy tax burdens. Elderly people living on social security often pay taxes based on the high value of their homes, not the low level of their incomes. Most states ease this burden through special tax-relief programs for the elderly poor.

The property tax is the one tax that voters can control directly at the ballot box. Voters choose to have more government services and higher taxes or lower tax rates and fewer public services when they vote on school and park plans. Voters in California sent their legislators a message when they passed the Proposition 13 property-tax limit—they did not want more government if it meant higher taxes.

The Total Tax Burden

You pay many different taxes. Income, social security, sales, and property taxes are the most important, but taxes on gasoline, liquor, tires, jewelry, corporation income, and automobiles all add to the total tax bill. How is the total tax burden distributed?

Benjamin Okner and Joseph Pechman of the Brookings Institution studied this question. Their answer depends in part on assumptions about the way taxes are shifted from one group to another. Do high-income investors pay the corporate income tax, for example, or does this tax get passed on to lower-income consumers who buy corporate goods?

When all the federal, state, and local taxes are added up, the sum looks to be approximately proportional, with the total tax bite averaging around 25 percent. If the benefits of government programs like social security and unemployment benefits are included, government's burden on the economy appears mildly progressive, placing heavier burdens on the rich than on the poor.

Tax Expenditures

Tax tools are used four ways in our fiscal system. Taxes raise tax revenues, alter the distribution of income, fight inflation, and fight unemployment. Taxes are also used as a substitute for government spending through tax expenditures. Tax expenditures? How can a tax be a form of spending?

Tax expenditures use the tax system to encourage people to spend their own money on government-approved goods and services. Suppose that you have just received a $100 raise and you are subject to a 50 percent tax rate. If you keep the money and spend it, the government takes half. If you give it all to the American Cancer Society or another government-approved charity, the IRS lets you deduct all $100 from your tax bill. Result? You pay no tax on the increased income. It costs you just $50 (your after-tax alternative) to give $100 to charity. Fifty dollars of your gift comes out of your after-tax pocket, the other $50 is money the government would have collected as tax.

It is unlikely that you will give away all of your paycheck to avoid taxes, but the special tax treatment reduces the cost of such gifts and so encourages you to channel your money that way. The government gets you to support cancer research through this tax-induced gift to the American Cancer Society.

Nonprofit groups like churches, universities, and food banks are not the only tax-expenditure recipients. Homeowners get a big break because mortgage interest payments and property tax payments are not taxed. Investors receive tax expenditures on long-term capital gains. These tax expenditures encourage people to buy homes, borrow money, and invest in long-lasting projects by reducing the after-tax cost of these activities. Private spending substitutes for public money.

Tax expenditures are a mixed blessing. You and I spend money instead of the government, so it looks like government projects are financed without cost. This appearance is a distortion. Government tax revenues decline when you take advantage of tax expenditures, so tax rates have to be raised to get as much money as before for government spending and transfer-payment programs. You end up paying for my tax expenditure indirectly through higher tax rates.

Too many tax expenditures make the tax system too complex and get in the way of economic growth. You might support a tax break for savers, for example, but dozens of tax breaks for dozens of groups boost tax rates and distort economic efficiency. Tax expenditures generate a deadweight loss. Families and firms spend their time working out elaborate schemes to minimize taxes rather than in producing and consuming good and services.

Why do we have so many tax expenditures? One reason is that tax breaks never show up as a spending item, so they are "invisible." Tax breaks are often justified in the name of equity, too. Tax expenditures remain a controversial tool of fiscal policy. Economists disagree about them, but their use has grown in recent years.

Automatic Stabilizers

Congress and the President actively use taxes, tax expenditures, transfer payments, and government spending to stabilize the economy. Some government tools do not need explicit direction, however. Automatic stabilizers act on cue to fight inflation and unemployment. An elaborate system of automatic stabilizers is one reason a deep depression is less likely today than it was 50 years ago.

How do automatic stabilizers work? Suppose that the economy slips into a recession. Many government programs automatically react to soften the blow to workers and their families. Jobless people receive unemployment benefits (not generally available 50 years ago) and welfare payments and qualify for food stamps or other subsidy programs. Lower income is subject to lower tax rates, too; consequently, people keep more of what they receive. This softens the blow to disposable income. Consumption spending does not fall as far as it otherwise would, so aggregate demand does not crash to the depression range.

This system also automatically limits increases in aggregate demand, thereby reducing the threat of inflation. Inflation boosts people into higher tax brackets, cutting disposable income and limiting demand-pull inflation. Transfer-payment programs like unemployment benefits phase out when RGNP rises.

The automatic-stabilizer system cannot prevent swings in the economy, but it does act to limit the size of booms and busts and so produces a more stable economic climate.

Advantages and Disadvantages of Fiscal Policies

Each fiscal tool has strengths and weaknesses. This makes fiscal choices difficult. Economists and politicians often disagree about what should be done—should we fight inflation or unemployment? Should we change aggregate demand or aggregate supply? Should we worry about the short run or the long run? Once agreement is reached about what to do, we still must choose how to do it—which tools to put to work. Let us look at the pros and cons of each fiscal tool.

GOVERNMENT SPENDING. Government spending's advantage is that it is powerful. The multiplier effect is large, so Congress can stimulate a particular area (say, unemployment in the northeast or in the defense industry) directly and then count on the multiplier chain reaction to increase spending in the rest of the economy.

An important disadvantage to government spending plans is that they can take a long time to get going. First there is a **legislative lag.** It takes months—sometimes years—for a newly introduced bill to make its way through congressional committees and subcommittees, get passed by both houses of the legislature, go through conference committee to iron out differences, and finally be adopted and signed by the President. Economic problems may be much different at the end of this process than at the start.

legislative lag: the lag in fiscal policy that occurs while legislators formulate policy.

Next comes the **implementation lag.** Rules and regulations, contracts and bids, and miles of red tape must be followed to their end before money is finally spent. The federal government has frequently found itself unable to spend money as fast as it wants (you and I do not have this problem). The **impact lag** is the final problem. It takes time for increased government spending to "hit" the economy and translate into consumption spending and aggregate demand.

implementation lag: the lag in fiscal policy that occurs while government policies are put into effect.

impact lag: the lag in fiscal policy that occurs before consumer spending responds to policy.

The combination of these three lags means that government-spending policies are not as reliable as they seem. The uncertainty of these lags reduces the effectiveness of fiscal policy.

TAXATION. Tax policies often escape the implementation lag and so are sometimes more useful than government spending. If Congress cuts tax rates today your disposable income rises in just a few weeks as payroll deductions are adjusted. Taxes are also useful because they have broad effects. Almost everyone pays taxes, so changing tax rates alter spending patterns throughout the economy. Tax expenditures can be used to increase spending on specific goods, too.

Tax policies have two important disadvantages, however. The tax system is so complicated that Congress sometimes has trouble getting through the legislative process quickly. President Ford's tax-rebate plan was passed in just a few weeks, but Jimmy Carter's tax programs hit wall after wall of committees. Carter recommended large tax cuts at one point as a way to reduce unemployment. By the time congressional committees were through, however, the unemployment rate was down and there was no reason to pass the bill (sometimes doing nothing is the best thing, but not always!).

The second problem is that tax policy depends on the actions of individual taxpayers for effectiveness. An increase in government spending directly boosts aggregate demand. A tax cut, on the other hand, gives people higher disposable income. Will they spend it all? Some of it? None of it? It depends in part on whether they view their disposable income raise as temporary or permanent. They might postpone new purchases until they are sure the tax cut is not going to be repealed, for example. This adds uncertainty to tax policy. Congress cut income taxes in 1981 and 1982, but aggregate demand still fell. Consumers feared a recession and so held on to their tax bonus, making the recession even deeper.

identification lag: the lag in fiscal policy that occurs while transfer payment recipients are identified and certified eligible.

TRANSFER PAYMENTS. Transfer payments suffer all the lag problems already discussed and one more: **identification lag.** Transfer payments are usually designed to aid specific needy groups. It takes time to identify and verify transfer recipients. Transfer payments have two important advantages, however. First, they often go to low-income groups who truly need the funds. Thus the distribution of income is improved. Second, transfer recipients are often powerful spenders—most or all the transfer goes to consumption spending. The size of the transfer-payments multiplier increases if the needy have a higher MPC than the MPC of the population as a whole. Transfer payments can be just as powerful as government expenditures if recipients spend all their government grant.

Deficit Spending and the National Debt

deficit spending: government borrowing; spending in excess of tax receipts.

national debt: total federal government indebtedness.

Deficit spending is not spending at all—it is borrowing. Government, like the rest of us, often spends more than it takes in. Spending in excess of tax revenues is called **deficit spending,** an indication that government has gone into debt to keep spending high. The **national debt** (now over $1 trillion and rising) is the total amount of debt the federal government has accumulated over the years.

From whom does the government borrow? From everyone. Government bond sales attract lenders from all walks of life and many foreign countries. You lend money to the government when you purchase a U.S. Savings Bond, for example. By buying the bond, you lend the government money to finance its deficits. Your bond is not a "piece of the rock," it is a chunk of the national debt.

Deficits in years past were generated by national emergencies: wars against foreign enemies and wars against poverty and unemployment. Deficits these days are high by historical standards, as Figure 8-6 shows. The last time the federal budget was balanced (taxes covered spending needs) was in 1969. Deficits have been the rule, not the exception, since the Great Depression.

Are high deficits and a rising national debt an economic problem? As usual, economists give at least two answers. On one hand, the national debt is not a problem because "we owe it to ourselves." This sounds silly, but it is at least partially true. When the government needs to pay back Mr. A's loan, it sells bonds to Mr. B to get the cash. Debt replaces debt. This is like paying off

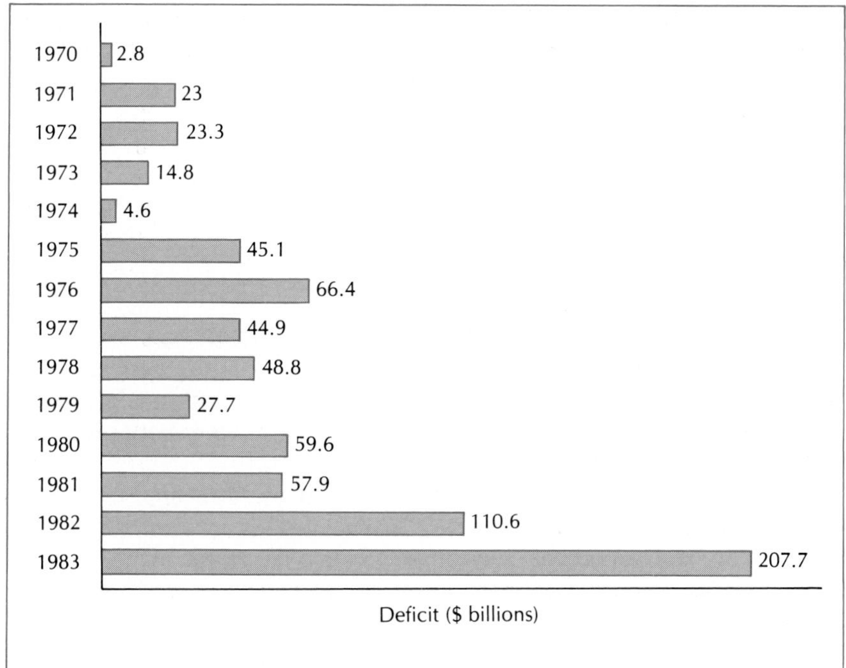

FIGURE 8-6 DEFICIT SPENDING 1970–1983. Modest deficits in the early 1970s have grown to massive debt in the 1980s. The federal government has not balanced its budget since 1969.

your Mastercard bill by putting the debt on your Visa card—a slick trick if you can get away with it. The national debt never "comes due" the way a private loan does so long as government remains a good credit risk. The national debt only becomes a problem, according to one view, if people refuse to lend money to the government.

Deficits do have a dark side, however. Massive government borrowing has two detrimental economic effects. The first is higher interest rates. Government bids up interest rates when it competes for loans. Higher interest charges are a burden to private borrowers and to taxpayers, too. Higher interest costs mean government must tax more, spend less, or borrow even larger amounts to keep up its interest payments. Interest payments alone were $100 billion for the federal government in 1982! One hundred billion dollars is roughly the size of West Germany's federal-government budget. The U.S. government borrowed as much as the German government spent!

The second problem is that government borrowing tends to *crowd out* private investment spending. Loanable funds are limited, so increased government borrowing leaves less for consumers and business investors. Many economists blame low productivity and falling aggregate supply on government deficits. Government borrowing crowded out investments in the 1970s and reduced economic growth.

Deficit spending and the national debt are another mixed blessing. On one hand, deficit spending increases aggregate demand by making it possible to have higher spending and transfer payments in conjunction with lower taxes. On the other hand, government borrowing is a drag on the economy when high interest costs and crowding out limit economic growth.

ECONOMIC CONTROVERSY:

Supply-Side Economics

Are high taxes a roadblock to economic growth? Are high taxes forcing people to the underground economy? Should the federal government cut taxes to stimulate aggregate supply? These are the questions that supply-side economics raises. Supply siders view tax cuts as the solution to both inflation and unemployment.

Supply-side economics is based on two ideas. The first is that taxes destroy incentives to save and invest, produce and innovate. Why should a worker put in overtime if the government gets most of his or her pay? Why should a firm install new machinery if profits are heavily taxed? Reducing tax rates, supply siders argue, increases incentives and generates growing aggregate supply.

Laffer curve: graph showing the relationship between tax revenues and tax rates.

Will not massive tax cuts bring equally large deficits that discourage investment and innovation? No, answer the supply siders, citing the **Laffer curve** relationship shown in Figure 8-7. The Laffer curve (named for Arthur Laffer who drew it on a cocktail napkin) shows how tax revenues and tax rates are related. It says that tax cuts might bring in more revenue than before—reducing the deficit, not increasing it!

A zero tax rate generates no money for government. Tax revenues rise when rates are increased but not by as much as you might guess. Higher tax rates discourage production and investment and encourage people to take their business underground where they pay no taxes at all. Higher tax rates hit

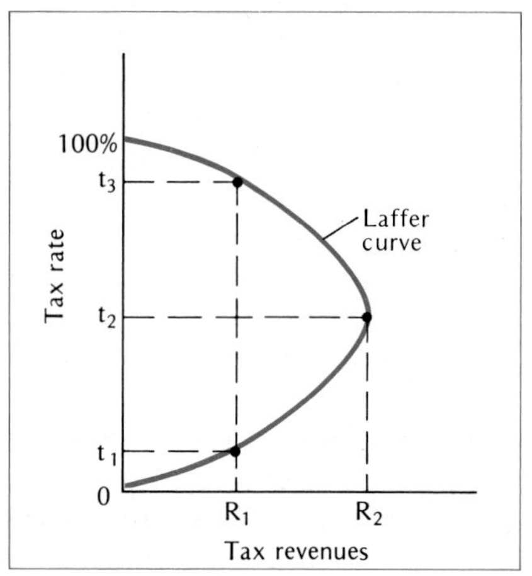

FIGURE 8-7 THE LAFFER CURVE. You can raise R_1 tax revenue with a low tax rate like t_1 or with a high rate like t_3. Higher rates discourage production and send people to the untaxed underground economy. Higher taxes actually result in lower revenues at rates above t_2.

diminishing returns and, eventually, increasing rates reduce tax collections as fewer people work and more people flee underground. Finally, a 100 percent tax rate collects nothing—no one bothers to pay it.

The moral of the Laffer curve is that low tax rates often collect as much money as higher ones. Where is the maximum revenue point? Economists are not sure and that is part of what this debate is about.

Cut Taxes Now!

Tax rates in the United States have crept into the top part of the Laffer curve. Taxes this high discourage investment and innovation and bring higher inflation and unemployment rates. High taxes are the cause of today's economic woes and the solution is to cut taxes now!

Tax cuts are good for people. High taxes take purchasing power away from people and give it to faceless government bureaucracy. People have no incentive to improve themselves and Jimmy Carter's "economic malaise" surely follows. Tax cuts increase aggregate supply and bring on balanced growth.

Some people argue that tax cuts will only lead to big deficits. This is hogwash. Fuddy-duddy demand siders say that we do not know which part of the Laffer curve we are on. It takes a lot of education, as Irving Kristol has said, not to know that we are on the top part of the Laffer curve. Lower tax rates now pay off with increased tax collections. You have only to look at your pay stub to feel the burden that government has imposed on your life. Lifting that burden would make us all better off.

Tax cuts now would give us even more government revenue. We can cut taxes and still have all the government services now available. Tax cuts are a supply-side bonanza.

Do Not Bet on the Laffer Curve

The supply-side argument sounds good—who does not want a lower tax bite? But do not bet the rent on the Laffer curve.

The supply-siders' argument is wrong in two important ways. First, they view tax cuts as supply-side stimulants. But taxes affect aggregate demand through the multiplier process. A big tax cut would fuel consumption spending, sending demand-pull inflation rates through the roof. Higher inflation pushes up interest rates, so investment spending and aggregate supply fall. No good comes of this in the long run.

There is no guarantee that their Laffer-curve analysis is correct, either. We are probably on the lower part of the Laffer curve now. Cutting taxes means less revenue, bigger deficits, and additional crowding out. These big deficits make it even harder for business to invest and grow. The tax-cut plan spells disaster for the economy.

Supply-sider tax cuts are like a nuclear power plant. If everything goes exactly as planned the result is great. But if something breaks down, we end up with an economic China Syndrome of high demand-pull inflation and falling aggregate supply. If tax cuts are not the answer, what is? Many people think we should raise taxes—especially taxes on consumer goods. Higher taxes would reduce the deficit, leaving more credit for investment spending. Taxes on consumer goods give people an incentive to save their money instead, putting more credit into the system. Economic growth requires tax increases, not silly supply-sider tax cuts.

SUMMARY

1. Fiscal policies use government-spending, tax, and transfer-payment tools to fight inflation and unemployment. Stabilization policy is only one function of government, however. Allocation, distribution, and public-choice needs must also be met.

2. Multiplier analysis describes the effect of fiscal policies on aggregate demand. A small change in government spending, for example, makes a big difference in aggregate demand because of induced consumption effects. Investment spending has the same multiplier as government spending. Taxes and transfer-payments multipliers are smaller because they influence consumption indirectly through disposable income.

3. The same fiscal policy has different effects depending on the shape of the aggregate supply curve. Government spending reduces unemployment, causes inflation, or both, depending on the prevailing AS curve.

4. All government spending has the same multiplier, but that does not mean that all spending is the same. Government investments increase aggregate supply as well as aggregate demand. Some government programs reduce economic efficiency and production potential.

5. All taxes are not the same, either. Taxes have different AS effects and are paid by different people. Taxes can be progressive, proportional, or regressive. The major taxes in the United States are income, social-security, sales, and property taxes.

6. Tax expenditures are special tax breaks that encourage people to spend their own funds on government-approved programs. Tax expenditures are a controversial tool of fiscal policy.

7. Each fiscal policy tool has both advantages and disadvantages. Much of this discussion centered on lags that make economic policy uncertain.

8. The government borrows money (deficit spending) when it spends more than is provided by available tax revenues. These deficits are acceptable, some think, because "we owe them to ourselves." But deficits bid up interest rates and crowd out private investment spending, reducing growth in aggregate supply.

9. Are big tax cuts a good idea? Supply siders say they stimulate aggregate demand and reduce the deficit. Others say tax cuts increase aggregate demand and, through higher deficits, reduce aggregate supply—bringing only more stagflation. Much of the debate dealt with the Laffer curve.

10. What happens if taxes and transfer payments are both cut by $100,000? You were asked this question earlier in this chapter. This policy pair has no effect on aggregate demand if all groups in the economy have the same MPC. The AD increase resulting from the tax cut is wiped out by falling aggregate demand from the transfer-payments reduction. The two multipliers are the same size. Aggregate demand might fall, however, if poor transfer recipients have a higher MPC than taxpayers or if taxpayers fail to spend their tax bonuses.

DISCUSSION QUESTIONS

1. The President's economic advisors have announced that a $40 billion increase in aggregate demand would lower unemployment to an acceptable level. The MPC is 80 percent. How should this increase in aggregate demand be accomplished?

- **a.** How big an increase in government spending would be necessary? Explain.
- **b.** How much would transfer payments have to increase to boost aggregate demand by $40 billion? Explain.
- **c.** How much should taxes be cut to accomplish this goal? Explain.
- **d.** How big an increase in investment spending (induced by a tax expenditure) would be needed? Explain.
- **e.** Which is the best plan? Explain how you arrived at your conclusion.

2. Economic policies are sometimes complex. The following events took place in the same year:

- **a.** social security taxes increased by $20 billion;
- **b.** social security benefits increased by $20 billion;
- **c.** government spending decreased by $10 billion;
- **d.** taxes decreased by $10 billion.

Explain how each of these policies affect aggregate demand and aggregate supply by themselves. What is the combined effect? Is this policy combination inflationary? Defend your answer.

3. President Reagan's tax-cut package reduced tax rates for most people. How should this policy affect:

- **a.** tax revenues (Hint: look out for the Laffer curve);
- **b.** the effectiveness of tax expenditures;
- **c.** the size of the deficit.

4. Where do you stand on the tax-cut debate? Would a big tax cut improve economic conditions? Which of the four taxes discussed in this chapter should be cut? Explain.

5. Should taxes be progressive, regressive, or proportional? What makes a "good" tax? Explain.

TEST YOURSELF

Circle the best response to each question.

1. The federal government increases spending by $10 billion. The MPC is 80 percent. The economy is in the depression part of the AS curve. This fiscal policy results in:

(X) aggregate demand rises by $50 billion
(Y) consumption spending rises by $40 billion
(Z) RGNP rises by $50 billion

a. all of the above
b. none of the above
c. only (X)
d. only (Y)
e. only (X) and (Z)

2. Taxes have just been cut by $10 billion. The MPC is 80 percent. The economy is on the full capacity part of the AS curve. This fiscal policy results in:

(X) aggregate demand rises by $50 billion
(Y) consumption spending rises by $40 billion
(Z) RGNP rises by $40 billion

a. all of the above
b. none of the above
c. only (X)
d. only (Y)
e. only (Z)

3. Congress has just enacted a new tax expenditure. It is an investment tax credit that provides lower taxes for firms that increase investment spending. This tax expenditure:

(X) encourages investment by reducing its cost
(Y) reduces aggregate demand because firms spend less on investment
(Z) increases the federal deficit because less tax revenue is received

a. all of the above
b. none of the above
c. only (X)
d. only (Z)
e. both (X) and (Z)

4. Two neighbors are comparing state-tax returns. Dr. Morrell's income is $50,000 and his state tax bill totals $5000. Ms. Eaton's income is $25,000 and her state taxes total $2500. If these taxpayers are typical, this state's tax is:

a. regressive
b. progressive
c. proportional

d. equitable
e. inequitable

5. Which of the following proposals could be adopted without an increase in the deficit *only* if the economy is on the top part of the Laffer curve?

a. increase both tax rates and defense spending
b. increase both tax rates and transfer payments
c. increase both defense spending and transfer payments with no change in tax rates
d. increase tax rates and decrease defense spending
e. increase defense spending and decrease tax rates

SUGGESTIONS FOR FURTHER READING

The Brookings Institution has long been a center for the study of government and the economy. *Setting National Priorities* looks at fiscal policy every year. A conservative view can be found in yearly volumes of *Contemporary Economic Problems* (Washington, D.C.: American Enterprise Institute for Public Policy Research). *How Taxes Affect Economic Behavior* (Washington, D.C.: Brookings Institution, 1981), edited by Joseph Pechman and Henry J. Aaron, tells the current tax story. Aaron and Michael S. Boskin's (eds.) *The Economics of Taxation* (Washington, D.C.: Brookings Institution, 1980) is an excellent tax primer. The author's *Public Finance* (Reston, Virginia: Reston Publishers, 1984) is another good reference. Jude Wanninski is a famous popularizer of supply-side economics. This view is well presented in his *The Way the World Works* (New York: Simon and Schuster, 1978).

III

MONEY, CREDIT, AND THE ECONOMY

9

MONEY AND BANKING

Preview

What is money? From where does money come?

How do banks create money?

What is the interest rate? Why are there different interest rates for different loans?

What makes the interest rate rise?

How does a fractional reserve bank work?

What is the Federal Reserve System? Why was it invented?

What does the FRS do?

Should the United States return to the gold standard?

money: anything generally accepted in exchange for goods and services and in payment of debt.

WHAT IS **money?** Well, you might say, money is . . . money! Greenbacks, dollar bills, those valuable pieces of paper you carry around in your wallet or purse. You know . . . MONEY!

This definition is good enough to get by at the supermarket, but it does not describe money as it existed for most of our history. Paper money—the currency you covet—is a relatively recent invention. Your great-grandfather probably would not have thought your idea of money worth the paper on which it is printed. Most of our monetary roots are buried in "real" money—money with intrinsic value. Gold and silver.

Money has taken many forms. The list of money used in North America alone includes paper bills, gold and silver, coins made of everything from copper and nickel to aluminum and plastic, seashells, and tobacco (money you could spend, save, or smoke!). Beer has even served as money in some cultures—cash with a head! (Drink up so your assets do not go flat.)

A Financial Fable

barter: a system where goods are exchanged directly without the use of money.

Stones were money on one Polynesian island. It all got started when the natives discovered that **barter** is not an efficient way to exchange goods and services. Barter depends on a coincidence of wants. You have coconuts and you would like to have pineapples, for example. Making this exchange in a barter economy means you need to find someone with pineapples who wants to trade for coconuts. If you cannot match desires, you might have to trade your coconuts for some other good, like guava fruit, that the pineapple grower does desire. Exchange using barter can be time consuming and difficult. You might spend all of your time searching for trading opportunities and little time in production.

The islanders soon discovered the advantages of money. They picked one good and valued everything by the common unit of measure (stones might have been chosen because of their scarcity or durability or because of the ease of making change—one big rock equals a dozen pebbles). Coincidence of want is no longer a problem. If you want a haircut, you do not have to worry about finding something that the barber wants to trade. Money can be exchanged for all other goods. All you have to do is pay the barber money and he or she can exchange that for any desired good or service.

The island economy prospered with the invention of money. Exchange was much simplified, so the islanders spent more time producing goods and less time searching for exchange. Assembly-line industries were started. These were not possible under the barter system—it was just too complicated to pay everyone a desired good. Large projects could now be constructed because all payments were made in the universally desired rocks.

New institutions sprang up to finance these large projects. Islanders deposited rocks in banks (located on river banks—hence the name). The bankers made loans, so savers earned pebbles as interest on their boulders. The island accounting profession was born so that debit rocks and credit rocks could be tallied. Economic activity picked up; the RGNP and the standard of living increased. The island economy worked just like ours, with one or two exceptions.

The biggest boulder on the island was a massive rock perched on a cliff overlooking the lagoon. The rock was too big to move. It was, therefore, impossible to spend it. This should have caused problems for the island financial community, but it did not. Everyone knew who owned the rock (the Rockerfellows). Everyone knew that the rock had value. All the merchants on the island were willing to take the Rockerfellows' IOUs in exchange for goods and services. The paper IOUs were not rocks, but they were just as good because they were "backed up" by rock-wealth. The paper money represented a "piece of the rock."

This rock system rolled on for years, gathering no moss, until the local volcano erupted. This had two interesting effects. First, the volcano spewed more rocks onto the island, increasing the money supply and bringing rock inflation (too many rocks chasing too few coconuts). The more interesting problem was that the Rockerfellows' wealth was shaken off its precarious perch. The massive boulder tumbled headlong into the lagoon and was never seen again.

Were the Rockerfellows wiped out by the boulder's crash? Not a bit. In fact, nothing changed. Everyone knew that the rock was there, even if they could not see it or touch it (or spend it). Everyone knew who owned the rock and everyone believed that the Rockerfellows' IOUs were backed up by a piece of the rock. The paper money continued to circulate exactly as before.

What is the moral of this silly story? The islanders' monetary system was much like our own. Our money is backed up by a precious commodity—gold. Right? Wrong! Look at your money. Who issued it? The U.S. government—right? Wrong again. The Secretary of the Treasury signed your dollar bill, but the **Federal Reserve System** issued it—it is even called a Federal Reserve Note. Well, the Federal Reserve is part of the federal government, is it not? No, the FRS is an independent agency. It is not controlled by Congress and it does not even get government funding. The Federal Reserve is a private institution owned and operated by the banking industry.

Federal Reserve System: the organization that regulates the national banking system and controls monetary policy in the United States.

What backs up the Federal Reserve Notes? Gold? Silver? Rocks? No physical asset stands behind the money you carry around. In a real sense it is worth no more than the paper on which it is printed. Is it worthless then? If you think so, please send your dollar bills to the author, in care of Academic Press. I will gladly dispose of this worthless trash for you!

Your money has value for the same reason the islanders honored the Rockerfellows' IOUs. Their paper money had value because they thought it did. They trusted that the IOUs could be traded for valuable goods and services. Trust is what really backs up your Federal Reserve Notes. Trust is the invisible foundation of the financial system.

The Money Supply

Anything generally accepted in exchange for goods and services and in payment of debt is money. Two types of money best fit this definition today: currency

demand deposits: checking account balances.

money supply: the amount of money available for spending.

(including coins) and **demand deposits.** Demand deposits are bank checking-account balances. They are called demand deposits because they can be withdrawn immediately ("on demand") and spent quickly—just like currency.

These two money types make up the **money supply.** Demand deposits amounted to $318 billion in 1981 and currency added another $123 billion to the money supply. Dollar bills are the way we think of money, but checking accounts are the way we spend it; they amount to over 70 percent of this total.

The money supply is an important economic statistic. How much are you likely to spend this month? Your personal money supply is an indication of your intention to make purchases. Economists keep track of the money supply and the FRS tries to control it because money and spending are so tightly intertwined. Spending and aggregate demand generally rise with an increase in the money supply and fall when this total declines.

M1 money supply definition: currency and demand deposit balances.

Economists measure the money supply in different ways to gauge the spending capacity of the economy. The money supply definition you have just learned is called the **M1 money supply definition.** This definition comprises money that people can spend as easily as writing a check. It includes cash, demand deposits, and travellers' checks.

time deposits: savings account balances.

money market funds: investments in short-term government and corporate bond pools.

M2 money supply definition: currency, demand deposits and time deposits, and money market fund balances.

The M1 money supply is a good indication of how much the economy can spend this minute, but not a perfect one. People can also spend money they hold in **time deposits** or in highly liquid financial investments like **money market funds.** It takes a little longer to get this money and spend it, but buying plans certainly take these funds into accounts. The **M2 money supply definition** includes all of M1, plus time deposits, money market balances, and similar highly spendable assets. The M2 money measure has become important because more and more money is now being held in these two additional types of accounts. Over $1 trillion sat in time deposits in 1981, while another $185 billion was held in money market funds.

M3 money supply definition: M2 money definition plus large certificates of deposit.

The **M3 money supply definition** adds large-denomination time deposits (like $100,000 certificates of deposit) to the monetary soup. These large deposits also measure the ability to spend, although large time deposits generally remain untouched in banks for long periods of time.

L money supply definition: broadest measure of money; includes M3 plus short-term government securities held by the public.

The L (for liquidity) money measure is the broadest measure of the spending capacity of the economy. The **L money supply definition** includes everything in M3, plus liquid assets like short-term Treasury securities, savings bonds, and the like.

What do these money measures really mean? Economists are not as sure as they used to be. The banking industry has changed radically in the last few years. We used to be able to divide the financial world into commercial banks (that offered demand deposits and made automobile, boat, and small-business loans) and savings banks that featured time deposits and made home loans. Now credit unions offer interest on demand deposits, other banks have time deposits that you can write checks on, stock brokers make available a full line of financial services, and money market funds that do not fall neatly into any category compete for savers' dollars.

The money supply is getting harder and harder to measure and interpret. Economists sometimes do not know just where to draw the line between time and demand deposits. Is it important if people pull money out of commercial bank checking accounts and put it into savings and loan time deposits they can draw on with a credit card? Does the fall in M1 this produces really mean anything? Questions like these frustrate money measurers and economic forecasters.

Most economists are M1 and M2 watchers. These two money measures tell us much about the spending potential of businesses and consumers even if they are not the perfect measures we would like them to be. Economists debate how important the money supply is and how changes in the money supply affect the economy. Economists agree, however, that money is important. You will hear more about money's controversy in the next three chapters.

Money Substitutes

Money makes the world go around, but many money substitutes grease the wheels. **Near money** is not money, but acts like money in specific circumstances. Bus tokens, grocery store cents-off coupons, and gift certificates all act like money at appropriate times but are not widely accepted nor useful in paying debts.

near money: assets with high liquidity that sometimes take the place of money.

Credit cards are an important near money. Many people view their bank card's limit as a more binding spending constraint than demand or time deposit limits. Credit cards are not money. They often pay bills, but are not acceptable in most buying circumstances. Credit cards are just a convenient way for consumers to borrow for short periods of time.

How do credit-card companies make money from these financial services? Most people assume that interest charges are what credit cards are all about. Unpaid balances earn interest charges of 18 percent and more in many states. Interest on these credit card loans is an important source of revenue to Mastercard and Visa banks and for companies like American Express and Diners Club. But credit card economics is deeper than this.

Consumers and merchants both pay for credit-card services. Consumers often are billed an annual fee by card companies. Merchants pay a fee to the companies, too, collected as a **discount.** If you charge $100 worth of economics books using your credit card, the bookstore might receive only $95 to $97 from the credit card company. The difference is a fee the card company collects for its services. Why would the bookstore agree to pay this fee? Many merchants feel they have to honor credit cards to be competitive and to lure impulse buyers who would not spend as freely with cash or a check. Credit card costs, however, eventually show up in the prices that all buyers pay.

discount: goods sold for less than their face value.

Credit cards also make money through the **float.** Suppose you bought those economics books on the first of January. You promptly pay the credit-card firm $100 on the first of February. The card people now have your funds, but they may not credit the bookstore's account until the first of March because of accounting delays. They have $100 cash to loan or invest during that one month period.

float: the time when two individuals temporarily own the same asset.

So what? What does it matter if American Express or Mastercard has $100 for an extra month? Multipy this one transaction by millions and millions of sales and payments and you will see that credit-card companies can invest literally billions of dollars and earn hundreds of millions of dollars interest from the floating funds. Floating funds are "free," but the profits they earn are real.

The float is a frequently used financial tool. Travelers'-check companies are built on the float. You buy a travellers' check today and spend it tomorrow. But merchants may not receive the funds for weeks or months. Floating dollars earn interest in the meantime.

The Interest Rate

credit: the temporary exchange of money among individuals, as when loans are made.

Money's services are exchanged when money is borrowed and lent. Money exchanged in this way is called **credit.** The interest rate is the price of credit—the cost of borrowing and the payment for lending.

Why is there an interest rate? Why should you have to pay to use money (so long as you pay it back)? This is a more important question than you probably think. Plato thought that interest payments were unethical. He did not think that money should gain in value through exchange. People work to earn money, he concluded, money cannot earn money. Muslims think interest payments are immoral. Banks do not pay interest in Islamic nations and Muslims in the United States are faced with a moral dilemma every time they receive their bank statement. **Usury laws** in the United States make it illegal to charge interest rates above some legal maximum—these laws are remnants of long-held prejudices against borrowing and lending.

usury laws: laws that set maximum legal interest rates.

Modern economists hold that an interest rate makes sense for five reasons. These five interest rate determinants explain why interest rates exist, why some loans carry higher interest costs than others, and why interest rates rise and fall.

time preference: interest rate due to the preference for present over future consumption.

opportunity cost: the value of the best foregone opportunity when a choice is made.

1. TIME PREFERENCE. Most people prefer to have things now rather than at some time in the future. This **time preference** is at the heart of all interest rates. Lenders give up the use of their money for the term of the loan—they give up the power to buy goods and services and take advantage of investment opportunities now in return for higher payments in the future. The items that the lenders forego in the present are the **opportunity cost** of the loan. These opportunity costs are real, and interest rates reflect the cost to lenders—who would prefer to have things now—of waiting for payment in the future.

A time preference interest rate would exist even if the remaining items on this list disappeared. The interest rate stemming from pure time preference is low—perhaps just one or two percent—and constant over time.

risk premium: interest rate due to uncertainty of loan repayment.

2. RISK PREMIUM. Loans are risky propositions. There is always a chance that the lender will not be repaid and must resort to costly legal means to gain his or her due. A **risk premium** is automatically included in each loan as a kind of insurance policy against default. The added interest on repaid loans compensates the lender for those that are not paid back.

The risk premium helps explain why some loans have higher interest cost than others. A credit card loan carries a high interest rate, for example, because there is a high probability of default. The typical credit card loan is not secured by **collateral.** What can the bank do if you do not pay your credit card bill? They cannot come and repossess your house or car. They can sue you, but this is costly and unlikely to generate cash quickly. The high risk of nonpayment translates into high risk-premium interest rates.

collateral: items held as security for a loan.

Home mortgage loans have a lower interest rate. Why? Most banks require large down payments for these loans, so poor risks often cannot get a loan. What happens if you do not pay your mortgage? The bank repossesses the house and probably sells it for more than the loan amount. There is small chance of the bank taking a loss even when the lender defaults. The lower risk is reflected in lower interest cost.

Loans on new or used cars fall somewhere between these two extremes. A car provides collateral for the loan, but risk remains. Cars, unlike houses, can be simply driven away, making repossession difficult or impossible. The higher interest rate car loans receive reflects higher risk.

The reputation and economic status of borrowers contribute to the risk premium. The risk premium is nil when General Motors goes to the bank. Repayment is nearly certain (except maybe in case of intergalactic nuclear war). Poor people are often considered such a bad credit risk that they cannot get loans at any price through legal lenders. They are forced to go to illegal loan sharks who demand astronomical interest payments for even modest, short-term loans.

Risk premiums also depend on the prospective use of the funds. A firm that wants to build a McDonald's across from a college campus probably pays a lower interest premium than another investor who wants the money to bet on horses.

The government helps set interest rates through the risk premium. Some loans are guaranteed by the government. If the borrower does not pay up, the federal government will. This shrinks the risk premium to zero and accounts for the lower interest rate on some student and mortgage loans.

3. ADMINISTRATIVE COSTS. The cost of setting up, processing, and administering a loan adds to the interest rate, too. Costly loans bear a higher **administrative-cost premium** as part of the interest rate. Home loans have substantial front-end costs, for example, but these are spread out over a 10 to 20 year term of the loan. A low-interest premium covers these costs.

administrative-cost premium: interest rate due to cost of administering loan.

Credit card loans, on the other hand, require costly monthly collection and billing. These higher costs are reflected in a higher interest fee.

Administrative cost and risk premiums explain why some loans (and some borrowers) are subject to higher interest rates than others. These two factors do not explain why the interest rate on a given loan might increase or decrease in the coming months. For the answer to why interest rates change we need to look to the last two determinants.

4. INFLATION PREMIUM. Inflation rates get built into the interest rate—borrowers and lenders react to the expected inflation rate over the period of the loan. The **inflation premium** is a practical necessity. Higher prices, as

inflation premium: interest rate due to expected future inflation.

noted in Chapter 4, reduce the real value of the loan repayment. Banks and other lenders must raise nominal interest rates to maintain constant real returns.

prime interest rate: interest rate on short-term, low-risk loans.

The inflation premium has been a powerful force setting interest rates in recent years. Figure 9-1 shows how the **prime interest rate** varied with the inflation rate. The message this figure tells is clear: interest rate and inflation rates rise and fall together.

This is one reason businesses fear inflation so much. Inflation bids up interest costs and makes inventories and investments more expensive. Higher interest rates also discourage consumer purchases. The U.S. automobile industry found itself impaled on the double-edged sword of inflation and interest rates in the early 1980s. High inflation-induced interest rates not only made modernization and "down-sizing" expensive but also prevented consumers from buying the new products. Auto manufacturers lost millions of dollars.

Politicians and business people were puzzled in 1982 when the inflation rate dropped substantially but the interest rate did not. What, they thought, can possibly be keeping interest rates so high? Figure 9-1 certainly suggests that lower inflation and reduced interest rates should go together. These puzzled people forgot two important things. The first is that the inflation premium depends on the expected future inflation rate, not the current one. Lenders

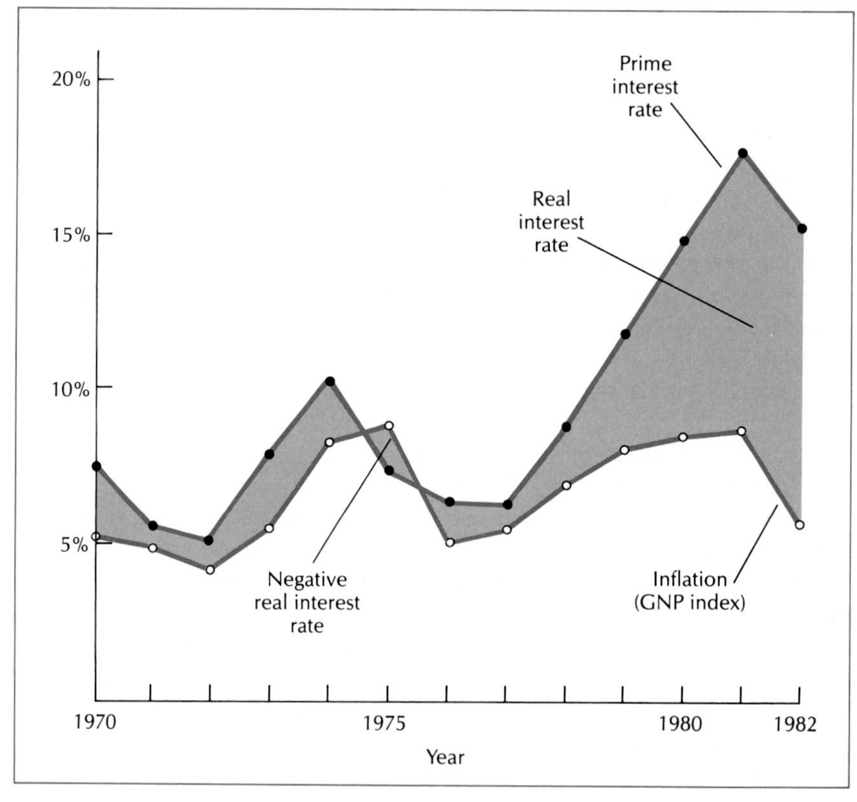

FIGURE 9-1 INFLATION AND THE INTEREST RATE. The prime interest rate is shown here along with inflation as measured by the GNP price index. The difference between the two lines is the real interest rate. Note the high correlation between inflation and interest rates.

who do not expect inflation to stay low are not likely to make low interest loans. The second key to the puzzle is that inflation, while important, is not the only thing changing interest rates. The other is scarcity.

5. SCARCITY PREMIUM. What happens to the price of apples if everyone wants to buy but no one wants to sell? Answer: scarcity bids up the price. So, what happens to the interest rate if everyone wants to borrow but few people care to lend? Same answer. Scarcity forces interest rates up during tight-money times and bids them down when easy money prevails.

The **scarcity premium** kept interest rates high in 1982 despite lower inflation premiums. The Federal Reserve restrained credit growth while the federal government borrowed tens of billions of dollars to finance the deficit. So much borrowing with little lending made credit scarce and kept nominal interest rates high while real interest rates hit record levels.

scarcity premium: interest rate due to relative scarcity of loanable funds.

The interest rate you pay on a loan is the combination of all five of these determinants. Your interest rate depends on time preference (treat this as a constant), cost and risk premiums that vary with the type of loan and the borrower, an inflation premium that depends on expected inflation rates, and the scarcity premium. Government guarantees and usury limits make some rates lower than they would otherwise be. Government borrowing makes money tight and drives up interest rates in general.

The Prime Interest Rate

Interest rates are in the news these days, and the prime rate gets most of the attention. The prime interest rate is the interest rate that banks charge their most prosperous customers for short-term, low-cost loans. You can think of the prime as the minimum interest rate a bank would consider.

Prime-rate loans have little risk or cost associated with them. The prime rate therefore reflects the important inflation and scarcity premiums that affect other loans. An increase in the prime rate means that expected inflation rates have increased or money is tighter. If these trends continue, rising prime rates lead to higher interest rates for cars, houses, and consumer loans, too. Lower prime interest rates eventually translate into lower interest costs on other loans (except those where government controls prevent price movements).

The prime rate has an interesting history. The prime rate was invented during the Great Depression when interest rates were low and dropping—government securities earned just one-half percent interest in 1933! Why such a low interest rate? Deflation was part of the problem. Falling prices brought interest rates down with them. It is hard to make money borrowing and lending with interest rates of one percent or less. The banking industry invented the prime rate as an interest rate floor. They used the prime rate to hold the line on falling interest charges. These days the prime rate is not so much a floor as a flag: it tells which way financial winds are blowing. You will learn more about interest rates in the next chapter.

Money and Banks

All this money, credit, and interest rate business revolves around banks. Banks hold most of the money supply—demand and time deposits. Banks create credit when they make loans. And interest rates like the prime rate also depend on banks. Just how does a bank work?

Banks are financial intermediaries. They make both borrowers and lenders better off by bringing them together. Banks collect funds from individual savers and pool their money into a diversified loan portfolio. This minimizes administrative cost and reduces risk compared with loans made by savers acting alone. The result of the bank's actions is that lenders receive higher, safer returns and borrowers pay lower interest charges.

Banking has a long history. The Roman empire boasted a working bank system. The Medicis were bankers to the Pope, and the financial houses of renaissance Genoa and Venice invented banking as we know it today. But banks did not always exist.

The closest thing to a bank in the ancient days of gold and silver coinage was probably a gold warehouse or jeweler's vault. Holding money was a risky business in early days. You had to be on the constant lookout for robbers and thieves; protecting your money was difficult (Robin Hood took advantage of this to promote his socialist schemes for redistribution of GNP in Sherwood Forest!). Baggy pockets gave away the size of a rich man's purse.

People paid the goldsmith (and others like him) a fee to keep and protect their savings. They put their coins and bullion in his vault and received, in exchange, a receipt that could be redeemed in gold at some future date.

The gold warehouse system reduced risk, but was still inconvenient. Suppose you wanted to spend a few doubloons on root beers with King Arthur. What a pain to have to go to the goldsmith, present your receipt, get your gold, take the gold to the pub and pay for the root beer. Risky, too—robbers did not take long to discover that the warehouse attracted gold like some gourmet magnet. How much easier it would be to make the gold receipts transferable!

Two solutions were found to the inconvenience problem. Some gold warehouses issued "bearer receipts" to depositors. This note said,

Pay to the bearer one piece of gold.

These receipts were the first form of currency. The receipts of well-known goldsmiths circulated alongside real gold coins and were equally valued (notes from unknown goldsmiths often traded at a discount—rightly so, since many of them were fake).

The second solution was even simpler. Instead of printing notes, the goldsmith simply agreed to disperse gold on written authorization of the depositor. When the Sheriff of Nottingham wanted to pay his troops, for example, he did not have to march all over England to collect the coins. He gave each of his men a note like the following

> Dear Goldsmith,
> Please pay to the order of SIR GAWAIN:
> Ten pieces of gold
> Sincerely,
>
> Sheriff of Nottingham

This was, as you can see, the first bank check. The checks we write today still take the general form of a note to the bank, although computers are now the principal readers.

Did Sir Gawain have to run to the goldsmith for payment? Not necessarily. He probably deposited this check with his own goldsmith. Every few weeks the goldsmiths met and exchanged notes to balance their accounts. They did not think of themselves as banks, but they functioned much the same way as banks do today.

Currency and check innovations made transactions easier, safer, and more convenient (especially payments involving great amounts or long distances). This benefited depositors, but led to an unexpected discovery for the goldsmiths themselves. Every day some people took money out of the goldsmith's vault, but others put gold and silver back in. The money coming in on an average day balanced out the money going out. The goldsmith's bank was busy, but his vault was not. Most of the gold and silver just sat there, collecting dust. New deposits took care of withdrawals, and only a little of the gold got any use.

Clever goldsmiths figured out that they could lend this dusty gold reserve and earn interest. No one would be the wiser and nobody's deposit would be threatened so long as day-to-day inflows and outflows roughly balanced. This discovery was the creation of the modern system of **fractional reserve banks.**

fractional reserve banks: modern system of banking where only a fraction of deposits are held as reserves, the rest are used for loans and investments.

Fractional Reserve Banking

Today's banks operate on the same principles as the gold warehouses. You deposit money in a bank and trust it will be there when you need it. But you know that the bank uses your deposit to make interest-producing loans. Mark Twain defined "faith" as believing what you know ain't so. If that is true, then banks run on faith. The normal balance of inflows and outflows is sufficient to deal with any problem—with faith!

What happens if all the bank's customers show up to withdraw their money at the same time? Such a bank run would close the bank since most of its funds are lent to others (often to the bank's own depositors). Many banks failed during the Great Depression when trust in the banks failed. Most banks these days are insured by a federal agency like the Federal Deposit Insurance Corporation (FDIC). The FDIC shuts down failing banks for a few days, then pays depositors from its insurance pool or arranges for a weak bank to merge with a healthier one. In either case the bank's depositors are protected.

Trust is the key to a fractional reserve bank. As long as each of us believes that the bank is sound—that deposits and withdrawals balance—the bank *is* sound, and any individual or small group can withdraw funds with no ill effects. If we lose faith in the bank, it must fail.

reserve requirement: fraction of bank deposits that must be held as reserves.

The Federal Reserve System regulates major banks in the United States (state governments regulate the rest). The FRS decides what types of loans banks can make, puts ceilings on interest paid to depositors, and limits bank investments. The FRS also sets the **reserve requirement** for member banks. The reserve requirement is different for different kinds of financial institutions and for different accounts, too. Demand deposits have a higher reserve requirement than time deposits, for example, since daily withdrawal and deposit needs are greater for checking accounts.

What happens when a fractional reserve bank receives a deposit? We can trace the path through Figure 9-2. Suppose that a new $100,000 demand

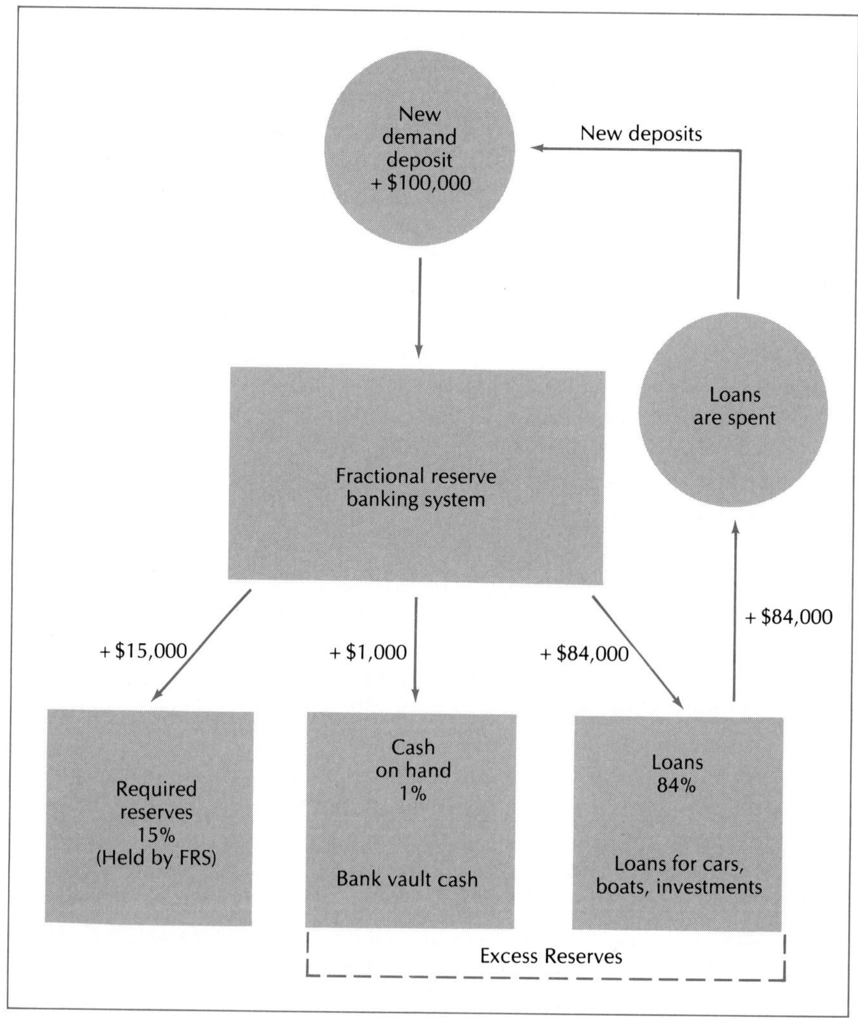

FIGURE 9-2 Fractional Reserve Banking. The $100,000 new deposit is first divided between required and excess reserves. Excess reserves can be held by the bank or used for loans. Loans, once spent, eventually reenter the bank as additional deposits.

deposit enters the bank. Part of the new deposit is set aside as required reserves. The example in the figure assumes a 15 percent reserve requirement on demand deposits, so \$15,000 is deposited with the FRS for this purpose. The remaining \$85,000 is put into the **excess reserves** account. This money is available for any income-producing activity allowed by law. Some of the money in the example is retained by the bank as cash on hand; that is, it is kept for potential future use. But profit-seeking banks use most of their excess reserves for loans. The bank in the figure lends out \$84,000 based on the \$100,000 deposit.

excess reserves: bank reserves over and above the reserve requirement; generally used for loans.

Demand deposits (money) create loans (credit). A \$100,000 new deposit generates up to \$85,000 in new loans, given a 15 percent reserve requirement. What happens to the loan money? Borrowers take the money and spend it. This \$85,000 eventually ends up with someone who takes it and deposits it in his or her bank, creating another new deposit.

How Banks Create Money

Hold on a second! Re-read that last paragraph. The bank starts out with a \$100,000 deposit and makes up to \$85,000 in loans. The loans end up as another bank deposit. We started out with \$100,000 and suddenly we have \$185,000. Where did the extra \$85,000 come from? Who created the extra cash?

Banks have the magical power to create money by making loans. The initial \$100,000 is still "in" the bank. The 15 percent reserve plus normal deposits guarantee that its owner can withdraw it at any time. The \$85,000 loan this makes possible is money in the same way. And the \$85,000 deposit makes even more loans and money possible.

Figure 9-3 shows the money creation game—and it is a mighty popular game. The \$100,000 initial deposit makes possible up to \$85,000 in loans that are spent and eventually deposited somewhere in the banking system. The \$85,000 new deposit is divided into required reserves (15 percent or \$12,750) and new loans (up to 85 percent or \$72,250). These new loans are spent, deposited, and the game continues. Fifteen percent of each new deposit goes to the FRS for required reserves. The remaining 85 percent can be used for loans. A small new deposit has a big multiplier effect on the supplies of money and credit.

How big is the **money multiplier?** Loans are like injections into the banking system, and required reserves are like leakages. The loan–deposit–loan process can be summarized by the following formula:

money multiplier: the relationship between a new deposit and change in the money supply.

$$\text{Change in money supply} = \frac{1}{\text{Reserve requirement}} \times \text{Initial deposit}$$

The initial deposit in this example is \$100,000. The reserve requirement is 15 percent or 0.15. The total change in the money supply is

$$\frac{1}{0.15} \times \$100{,}000 = \$667{,}000$$

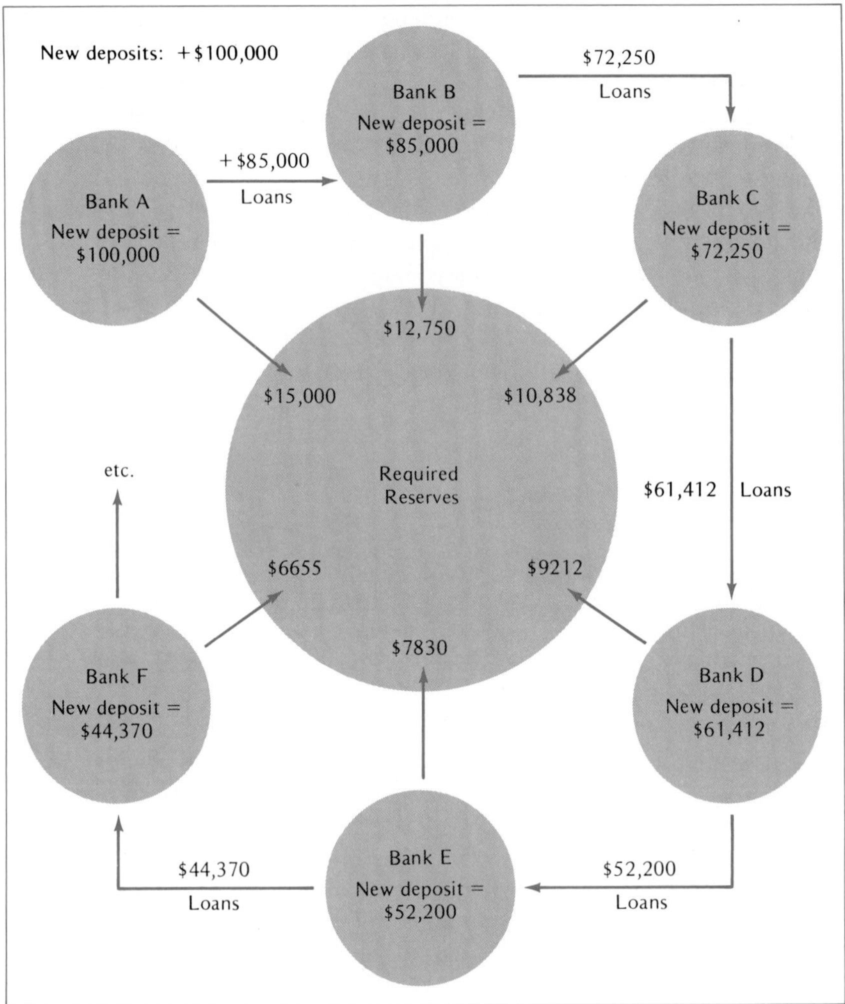

FIGURE 9-3 THE MONEY MULTIPLIER GAME. New deposits go from bank to bank, creating additional money and credit. The total effect is given by the money multiplier discussed in the text. The loan/deposit game ends when all of the original deposits have been placed in required reserves.

Where did all this money come from? The initial $100,000 deposit already existed, so the banking system must have created the remaining $567,000 by making loans. The money supply grows by up to $667,000 and the credit supply (supply of loans) rises by up to $567,000 when a new $100,000 enters the banking system with a 15 percent reserve requirement.

The money multiplier sets an upper limit on the amount of money and credit banks can create. The actual amount is usually much lower because banks hold some new deposits as excess reserves instead of making more loans. Not all money ends up in demand deposits, either. Some people hold large sums of cash or deposit the funds in other accounts. Money deposited in a savings account, for example, is not counted in M1 (so it has a smaller M1 money-supply effect), but it is subject to a smaller reserve requirement (so it has a bigger credit-supply effect). Some money even leaves the country, adding to the confusion. The money multiplier gives just a rough estimate of the result of money creation.

The money multiplier is a useful estimate of the outcome of monetary expansion, but it does not predict contractionary effects very well. What happens if $100,000 leaves the banking system? Money and credit supplies fall, but by far less than the money multiplier total. Banks use cash on hand and excess reserves to meet these needs rather than "destroying" money and credit.

Where do these new deposits come from, anyway? We know that banks create money through loans, but who starts the ball rolling? Look at a dollar bill again and you will think of the answer: the Federal Reserve System.

The Fed

The Federal Reserve System (affectionately called "the Fed" by economists and other romantics) was invented by Congress in 1913 to be a "Supreme Court of banking." Congress acted in response to the bank panic of 1907. The banking problem at the turn of the century was an inelastic money supply. Money and credit totals were fixed by the size of the national debt, not the money needs of the nation. What if banks needed more reserves to fight off runs or deal with bad loans? Sorry—nothing could be done and bank after bank failed. The FRS was given the power to regulate banks and create money when needed so that money and credit supplies could be adjusted to economic needs.

The Federal Reserve is a system of 12 banks that deal with monetary matters by geographical regions. Look at a Federal Reserve Note and you will see that it was issued by a specific regional bank: Boston, New York, Philadelphia, Cleveland, Richmond, Atlanta, Chicago, St. Louis, Kansas City, Minneapolis, Dallas, or San Francisco. Major monetary policies are set by the FRS Board of Governors based in Washington, D.C. The Fed facilitates check clearing among banks and lends money to needy members. This decentralized operation was designed to let money and credit expand and contract smoothly with economic activity.

Has the FRS been a success? Many banks have left the FRS because they feel unnecessarily constrained by its regulations. John Kenneth Galbraith points out that the FRS made little difference in its early days. The Fed failed to stop a bank panic in 1920–1921 and contributed to the banking collapse in the Great Depression. The Fed's role and performance will be discussed in more depth later.

The Fed's Board of Governors is appointed by the President, but they serve for a longer term than the President and cannot be easily removed. The FRS is independent of Congressional control, although it sometimes responds to political pressures.

The FRS is important because it controls money and credit supplies. Other banks create money with loans. Only the Fed, the "bankers' bank," can create money out of thin air. The Fed uses three tools to perform its monetary tasks: *open market operations*, *reserve requirements*, and the *discount rate*.

Open Market Operations

open market operations: FRS purchases and sales of bonds on the open market; used to regulate money and credit supplies.

The Fed changes money and credit supplies by buying and selling government bonds. These bond transactions are called **open market operations.** The Fed has purchased billions of dollars of government bonds over the years—it is the biggest single holder of the national debt. How does the Fed pay for the bonds it buys? By creating money—printing bills if it has to, or just attributing increased reserves to member bank accounts.

Here is how it works: Suppose the Fed's Open Market Committee thinks the economy needs more money and credit. They arrange to purchase $100,000 (or any other amount) of bonds on the open market. They pay for the bond by writing a $100,000 check on the FRS account, which the bond seller eventually deposits in a bank. The Fed attributes $100,000 more reserves to the bank's required reserve total and the transaction is complete. One hundred thousand dollars enters the system and the bank can start making new loans. The money multiplier begins. A $100,000 open market purchase increases the money supply by up to $667,000 and adds up to $567,000 more credit (assuming a 15 percent reserve requirement).

An open market sale has the opposite result. The Fed sells one of its bonds. The bond leaves the FRS vault, being replaced by the money that paid for it. This money is no longer part of the money supply because no one can spend it. An open market sale reduces the money supply and leaves banks with fewer reserves available for loans.

Open market operations are the Fed's main monetary tool. The FRS enters bond markets every week to buy and sell bonds. Stock and bond traders wait nervously for the Friday afternoon money supply announcement to see what the FRS is up to. The money multiplier results are made public, but the Fed's specific activities remain secret.

These days the Fed is having trouble controlling the money supply by means of open market operations. Control problems stem from two sources. First, many banks are not Fed members, so they have different reserve requirements and different money multipliers. Many loans and financial services are provided by nonbank firms like credit-card companies and brokerage houses. The Fed controls the biggest actors in this play, but not all of them.

The second problem source is that the Fed can increase or decrease bank reserves through open market actions, but it cannot control what the banks do with the reserves. The FRS can pump new reserves into the system, but the system stops there unless banks can find qualified borrowers ready to pay market interest rates. The result? Sometimes an open market sale has little effect on the money supply because all the money goes into excess reserves. But the money supply can rise when the Fed puts on the brakes with an open market sale if banks have used excess reserves to make more loans at the same time the Fed has sold bonds to tighten credit supplies.

A final problem is that money supply measures are becoming harder to interpret in our changing financial world. Fed watching is a nerve-racking profession.

Reserve Requirement Policy

The second FRS tool is the reserve requirement. The Fed indirectly affects money and credit supplies when it changes the reserve requirement. Suppose the Fed wants to expand money and credit supplies. A visible alternative to an open market purchase is to cut the reserve requirement. This does not change total reserves in the banking system; it allows banks to shift funds from required to loanable excess-reserve piles. Bank lending generally rises with the increased excess reserves.

The FRS restricts money growth when it raises the reserve requirement. Banks have to take loanable excess reserves and use them to meet the higher reserve requirement. Total reserves are not affected, but fewer loans are made and credit supplies tighten up.

Reserve requirement changes are powerful. A small change in reserve requirement affects billions of dollars of loans and reserves. Reserve requirement policy is infrequently used by the FRS. Sudden shifts in required reserves can catch bankers off guard. Some banks are hard pressed to dig up money to meet higher reserve requirements. A change in the reserve requirement means that the Fed is up to something important enough to shake a few trees in the financial forest.

Discount Rate Policy

The **discount rate** is the interest rate the Fed charges on loans to its member banks. The Fed is a "lender of last resort"—banks borrow from the FRS when they cannot otherwise meet reserve requirements or when they want to expand loans beyond current reserve limits. But the Fed is not the only place banks borrow. Banks with uncommitted reserves constantly lend to those with reserve shortages, too.

discount rate: interest rate on FRS loans to member banks; a signal of FRS policies.

Why is the discount rate so important? The Fed uses its discount rate to signal its intentions. The discount rate is the most visible sign of FRS policy swings. Suppose, for example, the FRS wants to announce an expansionary policy. It might begin by lowering the discount rate. This signal tells banks that the interest penalty for making too many loans is reduced. Bankers interpret the signal to mean that other policies—like open market purchases and reduced reserve requirements—are likely to follow, further increasing money and credit availability. Economists and business people interpret the discount rate drop to mean that the Fed is going to open the money spigot a bit; money should be less scarce and interest rates may drop when this happens.

An increase in the discount rate sends the opposite message. Higher discount rates signal banks to make fewer loans since open market sales or reserve requirement increases are likely to drain credit out of the banking system soon. Economists look for tight money and higher interest rates to result.

The discount rate is a little thing, but it gains stature because it signals the mighty Fed's intentions. The Fed's three tools exert considerable force on money, credit, interest rates, and consumer and business spending. Senator Hubert Humphrey once said that, "The guy who controls the money supply, he's in charge, and the rest of us are just playing ring-around-the-rosy." The game might be more complicated than this, but the Fed's ability to call the tune should not be ignored.

ECONOMIC CONTROVERSY:

Return to the Gold Standard?

What backs up U.S. currency? Faith and trust stand behind the monetary system these days. Many people do not think this is a sound foundation for our economy. They propose a return to the gold standard.

The United States left the gold standard in two steps. Anyone could trade $32.00 in coins or bills for an ounce of gold until 1933. Some coins were even made of gold. FDR changed all that—U.S. citizens could no longer trade paper for gold at the Treasury. Richard Nixon severed what was left of the gold link in 1971 when he ended the policy of backing dollars with gold in international transactions. The dollar began to "float"—the value of the dollar as defined by gold varied according to supply and demand forces.

Should we go back to a dollar defined by a fixed amount of gold? Let us hear both sides of the issue.

Return to the Gold Standard!

There are two important reasons for us to return to the gold standard; both involve inflation. Why do we have high inflation rates these days? One reason is simple psychology. Money loses its value when people do not believe in its value. If you think money is worthless—just filthy paper—you quickly trade it for valuable goods and services. What a swap! Paper for real assets! This drives up prices and reduces money's value. This psychological spiral can only end in two ways. Either we tie the dollar to gold, so that it really does have value, or we let the economy plunge into hyperinflation, panic, and eventual collapse. Which of these do you want?

Another reason we need a gold standard is to restrain the Federal Reserve. Right now these unelected money czars go around creating money right and left whether it needs to be created or not. Their uncontrolled acts pumped billions of unneeded dollars into the system during the 1970s. Too many dollars chasing too few goods can only cause prices to rise.

How would a gold standard check the Fed's actions? The money supply would be limited by the government's stock of gold. You could not issue more

TEST YOURSELF

Circle the best response to each of the following questions.

1. Which of the following items is/are accurately classified as money?

(X) an IOU signed by Ronald Reagan
(Y) demand-deposit balance
(Z) credit-card balance

a. all of the above
b. none of the above
c. only (X)
d. only (Y)
e. only (Z)

2. You observe that a 30-year house loan has a higher interest rate than a 2-year used car loan made on the same date. Which of the following best explains this interest rate difference?

a. the house loan has a higher time preference premium
b. lower inflation is expected over the term of the car loan
c. the car loan has a higher risk premium
d. the car loan has a higher cost premium
e. the house loan has a lower scarcity premium

3. The prime rate has just risen. Which of the following events would accurately explain this change?

(X) FRS has acted to tighten the credit supply
(Y) inflation is expected to increase in the future
(Z) prime interest rate loans are now guaranteed by the federal government, increasing the risk premium

a. all of the above
b. none of the above
c. (X) or (Y)
d. (X) or (Z)
e. (Y) or (Z)

4. The FRS has just made an open market purchase of $50 billion. The reserve requirement is 20 percent. Assume full money multiplier effects. At the end of the process, which of the following changes should be observed?

(X) money supply rises by $250 billion
(Y) credit supply rises by $200 billion
(Z) bank required reserves rise by $50 billion

a. all of the above

b. none of the above
c. only (X) above
d. only (Y) above
e. (X) and (Y)

5. The banking system currently has $100 billion in total deposits. The reserve requirement is 20 percent. Banks lend all excess reserves. Now suppose that the FRS cuts the reserve requirement to 10 percent. Assume the full money multiplier effect. This policy results in:

(X) money supply growing by $100 billion
(Y) credit supply growing by $100 billion
(Z) total required reserves growing by $10 billion

a. all of the above
b. none of the above
c. only (X)
d. only (Y)
e. (X) and (Y)

SUGGESTIONS FOR FURTHER READING

John Kenneth Galbraith has written an interesting and understandable history of this whole money business: *Money: Whence It Came, Where It Went* (Boston: Houghton Mifflin Company, 1975). Lawrence W. Ritter and William L. Silber have written an amusing little book that puts cash in perspective. It is simply called *Money* (New York: Basic Books, 1981). The gold standard is the topic of Tom Bethell's "Hard Money Men" in *Harper's* (February, 1981). This issue is further debated in an interview contained in "Should We (and Could We) Return to the Gold Standard?" (*New York Times*, September 6, 1981) and in "The Point of Linking the Dollar to Gold" by Arthur B. Laffer and Charles W. Kadlec (*Wall Street Journal*, October 13, 1981).

10

CREDIT MARKETS AND MONETARY POLICY

Preview

How do financial markets work? What is the difference between the stock market and credit markets?

How are interest rates set?

What determines the demand and supply of credit?

How does inflation get built into the interest rate?

What is disintermediation and why is it important?

Do government deficits affect interest rates?

How does monetary policy work?

What are the advantages and disadvantages of monetary tools?

Are interest rate ceilings a good idea?

SOMEBODY ONCE ASKED Willie Sutton why he robbed banks. "Because that's where the money is," he replied. Economists study banks for the same reason.

But banks should not be viewed as safe brick bins where money is locked away. It is better to think of a bank as a gateway to the carnival of financial markets.

The Stock Market

Pick up a newspaper and you will discover a merry-go-round world of financial markets hidden in the dreary columns of the business section. Financial markets are places where money is exchanged for credit, assets, and commodities. Speculators try to profit by guessing which way the market is headed. Savers hope to gain a healthy return on their financial investment. Others use these markets to hedge against future events.

credit markets: markets where loanable funds are exchanged.

This chapter concentrates on **credit markets** where loanable funds are exchanged. This market is a key to all the others, so our preoccupation with credit is justified. But, to begin with, let us look at three other important financial markets: stocks, commodities, and bonds.

stock markets: markets where shares of ownership in corporations are exchanged.

Stock markets, like the New York Stock Exchange on Wall Street, are places where shares in corporations are bought and sold. Stock shares represent partial ownership in a corporation.

equity: ownership of an asset.

Mike's Livestock, Inc. (a corporation that buys sheep and sells deer) issued 1,000 shares of stock when it was formed. Why did it sell stock? The people who originally bought the stock provided the cash Mike needed to get his firm rolling. Sales of **equity** shares are an alternative to borrowing to obtain investment cash.

dividends: corporate profits paid to stockholders.

capital gains: profits from the sale of assets.

Why would anyone want to buy corporate shares? There are two ways to gain from stock ownership. If you own one share of Mike's Livestock, then you theoretically own one-one thousandth of the business and have a claim on one-one thousandth of Mike's annual profits. Some of these profits are distributed to shareholders as **dividends.** There is no guarantee of profit or that the board of directors will vote to pay dividends (they might use profits to expand the business instead). Dividends are not as certain as interest payments.

Capital gains are the second road to stock market profit. If Mike's Livestock is profitable, you might be able to sell your stock for more than you paid for it. This gain is also never guaranteed, so stock investments are riskier than some other financial investments, but the profit potential is greater, too.

Who owns stock? Most people imagine stock traders as rich Diamond Jim Brady types, with pinstripe suits, fat cigars, and three-martini lunches. The true picture is less gaudy. Millions of people own stock directly and even more own it through pension plans and life insurance policies. Almost everyone has a stake in the stock market in some way. That is why stock prices are in every newspaper and are announced frequently on television and radio. Remember what happened in the 1930s when the stock market crashed!

Why do stock prices rise and fall? The fate of an individual company's stock depends much on its management and profit prospects. Forecasting the stock market is tough because so many people buy and sell stocks for so many different reasons. Many economists focus on the link between stocks and interest rates. Investors can either buy risky stocks or earn more certain interest returns. They sell stocks and put their money in financial institutions when interest rates are high. They take money out of banks and use it to buy the substitute stocks when interest rates fall. This produces an inverse relationship between stock prices and interest rates. Many people buy stocks "on margin" with borrowed money, making the interest rate–stock price link even more direct.

The relationship between interest rates and stock prices frequently explains trends on Wall Street. Three other theories have their proponents, too. Chart-keepers think the market runs in cycles. They try to spot turning points by keeping accurate charts of stock prices. The market psychologists view stock traders as pathological beings. They try to sense "the mood of the market" and respond accordingly. Expectations and social relations figure prominently in their analysis. Finally, many people think the market is a crap shoot. The **random walk theory** holds that there is no systematic relationship between stocks and the real world.

random walk theory: the theory that changing stock market prices have no systematic cause.

Which theory is best? Do not bet the rent on any of them. The interest rate hypothesis is based on sound logic, but the random walk theory works just as well in the real world.

Commodity Markets

Futures contracts for things like wheat, soybeans, silver, orange juice concentrate, frozen pork bellies, and even Treasury bills are exchanged on the Chicago Board of Trade and other commodities markets. People buy futures contracts for two reasons. Some people use them to hedge against uncertainty. A wheat farmer, for example, might sell a futures contract for his wheat now so that he is sure of the price he will get so that he will not have to worry about price fluctuations come harvest time. He agrees to supply a fixed quantity of wheat on a specific date for a price he agrees to today. Speculators try to guess which way prices will go and bet accordingly. **Commodity markets** are fast-moving and risky, but they play an important role in stabilizing markets for minerals and agricultural goods.

futures contracts: contracts promising future delivery of an asset at a set price.

commodity markets: markets where futures contracts for agricultural, mineral, and financial assets are exchanged.

What determines the price of a commodity contract? Interest rates and real market actions have a lot to do with it. An unseasonable frost in Florida, for example, sends the price of orange juice concentrate futures sky high because falling supply might bid up the price of oranges. There is direct relationship between the price of a good and the price of its futures contract. But psychology gets involved, too. Orange juice futures often rise when it snows in Chicago, for example, even if it's sunny and warm in orange-growing Miami. Commodity traders "think snow" and it changes their behavior in irrational ways.

Bond Markets

bond market: market where bonds (IOUs) are bought and sold.

The **bond market** is part of the credit market. We look at it here because bonds have a vocabulary all their own. A bond is just an IOU—a promise to pay a specific sum on a certain date in the future. People who sell bonds are borrowing money by selling their IOUs. Bond buyers are lenders who expect to be repaid when the bond comes due.

Interest is paid on bonds through a discount. Here is how a typical bond transaction might work. The Noah County School Board needs to raise money to buy economics books. They float a bond issue to get the money. Their bond is a promise to pay $1,000 one year from today.

How much would you pay for the Noah County bond? One thousand dollars? There is no profit in paying face value for the bond—you would give up $1,000 and get back $1,000 a year later. That is a zero interest loan. Would you buy the bond for $900? Here you would lend $900 and get back your $900 plus $100 interest. That is an interest rate of $100/$900 or 11 percent.

The interest rate and the bond's price vary inversely. Suppose the bond's price drops to $800. The $800 loan and $1000 total repayment means you would earn $200/$800 or 25 percent interest on the deal! Lower bond prices mean higher interest returns. Higher bond prices force down interest payments.

Bonds start life raising money for governments and corporations, but they are traded again and again. Bonds earn a capital gain when interest rates fall because the bond can be sold for more than it originally cost. Bond traders lose when interest rates rise because the selling price of already issued bonds drops.

There are many bond markets: short-term, long-term, business, and government bonds are all actively traded. Do you want to know what is happening to interest rates? The bond market is the best place to look for the answer.

Credit Markets

federal funds market: market for short-term government securities.

mortgage credit market: market for long-term loans used for housing loans.

Credit markets are places, like the bond market, where loans are made and credit exchanged. We can look at the whole market or focus on submarkets like the **federal funds market** where short-term government securities are traded or the **mortgage credit market** where interest rates for home loans are set.

The most important reason for studying the credit market is that it sets the interest rate. Why is the interest rate so important? Firms considering inventory or plant expansion compare potential profits to interest cost before they make a decision. Consumers decide whether to spend or save (and how much to spend) based on loan costs and the interest rate on savings accounts. Interest is a big cost for government, too, so the interest rate affects fiscal policy. Interest rates also help determine foreign exchange rates (as we will see in Chapter 14), so international trade hangs in the balance.

Who sets the interest rate? A few rates are determined by law or rule (interest rate ceilings, for example, fix the rate on passbook savings accounts). Most interest rates, however, fluctuate with supply and demand. To see what makes interest rates tick we must first look at credit demand and supply.

The Demand for Credit

Three groups dominate the demand side of the credit market: consumers, businesses, and governments. Consumers borrow to buy the goods and services they want now. They borrow for houses, cars, education, and many other things. Businesses borrow to finance investments like trucks and factories or to pay for inventories.

Governments borrow for equally varied ends. The federal government's borrowing goes for defense spending, social programs, and yes, to pay the interest on old debt. The government also acts as a conduit to enable others to borrow. Federal agencies borrow funds and then lend them to small businesses, farmers, low-income home buyers, and others. These people get better interest rates because they have access to the government's low-risk, highly efficient bond market.

State and local governments borrow to build schools, bridges, and highways. Some of this money ends up with private borrowers, too. Income from state and local interest is not subject to federal income tax, so governments get lower interest rates than private borrowers. Governments supply funds raised this way to private firms as an inducement to build and hire workers in their area. Governments are active in credit markets, but a lot of government borrowing ends up in private hands.

What determines the amount of credit demanded today? All kinds of things enter the borrowing decision. We can, however, whittle this list down to four main determinants:

1. INTEREST RATES. Interest rates are the cost of a loan, so desired borrowing is inversely related to the interest rate, all else being equal. Business firms borrow more, for example, at low interest rates than when interest costs are high.

The inverse relationship between interest and credit demand is complicated by two problems. The first is that government borrowing sometimes increases along with the interest rate. The national debt, as you read in Chapter 8, is continually refinanced. The interest on old debt is paid by new borrowing. High interest rates increase this expense, forcing the federal government to borrow even more to pay high interest costs. This vicious cycle keeps government borrowers busy even when rates are high.

The second problem is that borrowers often respond to real, instead of nominal, interest rates. Suppose that the nominal interest rate rises from 10 to 15 percent at the same time that the expected inflation rate jumps from 5 to 10 percent. Will people borrow less at the high 15 percent rate? Borrowing declines if loan-seekers respond to nominal rates. But the real interest rate has remained the same—5 percent—in this example. Borrowers and lenders still get the same real deal.

2. INFLATION AND INFLATION EXPECTATIONS. Inflation is an important fact to borrowers. First, higher prices mean that more money must be borrowed to buy cars and houses or to pay tuition bills. This forges a direct link between inflation and credit demand.

Inflation expectations are important, too. Borrowers gain from unexpectedly high inflation. People who anticipate higher inflation borrow now to lock in low real rates and purchase goods before prices rise. Borrowing declines when inflation is expected to slow.

3. INCOME AND INCOME EXPECTATIONS. Consumers and firms borrow more when they foresee rising incomes. Consumers borrow when income goes up and they can afford higher monthly car or mortgage payments. Businesses borrow to expand production and sales when income and product demands rise. Both groups "pull in their horns" and borrow less when unemployment rises or they anticipate hard times. Neither consumers nor firms want to be saddled with loan obligations during recessions.

This inverse relationship between income and credit demand does not extend to the government. Governments borrow less during boom times because tax revenues increase and transfer needs fall, thereby shrinking the deficit. Government borrowing increases during economic busts because spending needs go up and tax collections decline. We will assume in the next few chapters that income and credit demand rise and fall together because of the power of consumer and business borrowing. But we cannot forget that government actions weaken this relationship.

4. GOVERNMENT POLICIES. Government is such a big part of the credit market that a little government push brings a big interest rate jump. Credit demand changes with fiscal policies (as when Congress votes for higher or lower deficits) or when government lending programs, like Farm Home Loans, change. Credit demand depends on state and local government borrowing policies, too. The Washington Public Power Supply System (a group of public utilities) borrowed over $5 billion dollars in the early 1980s to build power plants, for example.

The Credit Demand Curve

All this information is packed into the credit demand (CD) curve shown in Figure 10-1. This curve maps the relationship between the interest rate and quantity of credit demand (the dollar amount of desired loans). A change in the interest rate brings a movement along the CD curve. Consumers, businesses,

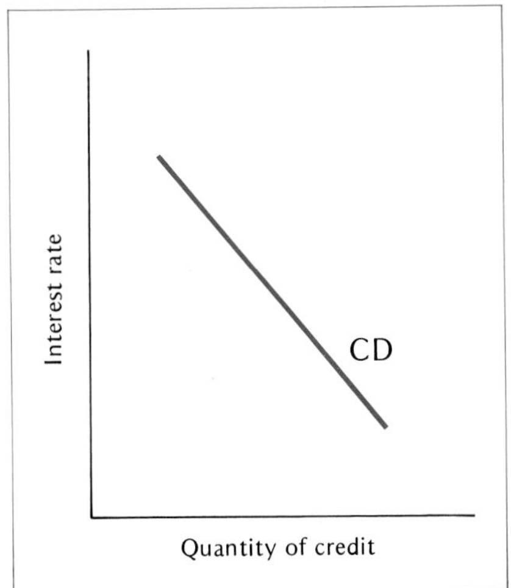

FIGURE 10-1 THE CREDIT DEMAND CURVE. The quantity of credit demanded rises with lower interest rates. Changes in government policies, income, and inflation expectations shift the credit demand curve.

and many governments seek fewer borrowed funds when interest costs are high. These groups want to borrow more at low interest rates.

The credit demand curve shifts whenever something besides the interest rate moves to change borrowing plans. An increase in credit demand (the CD curve shifts out and to the right) might result if:

- Consumers anticipate an increase in inflation rates;
- Unemployment rates fall, giving consumers more income;
- Firms borrow to expand stores in anticipation of higher future sales;
- Congress votes increased deficit spending for social programs.

Credit demand falls (the CD curve shifts back to the left) if something besides the interest rate changes to reduce intended borrowing. Credit demand would fall if:

- Inflation rates fall, reducing both the need and the desire to borrow;
- Unemployment rates rise; jobless workers buy fewer new cars and so do not need additional car loans;
- Businesses anticipate lower Christmas sales, so borrow less for inventory purchases;
- Congress finally balances the budget and government borrowing thus falls.

Demand is not the only side to any market, so let us move on to explore credit supply.

The Supply of Credit

To find the supply of credit we have to ride with Willie Sutton to the bank. Credit exists because many people want to save (put funds in the bank) and lend. What determines the amount of credit available?

1. **INTEREST RATES.** Savers and lenders react to interest rates. Interest is, after all, the payment lenders receive. Why part with your cash if the interest rate is low? People and banks hang on to their funds at low interest rates, but supply more loans when interest returns are high.

2. **INFLATION AND INFLATION EXPECTATIONS.** Inflation hits the supply side of this market, too. Unexpectedly high inflation hurts lenders, while unexpectedly low inflation makes savers better off. Fewer loans are offered when inflation is high because rising prices shrink real interest returns. Lower inflation rates temporarily boost real returns, so credit supply increases. Credit supplies are inversely related to inflation rates.

3. **SAVINGS.** Saving is the credit supply genesis. Higher saving rates boost credit supply. What determines saving behavior? Income is one factor—savings accounts grow when income rises and fall when unemployed people withdraw funds to pay the rent. Expectations are another variable. Americans who fear the social security system's collapse save more for their own retirement, for example. Tax laws are important, too. Congress enacted several tax expenditures in 1981 to encourage consumers to save instead of spend.

4. **FEDERAL RESERVE POLICIES.** Last—but not least—on this list is the Federal Reserve. The Fed uses its powerful tools to manipulate the credit supply. Open market operations, reserve requirement policies, and the discount rate all affect the availability of credit.

The Credit Supply Curve

The credit supply (CS) curve (shown in Figure 10-2) maps the relationship between the interest rate and the quantity of credit supplied. Higher interest rates bring more loanable funds to the market. Banks want to make more loans with higher returns. Savers shift money from stocks to bank accounts when interest rates are high, further boosting the credit supply. Lower interest rates reduce the amount of money lenders offer.

What makes the credit supply curve shift? The credit supply increases when anything except a change in the interest rate brings more loanable funds to the market. The CS curve shifts to the left if:

- The FRS makes an open market purchase, cuts the reserve requirement, or lowers the discount rate;
- New types of savings accounts attract higher saving rates;
- Lower inflation is anticipated.

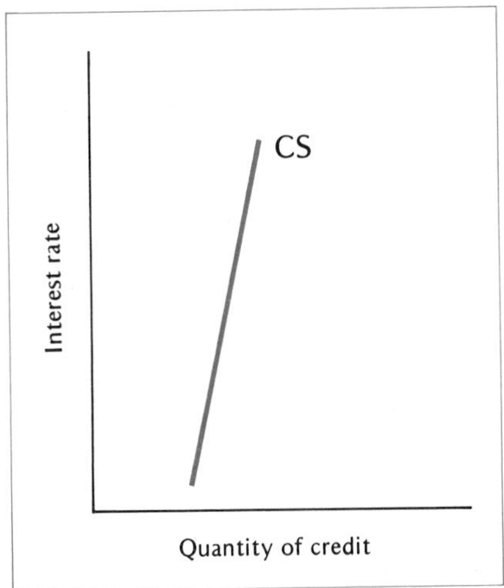

FIGURE 10-2 THE CREDIT SUPPLY CURVE. More loans are available at higher interest rates. The policies of the FRS, savings rates, and inflation expectations shift the credit supply curve.

The credit supply falls (the CS curve shifts back and to the right) if something besides the interest rate changes to discourage lending. The CS curve falls if:

- Savers expect higher inflation, so withdraw their money and spend it;
- The FRS makes an open market sale, raises the reserve requirement, or increases the discount rate;
- A new tax on interest income discourages saving.

The FRS is the most important actor in this monetary play, because small Fed movements are magnified through the money multiplier. But the Fed is not the whole show. Many of Ronald Reagan's supply-side policies were meant to increase credit supply by encouraging saving. It takes time for higher savings to accumulate and have a big effect on credit supply, however.

The Credit Market at Work

Demand and supply come together in the credit market shown in Figure 10-3. This figure shows a single credit market, but there are really many markets for different types of loans, all carefully intertwined. The forces of supply and demand we will explore in this single market show up in each of the many submarkets.

The first job of any market is to find equilibrium. This market clears at an interest rate of 14 percent. The quantity of credit supplied at this interest rate just equals the number of loans demanded.

Shortage and surplus force the market to this equilibrium. Suppose, for example, that interest rates were above equilibrium—at 18 percent in the figure. Banks and savers offer many loans at this high rate, but few consumers

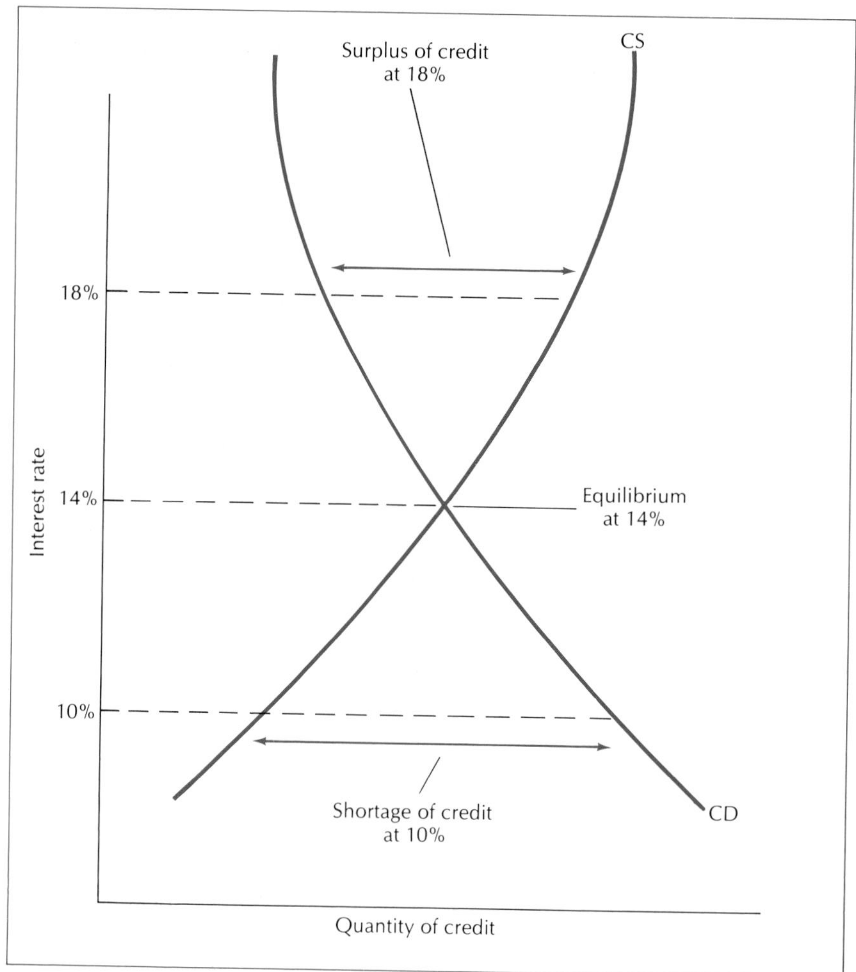

FIGURE 10-3 THE CREDIT MARKET. Credit demand and supply determine market interest rates. The forces of shortage and surplus bring the market to equilibrium.

or businesses want to borrow. The surplus of funds puts bankers in a bind. They need to make loans to pay the interest on their deposits. How should they attract more borrowers? They chop interest charges! Lower interest rates reduce the quantity of credit supplied (a movement along the CS curve) but increase the number of loans demanded (a movement along the CD curve). The surplus of credit shrinks until equilibrium is found.

The force of shortage works when interest rates are below equilibrium. Many people want to borrow at 10 percent interest, but few folks want to lend. Banks cannot please all their loan customers. How should they allocate their scarce funds? They lend to only low-risk customers and raise interest charges. Higher interest rates make a greater supply of credit available (a movement along the CS curve) and reduce the number of loan applicants (a movement along the CD curve). The shortage shrinks until interest rates hit equilibrium.

Once at equilibrium, the interest rate stays put until an outside force changes either supply or demand. What can happen to alter interest rates? Figures 10-4 and 10-5 show two possibilities.

Federal government deficits in the $100 billion range increased credit demand in 1982. The CD curve shifted out to reflect the higher government borrowing. A shortage of credit at 16 percent was solved by rising interest rates. More credit was supplied, but less demanded as interest rates increased. The result? Figure 10-4 shows that this demand-pull force bid up interest rates and increased the amount of credit exchanged. The same market result occurs when higher incomes and changing expectations produce an increase in the demand for credit.

The Federal Reserve fights high interest rates on the supply side of the credit market. An open market purchase increases credit supply through the money multiplier. The CS curve shifts out as Figure 10-5 shows. Now there is a surplus of loanable funds at the original interest rate. Banks and other financial institutions cut interest rates to make loans (this happens while the money multiplier is shifting credit supply). Lower interest costs attract more borrowers (a movement along the CD curve); the shortage disappears as the market moves to a new equilibrium.

Why does the FRS not keep interest rates low all of the time? Part of the problem is that monetary policies do not always work as efficiently as Figure 10-5 indicates. Sometimes expectations get in the way. Figure 10-6 shows an

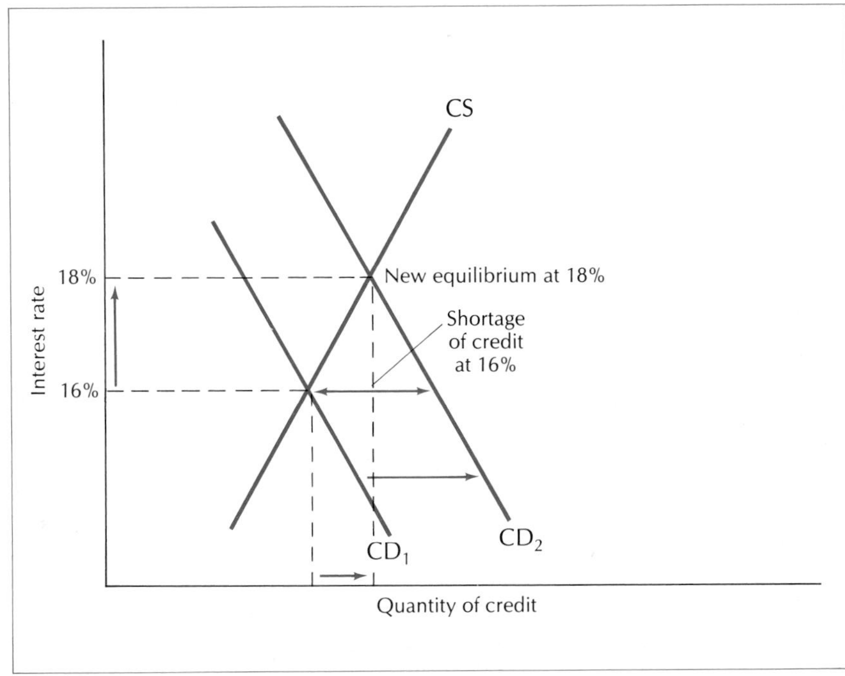

FIGURE 10-4 DEFICITS AND THE CREDIT MARKET. Deficits mean the government must enter credit markets, thereby increasing credit demand. Higher interest rates are the result.

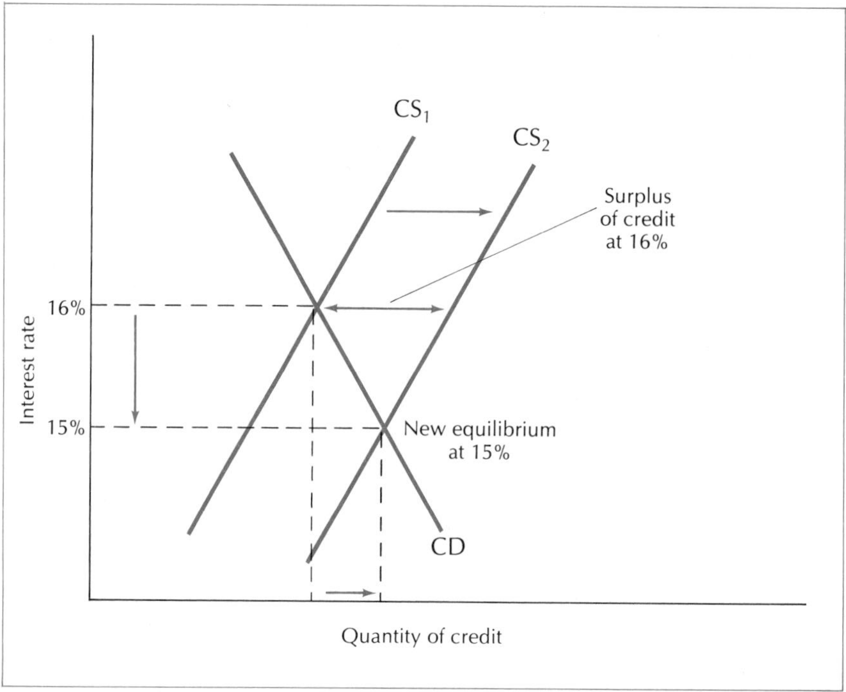

FIGURE 10-5 AN INCREASE IN CREDIT SUPPLY. An open-market purchase by the FRS increases the credit supply. Interest rates are bid down by the resulting credit surplus.

alternative result. The Fed's open market purchase still shifts the CS curve, but in this instance borrowers interpret the increased money supply as a harbinger of higher inflation rates. Credit demand rises on the expectation of inflation. The result? More credit is exchanged, but the interest rate does not fall and it could even increase. Expectations are an important part of any economic policy.

The Inflation Premium

The last chapter introduced the notion of the inflation premium: interest rates rise and fall with the expected inflation rate. This idea makes sense, but how does it happen? Who sets the inflation premium?

The inflation premium is the result of supply and demand forces illustrated in Figure 10-7. Suppose that yesterday's prime interest rate was 16 percent. This rate was consistent with scarcity and expected inflation rates. But things are different today. This morning's announcement of a higher Producer Price Index increases inflationary expectations.

Lender reactions are easy to predict. Higher future inflation rates shrink the real return of a 16 percent interest rate. They are less willing to lend at 16 percent (the CS curve shifts back as fewer loans are offered). Borrowers react in the opposite way. Inflation reduces the real burden of repaying a loan. It makes sense to borrow now, buy at today's prices and repay the loan with

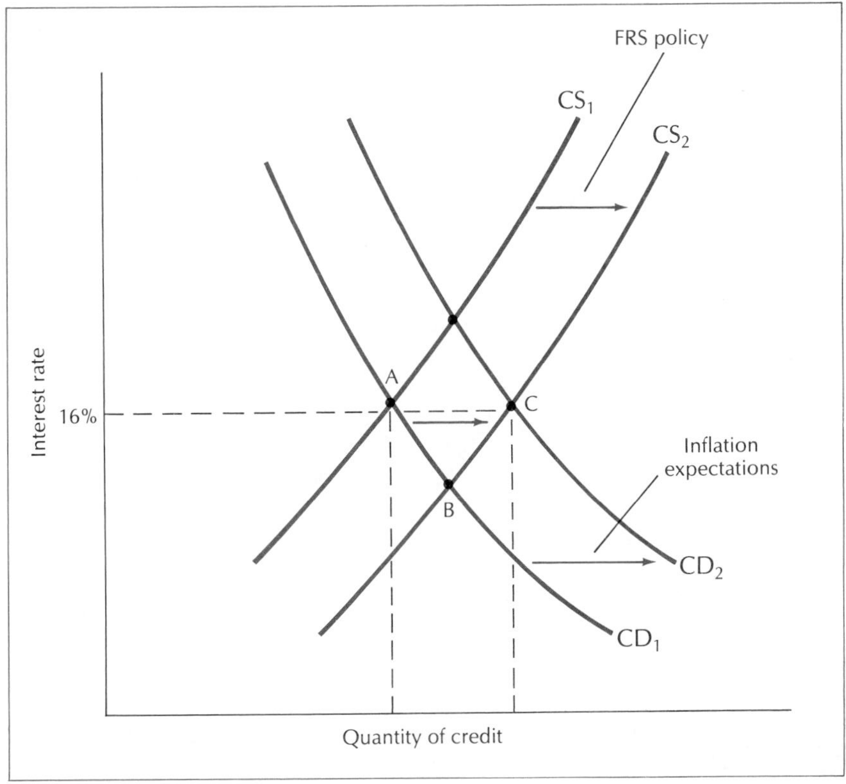

FIGURE 10-6 THE FRS POLICY AND EXPECTATIONS. The open-market purchase fails to force interest rates down when borrowers interpret FRS actions as an indicator of higher future prices. The credit demand curve shifts due to higher inflationary expectations. Instead of moving from A to B and lowering interest rates, expectations force the market to C.

inflation-reduced future dollars. Credit demand rises (the CD curve shifts to the right in the figure).

What is the result of this combination of events? Higher credit demand coupled with reduced credit supply serves to bid up interest rates. Expectations of future inflation boost interest rates today.

Who wins and loses in this market? If borrowers and lenders have the same expectations—and both groups guess correctly—no one is better or worse off. The higher nominal interest rate reflects higher inflation atop a constant real interest rate. The winners and losers discussed in Chapter 4 show up if borrower and lender expectations differ or if they guess wrong and are surprised by the true inflation rate.

High Interest Rates and Disintermediation

Interest rates were high in the late 1970s and early 1980s. The Prime interest rate, which averaged about five percent in the 1960s, went over 20 percent several times in this period (and the Prime is the lowest interest rate a bank offers!).

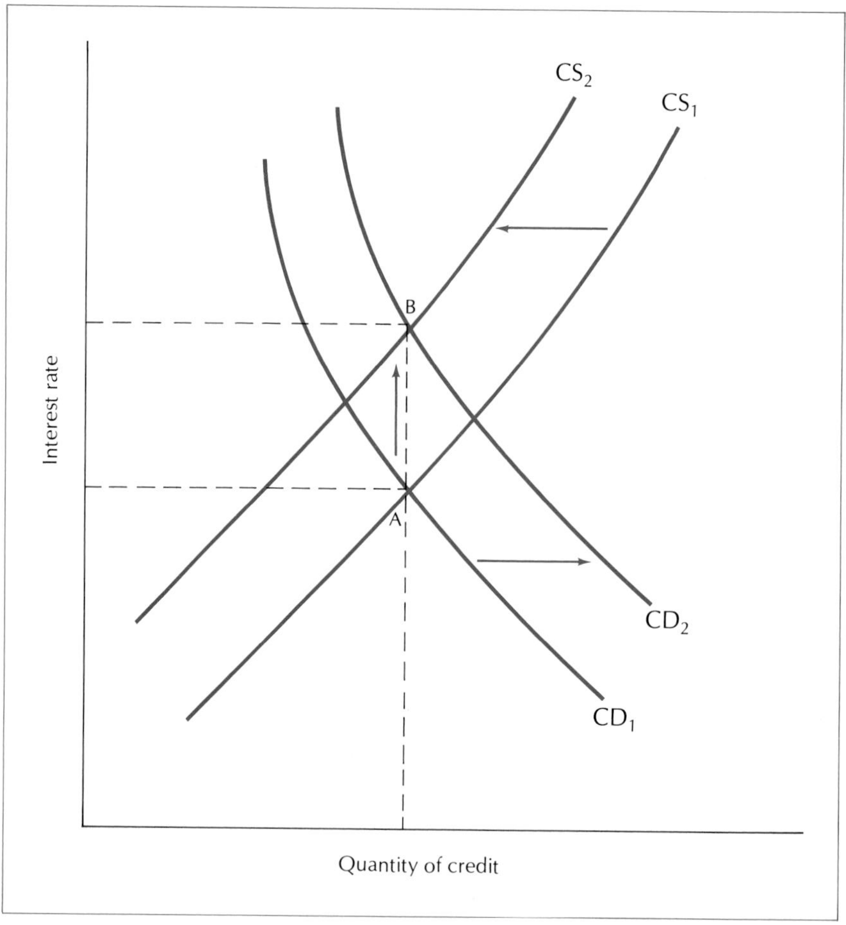

FIGURE 10-7 THE INFLATION PREMIUM. Inflation reduces credit supply and increases the demand for loans. The inflation premium results from these market forces. The credit market starts at A and ends up with higher interest rates at B.

Why were interest rates so high? You have already seen a few of the reasons. High inflation rates during the period reduced credit supply and increased demand forcing rates higher. Massive federal government deficits increased credit demand, too. And Federal Reserve policies kept credit supplies low in an attempt to fight inflation. Where could interest rates go but up?

High interest rates are bad enough, but their problems compound when combined with interest rate ceilings. Federal Reserve rules put a lid on the interest rate banks can pay their depositors. Checking account balances at most banks earn no interest at all. Savings account balances are limited to about 5 to 6 percent at commercial and savings banks. But interest returns on bonds and Treasury bills are not limited by anything except the forces of supply and demand.

Which would you rather have—a 5½ percent return or 15 percent on your money? Many people in the 1970s answered this question just as you did. They pulled their cash out of commercial banks and savings and loan associations and bought government bonds and money market funds. Economists call this movement out of financial intermediaries and directly into unrestricted credit markets **disintermediation.**

disintermediation: situation where savers take funds out of banks and deposit them directly in credit markets to avoid interest rate ceilings.

Disintermediation raised havoc with the financial system. Money flowed out of banks where small businesses and home purchasers borrow and into credit markets where governments and corporations seek loans. New home construction ground to a standstill because banks did not have money to lend. Housing is an important part of the economy, so the effect of disintermediation spread to such industries as lumber, plumbing, furniture, and carpet. Workers and business owners around the economy suffered the home-buyers' blues.

The FRS reacted to the disintermediation problem by allowing banks to offer higher interest rates on certain kinds of deposits (such as on six-month $10,000 certificates). This helped savings and loans attract some of the funds they had lost, but at a high interest cost to the banks. Bankers found themselves paying 14 percent for new deposits while receiving 8 percent interest on loans made just a few years before. Bank profits plunged. The banking system still has not fully recovered from disintermediation and its side effects.

Investment and the Credit Market

So far we have focused on the credit market's role in setting interest rates. One reason for this emphasis is the importance of interest rates to investment decisions.

The interest rate affects investment decisions in two ways. First, the interest rate is the cost of borrowed funds. Loans finance most business investments, so net profits vary inversely with the interest rate. A fleet of new trucks that makes profit sense at a 12-percent interest might be unprofitable at a higher 15-percent borrowing cost.

The interest rate is also an opportunity cost. Firms that invest in machines or new factories give up the money they could have earned if the same funds had been invested in bonds or bank accounts. Does it make sense to build a new store that returns 14 percent on investment if safer government securities pay 16 percent? No. The interest rate sets a lower limit on investment projects. No profit-seeker builds a factory or buys a machine if he or she can get a better return from the bank.

Business investments are made according to the following rule:

> Make *all investments that have an expected rate of return greater than or equal to the interest rate on securities of the same period (time frame) and risk.* Reject *all investments that have an expected return less than the interest return on securities of the same period and risk.*

investment rule: firms invest in projects with expected rates of return greater than or equal to the interest rates of bonds of equal period and risk.

This **investment rule** makes both intuitive and business sense. If the current interest rate is 14 percent (for corporate bonds of a given period and risk), then smart businesses invest only if they can beat this return—the list of profitable investments is limited by this interest cost. The investment list grows shorter when interest rates rise. Fewer investments pass the profit test at 18 percent interest. Lower interest costs, on the other hand, increase the number of investments businesses consider profitable.

Investment spending varies inversely with the interest rate; this relationship is an important one in macroeconomics. Interest rates are not the only thing that affects investment, of course. You learned in Chapter 6 that expectations, the health of the economy, tax policies, and many other variables enter the investment choice.

Investment spending is the key link between the credit market and the RGNP market. The credit market determines the interest rate. The interest rate affects investment decisions. Investment spending alters aggregate demand in the short run and changes aggregate supply in the long run. Investment spending links money and credit with aggregate demand and supply through the **monetary transmission mechanism.** Let us see why this is important.

monetary transmission mechanism: the link between changes in interest rates and investment spending; the key to monetary policy.

Monetary Policy

Federal Reserve policies like open market purchases, reserve requirement movements, and discount rate changes alter interest rates and, through the monetary transmission mechanism, influence aggregate demand. Here is an example of an **expansionary monetary policy.**

expansionary monetary policy: FRS policies that increase credit supply to stimulate aggregate demand.

Suppose FRS leaders decide it is time to stimulate aggregate demand. Expansionary policies like open market purchases, lower reserve requirements, or a cut in the discount rate have the effects shown in Figure 10-8. Any of these actions increase the credit supply, shifting the CS curve to the left. The Fed has created a surplus of credit and, all else—especially expectations—being equal, interest rates fall to relieve the market of surplus funds.

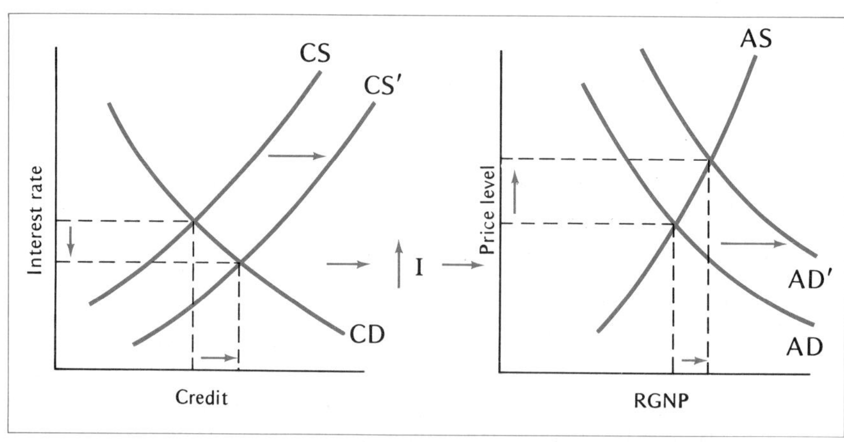

FIGURE 10-8 EXPANSIONARY MONETARY POLICY. The policies of the FRS increase the credit supply, bidding down interest rates. Investment spending rises and aggregate demand increases. Demand-pull inflation results.

Lower interest rates lengthen the list of profitable investments. Firms crank up their investment programs. Higher investment spending increases aggregate demand through the spending multiplier. Demand-pull inflation is the result, with higher RGNP but more inflation. The FRS policy has reduced unemployment (just as an increase in government spending or a tax cut would) through interest rates and investment spending. Aggregate supply rises in the long run (not shown in the figure) as investment spending adds to capacity.

We can summarize this process using a chain reaction notation:

Expansionary Monetary Policy
Open market purchases → ↑ CS → ↓ i → ↑ I → ↑ AD → ↑ RGNP → ↑ Price level
Long run: rising AS

where "i" stands for the interest rate and "I" means investment spending.

Expansionary monetary policy is an attractive option. Aggregate demand rises in the short run, boosting RGNP and fighting unemployment. Increased investment spending pours the foundation for future aggregate supply growth. The outlook for the long run is the balanced growth of aggregate demand and aggregate supply, with rising income and more stable prices. This is an appealing economic picture.

contractionary monetary policy: FRS policies that reduce credit supply to reduce aggregate demand.

Contractionary monetary policy uses open market sales, higher reserve requirements, or an increased discount rate to reduce aggregate demand. An example of a contractionary FRS policy is shown in Figure 10-9.

An open market sale reduces the money and credit supplies. Interest rates are bid up by the shortage of credit that results. Higher interest rates

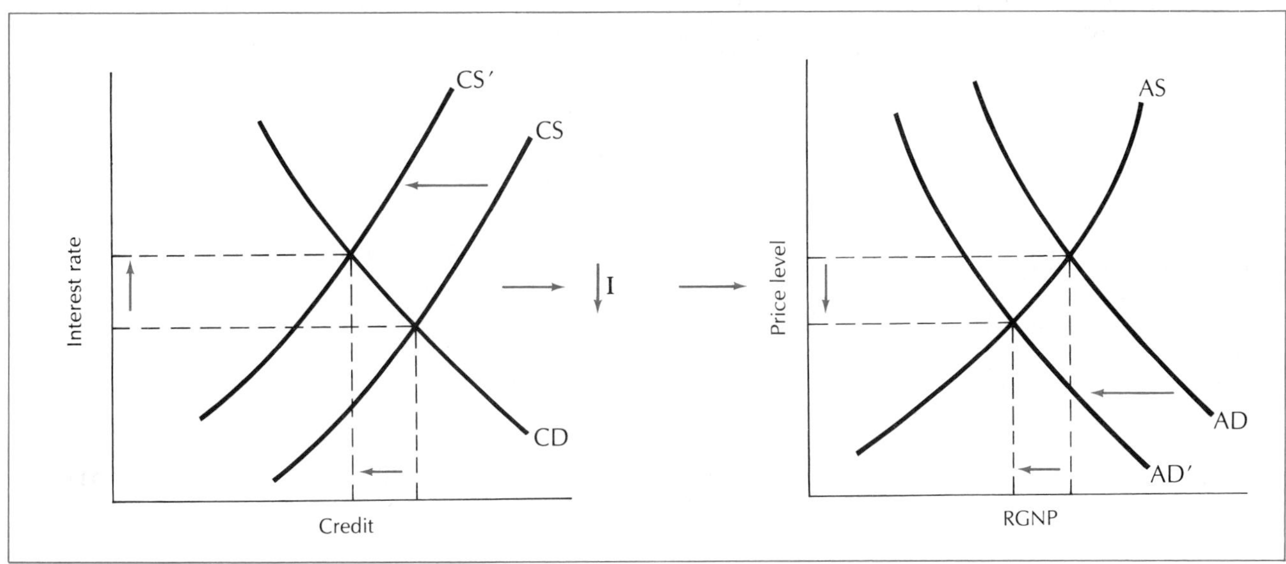

FIGURE 10-9 CONTRACTIONARY MONETARY POLICY. A contractionary FRS policy reduces the credit supply, bids up interest rates, and discourages investment. As a result, aggregate demand falls.

force firms to reconsider investment plans. Fewer investments pass the profit test at the higher interest rate. Investment spending falls, dragging aggregate demand down with it. RGNP falls in the short run—how much unemployment this causes depends on the shape of the aggregate supply and how sticky prices are. Aggregate supply might fall in the long run (not shown in the figure), too, if lower investment spending drains capacity.

This policy and its results are summarized by the chain reaction:

Contractionary Monetary Policy
Open market sale → ↓ CS → ↑ i → ↓ I → ↓ AD → ↓ RGNP → ↓ Price level
Long run: Falling AS

This contractionary policy looks like a good way to fight inflation, but it is a dangerous strategy. Tight money restrains investment and consumer spending in the short run, holding down aggregate demand and thus relieving price pressure. But high interest rates affect production choices in undesirable ways. Falling aggregate supply and cost-push inflation could result in the short run as higher interest costs increase production expense and reduce AS in the long run if investment spending falls so low as to damage production capacity. The FRS policymakers cannot ignore the possibility that they might trade current problems for cost-push misery through contractionary monetary policies!

The Pros and Cons of Monetary Policy

Federal Reserve policies are a powerful alternative to fiscal policies. They are especially important because Fed policies influence investment spending—a component of both aggregate demand and aggregate supply.

monetary policy: FRS policies that affect aggregate demand and aggregate supply by regulating money and credit supplies.

Monetary policy has several important advantages. It can be enacted quickly, not suffering as many lags as fiscal policies. Monetary policies benefit from the nonpolitical status of the Federal Reserve. Policymakers are economists, financiers, and business people—expert in money matters, not politicians trained in writing laws and partisan maneuvering. A final advantage of monetary policy is that, by focusing on investment spending, FRS policies are likely to influence both aggregate demand and aggregate supply. Fiscal policies sometimes forget about the long run AS problem.

Monetary policy suffers from two important disadvantages, however. The first is that it is so sensitive to expectations. The FRS has a hard time making an expansionary policy stick, for example, if borrowers view it as inflationary. You saw this in Figure 10-7. An increase in the credit supply cannot push interest rates down if inflation-worried borrowers increase credit demand at the same time. The expectations problem makes monetary policy less certain than it would otherwise be.

variable lag: the uncertain lag in the monetary transmission mechanism between changes in interest rates and investment spending.

Monetary policy is even riskier when the **variable lag** is considered. Federal Reserve actions rely on the link between interest rates and investment spending to move aggregate demand. Does investment spending rise when interest rates fall? Yes—eventually. But businesses might not run out and build new factories right away. They might act quickly, but they might wait to see if consumer spending patterns change or if interest rates fall even more or if tax laws will be changed. There is a lag of between a few months and a few years between monetary actions and their investment results. Is this variable lag important? You bet it is. Figure 10-10 shows what can happen.

The FRS intended to stimulate this economy out of the depression part of the AS curve. They increased the credit supply to fight unemployment, but investment spending did not respond because businesses were leery of expanding in a depressed economy. The FRS policy took hold a couple of years later, when the economy was operating close to full capacity. The result? This anti-unemployment policy ended up just adding to inflation.

The variable lag makes using monetary policy a little like driving a car with a variable lag steering gear. If you turn the wheel to the left you can be sure that the car will turn left—eventually. You might turn quickly and go exactly where you want. But the wheel might lag. The car could continue straight ahead for awhile, then suddenly lurch to the left. You might end up turning three blocks later and crashing through a taco stand!

Monetary policy has many advantages, but the problems of expectations and variable lag make it an uncertain choice for economic policy. Which is the better way to fight inflation and unemployment? Monetary actions or government fiscal policies? That is the topic of the next chapter!

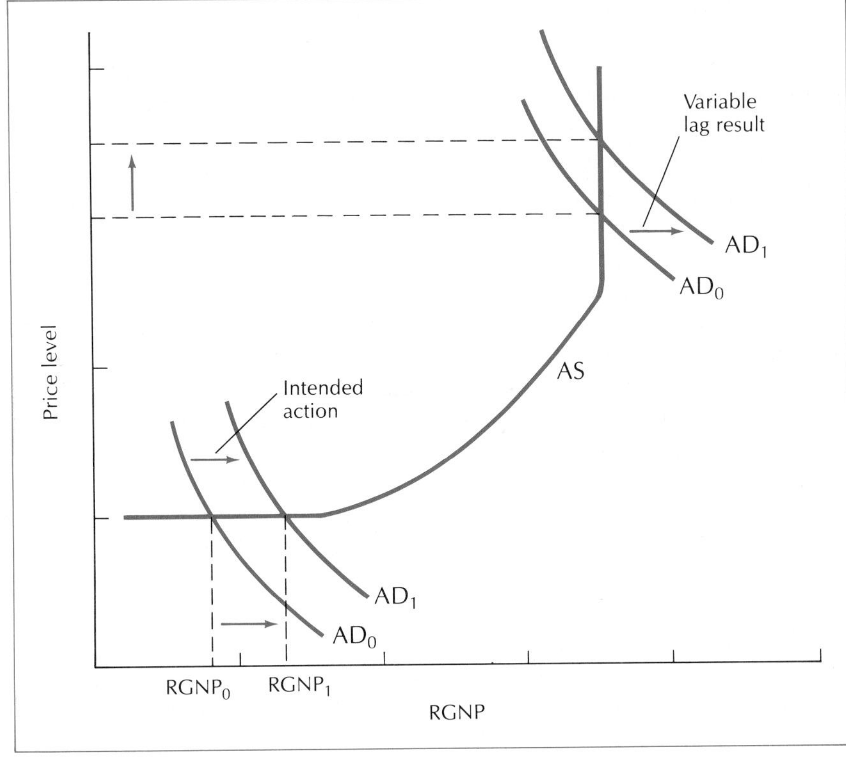

FIGURE 10-10 VARIABLE LAG PROBLEMS. The intent of monetary policy is to increase aggregate demand in a depression economy. However, investment spending does not rise until much later. The aggregate demand increases, but on the full-capacity part of aggregate supply. Consequently, the monetary policy has not accomplished its goal.

ECONOMIC CONTROVERSY:

Interest Rate Ceilings?

The credit market in general and the banking industry in particular are among the most heavily regulated parts of the economy. All manner of rules and regulations apply here to protect the public interest.

regulation Q: FRS regulations that limit bank interest payments.

Among the most controversial of these regulations are interest rate ceilings. The FRS' **Regulation Q** sets ceilings on interest rates banks pay their depositors. Commercial banks cannot pay interest on profitable checking accounts, for example, and are limited by a 5½ percent ceiling on regular savings accounts. Regulation Q is slowly being phased out, but limits still apply that keep savers from receiving as high a return as would otherwise exist.

Another set of controls limits interest rates on bank loans. Many of these interest ceilings are set by state governments to "protect" consumers from high interest cost. The purpose of the combination of these two sets of controls is to hold both interest earned on deposits and interest paid on savings at artificially low levels.

Are these interest rate ceilings a good idea? Here are two sides to the argument.

Ceilings Are in the Public Interest

We need a healthy, competitive banking industry and we need strong spending by consumers and investors. Interest rate ceilings assure both of these results.

Limits on interest rates paid for deposits prevents cutthroat competition among banks. Can you imagine the mess if banks could offer whatever interest rate savers demand? Competitive bankers would be forced to bid against one another. Cutthroat competition would drive banks out of business—taking depositors' savings with them! We would have an unstable banking system and higher interest rates on loans, too, since the higher cost of funds is eventually passed on to borrowers. Insecure bankers could not risk making long-term mortgage loans. Another bank panic would result!

Ceilings on loan interest rates serve two useful purposes. First, they encourage spending and investment by keeping interest rates at low levels that consumers and investors can afford. Unemployment threatens if interest rates get too high. Ceilings on loans also keep bankers from taking advantage of poorly informed consumers. Bankers have all the cards—money—in the credit game. Information about interest rates and credit availability is hard to find. Without interest rate ceilings, uncompetitive bankers could get away with murder—charging interest rates far above those justified by risk, cost, and other variables.

Interest rate ceilings protect the banking industry and protect borrowers. These ceilings should be retained.

Deregulate the Credit Market!

Did that make any sense to you? First bankers are so recklessly competitive that, without government restraint, they would drive themselves out of business. Have you ever met a reckless banker? Then banks are not competitive at all—government needs to protect us from this monopoly! The argument in favor of interest rate ceilings is confused.

Interest rate ceilings on loans are a bad plan, too. What happens when of credit and hurt the poor. Low interest rates on deposits discourage saving. Money in a 5 percent savings account loses real value quickly when inflation runs at 10 percent. Why save if inflation eats away at your nest egg? Low savings rates have kept the credit supply low, interest rates high, and caused both inflation and unemployment by discouraging growth in aggregate supply.

Interest rate ceilings on loans are a bad plan, too. What happens when the ceiling is set below the market equilibrium? A credit shortage results! Many people seek loans at the artificially low interest rates, but bankers lend only to low-risk customers. The money goes to the rich and profitable, not the needy who end up at pawn shops and loan sharks—they are forced to pay illegally high interest rates. The ceilings do little to protect them.

Interest rate ceilings are at the root of our current economic problems. Higher inflation, combined with credit market controls, gave us disintermediation in the 1970s. People could not borrow to buy houses and the construction industry collapsed. People could not borrow to buy cars and the auto industry collapsed. What industry is next?

Let the credit market set interest rates. Savers would get a higher return and borrowers might even pay less, since more credit would be available. Banks would not go bust in this competitive environment. We need market interest rates for long-term economic growth.

SUMMARY

1. Financial markets are an important part of the economy. Corporations raise funds by borrowing in the credit market or selling ownership shares on the stock market. The commodities market trades futures contracts in goods, stabilizing mineral and agricultural markets.

2. Bonds are an important part of the credit market. Borrowers sell bonds to the lenders who supply funds. Bond prices and interest vary inversely for reasons discussed in this section.

3. The demand for credit depends on the interest rate, expectations about inflation and income, and government policies.

4. The Federal Reserve System is the biggest influence on credit supply. The interest rate, saving behavior, and inflation expectations also affect the CS curve.

5. Interest rates are set by the forces of supply and demand. Borrowers and lenders compete and this competition brings interest to an equilibrium.

6. Inflation is built into the interest rate through market forces. Higher expected inflation rates increase credit demand but reduce the supply of loans. Interest rates must rise in this situation, unless government regulations intervene.

7. Interest rate ceilings cause disintermediation in inflationary times. Savers take their funds out of banks and invest in unregulated credit markets. Funds dry up for consumer and mortgage loans.

8. The monetary transmission mechanism is the link between interest rates and investment spending. Federal Reserve policies that alter the credit supply affect investments and aggregate demand through the interest rate link. Monetary policy is an alternative to fiscal actions.

9. Expansionary monetary policy increases aggregate demand in the short run as lower interest rates stimulate investment spending. Aggregate supply rises in the long run as capacity rises. The result is balanced growth with low inflation. Contractionary monetary policies bid up interest rates and discourage investment spending. Aggregate demand falls in the short run, but declining capacity might also reduce aggregate supply and lead to cost-push inflation.

10. Is monetary policy a good idea? These policies can be quickly enacted, but two problems persist. Expectations might wipe out interest rate changes, thereby handcuffing FRS policies. The variable lag between interest rates and investment spending adds to the uncertainty of monetary policies.

11. What do interest rate ceilings do in credit markets? Do they prevent competition or encourage it? Do they protect the poor or force them to go to illegal lenders? Do they discourage saving or prevent banking panics? The Economic Controversy debated these issues.

DISCUSSION QUESTIONS

1. What is the relationship between stock and bond prices? Should stock prices go up or down when bond prices fall? Explain your reasoning.

2. The FRS is nearly always increasing the money supply. Why are not interest rates always falling? Explain.

3. The FRS makes a $10 billion open market purchase. Explain how this action affects:

a. credit supply and credit demand
b. bond prices and interest rates
c. investment spending
d. aggregate demand and aggregate supply in the short run
e. aggregate demand and aggregate supply in the long run

4. What happens to the credit market if the FRS makes an open market sale at the same time as the federal government increases borrowing to finance higher deficits? How does this combination affect interest rates, investment spending, and the economy in the short run and the long run? Explain.

5. Where do you stand on interest rate ceilings? Are limits on deposit interest rates a good idea? Should limits on loan interest rates be retained? Defend your answer in each case.

TEST YOURSELF

Circle the best response to each of the following questions.

1. The financial reporter on the radio has just said he thinks the FRS is making open market sales. If he is right (and other things like expectations do not change) which of the following events should you observe soon?

(X) rising interest rates
(Y) rising bond prices
(Z) rising stock prices

a. all of the above
b. none of the above
c. only (X)
d. (Y) and (Z)
e. (X) and (Y)

2. The Federal Reserve has just cut the discount rate and lowered the reserve requirement. These actions together should:

(X) increase credit supply (shift CS curve)
(Y) increase credit demand (shift CD curve)
(Z) result in lower interest rates, all else being equal

a. all of the above
b. none of the above
c. only (Y)
d. (X) and (Z)
e. (X) and (Z), but cannot tell about interest rate

3. President Reagan's supply-side tax cut was supposed to increase income and give workers incentives to save more. If the tax cuts work as described here, how would they change the credit market?

a. increase both credit supply and credit demand—more loans are made, but cannot tell how interest rate changes
b. reduce credit demand but increase credit supply—interest rate falls, but cannot tell about number of loans
c. reduce credit supply and increase credit demand—interest rate falls and more loans are made
d. credit supply and credit demand both decrease—interest rates are constant and more loans are made
e. impossible to tell how credit supply and credit demand change.

4. How do increased inflationary expectations affect the credit market?

(X) credit supply rises to compensate for higher prices (CS curve shifts to the right)

(Y) credit demand falls because borrowers do not want to pay higher prices on loans (CD curve shifts to left)
(Z) interest rate rises because of credit surplus

a. all of the above
b. none of the above
c. only (X)
d. only (Z)
e. only (Y)

5. Your professor tells you that the FRS recently changed economic policies. Here are the economy's symptoms: lower interest rates, higher inflation, falling unemployment, and increased investment spending. Which of the following is a FRS policy that could have caused these changes?

a. income-tax cut
b. open market sale
c. increase in transfer payments
d. lower reserve requirement
e. increase in discount rate

SUGGESTIONS FOR FURTHER READING

Your best bet for analysis of money and credit is the daily *Wall Street Journal*. Check the editorial page and the section labeled "Credit Markets." Government influence on the credit markets is explored in "America's Other Budget" by William Barry Furlong (*New York Times Magazine*, February 21, 1982). The debate over credit-market ceilings rages still. Helen Frame Peters presents a good discussion of the pros and cons in a particular credit market in "The Mortgage Market: A Place for Ceilings" (*Federal Reserve Bank of Philadelphia Business Review*, July–August, 1977).

11

MONETARY VERSUS FISCAL POLICY

Preview

What are the important economic and political differences between monetary and fiscal policies?

Which policy is best to fight unemployment? Inflation? Stagflation?

Should Congress raise taxes or live with high deficits?

What is the best way to finance the deficit?

Do monetary and fiscal policies always work together?

What happens when Congress and the FRS disagree?

Should the FRS be independent of Congressional control?

MARK TWAIN tells the story of an amazing pair of Siamese twins (twins whose bodies are joined, sharing some body organs) named Angelo and Luigi. The twins had much in common, but differed in their views of the world. One was a Republican, the other a Democrat. One smoked like a chimney, the other could not tolerate tobacco.

Angelo was a teetotaler who could not stand strong drink. Luigi was an inebriate who could not resist a tumbler full of whisky. Their habits offended one another. Worse, their shared organs perversely refused to play fair. The sodden Luigi could drink all he liked and remain perfectly sober, a seeming paragon of virtue. The truly virtuous Angelo, however, felt all the ill effects of his twin's alcoholic binges—his speech slurred and he sang bawdy songs at the top of his lungs even though no liquor touched his lips. He was roundly (and wrongly!) condemned for his drunken behavior.

The U.S. economy is like the interdependent body of these amazing twins, Angelo and Luigi. Economic policy has two separate heads, each with a mind of its own. The Fed and the Congress make independent decisions. The economy feels the combined effects of the two separate policies. Decisions by one head affect the policies of them both.

Some people think that Congress, like Luigi, is drunk with the urge to spend and inflate prices. Others think the Fed, like Angelo, is unnecessarily prudent and afraid of stimulants that have beneficial effects. How does this peculiar division of economic labor work? This chapter gives you the tools to evaluate monetary and fiscal policies.

Fighting Unemployment

Suppose the economy is experiencing high unemployment rates (it should not be difficult to imagine this problem—more than 10 million people were unemployed in 1982). Which policy works best to fight unemployment? Monetary policies like an open market purchase or fiscal policies such as tax cuts or increased government spending? Let us compare the two options.

EXPANSIONARY MONETARY POLICY. The last chapter showed how monetary policies work. Here is how expansionary monetary policy increases aggregate demand and fights unemployment. The basics of this policy are shown in Figure 11-1.

An open market purchase hits the credit market first, shifting the CS curve to the right. Interest rates fall as the credit supply rises. Lower interest rates encourage higher investment spending totals, which stimulate aggregate demand through the spending multiplier process. The RGNP and the price level both rise when aggregate demand increases in the short run. Aggregate supply grows in the long run as higher levels of investment spending add to economic capacity. We can summarize this process by the chain reaction figure:

Expansionary Monetary Policy

$\uparrow$ CS $\rightarrow$ $\downarrow$ i $\rightarrow$ $\uparrow$ I $\rightarrow$ $\uparrow$ AD $\rightarrow$ $\uparrow$ RGNP $\rightarrow$ $\uparrow$ Price level

Long run: increased AS

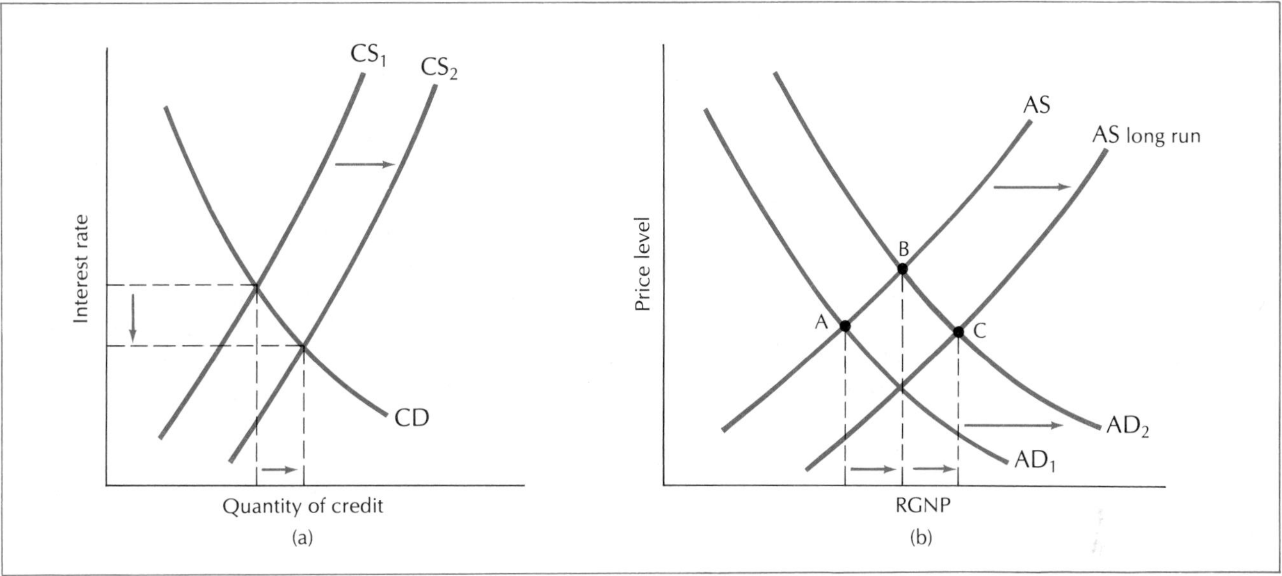

FIGURE 11-1 Expansionary Monetary Policy. (a) The FRS increases the credit supply. Interest rates fall and investment spending rises. (b) The economy moves from A to B as aggregate demand rises in the short run. Higher investment spending increases aggregate supply in the long run, moving the economy to C.

This chain reaction does not really end with the higher price level as shown above. The economy does not jump directly to its new equilibrium—it takes time to adjust. Higher income and prices, for example, encourage additional borrowing—credit demand rises. Higher credit demand pushes interest rates a little higher and thus keeps investment spending from growing as fast as it otherwise would. We could write out these secondary effects as:

Secondary Effects
Higher RGNP and price level → ↑ CD → ↑ i → ↓ I → ↓ AD

These secondary effects are quantitatively smaller than the first-order movements presented above. The economy oscillates back and forth like a guitar string as it seeks the new equilibrium. The secondary effects do not alter our conclusions about the direction of expansionary monetary policy—interest rates fall, investment spending rises, aggregate demand increases. The secondary effects reduce the size of these changes.

EXPANSIONARY FISCAL POLICY. What is the fiscal alternative? Government expands aggregate demand by increasing government spending and transfer payments or by cutting taxes. Suppose Congress decides to increase defense spending. How does this affect the economy?

Higher spending by government sets in motion the multiplier process discussed in Chapter 8. Aggregate demand grows by the combination of government spending and induced-consumption spending. Rising aggregate demand increases both RGNP and the price level. These effects are summarized by the chain reaction:

Expansionary Fiscal Policy
Increased G → ↑ AD → ↑ RGNP → ↑ Price level

where "G" stands for increased government and induced-consumption spending.

Demand-pull inflation makes unemployment lines shorter, but bids up consumer prices. The chain reaction does not end with higher prices—secondary effects need to be considered, too. Higher incomes and higher prices increase consumer borrowing, as Chapter 10 indicated. Increased credit demand bids up interest rates, which discourages investment spending. Falling investment spending reduces AD growth in the short run and slows AS growth in the long run. Capacity does not grow as fast as it otherwise would and might even be reduced (aggregate supply falls) if investment levels fall low enough. These secondary effects are summarized by the chain reaction:

Secondary Effects
Higher RGNP and price level → ↑ CD → ↑ i → ↓ I → ↓ AD
long run: lower AS

What do the secondary effects tell us? Changes in aggregate demand get smaller as we travel down the chains, so falling aggregate demand in this instance does not cancel out the expansionary effects of government spending. But we can see that increased government spending is partially offset by falling investment spending. This means that government spending's powerful multiplier effect is not so large as first indicated.

The secondary effects are also important because they tell us what happens to interest rates, investment spending, and aggregate supply. Government spending here increases aggregate demand in the short run but might reduce aggregate supply in the long run because higher interest rates discourage investment. This adds to our understanding of fiscal policy's effects. The complete picture of expansionary fiscal policy is shown in Figure 11-2.

Policy Options

Which of these policies is the best way to fight unemployment? The answer to this question depends on what you mean by "best policy." Suppose you think the best policy is the one that leads to the most long-run growth of the economy—the one that does the most to increase aggregate supply. If rising aggregate supply is the goal, then monetary policy is the better tool. Expansionary monetary policy bids down interest rates and encourages capital formation. Rising aggregate supply in the long run gives balanced growth—rising RGNP with lower inflation rates. Monetary policy is the choice over fiscal actions that balance demand-pull inflation in the short run with the potential for cost-push problems (if aggregate supply falls) in the long run.

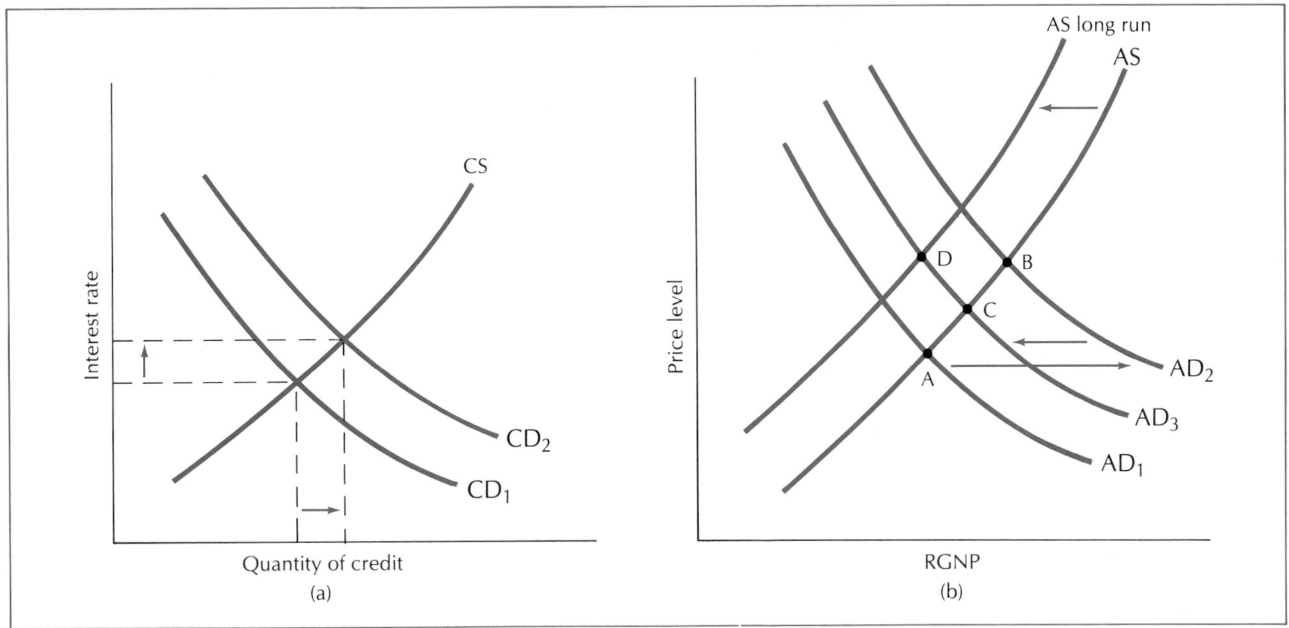

FIGURE 11-2 EXPANSIONARY FISCAL POLICY. An increase in government spending increases aggregate demand, moving the economy from A to B (b). Higher prices and income boost credit demand, however, driving up interest rates and forcing investment spending down (a). The aggregate demand falls back somewhat and the economy ends up at C in the short run. Lower investment totals may reduce capacity. The economy ends up at D in the long run (b).

Monetary policy looks good, but long-run aggregate supply concerns are not all that matters. People in unemployment lines might add another goal: they would like this policy to be certain and quick. They want a sure cure that creates more jobs in a hurry. Is monetary policy their choice? Probably not. The variable lag in monetary policy presents a problem. Businesses might start building projects promptly, but they might also wait to see what else happens. The recovery could be delayed for months or years. The long-run consequences of monetary policy are desirable, but they give cold comfort to impoverished families, bankrupt businesses, and jobless workers in the short run.

Monetary policy's success is sensitive to expectations, too. The money supply has to grow by more than borrowers expect if it is to bring down interest rates. Inflationary expectations, as we saw in Chapter 10, might keep interest rates from falling and so make FRS policies impotent.

Fiscal policies are subject to lags, too, but these are not so severe as with monetary policy. Fiscal policy's advantage is its relative certainty. It takes effect in the short run. Fiscal policy can also be tailored to meet the special needs of the unemployed—another advantage.

What is our conclusion? Economists and politicians face a trade-off in fighting unemployment. Monetary policy expands the private sector of the economy and creates more jobs through the long-run growth of aggregate supply. It is a good long-run strategy to fight unemployment. Fiscal policies discourage investment spending and so are not as desirable in the long run. But fiscal policy has the advantage of certainty and speed. Besides, no member of Congress has ever been turned out of office for creating jobs for his or her constituents. Which policy is best? The answer to this question is itself a question: Which goal of these goals is the most important?

Fighting Inflation

What is the best way to fight inflation? Most economic policies try to deal with inflation by reducing aggregate demand. Monetary policies accomplish this by reducing credit supplies and forcing interest rates up. Fiscal policies increase taxes, reduce government spending, or cut transfer payments. Let us look at each policy type.

CONTRACTIONARY MONETARY POLICY. The FRS cools off aggregate demand by cutting money and credit supplies. Interest rates rise and investment spending falls. Aggregate demand drops in the short run. This reduces the pressure of inflation but also lowers RGNP, so unemployment goes up. Lower investment spending in the short run limits AS-growth in the long run. The chain reaction is:

Contractionary Monetary Policy
$\downarrow$ CS $\rightarrow \uparrow$ i $\rightarrow \downarrow$ I $\rightarrow \downarrow$ AD $\rightarrow \downarrow$ RGNP
Long run: lower AS

The secondary effect of this policy is reduced credit demand that keeps interest rates from rising as far and thus cushions investment spending's fall. The contractionary effect is not as large as it might otherwise be.

CONTRACTIONARY FISCAL POLICY. Rising taxes or reduced government spending are the fiscal alternatives. Lower government spending reduces aggregate demand through the multiplier process (the same multiplier works for monetary policy's investment spending change). The RGNP falls and inflation rates go down. The secondary effects are important in this instance. Lower income and lower prices reduce credit demand. Interest rates fall and investment spending rises eventually (the variable lag shows up here). Rising investment spending once again cushions the AD fall and encourages long-run AS growth. The chain reaction (including both primary and secondary effects) is:

Contractionary Fiscal Policy
Lower G $\rightarrow \downarrow$ AD $\rightarrow \downarrow$ RGNP $\rightarrow \downarrow$ Price level $\rightarrow \downarrow$ CD $\rightarrow \downarrow$ i $\rightarrow \uparrow$ I $\rightarrow \uparrow$ AD
long run: increased AS

Remember that the spending effects are smaller at the end of the chain reaction than at the start. Aggregate demand falls here but by less than the multiplier amount because lower government spending is partially offset by increased investment purchases.

TRADE-OFFS. Which of these policies is best? The choice again depends on which goal you choose. Fiscal policy is the best choice if aggregate supply is the primary concern. A tax increase or government spending cut reduces credit demand. Lower interest rates encourage investment spending and so boost aggregate supply in the long run. But this policy has two limitations. The first is that investment spending might not increase quickly. Risk-averse firms do not want to expand capacity when production and sales are already low (as is the case with falling aggregate demand). The investment lag may be long. Lower interest rates are not much help, either, if business taxes rise. The benefits of fiscal policy are uncertain.

Political considerations present a second problem for contractionary fiscal policy. Members of Congress face voters every two years. Do they want to go on record as favoring higher unemployment rates? Probably not. Congress is therefore less likely to enact contractionary policies than is the insulated, unelected Federal Reserve Board. The Fed's conservative anti-inflation bias makes them likely to favor contractionary policies that fight inflation.

Why were inflation rates so high in the 1970s? These trade-offs illustrate why inflation is tough to beat. Both monetary and fiscal policies face important lags. Fiscal policies might work better, but monetary policies are more likely to be enacted. But contractionary monetary policies are a risky proposition. They might not work in the short run because of the variable lag. If they do work, they discourage investment spending and thus risk even more inflation in the long run due to falling aggregate supply. There is no obvious way out of this maze.

Fighting Stagflation

The economic policy riddle gets even tougher when stagflation is the opponent. What should we do if cost-push forces increase both inflation and unemployment rates at the same time? The ideal solution would be a short-run rise in aggregate supply. What is the best way to do this?

Supply siders (discussed in Chapter 8) suggest tax rate cuts to stimulate aggregate supply. This policy is risky in several ways. First, tax cuts might boost aggregate demand rather than aggregate supply. An increase in aggregate demand on top of falling aggregate supply would push inflation rates sky-high. Higher prices bring higher costs that further push up prices. This is not the solution we seek.

The second supply-side risk is that the silver lining of tax cuts might get lost in the dark cloud of higher interest rates. Tax cuts could boost the government's deficit. More federal borrowing bids up interest rates. Firms that face lower taxes and higher interest costs might expand—but they might not. We cannot tell which force is stronger.

Tax expenditures are another fiscal tool. Selective tax breaks for new investments (that do not reduce tax collections from other sources) might be a good alternative. Tax incentives encourage new investment but do not cause the same deficit problems as across-the-board tax cuts. But tax expenditures face problems, too.

The first problem is a political flaw: an investment tax expenditure looks like welfare for big business. Congress is often unwilling to cut business taxes unless consumer taxes fall, too. This increases the deficit, drives up interest rates, and reduces the tax expenditures' effects.

The second problem is that investment tax incentives are not a short-term solution. Capacity increases slowly over time. Tax expenditures, if they work, must be viewed as a long-term answer to stagflation. Policymakers often reject long-run answers to their short-term problems.

What are the other answers? We have already looked at most of them in this and other chapters. Wage and price controls hold down prices. Government can increase spending during a wage and price freeze without fear of higher prices. But wage and price controls discourage production and cause shortages. This is not the perfect solution we have been looking for.

Expansionary monetary policy boosts aggregate supply as a long-run result, but it brings demand-pull inflation in the short run. The Fed can therefore fight stagflation in the long run if it is willing to live with higher inflation rates in the short run. This is something the conservative leaders of the Federal Reserve are unlikely to do.

Congress can also vote for policies that stimulate long-run AS growth. But these contractionary policies, as we have just seen, add to unemployment lists in the short run. Is Congress willing to fight stagflation with restrictive policies that put voters out of work now but promise rising capacity and more jobs in the long run?

What is the key to this puzzle? Why is fighting stagflation so difficult? Trade-offs are the problem here. Which do you choose? Short-run or long-term effects? Certainty or riskier but possibly better policies? How important are political concerns? Which problem is more important—inflation or unemployment? Which do you fight if you cannot solve both problems in the short run?

Trade-offs make economic policy difficult because every desirable action has an undesirable side effect. It is no wonder that stagflation won its fight with Congress and the Federal Reserve in the 1970s.

Financing Government Spending

Trade-offs are the curse of economic policy. We can see these trade-offs by looking at a fiscal policy example. Suppose that Congress has decided to fight the unemployment part of stagflation by increasing government spending. They have made a choice: they are willing to live with higher inflation rates if they can cut unemployment. This choice does not end the matter, however. Congress must find the additional money it wants to spend. Spending decisions must be balanced by taxation or borrowing choices. Where will the money come from? Let us look at the three choices.

1. TAX FINANCE. Congress might choose higher government spending and increased taxes. Such a plan does not increase the deficit and does boost aggregate demand because the rise from government spending is greater than the contractionary result of higher taxes (the spending multiplier is larger than the taxation multiplier). Figure 11-3 shows how tax finance affects aggregate demand in the short run.

Tax-financed spending increases have relatively little effect on the economy. Increased government purchases stimulate spending, boost income, and bid up interest rates, but higher taxes counteract each step. Interest rates end up higher, so investment spending falls. This further reduces the expansionary effect on aggregate demand. Higher interest rates and higher tax rates might discourage AS growth in the long run, too. The dual chain reaction for this policy is given by:

Tax-financed Government Spending
Higher G $\rightarrow \uparrow$ AD $\rightarrow \uparrow$ RGNP $\rightarrow \uparrow$ CD $\rightarrow \uparrow$ i $\rightarrow \downarrow$ I
Higher tax $\rightarrow \downarrow$ AD $\rightarrow \downarrow$ RGNP $\rightarrow \downarrow$ CD $\rightarrow \downarrow$ i $\rightarrow \uparrow$ I
long run: lower AS

A policy like this one fights unemployment, but its stimulative strength is weakened by rising taxes and falling investment spending. Is there a more powerful choice?

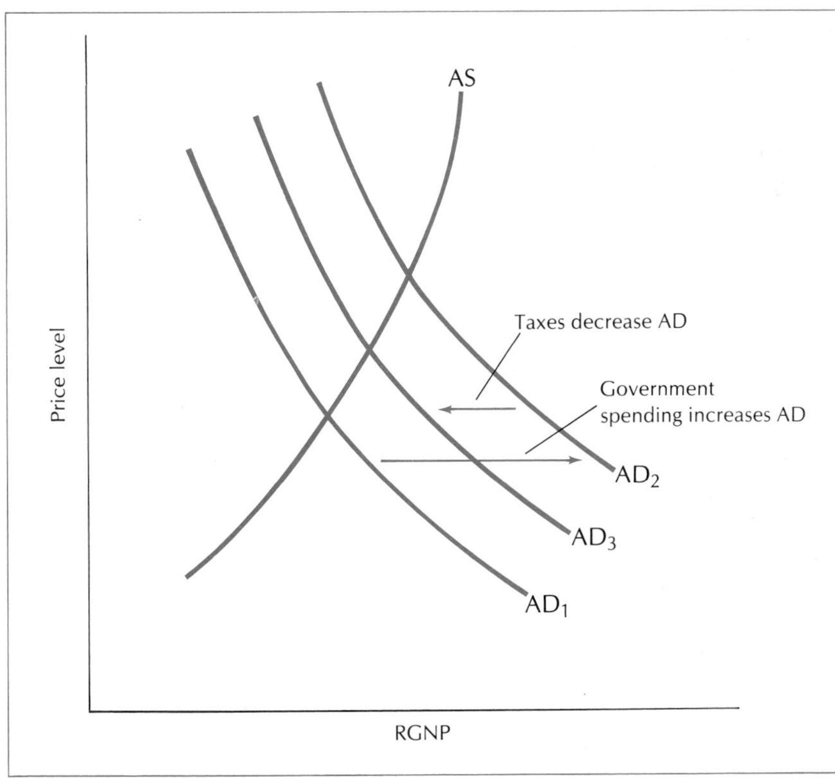

FIGURE 11-3 Tax-Financed Government Spending. Government spending boosts aggregate demand, but tax increases shift it back. Interest rates also rise. Falling investment spending further reduces this policy's effect.

2. BORROW FROM THE PUBLIC. One alternative is to increase government spending without raising taxes. The deficit is financed by borrowing from the public by selling government bonds to banks, investors, and households. The chain reaction here is:

Borrowing from the Public
Higher G $\rightarrow \uparrow$ AD $\rightarrow \uparrow$ RGNP $\rightarrow \uparrow$ CD $\rightarrow \uparrow$ i $\rightarrow \downarrow$ I
Deficit $\rightarrow \uparrow$ CD $\rightarrow \uparrow$ i $\rightarrow \downarrow$ I $\rightarrow \downarrow$ AD
long run: lower AS

This policy is not very powerful, either. Added government spending and federal borrowing to finance the deficit both bid up interest rates. Investment spending falls eventually and offsets part or all of the government spending rise. The result, as Figure 11-4 shows, is a smaller increase in aggregate demand in the short run. Higher interest rates and reduced investment spending might lower aggregate supply in the long run, too, making cost-push stagflation even worse.

The problem here is crowding out. Government borrowing takes the place of private sector borrowing. Government spending replaces private investment spending. Thus, we are presented with another trade-off.

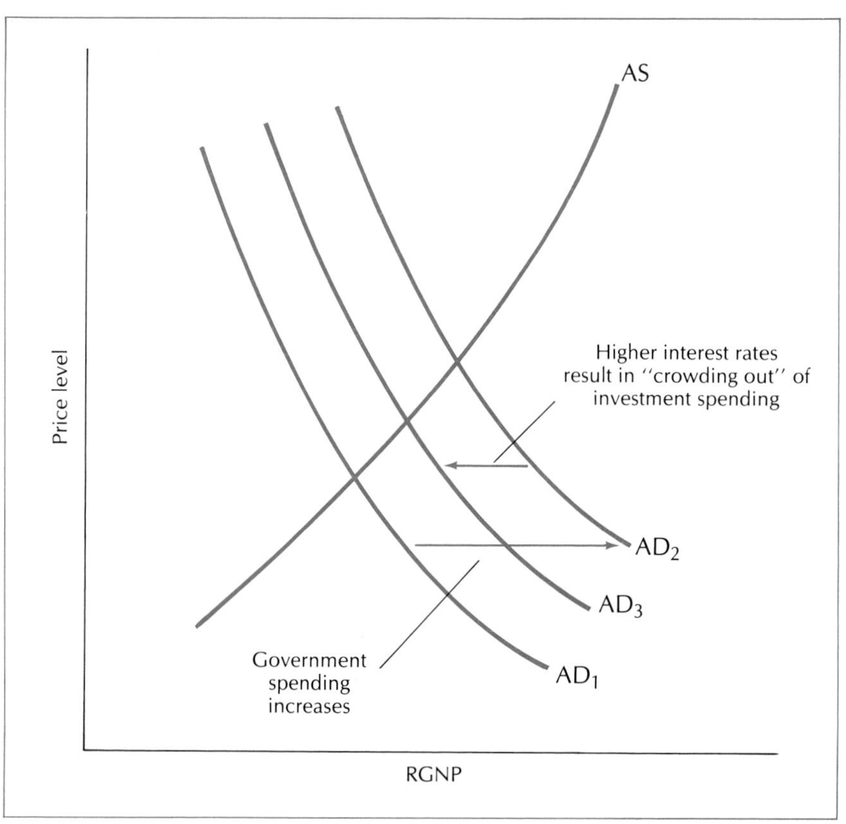

FIGURE 11-4 BORROWING FROM THE PUBLIC. In this figure, government spending makes aggregate demand rise. Borrowing from the public bids up interest rates and crowds out investment spending. Falling investment rates shift back the aggregate demand.

Is deficit spending a good way to stimulate aggregate demand? This question is answered with more questions. What kind of goods does government buy—investment goods like roads and research that add to aggregate supply or consumption goods that boost aggregate demand alone? Would private-sector businesses have used the funds to expand or would they have waited? Government borrowing in the right circumstances can successfully compensate for missing private-sector investment.

The economic effect of the deficit also depends on credit market conditions, as Figure 11-5 shows. The same deficit has different consequences depending on how tight the credit supply is.

The deficit is not a problem if loanable funds are readily available, as part (a) of the figure shows. The horizontal credit supply shows that banks have many excess reserves. The federal government can borrow $10 billion more without bidding interest rates higher. Additional government borrowing does not reduce funds available for private investment projects. No crowding out problem exists in this instance and government spending has its full multiplier effect.

Part (b) of the figure shows a more realistic case. The CS curve is upward sloping here. The same $10 billion deficit boosts interest rates and crowds out private investment spending. Available loan money amounts to $105 billion, but the government takes $10 billion, leaving just $95 billion—$5 billion less than at the start—for private firms. The net effect of government spending on aggregate demand is smaller because of the $5 billion crowding out.

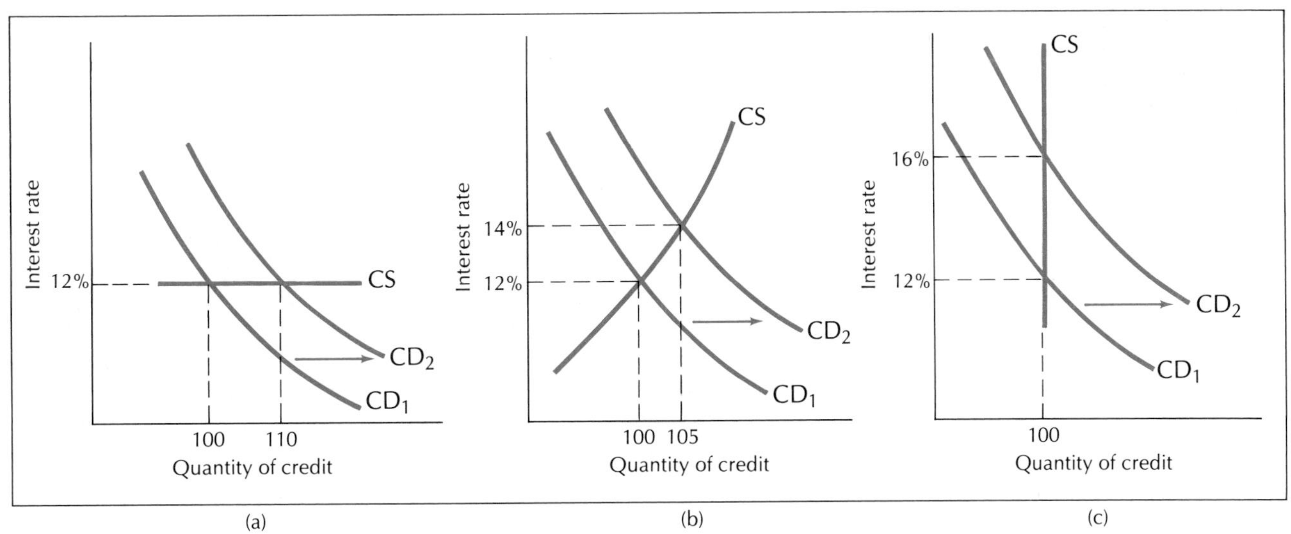

FIGURE 11-5 CROWDING OUT. In this figure, the government spends $10 billion more and borrows the money on the credit market. How much investment is crowded out? No crowding out occurs if the credit supply curve is horizontal, as in (a). Government deficits do not reduce private borrowing. Partial crowding out occurs if the credit supply curve is upward sloping as in (b). An additional $5 billion in loan money is available at the higher interest rate, but the government takes $10 billion more. Consequently, private borrowing and investment is $5 billion less than before. Complete crowding out is seen in (c). Deficits with fixed credit supply mean that government borrowing displaces an equal amount of private borrowing and investment.

complete crowding out: increased government borrowing leads to an equal decrease in private investment.

Complete crowding out is the final possibility. In part (c) the CS curve is vertical when credit supplies are tight and excess reserves are unavailable. Increased government borrowing in this instance sends interest rates soaring. A $10 billion deficit crowds out an equal $10 billion in private investment spending.

Government spending has no power to change aggregate demand when complete crowding out occurs. The $10 billion increase in government spending is completely wiped out by a $10 billion decrease in loan-financed business spending. Aggregate demand does not change in the short run, but aggregate supply might fall because of high interest costs and lower capacity. This policy makes the stagflation problem worse in the long run.

3. BORROW FROM THE FRS. The final option is really a combination of monetary and fiscal policies. The Treasury often finances deficits by selling bonds to the largest holder of government securities: the Federal Reserve. The government borrows from the Fed to finance increased spending. The Fed buys these bonds and "creates" money to pay for them. This FRS action increases credit supply just like an open market purchase.

This policy really has three parts: government spending, government borrowing, and the FRS bond purchase. All three are shown in this chain reaction statement:

Borrowing from the FRS
Higher G → ↑ AD → ↑ RGNP → ↑ CD ↑ i → ↓ I
Deficit → ↑ CD → ↑ i → ↓ I → ↓ AD
FRS purchase → ↑ CS → ↓ i → ↑ I → ↓ AD

This is the most expansionary way to finance a government spending increase. Government spending boosts aggregate demand directly. Credit demand rises as government borrows to finance the deficit, but credit supply goes up, too, as the FRS makes the needed funds available. Interest rates are held down, no crowding out takes place, and long-run AS growth is still possible.

Why is this policy not used to fight unemployment? One reason is that, while FRS finance is a powerful way to reduce unemployment, it is also a powerful force to increase the inflation rate! Rising aggregate demand trades off unemployment for higher prices. Is this a good trade-off? It depends on which problem you think is most serious. Disagreement on this issue slows policy action.

The second problem here is that borrowing from the FRS requires a joint effort—Congress must vote to spend more and borrow the funds and the FRS must be willing to create the necessary money. Both groups must favor expansionary policies. Is there any guarantee of this agreement?

Reviewing the Alternatives

Financing government spending is no easy choice. Raising taxes is one option. Congress is in control here, but the contractionary effects of the tax increase partially offset the AD boost of government spending. Increasing business taxes might add to cost-push inflation woes. Consumer-spending changes depend on whether households view the tax increase as temporary or permanent. Interest rates rise with this policy, too. Higher interest rates reduce investment spending and so slow aggregate demand's rise in the short run and hamper the growth of aggregate supply in the long run. Furthermore, voters might not appreciate the higher taxes.

Borrowing from the public gets voters off Congress' back, but not for long. Increased government borrowing bids up interest rates—consumers find that houses and cars cost more because of higher interest expense. Investment spending is crowded out, reducing the growth of aggregate demand in the short run and slowing aggregate supply in the long run. This policy might reduce unemployment in the short run, but it also might not. Complete crowding out is a real possibility. The burden of higher interest rates and lower investment spending could drag the economy into a high-inflation depression.

The final option involves borrowing from the Fed. There are no crowding out worries with this approach—the FRS creates the money and interest rates might even fall due to the money multiplier effect. But this policy is inflationary and requires joint Congressional–Federal Reserve action. Will the Fed's bankers be willing to add to the inflation rate? This policy is not guaranteed, either.

So what is the answer? The answer is that there are no easy answers—only choices and trade-offs. But the problem is compounded by the double system of U.S. economic policy. Two groups weigh these choices and trade-offs: fiscal policymakers and the FRS leaders.

Congress versus the Fed

The Federal Reserve System is separated from fiscal policies both by geography and, as often as not, by political and economic philosophy. The President appoints the Board of Governors of the FRS, but the FRS leaders are insulated by their long terms and their financial independence. Jimmy Carter took office when Republican Arthur Burns was in charge at the Fed and Carter-appointee Paul Volcker was Fed chairman during Republican Ronald Reagan's term.

The distance between monetary and fiscal policymakers is great. Members of Congress are often Keynesian or supply siders while the FRS leaders frequently follow the monetarist star. Congress often takes liberal political stands; the FRS is dominated by conservative financiers. Congress meets on Capitol Hill in Washington while the Fed holds its marbled court across town in the shadow of the Washington monument and implements policy in the capital capitol of New York.

Fiscal and monetary policies can either agree in purpose or work against one another. Let us examine the consequences of these policy combinations.

ACCOMMODATING MONETARY POLICIES. The first possibility is that the FRS chooses to fight the same fire as Congress and the President. Monetary policy is said to accommodate fiscal needs. The relationship between Congress and the Fed has often been cooperative—FRS actions in the 1950s, for example, were aimed at keeping government borrowing costs low.

accommodating monetary policies: FRS policies that have the same affect on aggregate demand as do fiscal actions.

Accommodating monetary policies make fiscal policy more powerful. Suppose, for example, that Congress fears growing unemployment lines and decides to cut taxes and borrow to finance the resulting deficit. The expansionary effects of the tax cut are partially or wholly offset by the contractionary results of increased borrowing. The Fed can either agree or disagree with this policy emphasis. If the FRS leaders also vote to fight unemployment, they use accommodating monetary policy to solve fiscal policy's problems:

Accommodating Expansionary Policies
Tax cut → ↑ AD → ↑ RGNP → ↑ CD → ↑ i → ↓ I
Deficit borrowing → ↑ CD → ↑ i → ↓ I → ↓ AD
FRS: increase CS → ↓ i → ↑ I → ↑ AD

An accommodating increase in the money supply keeps interest rates down. This makes the tax cut more potent in the short run and prevents undesirable aggregate supply effects in the long run.

Contractionary policies work best when both sides aim at the same target. Suppose that both Congress and the FRS view inflation as the biggest current threat to economic growth. Congress can vote a tax increase, for example. Lower RGNP usually forces interest rates down. Lower interest costs encourage borrowing and investing and so keep fiscal policy from having its full force. A contractionary monetary policy, however, keeps interest rates high. Aggregate demand falls and inflation is reduced. The chain reaction is:

Accommodating Contractionary Policies
Tax increase → ↓ AD → ↓ RGNP → ↓ CD → ↓ i → ↑ I
FRS: decrease CS → ↑ i → ↓ I → ↓ AD → ↓ RGNP

Agreement is not guaranteed, however. Congress and the Fed are separate bodies, chosen independently, with frequently opposing political and economic views. What happens when the economic twins disagree?

CONFLICTING ECONOMIC POLICIES. Stagflation combines inflation and unemployment in a sour soup. Which problem is the more important? The Fed and Congress frequently disagree on the answer to this question, with **conflicting policies** the result. Congress, reacting to the needs of unemployed voters, decides to fight recession by cutting taxes (and borrowing to cover the deficit). The Fed views this act as blatantly inflationary and redoubles its anti-inflation resolve. The Fed makes massive open market sales to cut credit supplies and reduce aggregate demand. How do these two policies affect the economy? These chain reactions tell the story:

conflicting policies: monetary and fiscal policies that are not intended to have the same effect on aggregate demand.

Conflicting Policies
Tax cut → ↑ AD → ↑ RGNP → ↑ CD → ↑ i → ↓ I
Deficit borrowing → ↑ CD → ↑ i → ↓ I
FRS decreases CS → ↑ i → ↓ I → ↓ AD

The two policies wipe each other out in the short run. Lower taxes from Congress meet a double dose of higher interest rates. Both Congress and the Fed force interest rates up by increasing credit demand when supplies are falling. Consumers find tax cuts only pay for higher interest charges. Aggregate demand could surge from the tax cut then plunge later when investment spending cuts are felt. The economy twists slowly in the wind.

These conflicting policies solved neither inflation nor unemployment. Congress and the FRS might increase their efforts, each trying to counteract the perverse reaction of the other. What happens? Bigger and bigger deficits meet smaller and smaller credit supplies. Crowding out is unavoidable and investment spending dries up. Figure 11-6 shows the probable result. Fiscal and monetary forces kill off one another in the short run. The AD curve does

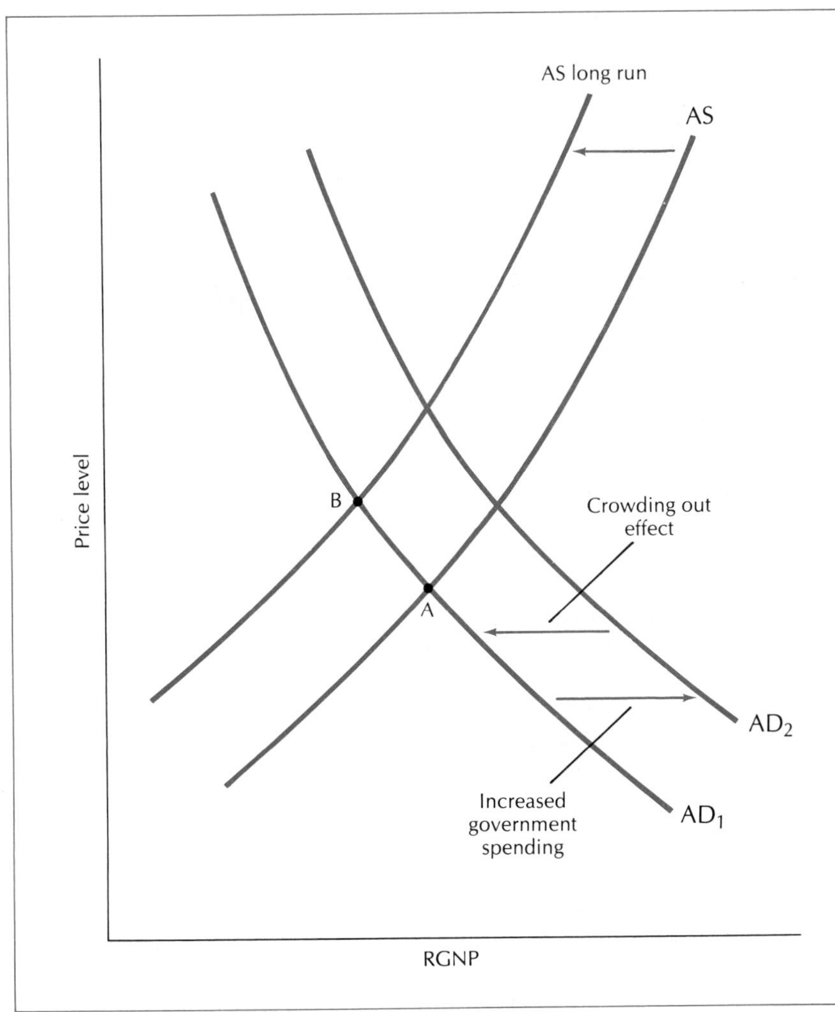

FIGURE 11-6 CONFLICTING ECONOMIC POLICIES. What happens if Congress fights unemployment while the FRS battles inflation? The policies oppose each other in the short run. In the long run, interest rates rise steeply and the aggregate supply falls, bringing more cost-push inflation and a movement from A to B.

not move. But investment decline (on top of higher business interest costs) forces aggregate supply back. Perversely, policies that sought to solve the problem of stagflation have made that problem worse by giving us more cost-push inflation!

Conflicting policies do not always have these bitter side effects. Assume for a moment that Congress and the FRS trade economic and political philosophies. Congress fears inflation and so increases taxes to reduce aggregate demand and lower deficit borrowing. The FRS, fearing the unemployment this causes, increases the credit supply. The chain reactions look like this:

Conflicting Policies

Tax increase $\rightarrow \downarrow$ AD $\rightarrow \downarrow$ RGNP $\rightarrow \downarrow$ CD $\rightarrow \downarrow$ i $\rightarrow \uparrow$ I

FRS:CS increase $\rightarrow \downarrow$ i $\rightarrow \uparrow$ I $\rightarrow \uparrow$ AD

Again the two policies work at cross purposes. The Fed's actions lower interest rates and encourage greater investment spending. Congress, by raising taxes, drives down spending. What happens in the short run? The answer depends in part on the length of the variable lag. If investment spending responds immediately to falling interest costs, the two policies cancel out. If investment lags for a time, aggregate demand might fall (tax increase) then rise later (investment increase), giving the appearance of a business cycle.

Smaller deficits mean less government borrowing. The Fed makes more credit available. Interest costs tumble and capacity grows as Figure 11-7 shows. Rising aggregate supply leads to long-run economic growth—a relatively happy ending to this economic policy conflict.

Economists are famous for finding dark clouds wrapped around silver linings. The beneficial aggregate supply result shown in Figure 11-7 is not likely these days. Deficits are at record levels and the Fed is still wearing its anti-inflation hat. Conflicting policies are the frequent rule and their result is more likely to be the stagflation of Figure 11-6 than the economic growth of Figure 11-7.

Economic policies work better when the Fed and Congress work together. Conflicting policies are risky. Are two heads really better than one? This topic is the subject of heated debate.

ECONOMIC CONTROVERSY:

The Independence of the Federal Reserve

Congress created the Federal Reserve in 1913 to be the "Supreme Court of Banking." It made the FRS independent of congressional control to insulate it from political pressures. The Fed's role in the economy has changed in the last 70 years, however. The Fed is now much more involved in setting economic policies.

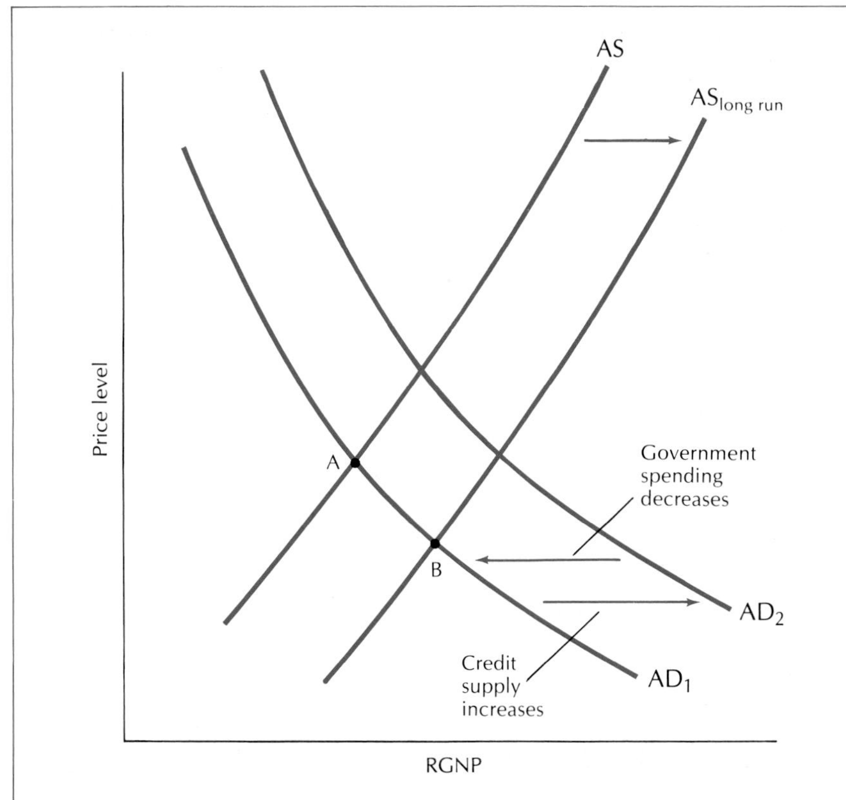

FIGURE 11-7 AN UNLIKELY POLICY WAR. What happens if the Fed fights unemployment while Congress battles inflation? Short-run policies have little effect, but the economy might move from A to B in the long run, as lower interest rates encourage increased aggregate supply capacity.

Has the independent Fed outlived its usefulness? Is conflicting policy too great a risk? Should Congress vote to put the Fed under its direct control? These are issues economists and politicians debate today.

End the Fed's Independence

The Federal Reserve System should be responsible to and under the control of the Congress. The current organization is a danger to the economy and to democracy.

One fundamental principle of democracy is the people's right to a voice in government policy. Members of Congress have to face voters regularly and justify their fiscal policy actions. They pay the price of their economic errors. The FRS leaders are not accountable to anyone. They can tax the economy by creating inflation or imposing unemployment and not answer for their misdeeds. This is a bizarre state for a democratic market economy!

Public policies ought to be the responsibility of elected officials who answer for their decisions. Congress and the President should control credit supplies.

The risk of conflicting policies is too great. We have lived through 10 years of the policies described by Figure 11-6. Higher and higher interest rates have been the consequence of big government deficits to fight unemployment and restrictive monetary policies to fight inflation. These conflicting policies simply serve to make both inflation and unemployment more serious. We cannot risk a continuation of these insane policies.

Let Congress control the monetary wheels. Congress might not always guess right, but the Fed's record has not been so good, either. At least the chance of conflicting policy disaster would be reduced. It is time for a change—the Fed has outlived its usefulness.

Keep the Fed Independent

There are two important reasons for keeping the FRS a separate and independent economic agent. First, the risk of conflicting policy is small compared with the risk of letting Congress play with the money supply. Money is simply too important to put in Congress' hands.

Members of Congress respond to short-term political pressures. If unemployment were too high they would crank up the money supply and make lots of inflation. If inflation were too high they would step on the monetary brakes and drag the economy into a deep recession. The economy would ride an increasingly unstable roller coaster. Worse, Congress might just vote more and more money to finance their deficit delights—hyperinflation would result and the economy would collapse.

The members of Congress do not understand economic policies and they focus on the short term. The FRS leaders are trained economists who understand the consequences of their acts. They can focus on the long run because they are insulated from political pressures. Thus, they make better decisions than would Congress.

The second argument for an independent Fed is that sometimes two independent heads are better than one—particularly if that one head is wrong! Suppose that Congress controls both monetary and fiscal actions. These two policies are always in agreement—they are always either very right or very wrong. The risk of accommodating both wrong policies is great.

Two heads are better than one. When the Fed and Congress act independently, there is a 25 percent chance that they will both pick the right policies. There is a 50 percent chance that their acts will conflict and wipe each other out. But there is only a 25 percent chance that both groups will pick the wrong policy and send us to either hyperinflation or deep depression. Are you not willing to live with conflicting policies if they reduce the risk of economic collapse?

Besides, conflicting policies are not all that bad. People on the other side of this issue ignore the fundamental strength of the U.S. economy. We can survive—and even prosper—when the Fed and Congress take each other out of the game. No doubt about it, the economy is better off with an independent Federal Reserve!

SUMMARY

1. Monetary and fiscal policies affect the economy in different ways. Both policies alter aggregate demand but through different means and with different aggregate supply effects. Lags and political factors make economic policy difficult.

2. Expansionary monetary policy increases aggregate demand in the short run and encourages investment spending that boosts aggregate supply in the long run. Balanced growth occurs. Expansionary fiscal policies discourage AS growth in the long run by bidding up interest rates. Which policy is best? The variable lag of monetary policy makes this a risky way to fight unemployment in the short term. Political considerations encourage fiscal policy in this instance.

3. What is the best way to fight inflation? Aggregate demand can be reduced through either monetary or fiscal means. The fiscal policy has better AS effects, but Congress does not want to vote higher unemployment rates. The FRS is insulated from these political concerns, but the variable lag might keep monetary policy from working in the short run.

4. The three ways of financing government have different economic and political consequences. Tax finance does little to shift aggregate demand. Borrowing from the public increases credit demand, driving up interest rates. Crowding out reduces fiscal policy's force and complete crowding out might wipe out Congress' actions entirely.

5. Borrowing from the FRS (an accommodating monetary policy) is the third way to finance government. Fiscal policies work best in this instance, but may be inflationary. There is no guarantee, either, that the Fed will cooperate.

6. Monetary and fiscal policies are either accommodating or conflicting. Policies work best when both groups aim at the same target. Congress and the Fed can offset one another in the short run, however. The long-run consequences of conflicting policies are important.

7. Should the FRS retain its independence from Congress? Are the risks of conflicting policies too great or is money too important to let Congress get into the act? Both sides of this issue were presented in the Economic Controversy.

DISCUSSION QUESTIONS

1. What is the best way to fight inflation? Justify your answer (Hint: what do you mean by "best"?).

2. What is the best way to fight unemployment? Justify your answer.

3. What is the best way to fight stagflation? Justify your answer.

4. You are the economics editor of the local newspaper. You have just received the following news items:

"Congress has just adopted a new budget calling for tax cuts and a $50 billion deficit."

"The FRS has just announced an increase in the discount rate, a signal that tight monetary policy is in the offing."

Write a brief news story describing how these policies will likely affect inflation and unemployment in the short term and in the long run.

5. Should the FRS remain independent? Take a side and defend your choice.

TEST YOURSELF

Circle the best response to each of the following questions.

1. Expansionary fiscal policy and contractionary monetary policy have the *same* impact on ________ but have *different* impacts on ________ . Choose the pair of phrases that best fills in these blanks.

- **a.** aggregate demand/aggregate supply
- **b.** interest rates/aggregate demand
- **c.** aggregate supply/interest rates
- **d.** aggregate supply/investment spending
- **e.** interest rates/investment spending

2. Suppose that you define the "best" economic policy to be that one that is the most *certain* to achieve its goals in the short run. Which of the following policies would be the best way to solve the unemployment problem?

- **a.** federal government increases spending
- **b.** FRS undertakes an open market purchase
- **c.** FRS increases the reserve requirement
- **d.** federal government cuts taxes
- **e.** federal government cuts transfer payments

3. President Carter increased government spending without also increasing taxes. We observed that aggregate demand did *not* increase. Which of the following best explains this seeming paradox?

- **a.** aggregate demand did not increase because of the variable lag
- **b.** aggregate demand would not have increased if there had been complete crowding out
- **c.** aggregate demand would not have increased if the FRS undertook an accommodating monetary policy
- **d.** aggregate demand would not have increased under any circumstance—aggregate supply should have increased
- **e.** none of the above explain this situation

4. The federal government is currently running an annual deficit of over $100 billion. This deficit is financed by borrowing from the public. Assume that the CS curve is *not* vertical. All else being equal, this deficit will cause:

(X) higher aggregate demand in the short run
(Y) reduced aggregate supply in the long run
(Z) higher interest rates

a. all of the above
b. none of the above
c. only (X) and (Z) above
d. only (Y) and (Z) above
e. only (Z) above

5. Suppose that you think that the long-run growth of the economy should be the most important consideration in making economic policy. Congress has just voted to spend less on defense this year. What should they do with the money that they save (choose the best answer)?

a. cut gasoline taxes
b. reduce the deficit
c. use the money to increase unemployment benefits
d. use the money to increase social security benefits
e. any of the above would be a good idea

SUGGESTONS FOR FURTHER READING

There are many views of the FRS, government, and their policy combinations. Chapters 3 and 4 of the *Economic Report of the President* (1982) give one view. "The Budget and the Economy" by Joseph Pechman and Barry Bosworth and "Long-Term Budget Strategies" by Charles Schultz (both in Brookings' *Setting National Priorities*, 1983) present a different view. "The Budget Deficit is a Red Herring" by Paul Craig Roberts (*New York Times*, February 14, 1982) gives one view of crowding out, while "The Reagan Deficit and Investment" by Benjamin M. Friedman (*Wall Street Journal*, January 13, 1982) takes the other side of this issue.

12

THE CHALLENGE TO KEYNESIAN ECONOMICS

Preview

How does the monetarist view of economic theory differ from Keynesian theory?
What is the monetarist view of fiscal policy?
What is the monetarist view of monetary policy?
What is rational expectations theory?
How does rational expectations theory differ from monetarism?
What is the rational expectations view of monetary and fiscal policy?
What is disequilibrium macroeconomic theory?
How should we fight inflation?

WHAT IS the best way to fight inflation and unemployment? The last chapter painted a bleak picture of economic policy. Two heads are not always better than one if they fail to act together. Every policy seems to have some risk of political or economic failure. Silver linings come wrapped in dreary dark clouds. Is there not another road to prosperity? This chapter looks at the maps that non-Keynesian geographers draw to guide economic policy.

The Keynesian economic theories you have been reading about have dominated economic theory in the 1980s, but a vocal minority of professional economists have proposed theories that challenge Keynesian orthodoxy.

monetarism: the school of economics that views economic theory as money demand and money supply; monetarists disagree with Keynesians about fiscal policy and the monetary transmission mechanism.

rational expectations theory: a macroeconomic theory built on microeconomic behavior; assumes individuals base rational behavior on expectations.

disequilibrium theory: the school of economics that thinks markets fail to clear; macroeconomics based on problems of disequilibrium.

Some, like Nobel Prize winner Milton Friedman, expound **monetarism;** their theories and policies focus on the role of money. Another group subscribes to the **rational expectations theory.** They suggest a different policy prescription. A third school has produced **disequilibrium theory.** Their economic policy advice differs from the first two. Add these three schools to the Keynesian and supply-sider's schools and you have a heated debate.

Each of these five groups subscribes to a different view of how individuals behave and how the macroeconomy works. Their different theories yield different views about proper government policy. Do these new theories open doors of escape from stagflation or do they lead up blind alleys?

Keynesian Doctrine

Let us begin this comparison of alternative theories with a quick review of Keynesian ideas. How does the economy work? What is government's role? These are difficult questions with complicated answers (as you should know by now), but we can collapse the basics of Keynesian theory into three propositions:

1. **MACROEQUILIBRIUM.** Keynes held that the economy automatically moves to an equilibrium, but that equilibrium is not necessarily desirable. Equilibrium with high unemployment (the depression experience) is as likely as full employment. The economy is stable, but stability with low income is not enough.

2. **ECONOMIC POLICY.** Macroequilibrium with high unemployment is possible, but it does not have to be permanent. Government can shift the economy to a more desirable equilibrium by regulating aggregate demand. In short, economic policies can fight unemployment.

3. **MONETARY AND FISCAL POLICY.** Both monetary and fiscal policies are effective. Fiscal policy works directly on aggregate demand through the spending, tax, and transfer payment multipliers. Monetary policy works through the monetary transmission mechanism: interest rates alter investment spending decisions.

Keep these three propositions in mind as we examine the challengers to orthodox Keynesian economics.

Monetarist Theory

Monetarism is both an old and a new theory. Economic textbooks written in the early 1900s presented only one view (in just one chapter!) of macroeconomics—the simple monetarist theory given by the **equation of exchange.**

equation of exchange: the simple monetarist view of the economy; M × V = P × Q where M equals money supply, V equals velocity of money, P equals price level, and Q equals RGNP.

The equation of exchange is an accounting identity: total spending equals total production. What happens when you buy a $1 loaf of bread? You spend $1 and a $1 loaf of bread is produced. What holds for individual transactions is also true for the economy as a whole. If we let P stand for the price level and Q represent total production (RGNP), then the money value of output is:

$$\text{Total production} = P \times Q = \text{Aggregate supply}$$

How much spending takes place? One way to view total spending is to take the money supply (M) and see how many times each dollar is spent during the year. The **velocity of money** (V) gives the average amount of spending per dollar of money supply (the velocity of money in 1981 was 6.6—each dollar of M1 accounted for almost seven transactions during the year). Using these definitions, we can write total spending during the year as:

velocity of money: the average number of times the money supply is spent in a year; GNP divided by the money supply.

$$\text{Total spending} = M \times V = \text{Aggregate demand}$$

The equation of exchange links these ideas. Total spending always equals total production (aggregate demand equals aggregate supply), so it follows that:

$$M \times V = P \times Q$$

The Equation of Exchange

Pre-Keynesian economists used this identity to derive policy predictions. What happens when the money supply increases because of FRS action or, in years past, if the gold supply suddenly rises as during the California Gold Rush? The equation of exchange tells us that an increase in M has three possible results (or some combination of the three).

1. RGNP RISES. The two sides of this equation have to balance, so an increase in M might result in an equal increase in Q (real output). Is this a likely outcome? Milton Friedman suggests not, using "Friedman's Helicopter" to explain why. Suppose a helicopter flies over the city and drops millions of dollar bills. Does this increase the amount of spending? Yes! Does this increase the number of cars in dealers' lots, the quantity of steel firms can produce, the proven reserves of oil, or the number of experienced mechanics in the labor force? No! At least not in the short run. Just having more money does not change the amount of real goods immediately available. So where does the extra money go? The second possibility is that velocity falls.

2. VELOCITY FALLS. The equation of exchange balances if an increase in the money supply brings an equal but opposite decrease in the velocity of money. People have more money but choose to spend less of it so total spending remains the same.

Does this sound likely to you? Would you not trade extra dollars for valuable goods if your money supply took a sudden jump? Monetarists think a decrease in velocity unlikely. The velocity of money, they say, is constant in the short run. More money means more total spending. If this is so, where does the money go? Only one place is left.

3. **INFLATION.** An increase in the money supply cannot change production in the short run and does not affect velocity—people spend more when they have more. The only possibility left is an increase in the price level. Inflation results if the money supply M grows faster than real output Q. Monetary policy is usually inflationary.

Monetarists think of money as being just like any other good. Try thinking of money as being like a particular kind of popcorn that everyone accepts as a medium of exchange. What would happen if someone suddenly increased the supply of this popcorn? Would people spend any less? No. Would people suddenly produce more of other goods to match the popcorn rise? No. Would the popcorn glut drive down the value of popcorn? Yes. An increase in the money supply drives down money's value (through inflation) in the same way.

This simple model of the economy was consistent with the laissez-faire attitudes of classical economists: The free market should be allowed to find the $P \times Q$ total output equilibrium. Monetary authorities should avoid causing inflation through sudden increase in the money supply. The best economic policy was moderation. Fiscal policy had no part in this drama.

Modern Monetarist Theory

Keynes' views overpowered this simple monetarism in the 1930s, 1940s, and 1950s. The monetarist challenge was renewed, however, when Keynesian policies failed to slay the stagflation dragon. This modern monetarist view dominates FRS policy today and has many proponents in Congress and academia.

Modern monetarism takes the equation of exchange one step further. It views the economy as a market for money and the equation of exchange as the equilibrium state of that market. Why do people produce and sell goods? Because they want the money that those sales produce. We can interpret the right side of the equation of exchange as:

$$\text{Money demand} = P \times Q$$

Buyers trade money for goods. They supply money to this market. The total amount of money available in a year is given by the amount of spending—the left side of the equation of exchange:

$$\text{Money supply} = M \times V$$

Put these two ideas together and we have a trio of important identities:

$$\begin{aligned} M \times V &= P \times Q \\ \text{Aggregate demand} &= \text{Aggregate supply} \\ \text{Money supply} &= \text{Money demand} \end{aligned}$$

The modern monetarist view is that the economy is made up of people who demand money (sellers) and people who supply money (buyers). Monetarists look at aggregate demand–aggregate supply analysis through these money-tinted glasses.

Money is the most important commodity in the monetarist world. The economy finds equilibrium where money demand equals money supply. This equilibrium determines both the quantity of money and goods exchanged (RGNP) and the price of money (its purchasing power).

What happens if there is a surplus on this market (as, for example, if the FRS suddenly increases money supply)? People try to trade surplus money for scarce real goods. Money's value declines (inflation) until the new equilibrium occurs. What happens if money is scarce? Producers bid more and more goods for scarce money. Purchasing power rises (money buys more—that is deflation) until another equilibrium is reached. All macroeconomic theory and policy can be analyzed as money demand versus money supply.

Money is the star of the monetarist drama. Monetarists and Keynesians disagree about money and the way the economy works. The following discussion is a simplified presentation of the monetarist view.

1. MACROEQUILIBRIUM. Monetarists agree that the economy seeks its own equilibrium. They disagree about the properties of that equilibrium. Keynes said that depression was as possible as full employment. Monetarists say that the economy is stable and strong if left free of government interference and destabilizing economic policies. No one wants to sell additional goods for money or exchange more money for goods at equilibrium. This equilibrium corresponds to the natural rate of unemployment discussed in Chapter 3. People who are still unemployed at equilibrium must not want to trade their labor for money at the going wage rate. If they did, there would be a shortage of money and its price would rise. The only people out of work are those who voluntarily forego employment (this type of unemployment is termed "natural" unemployment).

2. ECONOMIC POLICY. Can economic policy reduce the unemployment rate? Keynes said that aggregate demand policies like government spending and tax cuts could fight unemployment. Monetarists disagree; an increase in aggregate demand provides a temporary employment boost, at best, but does not do anything but cause inflation in the long run. We can see the monetarist view in Figure 12-1.

Suppose that the Fed increases the money supply. People take the monetary bonus and spend it, increasing aggregate demand. Aggregate supply is fixed in the short run, due to bottlenecks and physical limitations, so only inflation results. The increased money supply with no change in money demand bids down money's value.

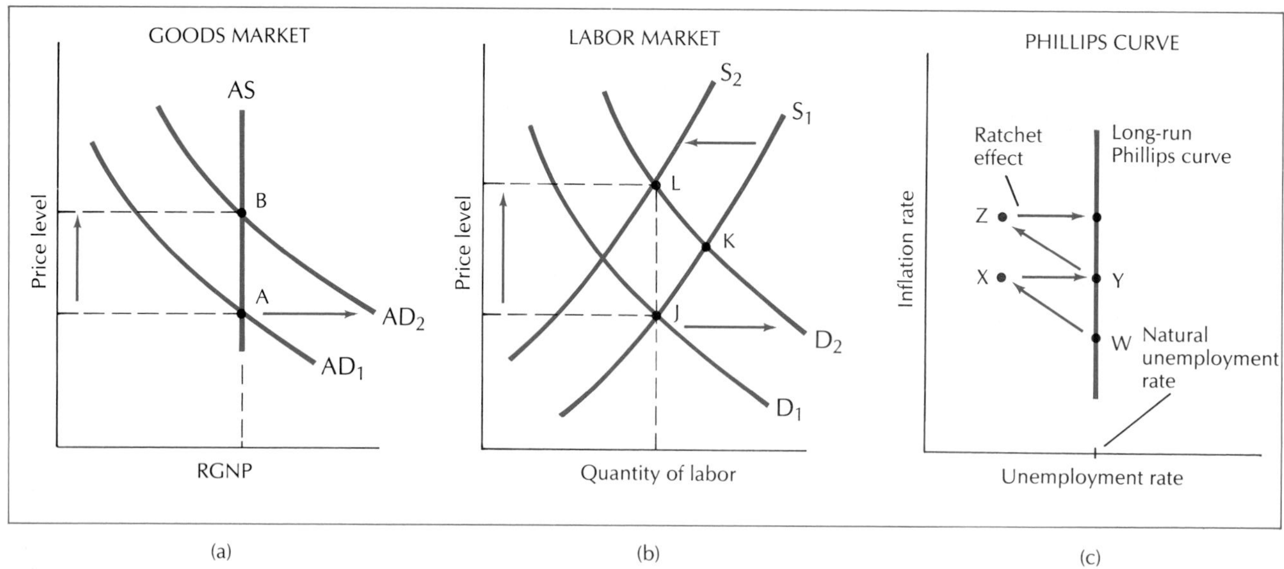

FIGURE 12-1 MONETARY POLICY, A MONETARIST PERSPECTIVE. Monetarists think that the aggregate supply curve is vertical in the short run. An increase in the money supply directly increases aggregate demand. The economy moves from A to B in the first part of the figure. Higher aggregate demand increases labor demand (temporarily increasing employment from J to K). However, inflation reduces labor supply and employment falls back to the old level (K to L), but with higher wage rates. This process makes a vertical Phillips curve, as shown in the third part of the figure. The economy starts at W and temporarily moves to X with higher inflation and lower unemployment. But employment falls as expectations adjust to higher inflation. The economy moves from X to Y. All that this policy does is increase the rate of inflation.

Does this policy reduce the unemployment rate? Any gain is only temporary, as the next part of the figure shows. Higher aggregate demand increases the demand for labor. But workers realize that inflation shrinks their real wages. They demand more pay and the labor supply curve shifts back. The result? The number of workers employed is the same as at the start. They receive higher wages, but inflation wipes out their gain.

Economic policies like this might temporarily reduce unemployment but not for long. No inflation–unemployment trade-off exists. The Phillips curve is vertical in the long run. Economic policies that stimulate aggregate demand have a **ratchet effect:** they push inflation to higher and higher levels without really changing production and employment.

ratchet effect: condition where economic policies result in ongoing increases in inflation with no permanent effect on unemployment.

3. MONETARY AND FISCAL POLICY. Only monetary policy works. Aggregate demand depends on the money supply alone in the monetarist view. A change in the money supply directly affects aggregate demand. Fiscal policies have no lasting effect.

Why does fiscal policy not work? Fiscal policy alters *who* spends money, but it does not change the *amount* of money or spending. Suppose, for example, that government decides to increase defense spending. Does this increase aggregate demand? It might, in the short run, if government spends faster than businesses and households (the velocity of money rises). But government's spending crowds out private spending, so the AD total remains unchanged. Increased government purchases are matched by lower consumer spending (if tax-finance is used) or by less investment spending (if deficits are financed by borrowing from the public). Fiscal policy does not affect either money supply or money demand. Government cannot alter the macroeconomic equilibrium in any lasting way.

Monetary policy is potent. An increase in the money supply boosts aggregate demand directly. Monetarists do not believe in the monetary transmission mechanism. An increase in the money supply, like that shown in Figure 12-2, boosts credit supply, but inflation eventually makes credit demand rise, too. Monetary polcy cannot force interest rates down in the long run.

Friedman's Policy of Rules

What economic policies do the monetarists recommend? A laissez-faire fiscal policy is best. Government cannot shift aggregate demand because it cannot change the money supply. Government policies can (and, monetarists think, frequently do) distort aggregate supply and set regulation roadblocks to eco-

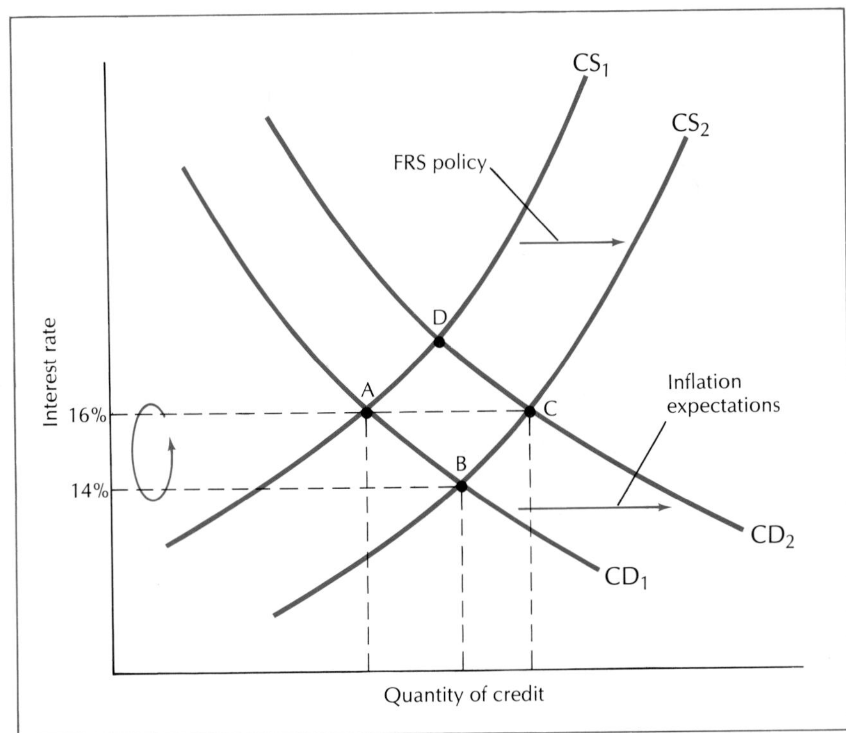

FIGURE 12-2 MONETARY POLICY WITH RATIONAL EXPECTATIONS. Federal reserve policy has no meaningful effect on the interest rate. The increase in credit supply initially moves the credit market from A to B. But borrowing increases in expectation of higher inflation rates, so interest rates rise back from B to C. Interest rates might even rise to D if savings are withdrawn from banks and spent, reducing credit supply in anticipation of inflation.

nomic growth. Government should balance its budget and deregulate the economy to promote AS growth.

Since fiscal policy is impotent, should the Fed step in to fight inflation and unemployment? No! the monetarists say. Most of our history of boom and bust has come from unwise activist monetary policies. The Fed cut the money supply during the 1930s (they raised reserve requirements to create "confidence" in banks), thereby making the Great Depression worse. Fed policies in the 1960s and 1970s tried to reduce unemployment. Inflation rates zoomed higher, but the unemployment problem was never really solved. Figure 12-3 shows the vertical Phillips curve of the 1970s and the results of expansionary Fed action.

According to monetarists like Milton Friedman, activist monetary policy has caused, not cured, our economic problems. They suggest a monetary policy of fixed rules. The Fed should steadily increase the supply of money at a fixed rate regardless of current economic conditions. This steady monetary growth makes aggregate demand grow at the same rate as aggregate supply. What happens when aggregate demand and aggregate supply grow together? Stable, high rates of economic growth are the result—with little or no increase in the price level.

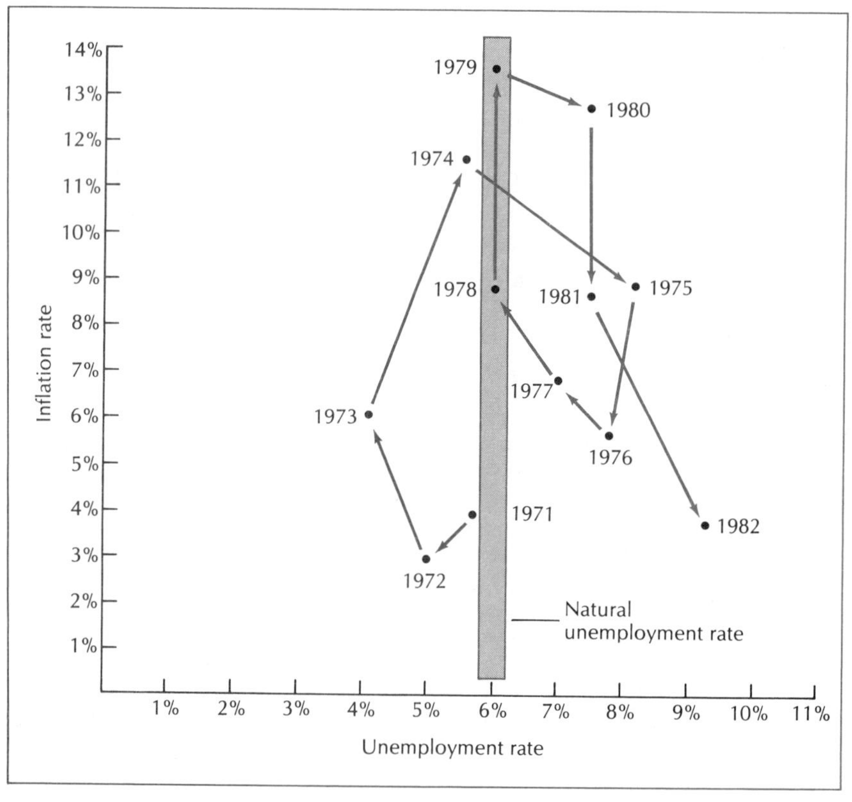

FIGURE 12-3 THE NATURAL-UNEMPLOYMENT-RATE HYPOTHESIS. The inflation and unemployment experienced in the period from 1971 to 1982 is consistent with a natural unemployment rate of about 6 percent. This does not prove that the natural rate hypothesis is correct, however. Other explanations for this relationship may be equally valid.

The exquisite paradox of monetarism is that the money supply is so important that monetary policy should not be used (even by the nonpolitical FRS!) to fight short-term fires. Keep your eye on the long run and aggregate supply growth, they advise.

What happens to interest rates if the **rules policy** is followed? Interest rates rise and fall depending on credit market conditions. Is this important? No, monetarist doctrine suggests. What is important is not the interest rate, which adjusts to match borrowers and lenders (and so determines *who* spends money), but the quantity of money—the amount of total spending in the economy.

rules policy: Milton Friedman's suggested FRS policy: money supply should grow at a constant rate to match AS growth.

The Monetarist Influence

Monetarism has been a powerful influence on economists and politicians. The economic programs of the Federal Reserve in the United States, the Bank of Canada, and the conservative government in Great Britain are based on the ideas presented here. Interest rates were high in these countries in the early 1980s as money supply targets replaced interest rates as a policy goal. Have these monetarist policies been successful? It is too early to tell. Falling inflation rates in the United States and Great Britain make monetarist claims credible, however.

Monetary policies face two important problems that weaken monetarism's power in today's world. Monetarist monetary policies and Keynesian fiscal policies, like oil and water, do not always mix. A monetarist FRS holds down money supply growth and ignores high interest woes. The Congress, in classic Keynesian form, fights unemployment with tax cuts and increased spending. These fiscal acts will not increase aggregate demand—if the monetarists are correct—but the huge deficits that result will still increase interest rates. Higher borrowing costs put shaky firms out of business, boost operating costs for those that remain, and discourage long-run growth. Important sectors like housing and automobiles bite the dust. Aggregate supply falls and the expansionary fiscal policy ends up with even more stagflation.

The second problem is more technical, but may be more important. Success in monetary policy, according to the monetarist creed, means setting money supply targets so that money supply (AD) grows at the same rate as money demand (AS). This is not an easy task, however. Which money supply should we use? The Fed currently sets targets for M1, M2, and M3, but the distinction between the different money measures is difficult to discern. Just what is the money supply and how is it measured? How do you set targets for variables that constantly change? Making good monetary policy today is like trying to hit a moving target while riding a merry-go-round. It is possible to score a bull's-eye—but success takes as much luck as skill!

These problems take some of the shine off monetarism's policy gems. Keynesian policies have uncomfortable trade-offs, but monetarist prescriptions are not guaranteed, either.

Rational Expectations Theory

The 1970s gave birth to a new economic theory based on the microeconomics of expectations. Rational expectations theory (Ratex, for short) says that individuals gather information about the state of the world, economic policies, and the like, and then plan their behavior accordingly so as to maximize profit, wealth, or satisfaction. Their individual behavior is rational, given their expectations of the future (hence, rational expectations theory's name).

One interesting conclusion of the Ratex theory is that expectations are always correct. If everyone expects higher inflation rates in the future, their rational behavior assures that result. Rational consumers borrow more, spend it quickly, and demand higher wages. Rational firms stock up on inventory goods and raise output prices. Aggregate demand rises, aggregate supply falls, and the expected inflation occurs.

Rational expectations theory differs from both monetarism and Keynesian doctrine in three important areas.

1. MACROEQUILIBRIUM. The economy is always in equilibrium, according to Ratex. This equilibrium is entirely dependent on individual expectations and rational behavior. The equilibrium does not depend on money or prices, since expectations can adjust for these.

2. ECONOMIC POLICY. Rational expectations theorists believe in the "natural unemployment rate" hypothesis. Government cannot, in their view, reduce the unemployment rate. How do they figure this? Suppose government fights unemployment by increasing social security payments. Everyone knows the effects that this will have: retired people expect their disposable incomes to rise, so they adjust spending plans. Merchants anticipate increased spending, so they raise prices. Workers expect labor demand and consumer prices to rise so they demand higher wages, and so on. Everyone anticipates and adjusts to these changes, so nothing really changes.

It is like the expectations problems you saw in Figures 12-1 and 12-2. If government increases labor demand, inflationary expectations (rational expectations, given a vertical Phillips curve) reduce the labor supply—nothing changes except prices. An increase in the credit supply (as Figure 12-1 showed) is matched by inflationary expectations. Once again, the only change is an increase in money prices. This means that the Phillips curve is vertical and that attempts to reduce unemployment from its natural rate only crank up the inflation rate, as Figure 12-3 showed.

3. MONETARY AND FISCAL POLICY. Keynesians think that both monetary and fiscal policy work against unemployment. The monetarists say only money supply changes are effective. Ratex proponents propose a shocking idea: nothing works.

Nothing? Any systematic monetary or fiscal policy, rational expectations claims, is powerless. Individuals find out about the policy, adjust future expectations to it and work around monetary and fiscal plans. The real variables of production, employment, and purchasing power remain unchanged! The only powerful action is a surprise policy—a sudden and radical tilt in monetary or fiscal policy that no one expects. This policy, by catching people off guard, succeeds in changing their behavior in the short run.

Surprise policies are the only effective ones, but there is little to be gained here. People soon adjust to the new policy and return to their old plans. A policy of random surprise policies would soon be discovered and expectations would adjust to this, too.

Rational Expectations Policies

Rational expectations theorists criticize both monetarists and Keynesians for believing that individuals can be fooled by widely publicized, systematic policies like tax cuts and monetary growth targets. They complain, as well, that other economic theories assume that consumers and producers act irrationally. Their main complaint is that other economists fail to fully incorporate expectations into their analysis of economic policy.

What economic policies do they propose? Ratex economists think that a goal of stability is more important than the particular policies Congress and the Fed adopt. They suggest that the "rules of the game" should be completely spelled out so that accurate expectations are formed. Government policy should hold a steady course. Tax laws should remain as is so that workers and businesses can plan with certainty. The Fed should not try activist policies unless they are consistent and well known.

Ratex policies aim to take government out of the economic game. Government lawmaking, national defense, distribution policies, and FRS monetary regulation are a necessary part of the economy. But activist economic policies are impotent and—worse—disruptive. Surprise policy changes (unexpected changes in the rules of the game) are responsible for booms and busts in the economy.

Disequilibrium Theory

Disequilibrium theory presents an eclectic view of the economy, bringing together elements from several other schools. This theory suggests that economic markets are not as competitive and flexible as the monetarists and rational expectations theorists think. Monopolies and large, powerful firms dominate some markets. Many barriers keep individual markets and, therefore, the macroeconomy from clearing. Here is how this still-developing theory views the world:

1. MACROEQUILIBRIUM. The economy is nearly always out of equilibrium. Markets fail to clear because of Keynes' sticky wages and prices, government floors and ceilings, widespread monopoly power, and because it is in the best interest of many individuals and firms to keep prices or output constant in spite of market conditions.

Why do wages not fall so low that unemployment disappears (or shrinks to the natural rate)? Hiring and firing are not costless. Firms that lay off workers now have to search for replacements later; they might also have to invest in expensive training. These firms have a vested long-term interest in keeping skilled employees. Unions with monopoly power try to keep wages high, too, because it gives them leverage in negotiations with powerful employers. Wages stay high during recession, and labor market disequilibrium (unemployment) results.

Why do the prices of some surplus goods not fall? Why do the prices of some scarce goods not rise? Buyers and sellers have a vested interest in retaining established trading patterns. Prices remain stable by custom or to encourage long-run commercial links. Firms with monopoly power sometimes absorb temporary losses to keep prices high in the future or hold prices unprofitably low to keep other firms out of the market. Price does not adjust and markets stay in disequilibrium. The economy cannot be in equilibrium when all of these markets are out of kilter.

2. ECONOMIC POLICY. Government should try to push the economy in the right direction, even if equilibrium is not likely. Monetary and fiscal policies work along Keynesian lines but are less powerful because prices and quantities do not respond to typical supply-demand forces. Government policies need to be stronger to achieve any given goal.

3. MONETARY AND FISCAL POLICY. Monetary and fiscal policies need to push the economy toward full employment and to help the economy achieve a more competitive structure. Government can do this in two ways. First, government rigidities that prevent markets from clearing need to be removed. Some market problems will not go away, so government's hand should strike a balance between the noncompetitive forces of monopolies and labor unions, for example.

Congress and the Federal Reserve may be forced to take a bigger role in the private sector. Monopoly power keeps wages, prices, and interest rates high and increases both inflation and unemployment. Many new price controls and market regulations might be needed to supplement traditional monetary and fiscal policies.

Disequilibrium analysis is still relatively new. The idea of macroeconomic disequilibrium is clear, but the specific policies disequilibrium requires are not well developed.

Supply-Side Economics

The final economic theory discussed here is supply-side economics. You have already read about supply-side theories in Chapters 7 and 8. Supply siders do not have a comprehensive theory. What they share is more a view of the world than a systematic model of the economy (their theories are still being developed, much like disequilibrium ideas). The following discussion outlines the views of supply-side economics.

1. MACROEQUILIBRIUM. Supply siders share the view that the macroeconomy finds its own stable equilibrium. They tend to follow the classical economists in believing that this equilibrium would be desirable if it were not for government interference. They see demand-management policies like taxes and open market purchases as roadblocks to aggregate supply. Monetary and fiscal policies prevent automatic adjustment to a high-employment equilibrium.

2. ECONOMIC POLICY. Government's activities should be limited to roles that private actors cannot play alone such as education, national defense, and a few public welfare functions. In general, supply siders think that government should get off the backs of workers and producers and allow their private actions to achieve prosperity. Supply siders view government as a potent force, but one that is more powerful in causing inflation and unemployment than in curing these ills.

3. MONETARY AND FISCAL POLICY. Full employment requires less government interference and more production incentives. Supply siders would deregulate most markets and cut tax rates to encourage greater production and to end underground activities. They view these tax cuts as expanding aggregate supply, not aggregate demand, however. Monetary policy should be designed to restore value to the dollar. Many supply siders favor returning to the gold standard as a way of reducing inflation and limiting monetary growth.

Who Is Right Here?

Which theory is the best? Which policy brings full employment and stable prices? If economists are so confused and divided, how can economic policy proceed? All these economic theories have something to offer and modern economists draw on the entire body of theory in suggesting policy.

Keynesian theory still forms the basis for most economic policy. Keynesian interest rates and monetary money supplies are both important. The money supply cannot be ignored—there is considerable evidence that monetary quantities exert strong influence on aggregate demand. But we cannot dismiss interest rates, either. Interest rates are important in helping to determine where spending goes. Expectations are important, too. The rational expectations theorists are right in saying that expectations and rational behavior can alter policy effects. Neither can economists ignore parts of the economy where markets fail to clear and disequilibrium prevails. Finally, the supply siders' emphasis on production, incentive, and aggregate supply must be taken seriously even by those who disagree with their specific policies.

The best model of the economy draws from all these theories. But merely adding these theories together still leaves important questions unanswered. Are monetary and fiscal policies impotent? Does the Phillips curve exist? Is it vertical?

So where does this leave us? What policy is best? It depends on which model you think most nearly describes the macroeconomy. If you think money is more important than anything else, you favor monetarist rules. If you think that expectations handcuff policymakers, you favor stable policies of whatever sort. Keynesians look for fiscal policies and watch interest rates. Supply siders seek lower tax rates and the gold standard as the way out of our economic box.

What is the right balance between these competing theories and policies? This question remains unanswered.

ECONOMIC CONTROVERSY:

How Do You Fight Inflation?

Inflation just will not go away. The high inflation rates of the 1970s have made themselves at home—even high unemployment rates have not permanently reduced inflation. What is the solution to the inflation puzzle?

This chapter introduced the theories of monetarism, rational expectations, and disequilibrium. You already know something about Keynesian and supply-side beliefs. Let us ask representatives of each school to answer the $64,000 question: How should we fight inflation?

Keynesian Economics

Fighting inflation in the short run is a problem of trade-offs. Lower inflation rates come at a high cost. How low do you want inflation to go? How much are you willing to pay?

Restrictive monetary and fiscal policies reduce aggregate demand and remove inflationary pressures in the short run. But they reduce RGNP and put people out of work. How severe is the inflation–unemployment trade-off? Economist Walter Heller estimates that RGNP has to fall by $200 billion (a loss of 3 million jobs) to reduce the underlying inflation rate by 1 percent! Do you want price stability? Are you willing to live with 15 to 20 percent unemployment? This is a high price to pay for lower inflation rates!

A second alternative is to impose wage and price controls and then use expansionary monetary and fiscal policies to handle any unemployment problem that shows up. While this policy directly addresses the inflation problem, it might cause shortages and reduce production incentives. This is not good, but this price seems more acceptable than high unemployment rates.

Other policies can be used to expand aggregate supply, but tax expenditures and interest-rate subsidies will not increase capacity immediately. There is no free lunch. Fighting inflation in the short run means paying a price—perhaps a high one.

The Monetarist View

Keynesians overstate the cost of anti-inflation policies just as they often underplay the costs of inflation itself. A successful anti-inflation policy has two parts.

First, Congress and the President have to learn to accept a less active role in fiscal policy. Government should balance its budget (to relieve deficit problems) and get down to the important business of making laws, planning national defense, and taking care of education and other public concerns.

Restrictive business regulations should be lifted because they only push up costs and prices. Government should limit its economic role to those few areas that the private sector cannot handle.

The main burden of anti-inflation policy falls on the Federal Reserve. The Fed needs to adopt a policy of orderly expansion of the money supply that matches the rate of aggregate supply growth. This policy limits inflation and achieves the goal of balanced growth. Friedman's policy of rules should be followed.

Will not these relatively restrictive policies cause unemployment? No—at least not for long. First, lower inflation rates (and the lower interest rates that follow) induce investment and aggregate supply growth. More and more permanent jobs in the private sector are born. Second, the unemployment rate quickly finds the natural rate. No fiscal policy is able to reduce unemployment from this natural level for long, anyway, and restrictive Federal Reserve policies will not cause it to rise above the natural rate for long, either. The unemployment rate might rise for a time, but lower inflationary expectations eventually increase labor supplies, bid down wage rates, and bring the economy into a low-inflation equilibrium at the natural unemployment rate.

The cost of fighting inflation is not so high. But spendthrift politicians are not willing to give up their illusions of power—they keep us from solving the inflation puzzle.

A Rational Expectations Policy

The monetarist is correct that fighting inflation need not drive up unemployment—the labor market quickly finds the natural unemployment rate. Both the monetarists and the Keynesians are wrong, however, about the effectiveness of economic policies.

Fiscal policy cannot fool people into reducing prices or inflation rates. Systematic monetary policies are similarly powerless. Activist monetary and fiscal policies have been the cause of inflation rates that have produced a ratchet effect on the vertical Phillips curve.

What is the solution to inflation? Inflation is whatever people expect it to be, but expectations are formulated on the basis of all available information—including information about government policies. Congress and the Fed both need to adopt moderate, stable long-run policies—and they need to convince economic actors that they will stick by consistent money, tax, spending, and transfer targets.

Will stable monetary and economic policies cure inflation by themselves? No. But these acts remove government as the cause of increasing inflation. Unemployment should return to its natural level and inflation rates should decline.

Disequilibrium Speaks

The rational expectations speaker is wrong about inflation and unemployment. There is no "natural rate" that results from efficiently clearing labor markets.

Many markets are consistently out of equilibrium with continuing shortage and surplus. Government does have a role in the disequilibrium economy.

Shortages and surplus can be effectively fought through monetary and fiscal policy. Government should step in to stimulate demand for labor and regulate prices. Regulation of uncompetitive markets and economic policies taken with market flaws in mind can bring inflation down without increasing the unemployment rate. These policies are complicated and require a larger government presence in the economy.

Let us face it, no force exists to bring the economy to a stable equilibrium—or to any equilibrium at all. The economics of the market fail to adequately describe the way the real world works. The rational expectations school, which says we are always in equilibrium and cannot do anything about it—is particularly wrong! Government can effectively improve on market disequilibrium. We must be prepared to actively intervene in the private sector to improve economic performance.

The Supply Side

All four of these views are wrong. Inflation can only be beaten through supply incentives. Two policies do the trick.

Taxes and government regulations discourage production and bid up costs. Government should cut regulatory strings and reduce tax rates dramatically. Lower tax rates slash production costs and give workers and firms the incentive they need to innovate, build, and produce. The supply side of the economy will grow quickly and bring prices down. Unemployment rates will shrink and the RGNP will grow. The United States should experience a new golden age of innovation and economic growth. Our standard of living will improve after many years of decline.

Monetary policy poses a threat to this supply-side expansion, however. Uncontrolled monetary growth debases the currency and removes production incentives. Why should anyone sweat to earn income or risk capital on innovation if all they earn are worthless paper dollars? We must restore faith in and value to the dollar. How can we do this? By returning to the gold standard!

Tax cuts, deregulation, and the return to the gold standard are the answer to inflation. What price must we pay for these benefits? No cost! Supply-side economics brings down prices by increasing production and RGNP and by reducing unemployment. This is the answer, we must only have enough faith in ourselves to enact it as policy.

SUMMARY

1. Keynesian theory says that the economy finds a macroequilibrium, but that equilibrium is not always desirable. Either monetary or fiscal policy can shift aggregate demand and fight inflation or unemployment. Fiscal policy works directly on aggregate demand; monetary policy works through the interest rate–investment spending link.

2. Monetarists see the economy as money supply and money demand. The economy finds its own macroequilibrium, but only monetary policy is able to shift aggregate demand. The equation of exchange, $M \times V = P \times Q$, shows the relationship between money supply ($M \times V$) and money demand ($P \times Q$).

3. Monetary policy shifts aggregate demand directly, not through interest rate effects. Spending depends on the size of the money supply, not on meaningless interest rates. Fiscal policy is impotent. Government taxing and spending actions do not change how much is spent, only who does the spending. At best, fiscal policy increases money velocity, bringing increases in short-term inflation.

4. Monetarists believe in the natural unemployment rate hypothesis. Economic policies cannot do much to change unemployment in the long run. The FRS should adopt a policy of steady expansion of the money supply in line with aggregate supply growth. This policy of rules, they think, brings low-inflation economic growth.

5. The rational expectations school agrees about economic equilibrium but disagrees about policy matters. The Ratex school holds that individuals form expectations and behave rationally, given those expectations. If policy changes, the new rules influence expectations and alter behavior. But the new behavior makes the policy powerless. In short, no systematic economic policy can change production and RGNP.

6. Rational expectations' policy prescription is stable, steady economic policy. Policy shocks, they claim, cause economic instability. The natural growth of the economy returns when activist economic policies are forsaken.

7. Disequilibrium macro theory is at the opposite end of the economic spectrum. Disequilibrium theorists suggest that many markets fail to clear because of high adjustment costs, monopoly pricing strategies, traditional business practices, and government policies. Shortage, surplus, and disequilibrium prices are the norm, not the exception. Powerful government policies are needed to alter output and encourage competition. Monetary and fiscal policies have an active role in this model.

8. Supply siders focus on the role of incentives in individual behavior. They see lower tax rates and a strong, stable currency as a way to achieve economic goals. They focus on policies that increase aggregate supply.

9. How can we fight inflation? The Economic Controversy presented five views and five policy prescriptions. No wonder Congress is confused!

DISCUSSION QUESTIONS

1. The equation of exchange can be used in many ways. Suppose that new oil deposits are discovered and there is no change in the money supply. How will this increase in RGNP affect the economy? Explain your reasoning. (Hint: what assumptions have you made about M, V, and P?)

2. Monetarists and Keynesians differ concerning the importance of interest rates to monetary policy. Why do Keynesians think they are important? Why do monetarists view them as irrelevant? What do you think?

3. What is the best way to reduce the unemployment rate? Answer this question from the perspective of a:

a. Keynesian
b. monetarist
c. rational expectations believer
d. disequilibrium theorist
e. supply sider

4. What is the best way to reduce the inflation rate? State your own views and defend them.

TEST YOURSELF

Circle the best response to each question.

1. The equation of exchange is M × V = P × Q, an accounting identity. This equation means:

(X) total spending (M × V) equals totals production (P × Q)
(Y) aggregate demand (M × V) equals aggregate supply (P × Q)
(Z) money demand (M × V) equals money supply (P × Q)

a. all of the above are correct
b. none of the above are correct
c. (X) and (Y) are true
d. (Y) and (Z) are true
e. (X) and (Z) are true

2. Suppose that economists agree that aggregate demand needs to be increased. Which of the following policies would a monetarist think most effective in shifting aggregate demand?

a. increase in government spending financed by borrowing from the public
b. increase in the reserve requirement
c. increase in government spending financed by borrowing from the FRS
d. open market sale
e. increase in government spending financed by higher taxes

3. Monetarists and proponents of the rational expectations view agree on some issues and disagree on others. Which of the following statements would cause disagreement?

(X) the Phillips curve is vertical—the economy tends toward a natural rate of unemployment
(Y) a desirable monetary policy is a stable, constant expansion of the money supply
(Z) fiscal policy is ineffective because it cannot change the money supply—only monetary actions affect the economy

a. they would disagree about all of these statements
b. they would disagree about (X)
c. they would disagree about (Y)
d. they would disagree about (Z)
e. they would agree on all of these statements

4. Which of the following groups view tax reductions as one way to reduce unemployment in the long run: Keynesians, monetarists, rational expectations theorists, disequilibrium macroeconomists, and supply siders?

a. all of them think tax cuts reduce unemployment
b. none of them think tax cuts reduce unemployment
c. only monetarists and Keynesians
d. Keynesians, disequilibrium theorists, and supply siders
e. rational expectations theorists and supply siders

5. Interest rates are falling. If you are a monetarist you think that:

a. investment spending will rise and increase aggregate demand
b. people must have expected lower interest rates and taken actions that resulted in an interest-rate decline
c. aggregate demand might grow, but only if lower interest rates are a sign of an increase in the money supply
d. aggregate demand might decline, but only if lower interest rates are a sign of contractionary fiscal policy
e. RGNP might increase, but only if falling interest rates are a sign of tax rate reductions

SUGGESTIONS FOR FURTHER READING

Daniel Bell and Irving Kristol are editors of an excellent volume that analyzes the theories discussed in this chapter: *The Crisis in Economic Theory* (New York: Basic Books, 1981). Daniel Bell's "Models and Reality in Economic Discourse" is particularly interesting. Mark W. Willes presents "Rational Expectations as a Counterrevolution" and Allan H. Metzler's article, "Monetarism and the Crisis in Economics," presents the monetarist view. Milton Friedman argues his monetarist views in "A Memorandum to the Fed," *Wall Street Journal*, January 30, 1981. An amusing and scholarly discussion of rational expectations is given in "A Child's Guide to Rational Expectations" by Rodney Maddock and Michael Carter, *Journal of Economic Literature* (March, 1982).

IV

INTERNATIONAL ECONOMICS

13

INTERNATIONAL TRADE

Preview

Why do nations trade? What are the economic effects of trade? Who gains from trade? How?

What are tariffs and quotas? What are the arguments for and against trade restrictions?

Who really pays the tariff?

Should we worry about balance-of-payments problems?

Why does the United States have a balance-of-payments deficit?

Are automobile import quotas a good idea?

THE LEADERS of the industrialized nations gathered together for a summit conference in Versailles in 1982. Which international issue do you suppose caused the most controversy? Peace and war? Nuclear weapons? Human rights? Political alliances? No. The key issue was high U.S. interest rates and their international trade consequences; such is the importance of international economics.

open economy: an economy that trades with other countries.

closed economy: an economy with no interaction with other countries.

You live in an **open economy.** The nations of the world are like so many toy boats in a bathtub. Political and economic waves in other countries rock you and your actions send ripples that are felt on faraway foreign shores.

The economic models discussed so far in this text have described a **closed economy**—international trade and payments have not played a major role in the macroeconomic theories discussed thus far. We have ignored just one thing—the rest of the world! It is time to correct this oversight. The next four chapters examine the causes and consequences of international economic interdependence.

The United States is such a dominant economic force that the traditional focus on closed economy economics is understandable. Other countries do not take this parochial view, however. If you were taking this course in England or Japan your study would have started here—international economic events often overshadow purely domestic matters in other countries.

This chapter sets the stage by looking at international trade and its economic effects. International economic interdependence is rooted in international trade. The obvious first question is "Why do nations trade?"

Why Do Nations Trade?

Why do nations trade? The obvious answer to this question is that we trade to get goods that we cannot produce ourselves. Is this a good answer? Look around. Make a list of imported goods you buy or use. You might discover imports of light bulbs, automobiles, clothing, textiles, televisions, radios and other electronic gear, typewriters, agricultural goods, and many more items around the house. Consumers in the United States bought over $333 billion in imports in 1982 (foreigners bought over $349 billion of our goods that year).

Are the goods on your list things that cannot be made in the United States—items that we must import? No. Most imported goods could be produced in the United States. In fact, technology permits us to produce almost any import (or a reasonable substitute) if we so desire. International trade is not based on necessity. Why do nations trade, then?

The Law of Comparative Advantage

This old question was posed by the nineteenth century English economist David Ricardo. Ricardo observed a peculiar pattern of trade between Great Britain and Portugal. Great Britain exported cloth and imported wine from the Portuguese. Why this particular pattern of trade, Ricardo asked?

Is necessity the answer? No. Ricardo found that both countries were able to produce both goods with the same technology. Tastes were not the answer either—the exporting Portuguese seemed to like the wine even better than the importing British. It was technically possible for Britain to export wine and import cloth from Portugal. Why did this not happen? Ricardo decided to find out.

Maybe there is some difference in productivity that decides trade patterns. Ricardo defined a basic "resource unit" (composed of fixed amounts of labor, capital, and natural resources) and studied productivity in each country. Ricardo found that his resource bundle, set to work in British mills, could produce four yards of cloth. Used in British vineyards, the same resources yielded six bottles of wine.

The story was different in Portugal. A bundle of resources used in Portuguese mills made five yards of cloth. The result was fifteen bottles of wine for each resource bundle used to make wine.

What a paradox! A bundle of resources employed in Portugal would make more wine than in Britain (the expected result), and more cloth, too. Ricardo said that Portugal had an **absolute advantage** in producing both wine and cloth. If Portuguese firms were more productive, why should they bother to import? Why should a highly efficient country buy goods from a less efficient neighbor? Why did Portugal buy cloth from Britain?

absolute advantage: the ability to produce absolutely more with given resources.

This puzzled Ricardo. The cloth–wine trade did not make sense. Portugal, with unlimited resources, would be better off making both goods itself and buying neither from the British. Ricardo found his answer by introducing the fundamental fact of economics into his analysis: *scarcity*. Neither Portugal nor Britain had unlimited resources. Land, labor, and capital are scarce. Labor used to make cloth must be pulled away from wine production. More cloth means less wine. In economic terms, the foregone wine is the opportunity cost of producing cloth.

Ricardo decided that international trade was based on cost—that is, on differences in opportunity costs. Opportunity costs measure what a nation gives up in production. Let us apply the idea of opportunity cost to the cloth–wine example.

Britain could use a bundle of resources to make either four yards of cloth or six bottles of wine. What did a yard of cloth cost? Every extra yard of cloth meant giving up six-fourths, or one and one-half, bottles of wine. What did a bottle of wine cost? Britain gave up four-sixths, or two-thirds, yards of cloth for every bottle of wine it made. Work out the math for yourself to be sure that you understand the origin of these numbers.

What were Portugal's costs? The Portuguese chose between five yards of cloth and fifteen bottles of wine each time they allocated a resource unit. If they made cloth, each yard cost them fifteen-fifths, or three, bottles of wine that could have been produced instead. When they made wine, however, they gave up just five-fifteenths, or one-third, yard of cloth.

Who had the **comparative advantage** in producing cloth? A yard of cloth cost three bottles of wine in Portugal but just one and one-half bottles in Great Britain. Britain is the cheaper producer. Ricardo said that Britain should spe-

comparative advantage: the ability to produce at lower opportunity cost.

cialize in its comparative advantage and export the relatively cheap cloth to those with higher comparative costs.

Who had the comparative advantage in wine? A bottle of wine cost two-thirds yard of cloth in Britain but only one-third yard in Portugal. According to Ricardo's **law of comparative advantage,** the Portuguese should have specialized in wine and exported it. Each country sells the good in which it has a comparative advantage and buys the relatively cheaper import.

law of comparative advantage: the theory that international trade and production specialization is based on differences in opportunity cost.

Gains from Trade

terms of trade: the ratio of two goods in international trade.

Can both nations gain from this pattern of trade? Suppose that the two countries agreed on **terms of trade** of one yard of cloth exchanged for two bottles of wine (one bottle of wine trades for one-half yard of cloth). In this instance, is trade mutually advantageous?

Great Britain produced cloth at a cost of one and one-half bottle of wine. Would they be willing to sell the cloth at this price? Yes! The cloth (opportunity cost equals one and one-half bottles) earns a profit when sold for two bottles of wine. Would Britain want to buy wine at this price? Yes again! Why produce wine that costs two-thirds yard of cloth if you can buy it for the equivalent of one-half yard at these terms of trade.

Great Britain gained from trade at these prices. They sold cloth for more than its opportunity cost and bought Portuguese wine for less than it would have cost to produce it themselves. If Britain gained, must Portugal have lost?

Portugal also gained from trade! The Portuguese were happy to sell wine for one-half yard of cloth—it only cost them one-third yard of cloth (the opportunity cost) to produce it. They were pleased to buy the cloth for two bottles of wine, too. They had to give up three bottles of wine to produce a yard of cloth themselves.

Savor the magic of international trade! Each nation sells at a profit and buys for less than the cost of home production. Both countries gain from international trade! You can see the potential for gain in Figure 13-1.

Each country has 100 resource bundles to use in production of wine or cloth. Britain can have either 400 yards of cloth (if they specialize totally in

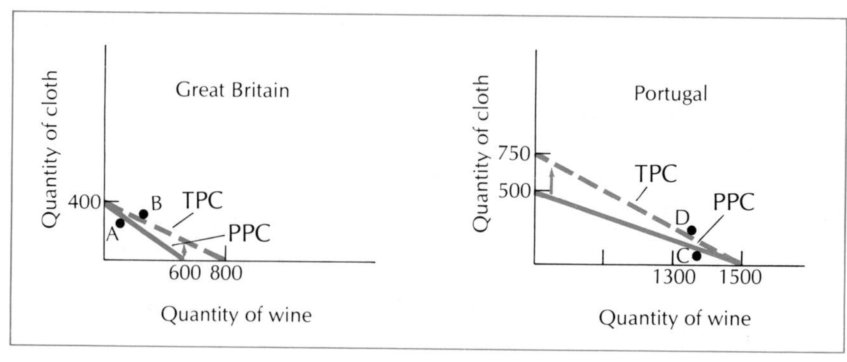

FIGURE 13-1 GAINS FROM TRADE. Production possibility curves (PPCs) show what each nation can produce and consume without international trade. Great Britain and Portugal are limited to points such as A and C. The trade possibility curves (TPCs) show the combinations of wine and cloth these countries can trade for at the exchange rate of 1 cloth = 2 wine.

textiles) or 600 bottles of wine, or any combination of the two given by the **production possibilities curve (PPC)** in the figure. The PPC shows the nation's production limits. Britain chooses a combination on the PPC, like point A, where they produce 300 yards of cloth and 150 bottles of wine.

production possibility curve (PPC): a graph showing the maximum amounts of two goods a nation can produce with scarce resources.

The British escape the bounds of their PPC through international trade. They specialize in cloth—their comparative advantage—and trade each yard of cloth for two bottles of wine. With trade they can have any point on the **trade possibilities curve (TPC)** in the figure. They can, for example, specialize in cloth and then trade 80 yards of fabric for 160 bottles of wine. This swap puts them at a point like B in the figure. They have 160 bottles of wine and can still keep 400 − 80 or 320 yards of cloth—they can consume more of both goods than if they produced them at home! Point B gives more wine and more cloth. Trade is advantageous to the British.

trade possibility curve (TPC): a graph showing the combinations a nation can trade for with given terms of trade.

The same idea applies to Portugal. The Portuguese can choose between 500 yards of cloth or 1500 bottles of wine or any point on their PPC (given 100 resource units and the productivity of this example). They consume the combination given by point C in the figure—1300 bottles of wine and 67 yards of cloth. Suppose they specialize in wine—their comparative advantage—and trade wine for cloth at the going terms of trade. Now they can have any point on their TPC—a point like D, for example. The Portuguese use all their resources to produce 1500 bottles of wine (complete specialization) and trade 160 of them to the British for 80 yards of cloth. They now have the 80 yards of cloth and the remaining 1500 − 160 or 1340 bottles of wine. They have more cloth than before trade, and more wine, too!

Economic Effects of Trade

Is this voodoo economics? How can both countries consume more with trade than they could without trade! Table 13-1 shows the puzzle.

Total cloth output was 367 yards before trade and 1450 bottles of wine were produced. Both totals grew after trade. From where did the extra goods come? Are more resources available? No. Both countries still have just 100 resource units, the same as before. Has technology changed? No. The productivity of each resource has remained constant. What has changed then? Each nation has specialized in its area of comparative advantage. Less wine is given up when cloth is produced in Britain. Less cloth is foregone when Portugal

TABLE 13-1 ECONOMIC EFFECTS OF TRADE

Country	Without trade			With trade		
	Point	Wine	Cloth	Point	Wine	Cloth
Great Britain	A	150	300	B	0	400
Portugal	C	1300	67	D	1500	0
Total		1450	367		1500	400

TABLE 13-1 PRODUCTION GAINS FROM TRADE. The same resources produce both more wine and more cloth when specialization and exchange take place.

specializes in the wine. The number of resources has not changed, but specialization (impossible without trade) means resources go where they are the most productive. Total output rises, thus more can be consumed and both nations gain.

International trade affects the economy in many ways. Trade allows countries to specialize and trade for goods not produced at home. This specialization allows firms to employ large-scale production techniques that further reduce opportunity costs. Everyone gains because one country produces a good at a lower cost instead of many small, costly factories dividing output.

International trade creates winners and losers. British wine drinkers gain in this example. Inexpensive imported wine costs less than expensive domestic goods. The Portuguese wine producers gain, too. They sell more wine and gain more profit with trade than without. Portuguese cloth buyers and British cloth producers likewise gain from lower prices and higher sales.

But trade makes losers, too, and the losers often call for trade restrictions to keep imports out. Who loses in this example? Import-competitors stand to lose here. British wine makers and Portuguese cloth manufacturers are both threatened by cheaper imports. Some consumers lose from the opening of trade, too. The price of cloth in Britain rises, for example, when Portuguese buyers bid prices up. Wine drinkers in Portugal pay a little more, too, because British oenophiles (wine snobs) add to the demand for their goods.

British buyers find that trade makes wine cheaper but cloth more costly. Portuguese consumers find prices going in the opposite direction. International trade tends to equalize prices across national borders. International trade increases production and consumption. Nations gain from trade, but individuals gain and lose as trade changes wages and prices and redistributes income within each country.

Comparative Advantage in the Real World

All this theory looks good on paper and probably made sense to Ricardo, but does it work in today's world? The surprising answer is—yes!

You need not look far to see comparative advantage at work. The United States buys oil from the OPEC nations and sells them agricultural goods, among other things. Does comparative advantage explain this pattern of trade?

Why does the United States buy costly oil from OPEC? Could we meet our own oil needs? Yes, but at a cost. Thousands of workers and machines would have to be diverted from production of other goods and put to work finding and producing oil. Could we do it? Yes, but the extra oil would cost us much more than OPEC's price. Thus, we gain from this trade.

OPEC gains, as well. Could OPEC meet its own food needs? Sure—but it would be expensive to make the deserts fertile. Resourses would need to be pulled away from competing uses. OPEC could grow its own food, but they would have to give up much more than they do with international trade.

The law of comparative advantage really works and its happy result is greater production and lower costs. We all have a stake in this miracle of exchange.

Tariffs and Quotas

Free trade benefits the majority but hurts important industries and worker groups in each nation. Firms and unions threatened by import competition lobby for trade restrictions like tariffs and quotas.

A **tariff** is a tax on imported goods. Tariffs were once an important source of government revenue. Their main function these days is to discourage international trade.

tariff: a tax on imported goods.

Here is how a tariff works: The market for imported scotch whiskey is shown in Figure 13-2. The free trade price is $10 per bottle. A $2-per-bottle tariff reduces import supply. Firms who pay the tariff supply less (because of their lower net price) or increase price—they need to charge $12 per bottle to take in a net of $10 after the tariff. The tariff produces a $2 vertical shift in the supply curve shown in this figure.

Falling supply bids up price and reduces the quantity imported. Price rises to $11 per bottle. Some consumers quit buying the import at the higher price; others switch to domestic substitutes. Employment rises in these import-competing industries.

A **quota** is a more direct way to keep imports out. Congress votes to limit imports to a specific physical quantity (and in some cases even sells the right to import these scarce goods). There is a big scotch shortage at the old

quota: a physical limitation on the quantity of imports.

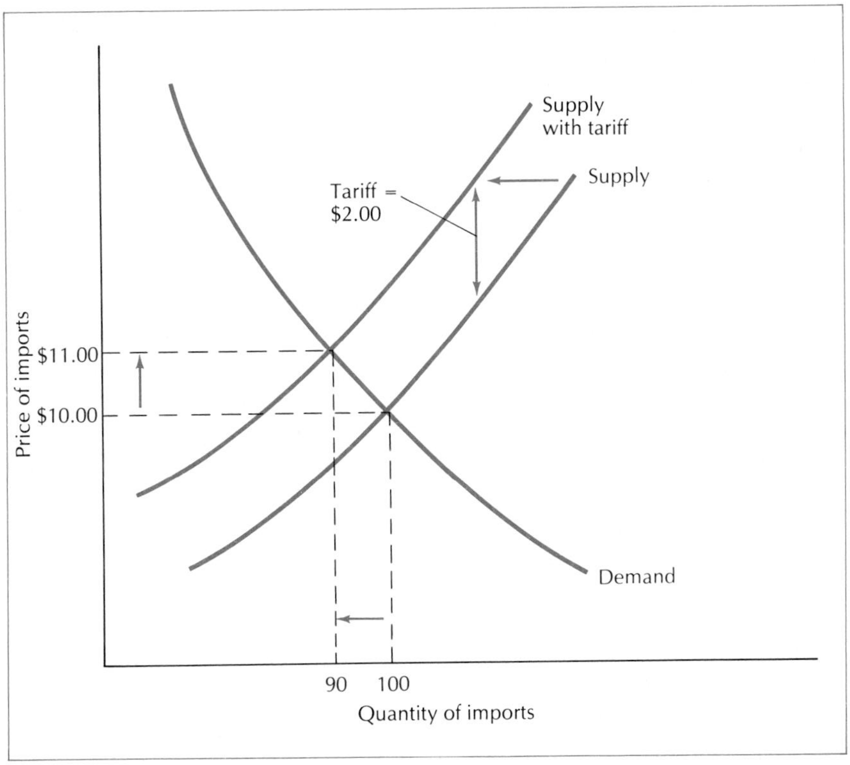

FIGURE 13-2 THE EFFECTS OF A TARIFF. A $2 tariff decreases supply. Firms supply less because their net receipts are reduced by the tariff. The import tax drives price up from $10 to $11 in this figure. The quantity of imports falls.

$10 price in Figure 13-3. The 50 bottle quota limit leaves many scotch drinkers dry. Price rises until quantity demanded falls to equal the quota limit of 50. The price goes from $10 to $18 in this figure.

Economists dislike tariffs and quotas. Both disrupt international trade. They raise import prices, discourage specialization, and disrupt the mutually advantageous system of comparative advantage. Both trade restrictions are bad, but quotas are the evil of two lessers. The market still works, after a fact, with tariffs. Consumers who want more imports can get them, if they pay tariff-inflated prices. But the market fails completely when quotas are imposed. An increase in demand by thirsty scotch drinkers in Figure 13-3 would bring only higher prices and monopoly profits to those permitted to import the quota amount. The import of extra goods to meet higher demand is illegal.

Who Pays the Tariff?

consumer burden: the part of a tariff paid by consumers as higher price.

Who bears the burden of trade restrictions? The tariff is levied against foreign producers, but do they really pay it? Look back at Figure 13-2. A $2 tariff was put on imported whisky here, but the price went up by $1. The **consumer burden** of this tariff was the $1 higher price (plus the value of the lost imports).

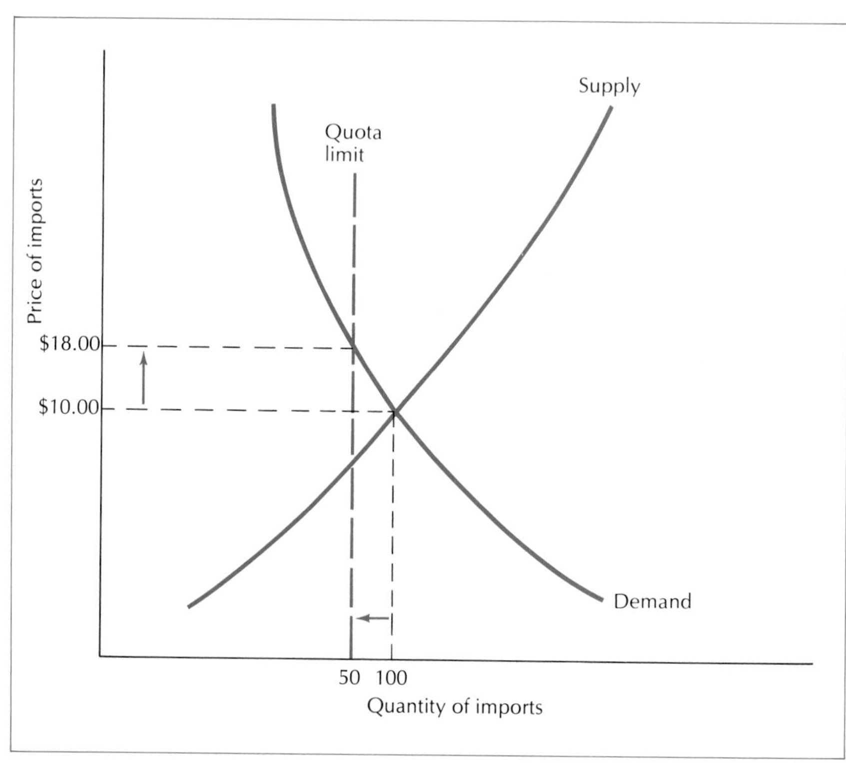

FIGURE 13-3 THE EFFECTS OF A QUOTA. A quota puts a lid of 50 on the number of goods imported in this market. The shortage disappears when price rises—to $18 here—high enough to adjust the quantity demanded to the limited supply.

Who paid the other half of the tariff? The **producer burden** falls on sellers as lower net price and reduced sales. Foreign producers receive $11 for the scotch but pay a $2 tax. They keep just $9—a dollar less than before. The lost net revenue (and the value of lost sales) is the producer burden.

producer burden: the part of a tariff paid by sellers as lower net price.

Is the tariff's burden always split as Figure 13-2 shows? The distribution of the tariff depends in part on the nature of import demand. Figures 13-4 and 13-5 tell the story.

Some imports face an **inelastic demand** curve like the one shown in Figure 13-4. Suppose that automobile buyers view imported cars as significantly different from domestic models. Since the two are not close substitutes, buyers do not switch from imports to domestic cars when the tariff is imposed. They will buy almost as many Toyotas as before when the price rises. Import demand is relatively unresponsive to price changes, giving the steep demand curve of this figure.

inelastic demand: demand relatively unresponsive to price changes; characteristic of necessity goods or goods with few close substitutes.

Who pays the tariff here? A $1,000 per car tariff reduces import supply and forces price up. The price here rises by $900 to $8,900 per car. Buyers pay most of the tariff as higher import prices. The producer burden is comparatively light. In general, a more inelastic import demand means a greater consumer tariff burden.

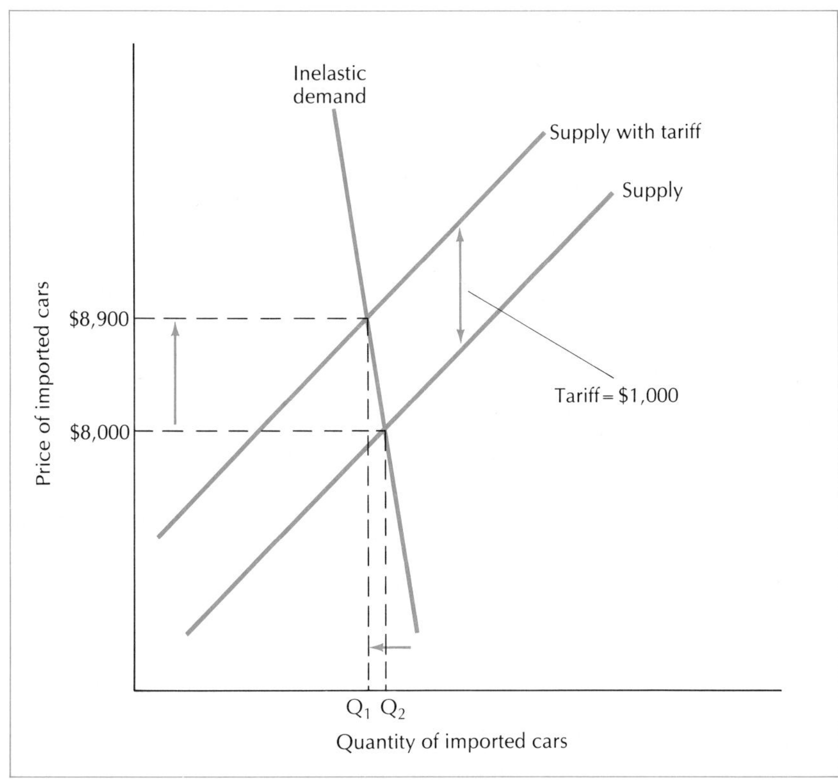

FIGURE 13-4 TARIFF WITH INELASTIC DEMAND. In this figure, demand is unresponsive to price changes. Most of the $1,000 tariff on new cars is passed on to consumers. Producers pay $100 of the tariff in lower net revenue, consumers pay the remainder.

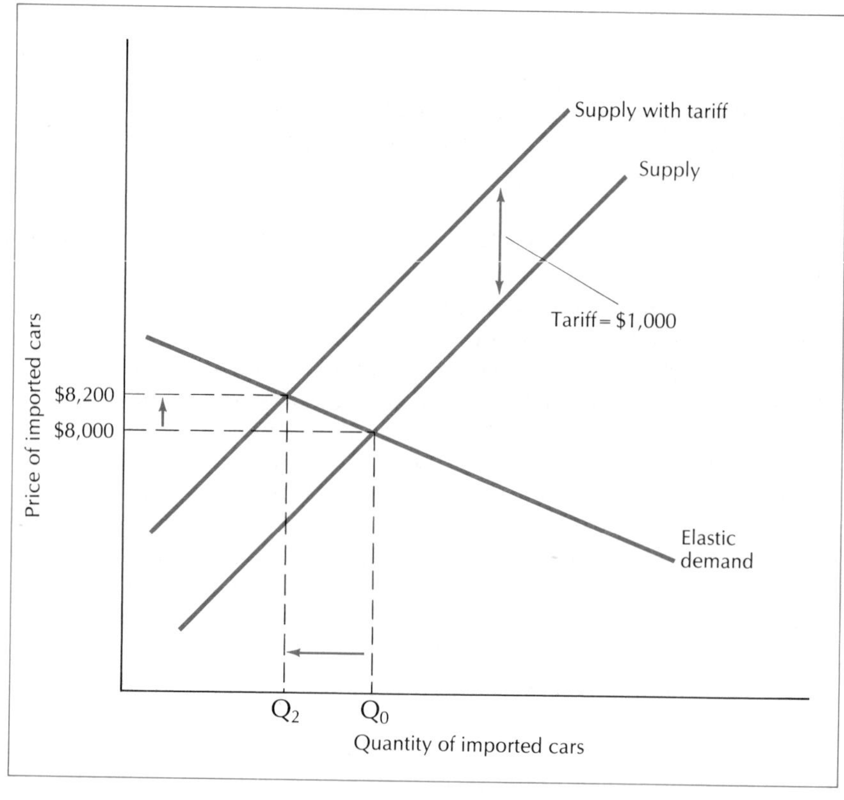

FIGURE 13-5 TARIFF WITH ELASTIC DEMAND. Producers pay more of the tariff when demand is responsive to price changes. Price rises by $200 in this market when the $1,000 tariff is imposed. The rest of the tariff falls on foreign producers. Compare this figure with Figure 13-4. Note the price and quantity differences.

elastic demand: demand relatively responsive to price changes; characteristic of goods with many close substitutes.

As can be seen in Figure 13-5, producers bear the brunt of the tariff in the case of **elastic demand.** Buyers in this market think that imports and cars built in the United States are much the same. They switch from one to the other depending on price. The flatter demand curve shows that the quantity demanded is highly responsive to changing price.

What happens when the tariff is imposed here? Importers again reduce supply when faced with higher tariff costs. Falling supply creates a shortage and bids up price. Does price rise a lot? No. Buyers switch to domestic substitutes when import prices go up. Sellers limit price increases or lose their market. The consumer burden is just $200—much less than in the inelastic demand case. Sellers receive $8,200 but pay the $1,000 tax, so their net price is $7,200 or $800 less than before the tariff. They pay most of the burden here.

Tariffs on goods with elastic demands collect relatively little revenue but successfully protect domestic industries by discouraging imports (look at the reduced quantities in the two figures). Tariffs on goods with inelastic demands do little to reduce imports, but they do bid up price and collect substantial revenue for the government. Perhaps this is why the British taxed colonial tea imports—to collect taxes paid mostly by colonial sippers. The Boston Tea Party that resulted shows how controversial tariffs can be!

Arguments for Tariffs

Most imported goods face some tariff or quota barrier. If tax revenue is not the main reason for trade barriers, why do they exist? Several arguments have been advanced in favor of these trade restrictions

1. PROTECTION. Many trade barriers exist simply to protect jobs and profits in U.S. industries. Tariffs and quotas divert demand from cheaper imports to domestic production.

Protective tariffs are enacted to save U.S. jobs from "unfair" foreign competition. Foreign firms are said to have an unfair advantage because wages or other costs are lower for them. Economists recognize that the "unfair" advantage is usually just comparative advantage at work. Opportunity costs are less in other lands, so their goods can be imported for less. Protective tariffs that disrupt free trade destroy comparative advantage.

Why does Congress pass protective tariffs that benefit a few groups but hurt the majority? Suppose that a $1 tariff on Italian shoes is up for a vote today. How much would this tariff hurt you? Unless you spend lots of money on Italian shoes, chances are you are not hurt much—you probably do not even know that Congress is considering the issue! Would you be informed if you were a U.S. shoe manufacturer? You bet your boots! You would have much to gain from this legislation, so you would lobby Congress and see that the trade barrier is erected.

Congress does not hear from the majority on issues like this. Individual shoe buyers pay too small a cost to make anti-tariff action economical (the total loss is high, however). Special interests stand to gain a bundle, however, so they make their feelings known. Congress responds to the "voice of the people," but the only voices they hear are those of pro-tariff special interests. Protective tariffs sprout like wheat in Kansas.

2. INFANT INDUSTRIES. A better argument for tariffs and quotas is that they provide protection for infant industries. Sometimes a country meets all the requirements for a new industry. Demand is there, the technology is available, capital and labor are ready, too. But start-up costs are high in many industries. Cheaper foreign imports keep domestic producers from starting factories that could, eventually, grow to compete in world markets.

A temporary tariff is sometimes justified to protect infant industries. The tariff protects the young industry while it grows and expands production to meet domestic needs. Consumers pay higher prices in the short run, but create additional jobs. Tariffs are lifted in the long run and prices fall back to world levels. Trade restrictions of this kind can be powerful. Japan protected its auto industry after the Second World War. Japanese firms grew to meet their domestic market and then conquered the world. Japan might not have such a potent automobile industry today if the initial quotas had not been imposed.

The problem with infant-industry tariffs is that they often outlive their purpose. Tariffs designed to protect weak infants often hang around to keep mature firms fat.

3. COMPETITION PROBLEMS. Some tariffs are imposed to deal with anticompetitive import practices. Sometimes foreign sellers *dump* goods on international markets for a lower price than they charge in their home countries. They do this to drive other producers from the market or to get rid of excess production abroad while keeping higher prices at home. Tariffs to limit this practice are justified in some cases. In the early 1980s, U.S. steel producers called for tariffs against foreign imports, citing dumping as their reason.

Some foreign producers receive subsidies from their governments. These side payments make imports cheaper than unsubsidized domestic goods. Governments "export" unemployment through subsidies that increase domestic production and exports and put foreign competitors out of work. Tariffs to discourage this practice are sometimes called for, too.

Trade barriers are also useful if the seller is a monopoly and thus able to extract a high price for imports. Many economists have called for a tariff on OPEC goods. Oil producers would bear much of the tax, they argue, and lower sales in the United States would remove some of OPEC's monopoly power.

Some experts favor tariffs for strategic reasons. The threat of tariffs, they claim, is a weapon. Tariffs, quotas, and other trade limitations help the United States meet its foreign policy goals and force other countries to keep their economies open to U.S. exports.

4. NATIONAL DEFENSE. Trade barriers are sometimes required for national security reasons. Here is an outlandish example of the national defense reasoning. Suppose Greenland has a comparative advantage in automobile production. Cheap Greenland cars flood our markets and finally put the U.S. car industry out of business. The United States specializes in making other goods and trades them to Greenland for cars. Now suppose that the United States and Greenland go to war. We would need a healthy automobile industry to make jeeps and tanks and other vehicles, but none would exist because of the effect of international trade. The United States would be at a comparative disadvantage in this war.

The national defense argument suggests that trade barriers be erected around industries vital to national defense so that they will be ready in case of war. Many countries keep otherwise uneconomic airline, aerospace, and shipping firms in business for defense reasons.

National defense tariffs are a trade-off. Consumers pay higher prices and lose the benefits of comparative advantage in time of peace. They gain an important advantage in wartime, however. This assumes that everyone is not vaporized in the first 15 seconds of a nuclear conflict! If this happens, the national defense argument goes up in smoke.

Arguments against Tariffs

The arguments against tariffs have already been stated. Free trade increases production and makes nations as a whole better off. Resources go to their best use. Most tariffs "protect" the public from the benefits of comparative advantage. Some protection! Is a particular tariff really justified by competition problems, national defense, or infant industry concerns? This question is often difficult to answer.

Customs Unions

Customs unions like the **European Economic Community (EEC)** are a successful compromise between protection and free trade. Members of a **customs union** agree to drop all trade barriers among themselves. Trade between France, Germany, and Britain, for example, takes place as if they were all part of one country. (The separate United States can be thought of as a big customs union—most trade barriers are forbidden between the states).

European Economic Community (EEC): a customs union composed of major European nations; also called the Common Market.

customs union: groups of nations having free trade among themselves and unified tariff barriers with other countries.

Free trade among members of the customs union generates the benefits of comparative advantage. Import prices drop and export employment rises. Productivity increases, too. A customs union creates trade among its members but erects a uniform set of trade barriers against nonmembers. Great Britain had to impose tariffs against Canadian goods, for example, when it entered the EEC but found that French trade restrictions were eliminated. Trade is created within the Common Market but reduced with outside trading partners.

The EEC has been largely successful, but some problems remain. While formal trade barriers among member nations have been dropped, more subtle barriers remain. Arbitrary quality and safety standards still prevent free trade. And a system of subsidies has replaced tariff barriers in some industries. The EEC finds itself in the peculiar position of granting subsidies to French farmers (to protect them from Italian competition) then giving subsidies to Italy, too, to protect them from the French. After more than 25 years, the EEC still has a few bugs to work out, but the benefits of even limited free trade outweigh the costs of this alliance.

Balance-of-Payments Accounts

Accountants keep track of money coming into a firm's coffers (payment for goods sold or return on investment) and money that leaves to pay for inputs or as payment on debt. The firm's books show its financial health—no company can exist for long if outflows persistently exceed inflows.

Economists keep similar records for the nation as a whole. The balance-of-payments accounts look at all international payments and the balance of trade keeps track of money involved in international trade.

BALANCE OF PAYMENTS. The **balance of payments** is the broadest measure of international financial health. Money enters the United States for four reasons: payments for exports, gifts (transfer payments) from abroad, investments (when the Japanese Sony company builds factories in the United States, for example), and profits and interest from U.S. investments abroad. Money flows out of the country for four similar reasons: imports (we get the

balance of payments: the record of all payments of a country; total inflows of money minus total outflows.

goods, foreign sellers receive the money), transfers (foreign aid to less developed countries), investments by U.S. firms in foreign lands, and interest and profit payments to foreign investors.

balance-of-payments surplus: total money inflows (for exports, transfers, investment, and profits) exceed total outflows for a nation.

balance-of-payments deficit: total money outflows exceed total inflows for a nation.

Some countries take in more funds than they pay out—their inflows of money exceed outflows. These countries are said to have a **balance-of-payments surplus.** This is something like a gross national profit. Other economies pay out more than they receive in these four categories. They experience a **balance-of-payments deficit.** The United States has been in the latter group in recent years. High payments for oil and interest payments to foreign lenders (among other things) have kept money flowing out of the nation.

Why do economists bother to calculate the balance of payments? What would happen to you if you had a personal balance-of-payments deficit? It would mean that you spend and pay out more than you earn or receive from others. How could you finance this deficit? You could pay the difference by withdrawing money from your savings or checking account. You could do this once or twice (assuming you have money in the bank!), but this is not a permanent solution since your bank account eventually dries up. A second option is to borrow. Others (people with a balance-of-payments surplus) might lend you money to pay the difference. This strategy, like dissaving, does not work forever since you cannot expect to continually borrow to pay the rent.

A third solution is to sell off some assets—furniture or your car or stocks and bonds. You can finance the deficit this way as long as your assets hold out. Eventually, however, you must do something to address the cause of the deficit—you must find a way to take in more money (take a second job, for example) or pay out less.

What does this little lesson in personal finance have to do with the balance of payments? A nation is like an individual in regard to its balance-of-payments. Deficit countries (like the United States) must eventually make up the difference between money coming in and money going out.

How does the United States pay its bills? For a time the United States sold gold from Fort Knox. As the gold supplies fell, borrowing became more important. Central banks in many nations agreed to hold dollars as IOUs against U.S. debts and interest rates rose in this country, in part to attract inflows of investment funds from abroad. These are temporary solutions to the balance of payments problem, however. The long-term key lies in making U.S. goods attractive to foreign buyers and U.S. markets profitable for foreign (and U.S.) investors. Curing a deficit is a complex task, as you will see in Chapter 16.

balance of trade: the record of international trade payments; exports minus imports.

BALANCE OF TRADE. The **balance of trade** is another indicator of international economic transactions. The balance of trade looks at just one piece of the puzzle: international trade. The balance of trade compares exports and imports of merchandise. Why is the balance of trade important? It paints a picture of the comparative health of producers in different countries. The balance of trade looks at trade in goods and services, ignoring investments, transfers, profits, and the rest.

The United States has a history of balance-of-trade surplus in the 1950s and 1960s. Exports of agricultural products and manufactured goods exceeded imports of raw materials and other goods during this period. Surplus turned to substantial deficit in the 1970s, however. Why the change? Oil is the first reason. Billions of extra dollars leave the country each year to pay for high-priced petroleum imports. This is bad for the balance of trade but good in a bigger sense: trade following comparative advantage makes both trading partners better off.

Some U.S. imports, like automobiles and television sets, are goods that the United States once exported. How did this trade reversal come about? Exchange rates (discussed in the next chapter) are part of the answer. Changes in the dollar's international value in recent years have made foreign imports cheaper and have raised U.S. prices abroad. Price changes resulting from fluctuations in the exchange rate encouraged imports, discouraged exports, and contributed to balance of trade deficits.

Another part of the puzzle is what Raymond Vernon calls the **product life cycle theory.** The United States has a comparative advantage in innovation and the free communication needed to bring new products to market. New products (exported by U.S. firms) eventually become standardized and production shifts to lower cost factories in other countries. Consumers in the United States now import goods that once were produced at home. Have high interest rates and low investment spending in the United States discouraged innovation and reduced U.S. exports of new high-technology goods? This is one possible explanation for U.S. balance of trade woes.

product life cycle theory: the theory that newly invented goods are first exported then imported when standardized and produced abroad.

Stages in the Balance of Payments

Why does the United States have a balance-of-payments deficit today? We can better understand today's international economy by looking to the past. The United States has gone through four balance-of-payments stages. Other countries may pass through these stages, too.

1. **IMMATURE DEBTOR NATION.** Many young nations have payments deficits. They have ample natural resources but lack the means to exploit these riches. They import investment funds, manufactured goods, and even some raw materials. Transfer payments flow into the country, adding to the deficit. Exports are few in the immature stage. This description of an **immature debtor nation** fits colonial America well.

immature debtor nation: a less developed nation with a balance-of-payments deficit resulting from high investment and transfer inflows.

2. **IMMATURE CREDITOR NATION.** Nations begin to export raw materials, minerals, agricultural goods, and other primary products in the second payments stage. Revenue from these exports exceeds the cost of imported technology and manufactures. The United States fit this description in the early 1800s and Saudi Arabia is probably an **immature creditor nation** today.

immature creditor nation: a nation with a balance-of-payments surplus from sales of raw materials and natural resources.

3. **MATURE CREDITOR NATION.** Nations in the third stage take advantage of their natural resources and use them to produce manufactured goods. Mineral and agricultural products are used by new industries at home rather than being sold to foreign factories. Exports of manufactures exceed imports of raw materials. The OPEC nations are building now for this **mature creditor nation** stage. Chemical factories and oil refineries in the OPEC nations

mature creditor nation: a nation with balance-of-payments surplus from export of manufactured goods.

will soon compete with similar oil-consuming firms in other nations. The United States fit this balance-of-payments category from the 1800s until World War II.

mature debtor nation: a nation with a balance-of-payments deficit from credit and investment outflows.

4. MATURE DEBTOR NATION. Nations in the final balance-of-payments stage export credit and capital, as well as manufactured goods and services. They invest in other nations and transfer production to more profitable factories abroad. They provide the money for the growth of other countries and profit from both trade and investment. Investment and transfer payment outflows lead to the payments deficit experienced by a **mature debtor nation.**

Is A Deficit Bad?

How much should we worry about a balance-of-payments or balance-of-trade deficit? This question, like so many in economics, has more than one answer.

International payments deficits are a cause for national concern because of their long-run consequences. A nation that runs a deficit one year and a surplus the next has no need to worry—debit and credit cancel out in the long run. But countries with continuing deficits must deal with the financial imbalance. A persistent deficit is a symptom of deep economic problems at home. Has comparative advantage shifted? Are domestic industries out of touch with the market? Is home technology obsolete? Why do investment funds flee abroad? These are the questions that deficits force us to ask. Nations sometimes find it less painful to run deficits and, say, borrow the difference, than it is to solve these nagging economic problems.

What does a balance-of-trade deficit mean? It says that a nation spends more on imports than others spend on its exports. Viewed another way, however, it means that the nation is trading a few of its goods (exports) for many more foreign goods (imports). In this light, a balance-of-trade deficit (in dollars) is a surplus when measured in real goods and services.

merchantilists: eighteenth century merchants and economists who favored trade restrictions to protect gold accumulations.

Which is more important—the money or the goods? Adam Smith answered this question in eighteenth century England. In Smith's day a group called the **merchantilists** dominated economic policy. They said that the goal of international trade should be to amass a fortune—to have a surplus of money and gold. Smith's answer, in his *The Wealth of Nations* (New York: Modern Library, 1937) was that the wealth of a nation was not its money, but the real things that its people had. Smith did not favor a balance-of-trade surplus if it meant giving up needed goods and services to get unproductive gold.

ECONOMIC CONTROVERSY:

Automobile Import Quotas?

Foreign imports dominate the new-car market in many parts of the United States. Imports of cars, especially from Japan, help cause balance-of-trade deficits and, some think, threaten U.S. jobs. Are automobile import restrictions justified?

The question of import quotas is a hot one. Workers and firms in importing countries claim they are beset by unfair competition that threatens their jobs. Exporting countries respond that their goods are selected because they are better or more economical. Most nations both import and export and so find themselves on both sides of this debate.

The debate over quotas became particularly heated in the early 1980s when unemployment rates in Detroit and other car-producing centers hit post-depression highs. The threat of trade restrictions was clear. Foreign producers reacted in three ways. Some (Volkswagen, Honda, and Renault) moved production facilities to the United States. Others (such as Toyota and Mazda) reached agreements to produce cars for U.S. firms. Finally, Japanese automakers agreed to voluntary (?) export restrictions—they decided to temporarily limit their U.S. sales and let the anti-import fever cool.

Are restrictions on automobile imports a good idea? Here are two sides of this continuing debate.

Keep Unfair Competition Out

There are three good reasons to restrict imports of foreign cars. The first can be summarized in one word: jobs. We need to protect U.S. jobs from foreign competition. Quotas are a simple way to be sure that U.S. workers make the cars that Americans buy. With unemployment rates of 12 percent and more, can we afford not to limit foreign imports?

Why have imports taken such a big chunk of the automobile market? Unfair government subsidies are one answer. Foreign car producers gain from many hidden subsidies that let them price lower than free-enterprise U.S. firms. Foreign firms do not provide their workers with the same benefits or standard of living as firms in the United States—lower wage rates give them an unfair advantage. Finally, U.S. firms are stuck with old factories that were designed to produce bigger cars. Firms in the United States need temporary protection while they build new, modern plants to produce today's smaller cars. Trade restrictions can be lifted when new plants are in full production and costs have come down.

No one likes quotas—and American workers are not afraid to compete in any fair market. But international markets are not fair these days—the Japanese and others use subtle rules to keep U.S. manufactures and agricultural goods out of their markets. If they will not buy from us, we should not buy from them. Maybe a taste of their own medicine—trade restrictions—will help convince them to open their markets to U.S. goods.

Free Trade Is the Answer

All the arguments you have just read are short-sighted and misleading. Free international trade is the answer—trade boosts income, reduces price, and increases choice. Trade restrictions, like those of the 1930s, only make the poor poorer. Automobile import restrictions are particularly undesirable.

What happens if we cut auto imports? Detroit autoworkers might be put back to work, but do not bet on it. Are U.S. cars and the foreign imports close substitutes? No. Most people agree that there is a big quality and reliability gap. Restrict imports and you will boost up their prices, but people will not switch to a costly and inferior American product. They will just delay buying cars. The quota would have the same outcome as the tariff in Figure 13-4—it would just tax U.S. buyers and not help domestic workers. Jobs in the U.S. industry will not be created until firms in the United States build better cars.

Trade restrictions do not create jobs, they destroy U.S. jobs. Thousands of people now work in the imported car industry—in ports, dealerships, repair shops, and elsewhere. Clamp on trade restrictions and you will put these people out of work. Trade restrictions will not solve our balance-of-trade problems, either. People who switch from gas-stingy imports to gas-hogging domestic cars force oil imports higher. Why trade Japanese cars for OPEC oil deficits?

Do you think the Japanese will buy our goods if we refuse theirs? The anti-import policy costs jobs in the export industries, too. We have already traveled this road—the punishing tariffs of the Great Depression proved the proverb, "beggar thy neighbor (through trade restriction), beggar thyself."

The final argument for free trade is that it makes consumers better off. Automobile quotas artificially bid up prices and limit choices. Why should consumers suffer because Detroit will not build sound cars for them? Forcing inferior domestic cars on U.S. buyers is not in the long-run interest of either car buyers or car producers. Free trade, with competition that forces improvement and economy on all sides, is the best choice.

SUMMARY

1. All nations gain from international trade. The theory of comparative advantage holds that mutually advantageous trade is based on differences in opportunity costs. The country with the lowest opportunity cost exports. Trade that follows this rule is good for both sides and increases total production and consumption.

2. Trade restrictions limit trade and increase import prices. Tariffs are a tax on imports. Quotas are a physical import limitation; they create a shortage and drive up prices.

3. Most economists favor free trade. The arguments against free trade center around protection, national defense, competition problems, and infant industries. Customs unions, like the European Economic Community (the Common Market) are a compromise. Free trade takes place within the customs union, but trade barriers still discourage imports from non-EEC countries.

4. Who bears the burden of a tariff? The answer depends in part on the elasticity of demand for imported goods. Consumers bear most of the tariff burden on goods with an inelastic import demand (few domestic substitutes).

Tariffs translate into price increases for these goods. Producers pay a larger share of the tariff on goods with elastic import demand, however. Consumers switch to domestic substitutes when the tariff is imposed. Price does not rise and foreign producers must pay much of the import tax.

5. The balance of payments and the balance of trade are two ways of accounting for international payments. The balance of payments looks at all international financial flows; the trade balance examines imports and exports alone. The United States has a balance-of-payments deficit. This may be natural, given the United States' stage of development, but the deficit must be financed somehow.

6. Should automobile imports be limited? One side claims that import restrictions create U.S. jobs and compensate for unfair foreign competition. The other side claims that restrictions destroy jobs for U.S. workers and hide the real problems of uncompetitive industry in the United States.

DISCUSSION QUESTIONS

1. Inexpensive shoe imports from Brazil and other newly developed countries have flooded U.S. markets and caused unemployment in the domestic shoe industry. A tariff on these inexpensive imports has been proposed to bring their cost up to that of comparable U.S. products. Who would gain from such an action? Who would lose? Make your lists as complete as possible.

2. The United States currently imports oil from Saudi Arabia (trade takes place according to the laws of comparative advantage). Congress is considering a tariff on imported oil. Can this tariff:

a. reduce oil imports?
b. end oil imports?
c. reverse trade (United States would sell oil to Saudi Arabia)? Explain your reasoning in each case.

3. Wade and Marti are thinking about swapping services. If Wade works one hour he can type two pages of a report or clean and gap four spark plugs. Marti, working one hour, can type three pages or clean and gap eight spark plugs. Who has the absolute advantage in typing? According to the theory of comparative advantage, who should do the typing? Give an example of an exchange rate that would prove mutually advantageous. Explain your reasoning for each question.

4. Who would bear the burden of a tariff on foreign-car imports—U.S. consumers or foreign producers? Defend your answer.

5. Should tariffs or quotas be used to restrict automobile imports? List the arguments on both sides of this issue and then state your own position.

TEST YOURSELF

Circle the best response to each question.

1. The United States can produce either 10 barrels of oil or 50 tons of wheat with a given amount of resources. Using the same resources, Saudi Arabia can produce 10 barrels of oil or 10 tons of wheat. Which of the following statements accurately describes trade between the United States and Saudi Arabia according to the law of comparative advantage?

(X) Saudi Arabia has an absolute advantage in producing oil
(Y) Saudi Arabia has a comparative advantage producing oil
(Z) the opportunity cost of a ton of wheat in the United States is 5 barrels of oil

a. all these statements are correct
b. none of these statements are correct
c. only (X) is correct
d. (X) and (Y) are correct
e. only (Z) is correct

2. Which of the following is a terms of trade or exchange such that both Saudi Arabia and the United States would gain from trade (assume opportunity costs from question 1):

(X) one barrel of oil equals three tons of wheat
(Y) one barrel of oil equals one-half ton of wheat
(Z) one barrel of oil equals six tons of wheat

a. trade would take place at any of these exchange rates
b. mutually beneficial trade is impossible at any of these exchange rates
c. only (X)
d. only (Y)
e. only (Z)

3. Tariffs and quotas are two ways to restrict imports. Which of the following statements about a quota is (are) *true?*

(X) tariffs and quotas tend to increase the price of imports
(Y) the burden of a quota falls completely on the producer
(Z) consumers bear more of a tariff's burden if demand is elastic

a. all the above are true
b. none of the above are true
c. only (X) is true
d. only (Y) is true
e. only (Z) is true

4. One argument in favor of tariffs is the infant industry argument. According to this view, trade restrictions are desirable if:

a. the protected industries employ large numbers of people (who have children to care for)
b. the protected industry is small relative to the world market
c. the protected industry uses goods supplied by poor, less developed countries
d. the protected industry is vital to the national defense of a new country
e. the protected industry needs time to grow so it can compete with imports

5. Some people think that Mexico is a mature creditor country. If this view is correct, then Mexico should have a ________ balance of payments and a ________ balance of trade. (Choose the answer that best fills in the blanks)

a. surplus/surplus
b. surplus/deficit
a. deficit/surplus
d. deficit/deficit
e. it is impossible to tell from the information given

SUGGESTIONS FOR FURTHER READING

Comparative advantage and the gains from trade are discussed in more detail in the author's *Introductory Microeconomics* (New York: Academic Press, 1981), Chapter 2, and *Introductory Economics* (New York: Academic Press, 1981), Chapter 18. The automobile import debate is well presented in "Car Wars: Protectionism Battle Over Imports of Autos May Head for Congress," an article on the front page of the February 15, 1980 *Wall Street Journal*. A different perspective is provided by "Quality: When Better Cars Are Built, Will America Be Building Them?" by Rich Ceppos, *Car and Driver* (March, 1981). The changing balance-of-payments stages are illustrated in "The Saudis Build a Pittsburgh" by Douglas Martin (*New York Times*, January 31, 1982).

14

THE FOREIGN-EXCHANGE MARKET

Preview

What is an exchange rate? Why is the exchange rate important?
Who gains and loses when the exchange rate changes?
Why does the exchange rate change?
How do interest rates affect the dollar's value?
Can exchange rates help solve balance-of-payments problems?
Which is better: flexible or fixed exchange rates?

MOST AMERICANS are happily oblivious of exchange rates. They feel a certain pride when they hear that the dollar is stronger and an uncertain shame when its value drops, but they do not know why. Is ignorance bliss? Not where exchange rates are concerned!

In other countries, the person in the street is a foreign-exchange wiz because a small fluctuation in the exchange rate makes a big difference in prices, real income, and buying habits. The rest of the world already knows this story; you need to learn it. The exchange rate is important to you because it affects the prices you pay, your job, your income, and national economic policy. This chapter helps you understand what the exchange rate is and how it works.

The Exchange Rate

Money complicates international economics because there is no single, universal currency. Each nation has its own standard of value and medium of exchange. Prices are denominated in dollars ($) in the United States. Great Britain uses the pound (£), France the franc (Fr), West Germany the deutsche mark (DM). The Japanese have a yen (Y) for their currency. Italians use the lira (L), Russia the ruble (R), and Venezuela the bolivar (B).

Currency is the yardstick we use to measure value. We use the dollar to compare the cost and value of different items. Foreign currencies perform the same functions in their home countries. It is as if each country has adopted a separate measure of length, weight, or volume. All these units are equally able to measure a given distance, but it is difficult to find your way in a foreign land without a conversion table—a way to go back and forth between the different measures.

The exchange rate converts value measures from one currency to another. Suppose you are visiting France and you find an attactive sweater that would cost $20 at home. The Paris price is Fr 150 (150 French francs). Is this a good buy? If the exchange rate is Fr 1 = $.10 ($1 = Fr 10) the answer is, oui! The Fr 150 sweater costs the equivalent of $15. Buy it in Paris tout de suite. What if the exchange rate is Fr 1 = $.20 ($1 = Fr 5)? Zoot alors! (That is French for "Holy cow!") The sweater now costs $30 (measured in U.S. currency). The sweater at home is a better buy.

French buyers of U.S. goods live in a mirror-image exchange-rate world. For example, a French exchange student is pricing a U.S. camera that sells for $50 (a similar model sells for Fr 400 at home). Should she buy it? At the Fr 10 = $1 exchange rate it is a bad deal. The camera costs the equivalent of Fr 500—she should buy it at home. But the camera only costs Fr 250 if the exchange rate is Fr 5 = $1. The U.S. camera is the better buy at this currency rate.

You have just learned the first use of the exchange rate—it helps determine the cost of imported goods. A change exchange rate means new prices for buyers figuring in another currency. The sweater is priced at Fr 150 and the camera costs $50 in either case, but they are bargains or bad deals depending on the exchange rate.

The franc is a "smaller" measure of value than the dollar—does this mean that the dollar is better than the franc or that the U.S. economy is stronger than that of France? Currencies just measure value in the same way that feet, yards, and meters just measure length. Is your shoe a different length if we measure it in meters instead of yards or feet? No. That is silly. Your shoe is the same length regardless of whether it is measured in fractions of a mile or in thousands of microns. Currency values evolved over time just like other standard measures. Great Britain measures value in pounds (worth about $2 each in 1982) and Argentineans use a tiny peso—it took over 30,000 pesos to buy a dollar in 1982! All measures are equally good; the choice of a currency "length" does not tell us anything about the health of different economic systems.

The Foreign-Exchange Market

Who picks the exchange rate? The President? Congress? The Federal Reserve? No individual or organization sets the exchange rate in most countries—that job falls to the foreign-exchange market. The exchange rate is the price at which foreign currencies are bought and sold.

A market for foreign currencies? Why would someone want to buy money from other countries? There are many motives. Some people collect **foreign exchange.** Money from other lands is colorful and interesting (economists like to collect money instead of stamps or beer cans). You can play with foreign money, paper the walls with it (the Argentinean peso looks like the best bet here), shred it, staple it, or smoke it.

foreign exchange: foreign currencies.

But mostly people spend it. People buy foreign currencies because they want to buy foreign goods. Sellers in France or Japan demand to be paid in their home currency. If you want to import their goods, you first have to buy the necessary foreign currency. The demand for foreign exchange is a **derived demand.** The demand for foreign exchange depends on the demand for foreign goods. Let us see from where the foreign-exchange market comes.

derived demand: demand for one good based on demand for its complement.

Demand for Francs

Congratulations, you have just entered the import-export business. You have decided to finance your college education by importing a particularly revolting brand of French wine (Chateau Attila the Hun). This wine sells for Fr 20 on the Paris export market. You are pretty sure you can sell it at home, but price is important. How much should you buy? The answer depends on the demand for the wine at home (shown in Figure 14-1) and the exchange rate.

Suppose that the current exchange rate is Fr 1 = $.20. How much does the wine cost? A Fr 20 bottle of this plonk costs $4 at this exchange rate. This is a high price for bad wine—not many bottles will be sold (point A on the wine demand curve in the figure). At this exchange rate you want to buy only a few bottles of wine. Since you do not want much wine, you do not need to buy many francs for your import purchases. There is a small quantity of francs demanded (point A on the franc demand curve in Figure 14-1).

depreciate: decrease in the relative value of a currency.

What happens if the exchange rate changes? Suppose the franc **depreciates** tomorrow—that it falls from Fr 1 = \$.20 to Fr 1 = \$.10. The franc is cheaper, so the Fr 20 bottle of wine is cheaper, too. The wine costs just \$2 now. You can sell more wine at \$2.00 (see point B on the wine demand curve), so you buy more wine and therefore need to buy more francs to pay the bill (point B on the franc demand curve).

appreciate: increase in the relative value of a currency.

What happens if the franc **appreciates** to Fr 1 = \$.25? The franc costs more dollars, so the French wine costs U.S. buyers more, too. The wine costs \$5 per bottle at this exchange rate. There is not much demand for bad wine that is this expensive; therefore, little of the wine is imported and there is only a small quantity of francs demanded at this exchange rate. The small wine demand at point C means a small currency demand at point C in the figure. The demand for the franc derives from the U.S. demand for French imports.

Demand for Dollars

This is only one side of the foreign-exchange market. To see the other side, we must travel to France. Thus, let us hop aboard the Concorde, don our berets,

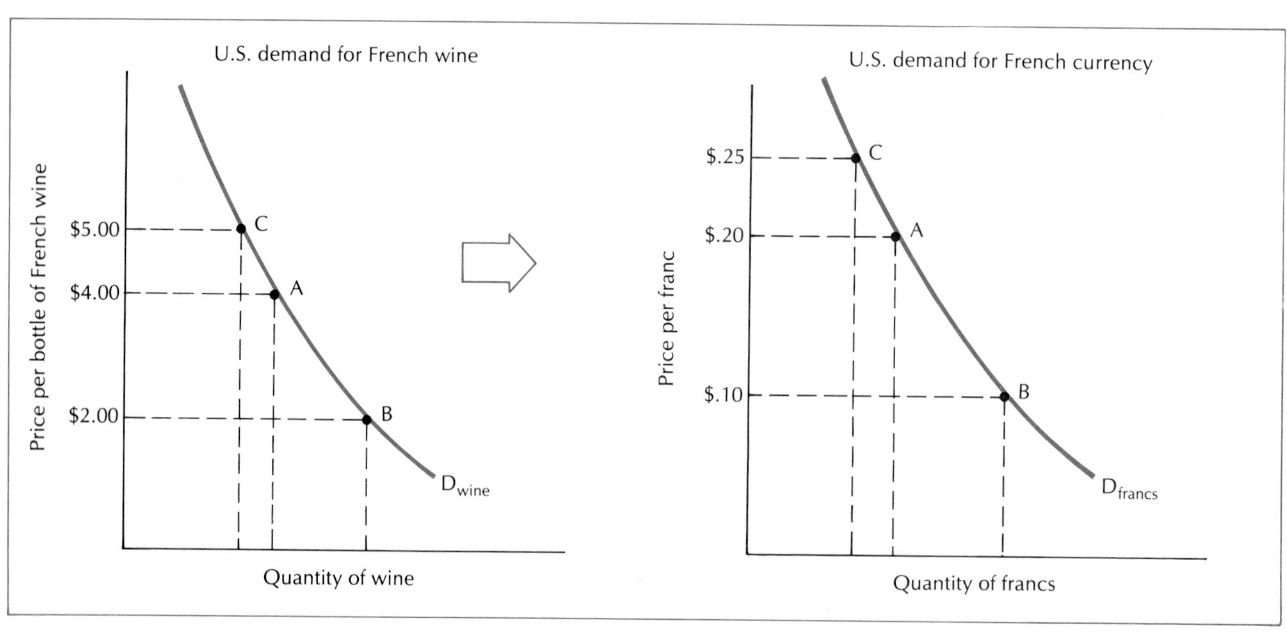

FIGURE 14-1 THE DERIVED DEMAND FOR FRANCS. The demand for the franc is derived from the demand for French imports. French goods become cheaper for U.S. buyers when the franc depreciates. Buyers in the United States want more imported goods, so more francs are also demanded. French goods cost more when the franc appreciates. Fewer French goods and less French currency are demanded. Points A, B, and C on the wine demand curve correspond to A, B, and C on the franc demand curve.

wax our mustaches, and sip a little champagne. Soon we will be in gay Paris, home of the Eiffel Tower, the Louvre, and French postcards!

The French are also busy in the foreign-exchange market. Some French students are paying their tuition bills by importing American blue jeans. They need to buy dollars to pay for the jeans imports. How many dollars do they need? This depends on how many jeans they want to import. This, too, depends on the exchange rate. Figure 14-2 tells the story.

Suppose the current exchange rate is 20 cents per franc (Fr 5 per dollar, in Parisian terms). Are the jeans a good deal? The $20 jeans cost Fr 100 at this price (point A on the jeans demand curve). Many French teens will pay this price. The amount of dollars demanded here depends on the number of jeans purchased at this price.

What happens if the dollar depreciates? If the dollar drops from Fr 5 to Fr 4 (it takes fewer francs to buy a dollar), the U.S. jeans are cheaper, too. The jeans now cost just Fr 80—a better deal for French buyers. More jeans are demanded (point B on the jeans demand curve), so the quantity of dollars demanded also rises (point B on the dollar demand curve).

Fewer dollars are demanded when U.S. currency appreciates. If the dollar rises to Fr 10 (10 cents per franc) it takes Fr 200 to buy the $20 jeans. Twenty million French cannot be that gullible—they will shun pantaloons this expensive! Only a few pairs are sold (point C on the jeans demand curve), so only a few dollars are demanded to make the deal (point C on the dollar demand curve).

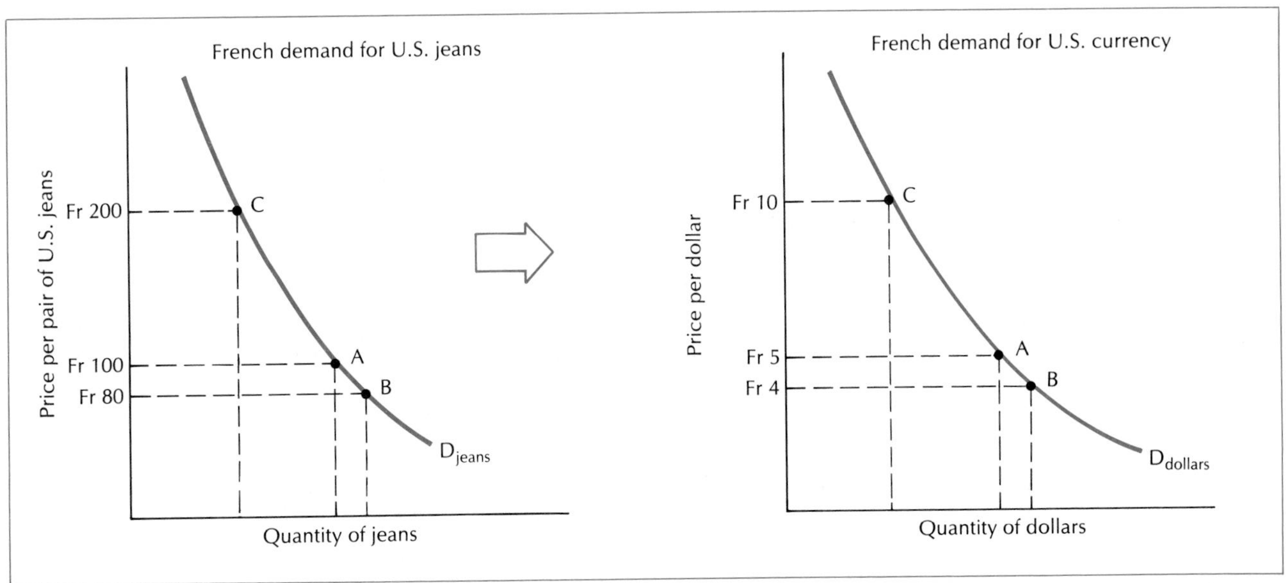

FIGURE 14-2 THE DERIVED DEMAND FOR DOLLARS. Dollar demand comes from the demand for U.S. goods. Exports from the United States are less expensive when the dollar depreciates. More dollars are demanded to buy more U.S. goods when the dollar's value is low.

Games Exchange Rates Play

This example illustrates the subtle way exchange rates affect economic activity. Look back at the two examples just given. What happened when the exchange rate changed from Fr 1 = $.20 to Fr 1 = $.10? The U.S. student said that the franc depreciated—became cheaper. His French rotgut wine was cheaper, too. Buyers in the United States found that French goods were cheaper. French wine makers gained; U.S. wine makers worried about cheaper imports taking their market.

The French students saw this exchange-rate shift differently. They said that the change from 20 cents to 10 cents per franc made the dollar appreciate. It took more francs to buy a dollar after the change. Thus, U.S. imports cost more in France. French import buyers suffered (along with U.S. export firms), but French firms that compete with imports were happy to see foreign prices rise.

Exchange-rate movements make some people winners and others losers. If the dollar appreciates (as in this example), U.S. firms sell fewer goods abroad, but foreign producers sell more goods in the United States. Unemployment grows in the United States. American buyers find cheaper imports when the dollar appreciates, so inflationary pressures subside.

A falling dollar brings the opposite result. Exporters in the United States sell more abroad because cheaper dollars mean cheaper prices in foreign markets. Unemployment falls in the United States when the dollar depreciates. Prices go up, however. Imports cost more, boosting the price level, when the dollar loses value against foreign currencies.

Here Is Demand, Where Is Supply?

So far we have seen what the exchange rate is, what it does, and why there is a demand for it. But a market cannot live with just demand! Where is supply? Who supplies French francs and U.S. dollars? We need supply curves, but they are nowhere to be seen. Has there been some mistake?

The supply curves have been here all along, we just have to look for them (as Figure 14-3 shows). Who supplies dollars to this market? People in the United States, that is who! Why do they sell their dollar? They sell them when they trade them for francs!

We Americans see ourselves as franc demanders. We want to buy the French currency so we can buy French goods. The French, in typical Continental fashion, look at our behavior from a different point of view. They see our acts as offering dollars for sale, in exchange for their francs. We see ourselves demanding francs, but they see us as the suppliers of dollars. Who is right? Both sides are correct!

Americans want to buy many francs when the exchange rate is 10 cents per franc (point C on the franc demand curve in Figure 14-3). View this from the other side of the Atlantic—the French see the Americans as offering to sell

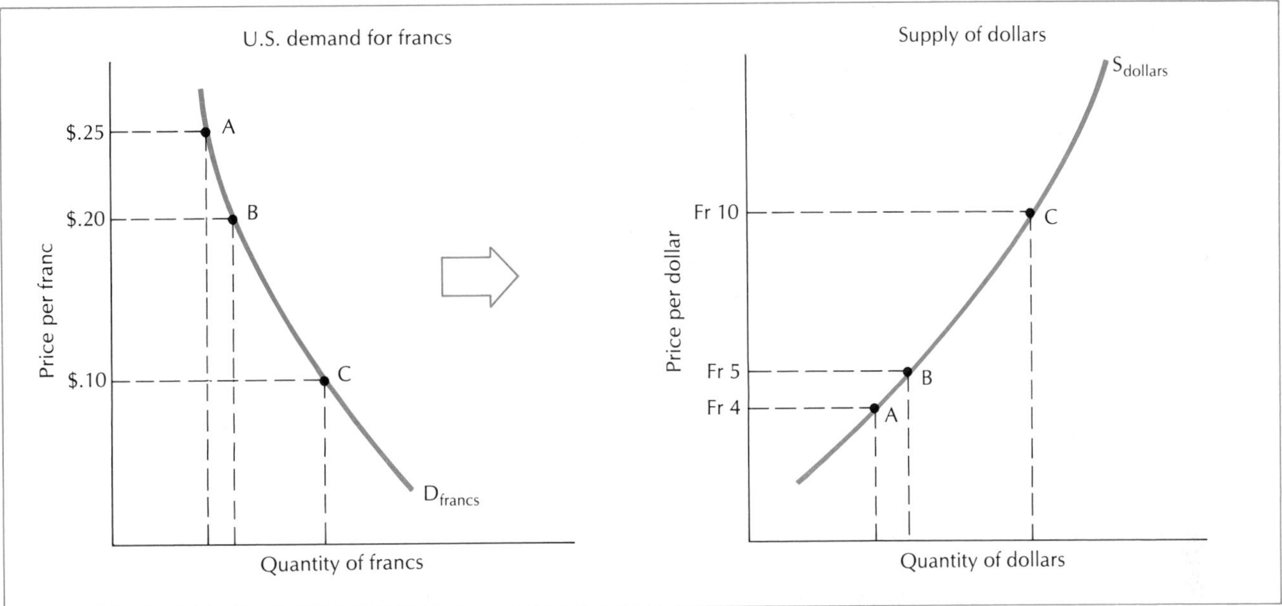

FIGURE 14-3 EXCHANGING DOLLARS AND FRANCS. Import buyers in the United States provide the supply of dollars on foreign exchange markets. High demand for the franc at an exchange rate of 10 cents per franc (point C on the Fr demand curve) means that many dollars are made available at the equivalent Fr 10 per dollar exchange price (point C on the dollar supply curve).

many dollars (in exchange for francs) at the equivalent price of Fr 10 per dollar (point C on the dollar supply curve). The large quantity of francs demanded translates into many dollars offered for sale on the foreign-exchange market.

What happens when the franc appreciates? Fewer francs are demanded at 20 cents per franc, so fewer dollars are offered in exchange at the equivalent rate of Fr 5 per dollar (point B on both curves). The lower demand for francs at this exchange rate translates into fewer dollars supplied.

Who supplies dollars to the foreign-exchange market? Groups in the United States who want to buy foreign currencies. Who supplies francs? French importers who demand U.S. dollars. The supply of francs is derived from the demand for dollars as Figure 14-4 shows. Points A, B, and C correspond to dollar demand and the corresponding franc supply at different exchange rates.

Exchange-Market Equilibrium

Supply and demand get together in the foreign-exchange market where dollars and francs (or any other pair of currencies) are exchanged. There are two ways to view this market—as supply and demand for francs or as a market for dollars. Both views give the same answers; you just pick one currency as "price" and

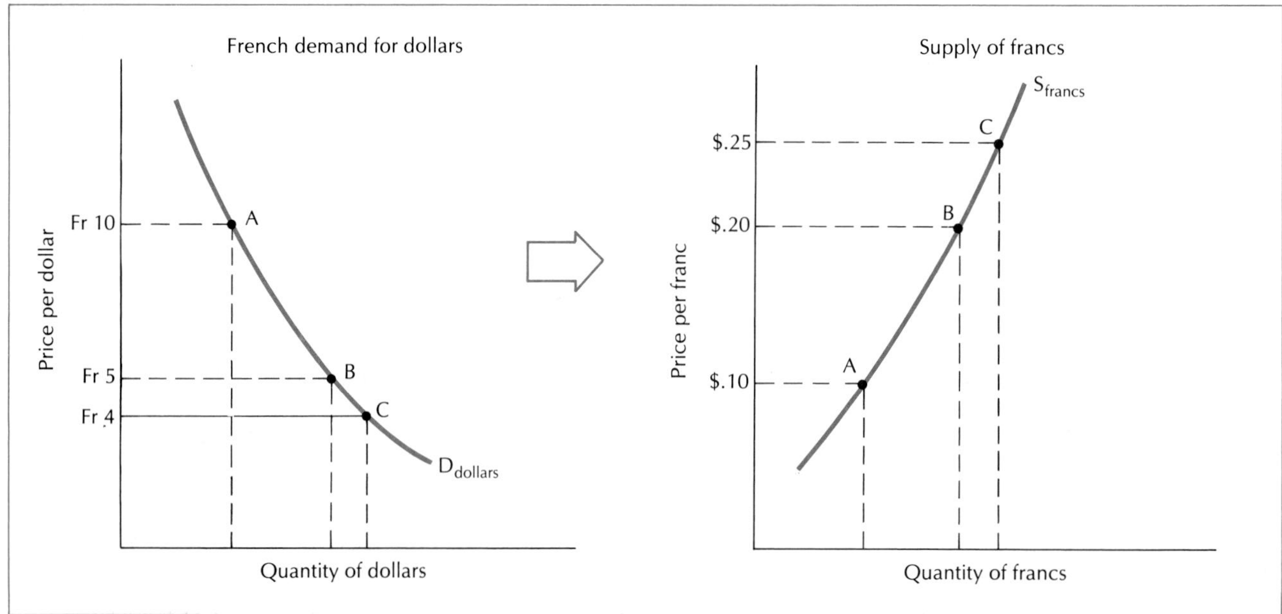

FIGURE 14-4 DEMANDING DOLLARS MEANS SUPPLYING FRANCS. French buyers who demand dollars provide the international franc supply. Only a few dollars are demanded at Fr 10 per dollar, so only a small quantity of francs is offered "for sale" at the equivalent 10 cents per franc exchange rate.

the other as "quantity." You can look at the market correctly either way. Figure 14-5 shows the exchange-market equilibrium.

This market is in equilibrium at an exchange rate of 20 cents per franc (the U.S. view) or Fr 5 per dollar (the French perspective). What happens if the exchange rate drifts away from equilibrium for some reason? The mechanisms of shortage and surplus force the exchange rate to its market-clearing level.

over-valued: an exchange rate above market equilibrium.

Suppose you wake up one morning and find that the exchange rate has moved to 25 cents per franc (as in Figure 14-5). At this price the franc is **over-valued.** There is a surplus of francs (and a shortage of dollars) at this exchange rate. Frustrated French import buyers bid the dollar up (the franc depreciates) until the equilibrium is finally restored.

under-valued: an exchange rate below market equilibrium.

The franc is **under-valued** at an exchange rate like the 10 cents per franc in the figure. There is a shortage of francs (and a surplus of dollars) at this exchange rate. Buyers in the United States bid up the franc's price; the franc appreciates (and the dollar falls) until equilibrium is reached again and quantity demanded equals quantity supplied.

arbitrage: riskless speculation; buying currencies on one foreign-exchange market to sell at a profit elsewhere.

Who makes sure that the market finds equilibrium? Foreign-exchange **arbitrage** dealers make it their business to find and destroy disequilibria. Suppose, for example, that the franc is selling for 19 cents in New York and 21 cents in Paris. Arbitragers quickly spot the difference and buy up cheap francs in New York, selling them for the higher price in Paris. Big deal—so they make

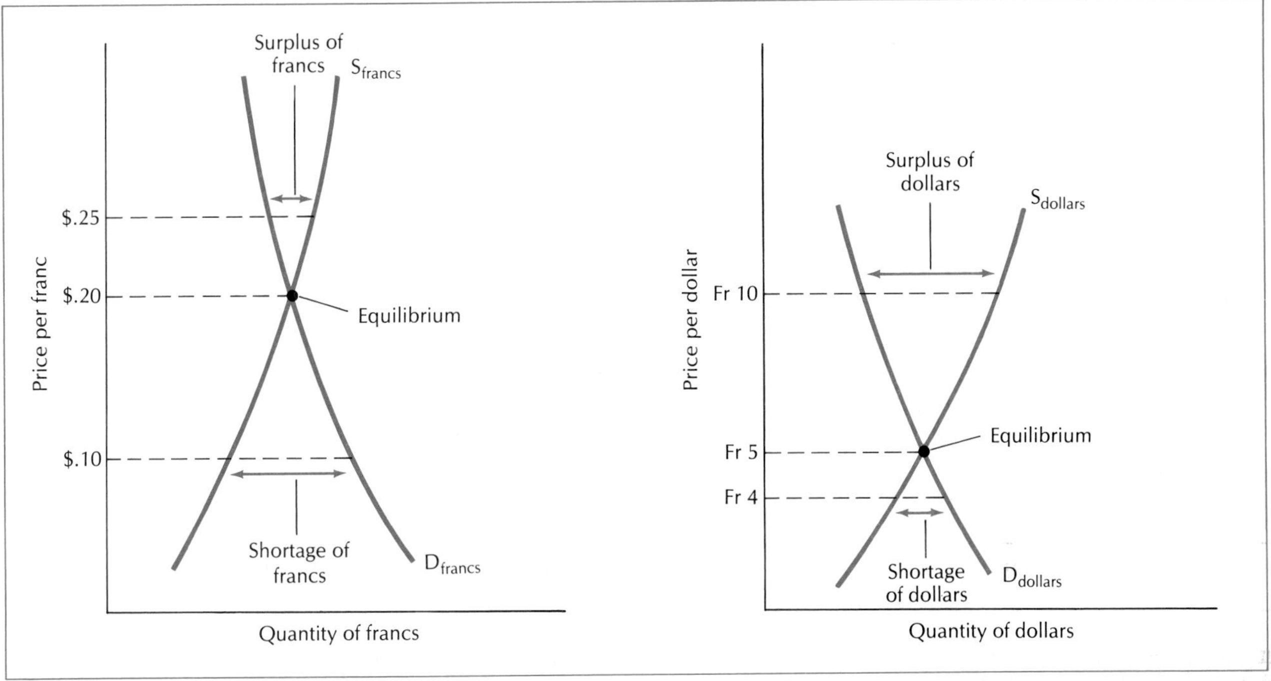

FIGURE 14-5 EXCHANGE-MARKET EQUILIBRIUM. The foreign-exchange market finds equilibrium at Fr 5 = $1 (20 cents per franc). As in any market, surplus and shortage act to assure equilibrium.

a 2 cent gain. So what? Multiply that small profit by the millions of francs that they buy and sell and you can see how profitable this work can be. Arbitrage brings the two markets to equilibrium. Increased arbitrage demand for francs bids up the price from 19 to 20 cents in New York. Increased arbitrage supply in Paris drives that price down from 21 to 20 cents. International equilibrium is restored and the arbitragers (who work for big banks and brokerage houses) collect the profit.

The Foreign-Exchange Market at Work

Why do exchange rates change? Many things shift supply and demand for foreign currencies. Here are some examples of important exchange-rate determinants. The figures used in these illustrations show just one side of each foreign-exchange market. You will get the same answer if you look at exchange from the other side.

1. TARIFF ON COFFEE. Tariffs and quotas reduce imports, but they have an unexpected side effect when exchange rates are involved. Suppose that the United States imposes a big tariff on a major import like coffee (in an attempt to weaken a coffee cartel or monopoly, perhaps). Coffee prices go up in the United States and Americans buy less coffee. Do economic effects end here? No.

Less coffee is demanded after the tariff, so U.S. coffee importers do not need to acquire as many Brazilian cruzeiros (that country's currency) for their import purchases. The demand for cruzeiros falls, as Figure 14-6 shows, and the cruzeiro depreciates against the dollar (or the dollar appreciates against the cruzeiro).

What do these exchange-rate effects mean? First, the tariff is not as effective as first thought. The tariff made coffee prices rise in the United States, but the falling cruzeiro means that all Brazilian imports (including coffee) fall in price. Coffee prices still go up, but not as much as before.

Coffee is not the only product affected, however. All Brazilian imports cheapen when the cruzeiro depreciates. United States firms that compete with Brazilian imports face hard sledding against cheaper imports. The U.S. firms that sell to Brazil are hurt, too. Appreciation of the dollar means their goods cost more to Brazilian consumers, who buy less of them. Thus, U.S. exports to Brazil decline.

The tariff was meant to reduce coffee imports. The exchange-rate side effects are that more noncoffee goods are imported from Brazil, but fewer U.S. goods are sold there. Unemployment rates rise in the United States as we buy more from Brazil and sell them less.

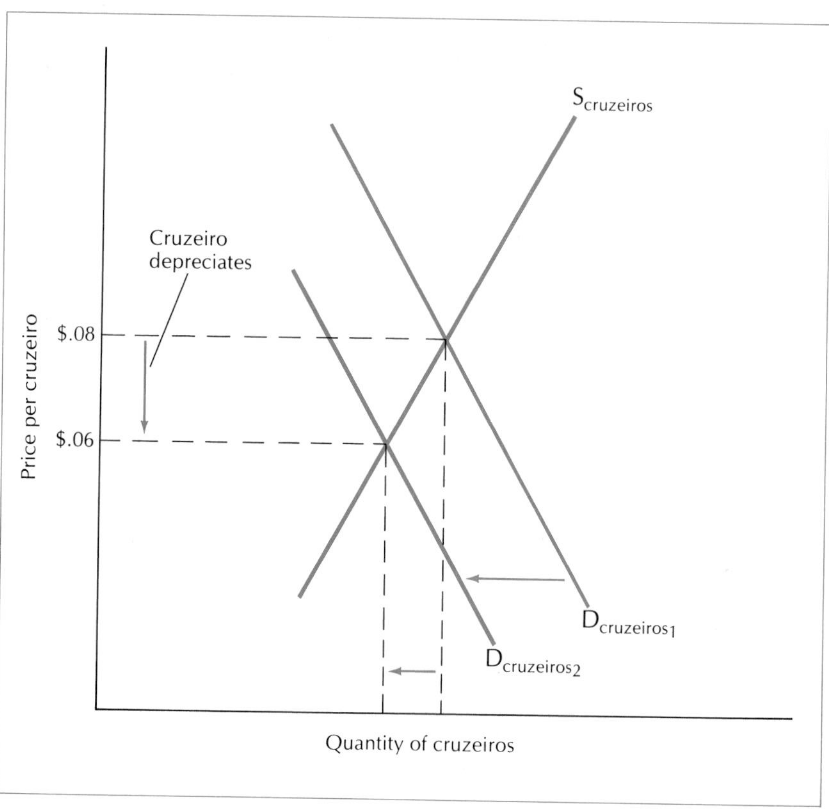

FIGURE 14-6 TARIFFS AND THE EXCHANGE RATE. This tariff on Brazilian imports reduces the demand for the cruzeiro. The Brazilian currency depreciates, with the unintended effects discussed in the text.

2. ECONOMIC GROWTH. The exchange rate is tied to economic growth in a subtle way. The U.S. economy grew more rapidly than other nations in the last years of the 1970s. How did the strength of the U.S. economy affect the exchange rate? The strong economy meant a weak dollar: the dollar fell!

What do people do with higher incomes that come with economic growth? They spend much of the increased income, that is what. And some of this spending goes for added purchases of imports, as Figure 14-7 shows. Consumers in the United States bought more Italian shoes, cars, wine, and electronic gadgets. This helped Italian industry, but disrupted exchange markets. Increased U.S. buying flooded exchange markets with dollars. The increase in the supply of the dollar bid down the dollar's value against the lira. The dollar depreciated and the lira appreciated.

Rapidly growing countries often experience depreciation of their currency. Oddly enough, this helps them grow even more. The falling dollar made U.S. goods cheaper in Italy and increased the price of Italian goods in the United States. Firms in the United States exported more due to depreciation,

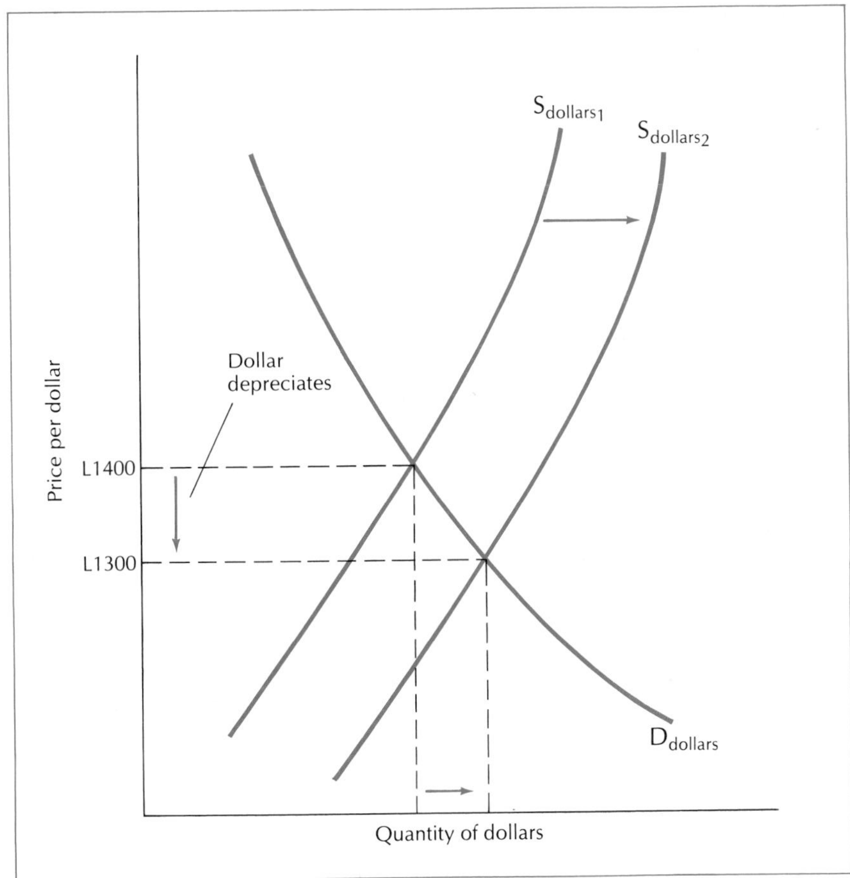

FIGURE 14-7 ECONOMIC GROWTH AND THE EXCHANGE RATE. Economic growth in the United States increases the demand for Italian imports. Consequently, the dollar depreciates against the lira.

while the rising lira encouraged some buyers to switch from, say, Italian soave to California chardonnay wine.

3. INFLATION AND THE EXCHANGE RATE. The exchange rate responds quickly to international inflation-rate differences. British inflation rates were as much as double U.S. inflation in the 1970s. High inflation rates push a country's currency down. Imagine, for example, you have the choice of buying a $100 U.S. radio or a similar British model that sells for £ 40. If the exchange rate is $2.50 per pound, you are probably indifferent between the two goods: they both cost 100 U.S. dollars. Now suppose that prices are stable in the United States, but that the British have 25 percent inflation. The U.S. radio still sells for $100 one year later, but the British model now costs £ 50—25 percent more. Which one are you going to buy now?

Falling demand for high-inflation British goods makes the demand for British currency fall, too, as Figure 14-8 shows. At the same time, buyers in England start to import more goods from low-inflation U.S firms. The supply of pounds rises as the British demand for U.S. goods increases. What is the result? A smaller demand for pounds coupled with an increasing supply means only one thing—depreciation. The exchange market moves from initial equilibrium at A to a new balance at B in the figure. The high-inflation pound falls in value while the lower-inflation dollar appreciates.

Exchange rates partially protect countries like Britain from their high

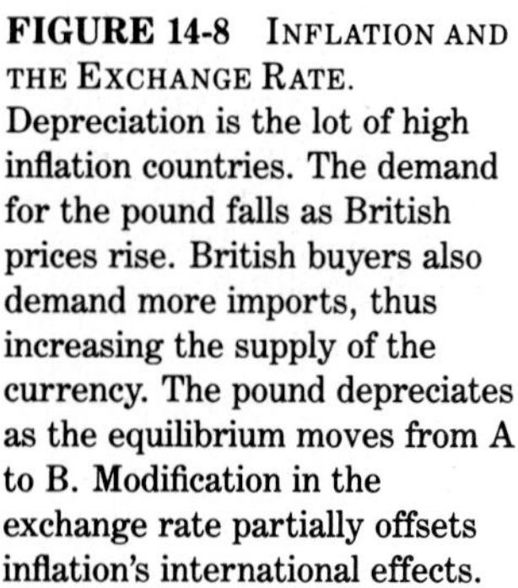

FIGURE 14-8 INFLATION AND THE EXCHANGE RATE. Depreciation is the lot of high inflation countries. The demand for the pound falls as British prices rise. British buyers also demand more imports, thus increasing the supply of the currency. The pound depreciates as the equilibrium moves from A to B. Modification in the exchange rate partially offsets inflation's international effects.

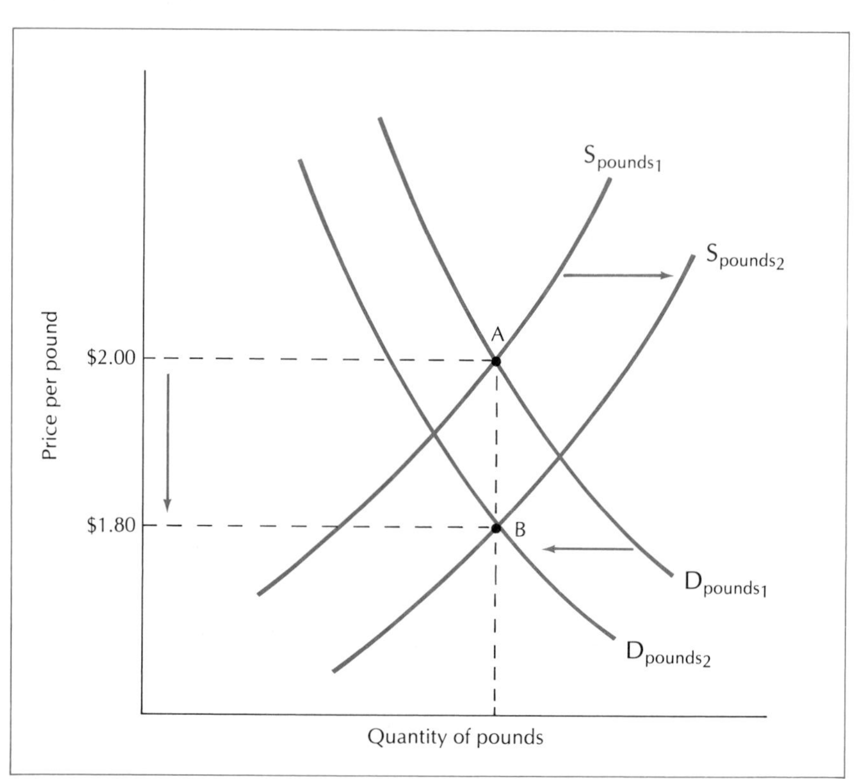

inflation woes. Inflation makes home prices rise, but the falling pound keeps the price of British goods abroad roughly the same. Exchange rates that adjust like this keep high inflation rates from killing export sales. Depreciation also means that low-inflation U.S. goods cost more abroad—since the dollar is more expensive, so are U.S. goods. The exchange rate also protects the British market from cheaper items from other low-inflation countries.

4. INTEREST-RATE DIFFERENCES. People do not buy foreign currencies for import purposes alone. Banks, insurance companies, and large corporations invest their funds in the credit markets of many countries. If interest rates rise in West Germany, for example, big firms jump to take advantage of the higher return. They buy German bonds or make deposits in German banks. There is a catch, however. They must exchange dollars for deutsche marks (to make German investments) before they can get the higher foreign-interest return.

Interest rate differences are an important part of the foreign exchange market. High U.S. interest rates are one reason for the dollar's appreciation in the early 1980s. Figure 14-9 shows what happened.

Real interest rates reached record levels in the United States in the early 1980s. Would you not want the higher return? Mexican investors pulled pesos out of their financial institutions and used them to buy dollars to put in

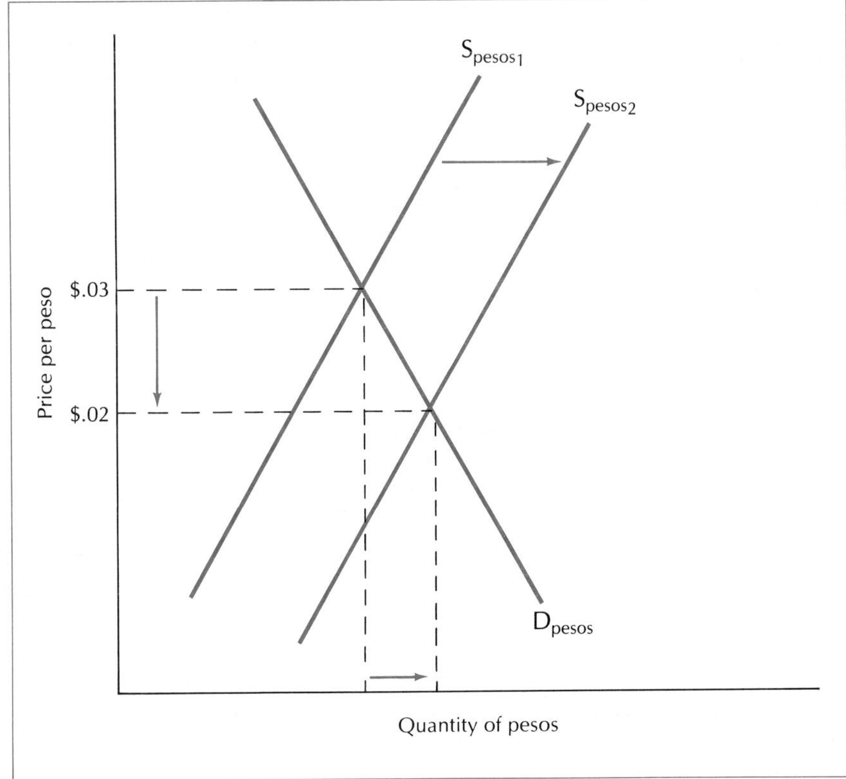

FIGURE 14-9 INTEREST RATES AND EXCHANGE RATES. High U.S. interest rates attract funds from Mexico. Increasing peso supplies drive down the exchange rate. The high-interest dollar appreciates while the low-interest peso falls in value.

American money-market funds. The supply of pesos rose on the foreign-exchange market and the Mexican currency fell in value against the dollar. The peso's depreciation meant that U.S. goods cost more in Mexico, but Mexican goods were cheaper in the United States.

Was this international credit flow good for Mexico? We must weigh the trade-off. Credit flowed out of Mexico, making loans harder to get and driving up that country's interest rate. Imports from the United States cost more in Mexico, too, so the shift in the exchange rate added to inflation. But there is a silver lining: Mexican exports to the United States rose because the dollar price of these goods fell along with the peso.

5. OFFICIAL INTERVENTION. Sometimes the Federal Reserve and foreign central banks intervene in foreign-exchange markets. They buy or sell foreign currencies to artificially alter exchange rates. They "prop up" currencies to end or limit depreciation.

Why would the FRS intervene to force the dollar's value higher? Pride could be the reason, but it is hard to imagine conservative FRS bankers pushing exchange rates around for ego gratification. Anti-inflation policy is a better reason for official **intervention.** Dollar appreciation lowers import prices and so reduces inflation. Falling exports and rising imports lower aggregate demand in the United States, thereby taking more pressure off inflation. Defending the dollar is another FRS economic weapon.

intervention: government or central bank foreign-exchange transactions intended to alter the exchange rate.

Here is another reason for U.S. intervention: Billions of dollars have flowed out of the U.S. economy over the years. Many of these have ended up in the vaults of foreign central banks where they are held as official reserves. Central bankers trust that their dollars have value, so they do not rush to exchange them for gold or their own currency.

What happens to this trust if the dollar starts sliding against other currencies? The risk is that foreign countries will spook and stampede: start an international bank run on the FRS. What happens if all these countries try to sell their dollar reserves at once? Collapse! The dollar is worthless. Part of the Fed's intervention concern is to keep the dollar strong enough to warrant international faith. So the Fed buys up dollars (using its reserves of foreign currencies or loans from other central banks) to keep the dollar strong.

Is the United States the only country that fiddles with foreign exchange rates? No. Most major countries intervene from time to time. This sometimes creates international economic conflict. The FRS might want to keep the dollar from falling in value. But other central banks sometimes try to make the dollar cheaper. Why? It could be an anti-inflation policy of their own—their currency appreciates and the dollar falls. Oil provides a better answer, however.

The members of OPEC demand payment for their oil in dollars, not francs, pounds, Saudi riyals, or some other currency. If the British, French, or the Japanese want to buy oil, they first have to buy dollars. This makes the value of the dollar an important economic statistic. If the dollar appreciates against the yen, for example, Japanese buyers find oil prices rising, too. Higher oil payments reduce aggregate demand and boost production costs, cutting Japanese aggregate supply. Stagflation follows this shift of aggregate demand and aggregate supply.

What happens when the United States intervenes to increase the dollar's value and other governments step in to make it depreciate? A financial World War III erupts, and no country's policy is particularly effective.

6. BALANCE-OF-PAYMENTS PROBLEMS. Market exchange rates are part of the solution to a country's balance-of-payments woes. The exchange rate (assuming no official intervention) automatically changes to reduce balance-of-payments problems. Figure 14-10 shows how this system works.

The United States has a balance-of-payments deficit with West Germany. What does this mean? The deficit is a sign that more dollars are leaving the country (exchanged for deutsche marks) than deutsche marks are entering (being exchanged for dollars). The market interpretation of this condition is simple: a balance-of-payments deficit means that there is a surplus of dollars (more dollars leaving the United States than entering it) and a shortage of deutsche marks (more deutsche marks demanded than supplied). The deficit might have resulted from a rising demand for German goods, like the shift shown in Figure 14-10.

How does the market react to this market imbalance? The surplus dollar depreciates and the shortage deutsche mark rises in value. This exchange-rate adjustment helps bring the balance of payments back into equilibrium. The

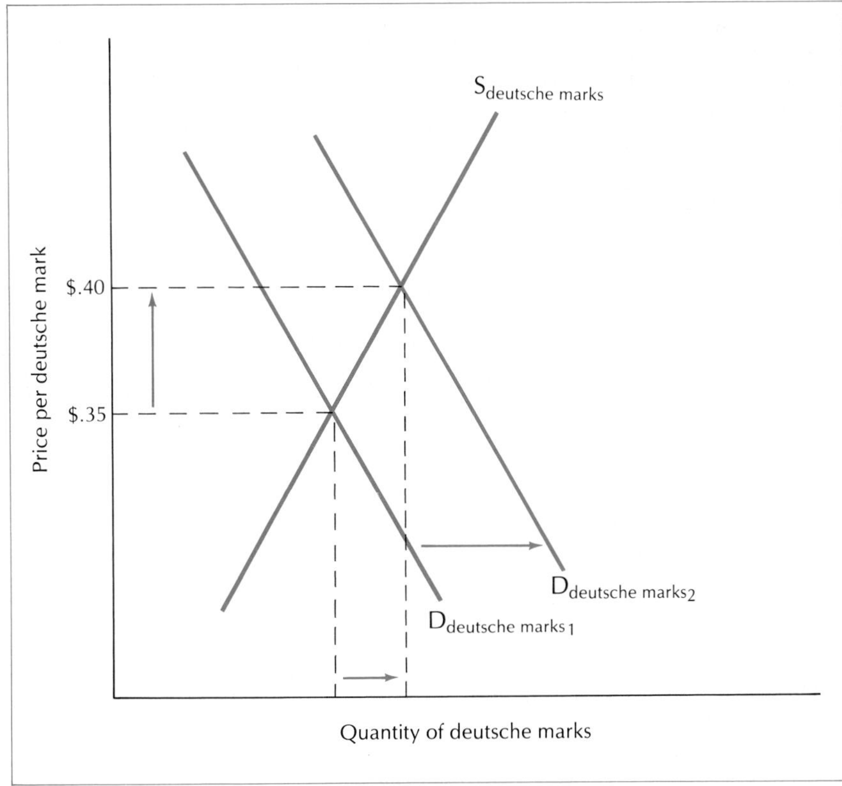

FIGURE 14-10 BALANCE-OF-PAYMENTS-ADJUSTMENT. An increase in demand for German goods causes the U.S. balance-of-payments deficit depicted in this figure. The deutsche mark appreciates and the dollar falls in value, automatically shifting trade patterns and adjusting for the payments problem.

falling dollar encourages U.S. exports (more money comes into the United States) and discourages the import flow of money to other lands. The result? The U.S. payments deficit shrinks and Germany's surplus grows smaller, too.

Automatic exchange-rate movements cannot solve all balance-of-payments problems—especially when official intervention keeps exchange rates from finding their own levels. But **flexible exchange rates** keep surplus and deficit from getting out of hand.

flexible exchange rates: exchange rates set by supply and demand.

The Traveller's Paradox

What is the dollar's worth today? Bill and Phil, two university professors, decided to find out. Bill visited rural India. He reports that the dollar is mighty and Indian prices low—his haircut cost just 40 cents abroad versus more than $10 at home. International trade tends to equalize prices, the textbook says, but Bill found bargains. Bill concluded that prices are lower abroad and the dollar's purchasing power is high.

Phil exported himself to Europe and imported different news when he returned. The dollar is weak, he said, and foreign prices are high. Hotel rooms, restaurant meals, and everyday goods are expensive—much costlier than at home. "How can Europeans afford to pay these prices?" Phil pondered, "Europe is no bargain anymore with the dollar so weak."

Here is a most peculiar paradox. Are prices high abroad or are they low? Is the dollar strong or weak? Does international trade not equalize prices (that is what the last chapter suggested)?

It is not hard to explain the traveller's paradox. International trade does tend to equate price across national borders but only for goods that are traded, like wheat, rice, or steel. The goods that Phil and Bill bought are nontraded goods—their prices are set by the forces of local supply and demand, not by vast world markets. Low income in India means a small demand for haircuts, so Bill got a bargain. But many tourists want to stay, eat, and spend along with Phil, so the prices he paid reflect high demand and limited local supply.

Differences in local demand and supply are not the whole story, however. Part of the saga of Bill and Phil is based on exchange rates. Both tourists based price comparisons on dollar values—the prices they paid depended on the exchange rates. The exchange rate, in turn, depends on trade patterns, interest rates, and official intervention, among other things. The prices of the nontraded haircuts and hotel rooms they bought were decided, in part, by exchange movements based on sales of traded goods.

Bill got a bargain because India has a balance-of-payments deficit with the United States. India buys a considerable amount of manufactured goods from the United States, so the demand for the dollar is high. The dollar appreciates against the rupee and Bill's bucks buy big in Bombay. Phil had the bad luck to travel in countries that had a payments surplus with the United States. Americans buy more European goods than they sell—the dollar depreciates against these currencies, so Phil's finances fail in Frankfort.

Fixed Exchange Rates

Flexible exchange rates, where currency values are set by market forces, have only been around since about 1973. **Fixed exchange rates** prevailed in the world for most of the post-World War II period. Many small countries still fix their exchange rates against a major currency and members of the European Economic Community have adopted a plan to fix exchange rates, within limits, for EEC currencies, while letting currency rates with non-EEC nations float on the market.

fixed exchange rates: exchange rates set by central banks.

How does a fixed-exchange system work? Central banks agree on an official exchange rate—something like an exchange-rate price control. When market forces start to push exchange rates away from the official rates, central bankers actively intervene, buying and selling currency, to make the official price stick.

Fixed exchange rates put an extra burden on countries with balance-of-payments deficits. A U.S. payments deficit, as explained earlier, pushes the dollar down when flexible exchange rates apply (see Figure 14-10). This cannot be allowed to happen under a fixed-rate regime. The FRS would be forced to step in and defend the dollar—buying up the surplus greenbacks with reserves of foreign currency or gold or by using its **special drawing rights** (a special currency used for transactions among central banks). How long can the FRS prop up the dollar? There is no problem if the deficit is short lived. A persistent deficit, however, means a continuing drain on U.S. reserves. Nations with long-term deficits are eventually forced to **devalue** their currency—change its official value to an exchange rate closer to the market-clearing price. The United States devalued the dollar several times in the early 1970s in the face of persistent payments problems.

special drawing rights (SDRs): an international central bank reserve: sometimes called "paper gold" because SDRs can be used like gold for central bank transactions.

devalue: to lower a currency's fixed exchange rate.

Are fixed exchange rates a good idea? Or are market-determined currency values a better system? This is the topic of this chapter's debate.

ECONOMIC CONTROVERSY:

Flexible or Fixed Exchange Rates

Which exchange-rate system is best? Fixed exchange rates worked well for most of this century, but flexible exchange rates are in use in most of the world today. European countries have their own semi-fixed-rate system, however—the exchange rates among EEC currencies are allowed to vary but only within a narrow band or "snake." Let us hear from both sides of the exchange-rate debate.

Markets Should Set Prices

The only rational way to set exchange-rate prices is through supply and demand. How can central banks possibly know which exchange rate is right? Flexible exchange rates should be retained.

Flexible exchange rates have several important advantages. First, they help automatically adjust for balance-of-payments problems. Internal economic adjustments were the rule under the fixed-rate regimes. The governments of deficit countries were often forced to boost unemployment rates to balance their payments account. Unemployed people do not buy as many imports, the logic went, so internal recession reduced external imbalance.

Can you imagine what would happen if this "classical medicine" were used today? Fixed exchange rates could not automatically adjust to the 1980s big oil deficits. How would government deal with huge payments deficits? Mass unemployment would keep people off the roads and reduce oil imports—thereby solving the payments problems. The medicine would work, but the patient (the U.S. economy) would be dead! Flexible exchange rates are valuable because they help us adjust to today's big deficits without paying this high price.

Inflation is a more important problem today than in the fixed-exchange past. Inflation rates rise and fall—and are much different among trading partners. Fixed exchange rates in this world would be a disaster. A country like Italy with high inflation rates would find itself facing high unemployment rates, too—who would buy its high inflation goods if exchange rates were stopped from their automatic adjustments? The rich would get richer and the poor would get poorer with fixed exchange rates.

Are there problems with floating exchange rates? Sure—no system is perfect. Market exchange rates vary daily, and this makes international trade uncertain. But traders today use the **forward exchange rate** to hedge against changing currency values. They make contracts among themselves to insure against unexpected money moves.

forward exchange rate: a contractual agreement that sets the exchange rate for a specific transaction at a future date.

Fixed exchange rates are uncertain, too. The small daily moves of the flexible exchange rate are easy to deal with compared to the huge swings when nations suddenly devalue currencies to solve balance-of-payments problems. No one can hedge against unpredictable official acts. Let exchange rates float!

Fixed Rates Are a Better System

Fixed exchange rates are a better system and many nations are realizing that a return to fixed rates is the only way to solve today's economic problems. Why? Flexible exchange rates let government policymakers run wild. Fixed exchange rates impose the discipline we need to fight inflation and unemployment.

What happens if the FRS goes crazy and prints too much money? Inflation is the clear result in the short run. The dollar depreciates under flexible exchange rates, making inflation worse! Higher import prices and increased demand for exports bid prices even higher. Inflation and depreciation are a deadly cycle and the economy spirals to hyperinflation. Only an artificial shock, like interest rate rises or official intervention, can end this cycle.

Compare this with the fixed-exchange rate alternative. If the Fed prints too much money, the dollar starts to depreciate and they have to buy back the excess bucks to keep the exchange rate level. The exchange rate stops central bank money binges and keeps the money supply at just the right level. Flexible exchange rates are not the cure for inflation, they cause inflation by removing the exchange-rate control on monetary actions.

Flexible exchange rates have a second flaw. Exchange rates have become a policy tool these days. Governments try to use the exchange rate just as they use taxes, transfers, and money supplies to achieve policy goals. These international policies are dangerous, however. If Japan depreciates the yen, more jobs in Osaka come at the expense of unemployment in Omaha. International economic competition in this game is sometimes fierce and always undesirable. Cooperation is the key, as the EEC countries have discovered. Their fixed-exchange rate system limits destructive exchange-rate strategies.

We need the certainty of fixed exchange rates, too. Currency differences do not matter under fixed exchange rates, so more international trade takes place and the gains from the additional trade benefit all. Flexible exchange rates make trade uncertain—an otherwise profitable deal might be wiped out by a sudden currency move. Common Market countries have seen that fixed exchange rates encourage international trade and investment.

What about balance-of-payments problems? It is true that fixed exchange rates do not automatically adjust for payments imbalances, but flexible exchange rates have not prevented these problems in the past, either. The discipline of fixed exchange rates should make deficits smaller, however, by tying the hands of unwise monetary authorities. Fixed exchange rates make a more stable world. Is that not what we need today?

SUMMARY

1. The exchange rate converts values from one currency to another. Exchange-rate differences do not mean that one country is better or stronger than another, only that they measure value on a different scale.

2. Shifts in exchange rates produce winners and losers. Cheaper imports benefit consumers when the dollar appreciates, but import-competing firms are hurt and exports fall. A falling dollar makes these domestic firms better off: more goods are exported and fewer imports are demanded because their prices increase in the United States.

3. The demand for foreign currency is derived from the demand for foreign goods. Exchange-rate movements affect import prices and so influence the quantity of imports demanded. The demand for foreign exchange rises and falls with the demand for imported goods.

4. The supply of dollars on foreign-exchange markets comes from the U.S. demand for foreign currency. When U.S. Traders buy pesos and yen they supply dollars in exchange. It is all just one big market, viewed from two different perspectives.

5. Why do exchange rates vary? Changing demands, economic growth, trade restrictions, inflation and interest rates, balance-of-payments problems, and official intervention are all important to a currency's international value.

6. Why does the dollar's purchasing power vary in different countries? The difference between traded and nontraded goods is part of the answer. Exchange-rate influences tell the rest of the traveller's paradox.

7. Fixed exchange rates are an alternative exchange system. Fixed rates impose discipline and add certainty to international deals. Flexible rates are favored by some for their automatic adjustments. The Economic Controversy presented both sides of this issue.

DISCUSSION QUESTIONS

1. Many Japanese car firms are considering moving production from Japan to the United States to escape U.S. trade barriers. How will this change imports and affect the demand for the yen? The supply of the yen? The exchange rate between the dollar and the yen? Explain.

2. Who gains and loses from the exchange-rate change in Question 1? Make your list as complete as possible. How could car firms that stay in Japan be affected? Explain.

3. Your firm has agreed to pay a Japanese supplier 100 million yen at the end of the month. You have just learned that the inflation rate in Japan is increasing (the U.S. inflation rate is stable). Should you buy the yen now or wait until the end of the month to make your foreign-exchange transaction? Explain your reasoning.

4. Income is growing in West Germany while France is suffering a recession. How does this affect a flexible exchange rate between the two countries? How does your answer change if the exchange rate is fixed? What official actions are required? Do these actions increase or decrease the income gap between the two nations? Explain.

5. Are fixed exchange rates better than flexible rates? List the advantages and disadvantages of each system. Which do you think is best? Defend your choice.

TEST YOURSELF

Circle the best response to each question.

1. One of Mexico's main exports is oil. Buyers must purchase pesos (the Mexican currency) to buy the oil. Recently the oil market has "softened"—the price of oil has fallen. All else being equal, how should this event affect the exchange market between the peso and the dollar?

(X) decrease the demand for the peso
(Y) increase the supply of dollars
(Z) cause the peso to appreciate

a. all of the above are true
b. none of the above are true
c. only (X) is true
d. both (X) and (Y) are true
e. both (Y) and (Z) are true

2. Use the information given in Question 1 concerning the exchange market between the dollar and the peso. How do these actions affect prices in the United States and Mexico? (Choose the *best* answer.)

a. the price of Mexican tomatoes rises in the United States
b. the price of U.S. apples rises in Mexico
c. the price of Mexican tomatoes falls in the United States and the price of U.S. apples also falls in Mexico
d. the price of apples and tomatoes does not change—only the price of oil has changed in this problem
e. the price of Mexican tomatoes rises in the United States and the price of U.S. apples also rises in Mexico

3. If the yen were to appreciate against the dollar, which of the following groups would *not* stand to benefit?

a. Japanese tourists who are vacationing in Seattle
b. people in the United States who hold yen
c. American exporters of wheat to Japan
d. U.S. autoworkers
e. Toyota dealers in the United States

4. Germany was shocked by Argentina's invasion of the Falkland Islands. The Germans pledged to boycott Argentinean goods (they would purchase no more goods from Argentina). They did, however, continue to sell goods to Argentina. How does this action affect the exchange rate between the German deutsche mark and the Argentinean peso?

a. both currencies appreciate
b. both currencies depreciate
c. the deutsche mark appreciates, the peso depreciates
d. the deutsche mark depreciates, the peso appreciates
e. there is no change in the exchange rate

5. Interest rates are falling in the United States, but the exchange rate does not change. Which of the following events would explain this situation?

(X) exchange rates are fixed
(Y) income is rising faster in the United States than in other countries
(Z) inflation rates are rising in the United States at the same time

a. all three suggested answers explain this situation
b. none of the above
c. (X) is the only good explanation
d. (X) and (Y) both work
e. only (Z) explains why the exchange rate does not change

SUGGESTIONS FOR FURTHER READING

Flexible and fixed exchange rates are discussed in *The Great Wheel: The World Monetary System* by Sidney E. Rolfe and James L. Burke (New York: McGraw-Hill, 1975). Peter Lindert and Charles Kindleberger's textbook *International Economics* (Homewood, Illinois: Richard D. Irwin, 1982) has one of the best presentations of foreign-exchange markets. What is the FRS up to in foreign exchange markets? The Fed reports its actions in its monthly *Federal Reserve Bulletin*. The world monetary system is analyzed by Gerald M. Meier in *Problems of a World Monetary Order* (New York: Oxford University Press, 1982).

15

INTERNATIONAL ECONOMICS

Preview

What happens to the economy when the exchange rate changes?

How do international credit movements influence interest rates and monetary policy?

What are Eurodollars?

How do economic policies work in an open economy?

Which policy is more effective against unemployment: monetary or fiscal actions?

Does it matter whether exchange rates are flexible or fixed?

Does exchange-market intervention alter the answers to these questions?

Should the FRS actively defend the dollar?

REMEMBER THE Gross National Bathtub? In Chapter 6 you learned to think of the economy as a big bathtub, with leakages that reduce income and injections that make spending grow. Exports are one injection. Spending on goods sold abroad flows into the U.S. bathtub—from where does it come? From another country; from another bathtub. Imports are a leakage—spending is piped from our economy to become an injection elsewhere.

The international economy is a plumber's nightmare of drains and spouts that connect national bathtubs in a giant interdependent system. Events in any one tub alter the equilibrium of the entire system. Pour a little extra water into one tub and the whole system adjusts. No nation is an island in this sea of tubs.

International economic interdependence is a fact of life. Nations are connected by trade flows of imports and exports and by credit flows—money crossing national borders seeking higher returns. Exchange rates tie together the currencies and economies of the world. This chapter asks the question, what does interdependence do to national economic policies?

Trade and the Economy

How do exchange rates and international trade affect the economy? Trade has many sides; it alters prices, the distribution of income, aggregate demand, and aggregate supply. Let us see how shifting exchange rates change these four faces of international trade.

1. TRADE AND PRICES. Let us review what we learned in the last chapter. What does a rising dollar (a dollar that has appreciated against other currencies) do to prices in the United States? The dollar buys more foreign currency, so dollars buy more foreign goods. Import prices fall (after a brief lag while declining prices work their way to consumer markets). Cheaper imports also mean lower prices for substitutes made in the United States. The demand for domestic products falls when people switch to cheaper foreign-made goods.

Many U.S. firms use foreign-produced inputs like raw materials and intermediate goods. The rising dollar is good for these firms because it lowers their production costs. Supply rises in these markets, bidding down price.

A strong dollar also lowers the price that American buyers pay for U.S. export goods, too. Why? Let us take wheat as an example. What happens to the price you pay for wheat when the dollar appreciates? American wheat costs more yen when the dollar's yen price rises. Foreign buyers switch to less costly grains (and wheat from other exporting countries). Falling world demand bids down the price of U.S. wheat. American buyers benefit from the reduced export demand—we pay fewer dollars for wheat because the exchange rate has reduced foreign demand for U.S. goods. An appreciating dollar forces U.S. prices down. Imports cost less, import-competing firms lower prices to hold on to customers, and exported goods are also cheaper for U.S. buyers.

What happens when the dollar depreciates? Work through the effects on U.S.prices for yourself. Imports increase in price and import substitutes made in the United States cost more, too. Prices rise, as well, for goods that use imported inputs. Higher costs reduce supply in these markets. Exports like Kansas wheat cost more when the dollar falls. The exchange-rate change boosts world demand for our products; buyers in Britain bid up the Boston price.

2. DISTRIBUTION OF INCOME. The price changes just discussed alter the distribution of income in trading countries. A rising dollar, for example, shifts income away from workers in import-substitute industries. Income falls in exporting occupations, too. Who gains? The rising dollar increases income in jobs that use cheaper imports as an intermediate good. Firms that import and process foreign steel or agricultural goods increase their share of domestic markets.

Dollar depreciation has the opposite consequences. Imports cost more, so incomes rise for workers in import-competing firms. Income rises in export industries, too. Export sales jump when the dollar slumps, increasing income among workers and firms in these industries.

3. AGGREGATE DEMAND. Dollar appreciation reduces aggregate demand. The rising dollar increases imports (an aggregate demand leakage) and reduces exports (an injection). Lower aggregate demand cuts inflation, but RGNP falls, too, and unemployment lines lengthen.

A falling dollar brings demand-pull inflation. Imports decline and exports increase when the dollar depreciates. More export injections and fewer import leakages increase aggregate demand.

4. AGGREGATE SUPPLY. How do exchange rates alter aggregate supply? Changing input prices are the most important effect. The dollar's appreciation tends to reduce production costs and increase aggregate supply by lowering the cost of foreign-made production goods. The falling dollar, on the other hand, makes imported intermediate goods more expensive. Production costs rise and aggregate supply falls.

The AD-AS effects are summarized in Figure 15-1. What happens when the dollar appreciates? Aggregate demand tends to fall, but aggregate supply rises due to lower import costs. The appreciating dollar is deflationary, but its unemployment effect depends on whether aggregate demand or aggregate supply shifts the most. The AD effect often dominates and RGNP falls.

Dollar depreciation means inflation, as Figure 15-1 shows. Aggregate demand rises, fueled by rising exports and reduced imports, but aggregate supply falls because imported inputs cost more. Inflation increases. The AD shift is often greater in the short run, as the figure indicates, so the falling dollar boosts RGNP and lowers unemployment.

This discussion has focused on exchange rates and international trade. It is important to remember, however, that exchange rates do not just shift—they move only in response to outside forces like inflation, official intervention, and the other causes discussed in the last chapter. These initial acts need to be considered when examining the trade implications of exchange-rate moves.

International Credit Movements

Interest rates are a key determinant of exchange-rate movements in the short run. Income differentials and changing patterns of comparative advantage alter

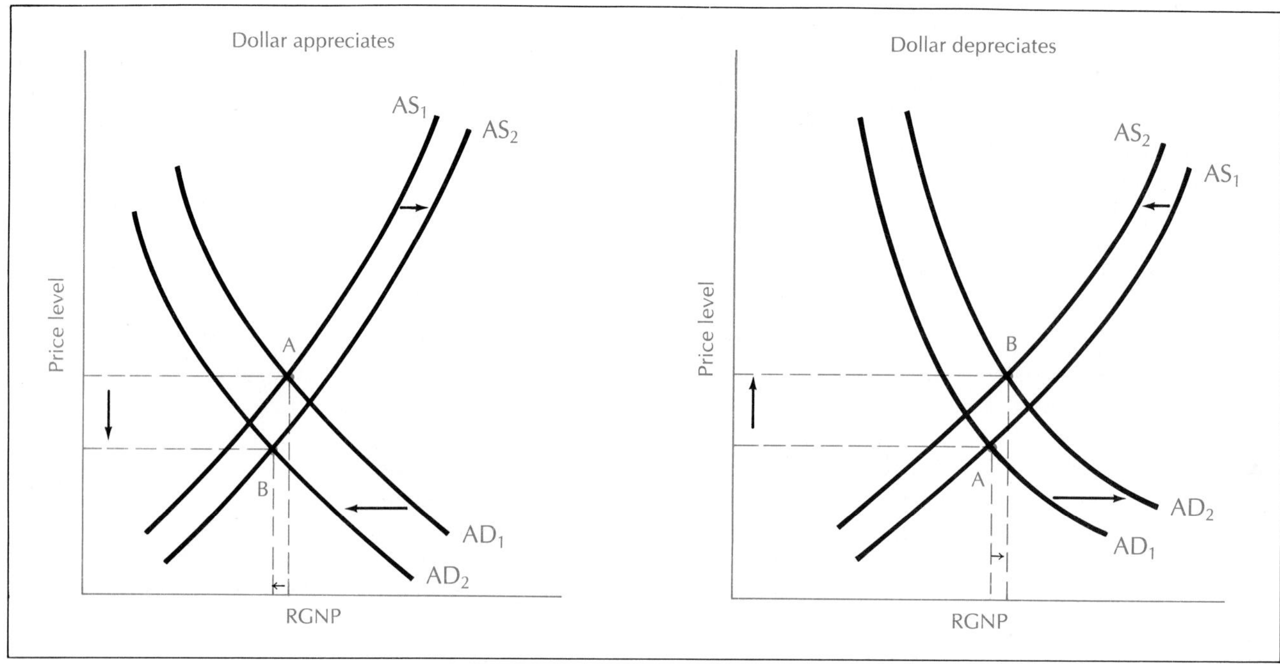

FIGURE 15-1 EXCHANGE RATES AND THE ECONOMY. **Aggregate demand falls when dollar appreciation discourages net exports. Less expensive imported goods reduce production costs, increasing the aggregate supply. The economy moves from initial equilibrium A to new equilibrium B in the first part of the figure. The aggregate demand rises when the dollar depreciates, but the aggregate supply falls if higher import prices boost production costs. The economy moves from A to B in the second part of the figure.**

exchange rates over long periods, but interest rates, inflation, and official intervention are the principal causes of short-term change.

Credit movements are important for two reasons. First, changing interest rates, as we saw in the last chapter, force exchange-rate movements. Second, and just as important, international credit movements alter interest rates and loan availability around the world. Let us look at two examples.

Suppose that interest rates drop in the United States because the federal deficit has been reduced and credit demand is thus lower. Investors shift funds to foreign credit markets where interest returns are now higher. The result? First, the credit outflow is a dollar outflow. The increased supply of dollars on foreign exchange markets makes the dollar depreciate (with the effects noted in the last section). The second blow hits the credit market itself: the exiting of credit reduces the U.S. credit supply, forcing interest rates back toward their original level. The result? Figure 15-2 shows that interest rates do not fall as much as originally thought. Falling credit demand (less deficit spending) is matched by lower credit supply (as credit leaves the United States, seeking higher returns in other countries). Lower deficits reduce interest rates, but international credit movements keep the changes small.

Huge federal deficits increased credit demand in the early 1980s, but international movements cushioned the interest-rate blow. Higher credit demand

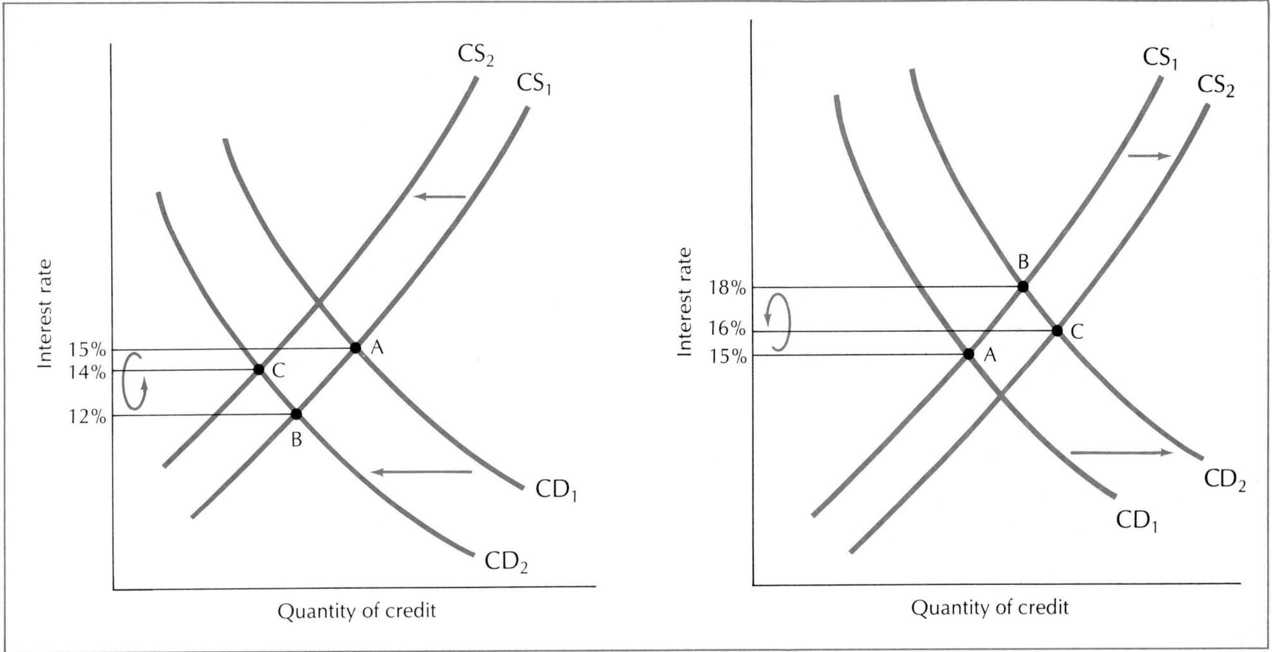

FIGURE 15-2 INTERNATIONAL CREDIT FLOWS. International forces limit interest rate changes in the United States. Lower credit demand drives interest rates down from A to B; however, credit exit brings equilibrium interest back to C. Higher credit demand initially increases interest rates to B in the second part of the figure, but credit inflows push rates back to C.

drives up the U.S. interest rate. Higher interest return, in turn, attracts credit from foreign markets. International financiers take funds out of foreign credit instruments and invest in U.S. bonds and bank accounts. The result? The dollar appreciates as demand for U.S. currency rises. The U.S. credit supply increases, too, as foreign funds add to domestic bank reserves. The credit supply rises, as the figure shows, and the deficit's crowding-out worries are reduced.

International credit flows keep interest rates in individual countries from drifting far from the world equilibrium. Funds exit low-interest economies and head for higher returns abroad. These movements drive up interest rates in source nations and drive down interest returns elsewhere. That does not mean that interest rates are the same everywhere, however. Differences in credit regulations and inflation rates among countries keep interest returns from finding the same level everywhere.

Eurodollars

Eurodollars are dollar-denominated accounts in non-U.S. banks. Imagine that your local bank allowed you to deposit Japanese yen, keep your bank account in yen amounts, and write checks in yen rather than in dollars and cents. That is how Eurodollar accounts work for people in other countries.

Eurodollars: dollar-denominated accounts held in foreign banks.

Who invented Eurodollars? The first Eurodollar accounts were created by Soviet leaders in the 1950s. They needed to keep dollars to buy U.S. exports, but they were afraid to keep them in U.S. banks—they feared the government might grab their money in a cold war strategy. Billions of dollars are held in Eurocurrency accounts these days for international trade and investment use.

Why would someone want to keep a Eurodollar account? Convenience is one answer. A German firm with a Eurodollar account does not have to worry about exchange-rate changes when making a U.S. deal—it already has the dollars it needs. Why not just keep the dollars in a U.S. bank? American banks are subject to strict Federal Reserve regulations. European banks can pay higher interest rates to depositors because they are not subject to Regulation Q interest-rate ceilings. Foreign banks have lower reserve requirements, too. They pay depositors more and still offer lower lending rates because less of each Eurodollar deposit sits idle in required reserves. The cold war gave birth to the Eurodollar, but restrictive FRS regulations keep it alive today.

Eurodollars show how freely money flows from one country to another. Are U.S. interest rates falling? Shift your funds into Eurocurrency accounts to get the higher world return. Is the FRS increasing U.S. interest rates? Move your dollars from outside accounts into the U.S. credit market. These movements make it more difficult for the FRS to control the money supply since any FRS act generates an opposing international money movement.

A final note about Eurodollars. Unlike other credit movements, Eurodollar credit flows do not change the exchange rate. Money moves to and from dollar-denominated foreign accounts but no foreign-exchange transaction is needed since dollars are used in both places. Eurodollars show just how "open" world economies have become.

Economic Policy with Flexible Exchange Rates

The first 12 chapters of this book focused on the closed-economy effects of monetary and fiscal policy. A complete view of economic policy needs to add the effects of exchange rates, trade, and international credit flows. Let us see how economic policy works in an open economy. Suppose that the United States is experiencing high unemployment rates like those that prevailed during the early 1980s. What is the best way to fight unemployment?

1. EXPANSIONARY MONETARY POLICY. Expansionary Federal Reserve policies bring both national and international effects for the U.S. economy. The dual impacts are listed in Figure 15-3.

The national or closed-economy results of monetary policy are well-known. An open-market purchase or other expansionary action increases money and credit supplies in the United States. This tends, all else being equal, to bid down interest rates and encourage greater investment spending. Increased investment spending boosts aggregate demand in the short run and increases aggregate supply in the long run. What is the closed economy result? Demand-pull inflation is the short run consequence, with growing aggregate supply in

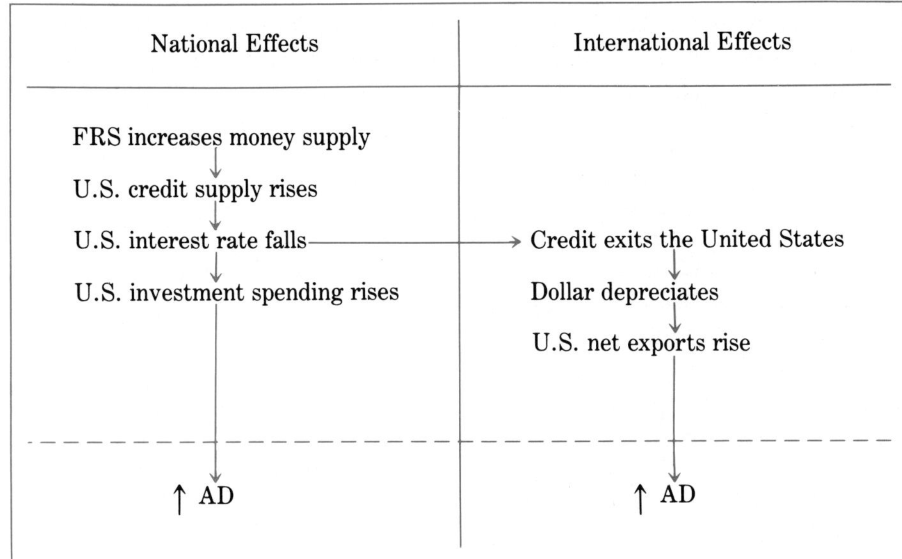

FIGURE 15-3 MONETARY POLICY WITH FLEXIBLE EXCHANGE RATES. Expansionary monetary policy drives down both interest rates and the dollar's foreign exchange value. Higher exports and lower imports make this policy an effective way to increase the aggregate demand.

the long run. This policy should reduce the unemployment rate as it pulls RGNP higher. (Review Chapter 11 if you have trouble with this chain reaction.)

Do international events alter these conclusions? Let us focus on the exchange rate for a moment. Does expansionary monetary policy make the dollar rise or fall? Lower interest rates in the United States bring on a credit exit—international investors seek higher returns elsewhere. They sell dollars and lend their credit abroad. The credit exit keeps interest rates from falling as far as they otherwise would and forces dollar depreciation.

The dollar's depreciation makes this FRS policy at once more expansionary (bigger RGNP effect) and more inflationary. Credit leaving the United States pushes the dollar's value down. This makes imports more costly and makes U.S. exports more attractive abroad. Increased exports and reduced imports further boost aggregate demand. Aggregate supply falls due to higher import costs, however.

What is the conclusion? Monetary policy still works, even when the international effects are included. Expansionary monetary policy has these effects:

- Interest rates fall (though by less than before because of credit exit);
- Investment spending rises (though by less because of smaller interest-rate drop);
- The dollar depreciates (the credit-exit effect);
- Net exports rise (the exchange-rate effect);
- Aggregate demand rises (higher investment spending plus increased exports and reduced imports);
- Aggregate supply falls in the short run (higher import prices boost production costs).

Monetary policy works in an open economy, but in a different way than closed-economy policymakers think. Does fiscal policy work in an open economy, too?

2. **EXPANSIONARY FISCAL POLICY.** You already know the national or open-economy effects of expansionary fiscal policy. Figure 15-4 shows what happens.

Increased government spending stimulates aggregate demand directly. Higher prices and incomes mean greater credit demand, so interest rates rise. The expansionary effect of rising government spending is partially offset by falling investment spending. Aggregate demand rises in the short run, but aggregate supply suffers in the long run. (Review Chapter 11 if you have trouble with this chain reaction.)

How does this fiscal policy influence exchange rates? Higher RGNP and rising U.S. prices tend to drive down the dollar. In the short term, however, interest-rate effects probably dominate, especially the high interest rates that come when deficits are financed by borrowing from the public. Higher interest rates attract credit from abroad. Foreign investors need to buy U.S. dollars before they can purchase U.S. bonds. The dollar appreciates as credit flows into U.S. banks and credit markets.

The appreciating dollar makes expansionary fiscal policy less inflationary than in a closed economy but less powerful, too, against the unemployment foe. Rising dollar prices reduce exports and increase imports. Net exports and aggregate demand fall. The international effects weaken fiscal policy in the United States (where the closed-economy effects are still important) and under-

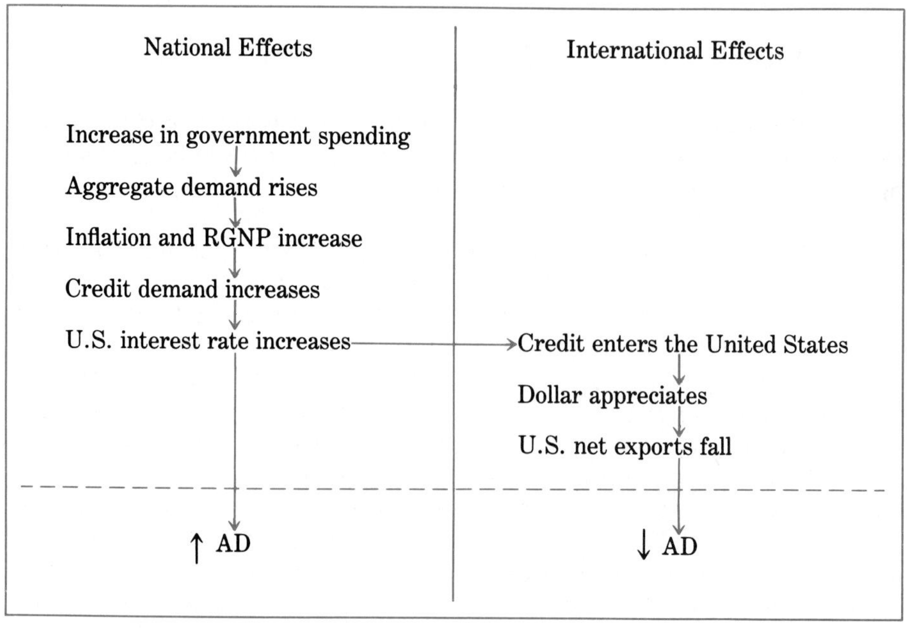

FIGURE 15-4 Fiscal Policy with Flexible Exchange Rates. Expansionary fiscal policy drives up interest rates and the dollar appreciates. Higher government spending is offset by lower investment and net export spending. This makes the policy less potent in moving the aggregate demand.

mines government actions in countries like Japan and Great Britain where international effects are larger.

Why is fiscal policy weak? The initial stimulus of government spending is offset by both falling investment spending and declining net exports. Government crowds out both investment and exports. The net effect is only modestly expansionary.

Economic Lessons for the 1980s

What are the implications of this open-economy analysis for the United States? Two lessons can be learned from our analysis so far. The first is that monetary policy is the most important tool for economic policy in these days of flexible exchange rates. Monetary policy gains strength from international effects; fiscal policy is diluted by exchange rate changes. This is not a comforting conclusion—monetary policy is risky and controversial. The variable lag between interest rates and investment spending makes FRS acts uncertain. Another lag between exchange rates and import–export changes adds to the uncertainty.

Monetary policy is controversial, too. Keynesians look at interest rates while monetarists seek money supply targets. The theory debate makes monetary policy uncertain in some investors' minds because it is hard to know which star is guiding Federal Reserve actions. Tight monetarist policies in the late 1970s brought high and highly variable interest rates that boosted dollar values.

Monetary policy is potent under flexible exchange rates, but government actions are still important. Fiscal effects on interest and exchange rates cannot be ignored.

Economic Policy with Fixed Exchange Rates

Economic policy prescriptions depend on the prevailing exchange-rate regime. Exchange rates were fixed between 1946 and 1973, and many countries (including the powerful EEC nations) use some variant of a fixed-exchange rate system today.

What is the biggest difference between flexible- and fixed-exchange rate policies? The central bank (the FRS in the United States) must intervene whenever the exchange rate moves if a fixed rate is to stick. This changes the way economic policies work.

1. **EXPANSIONARY MONETARY POLICY.** The United States was stuck in a deep recession in the early 1960s when exchange rates were fixed. How did monetary policy work then? Figure 15-5 sketches the main points.

An increase in the money supply bids down interest rates, all else being equal, and investment spending should increase. But, lower interest rates push credit out of the country. The credit exit tends to drive down the international value of the dollar. Dollar depreciation, however, cannot be allowed under fixed exchange rates. The FRS must intervene to restore the dollar's value. How do

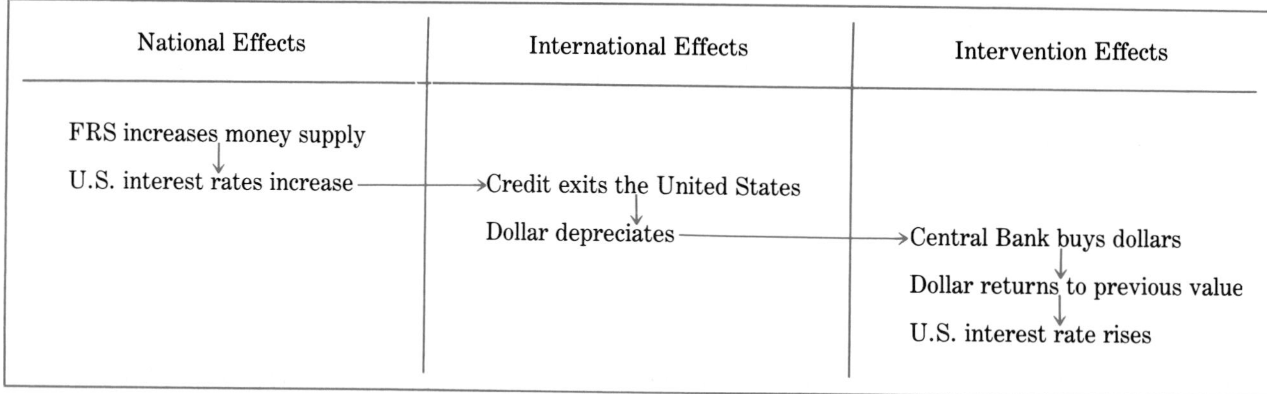

FIGURE 15-5 MONETARY POLICY WITH FIXED EXCHANGE RATES. Intervention makes monetary policy less powerful. The FRS money-supply increase triggers intervention to keep the exchange rate from dropping. This policy has little effect on exchange rates, interest rates, or aggregate demand.

they keep exchange rates fixed? By buying up the increased money supply they have just created! What is the net effect? Only small changes occur in the money supply and interest rate and no change occurs in the exchange rate. The FRS increases the money supply at the "open-market window" then buys it back at the "foreign-exchange window."

The fixed exchange rate effectively ties the FRS's hands. They can only expand the credit supply as fast as the U.S. credit demand increases—any monetary policy that increases the money supply faster than this must be neutralized later when the dollar starts to fall.

Monetary policy is impotent under fixed exchange rates. It is, at best, modestly stimulative. Fixed-exchange rate agreements prevent the FRS from discretionary monetary actions.

2. FISCAL POLICY. Do fixed exchange rates bind fiscal hands, too? Figure 15-6 sketches the basics of fixed-exchange rate fiscal policy. An increase in government spending has familiar closed-economy effects. Aggregate demand rises, credit demand rises, and interest rates go up. Higher U.S. interest rates attract funds from other countries, and the dollar starts to appreciate. The appreciating dollar makes fiscal policy less powerful under flexible exchange rates, but not here.

The central bank (FRS) must step in to keep the exchange rate fixed. How? By selling dollars to keep the exchange rate from rising. Federal Reserve intervention maintains the fixed exchange rate and makes fiscal policy more effective. Aggregate demand still rises due to the multiplier effect of increased government spending, but exchange-rate changes no longer get in the way. In fact, the fixed exchange rate makes fiscal policy more powerful because it forces the FRS to increase the money supply (by selling dollars on foreign-exchange markets) when government spending increases. The fixed exchange rate takes economic policy out of the Fed's hands and forces them into accommodating actions!

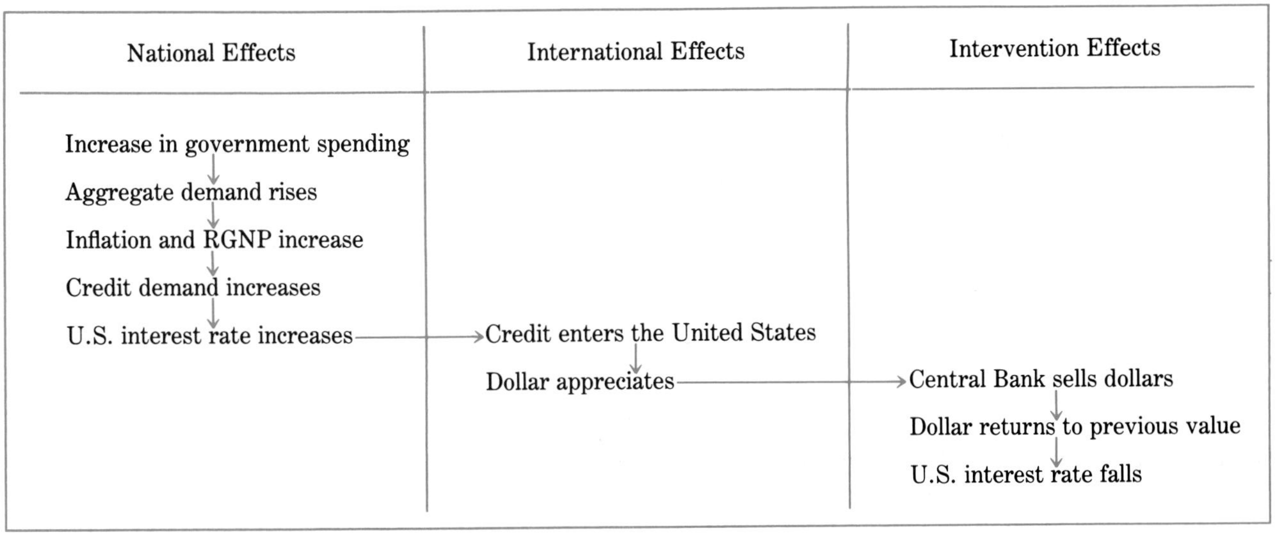

National Effects	International Effects	Intervention Effects
Increase in government spending ↓ Aggregate demand rises ↓ Inflation and RGNP increase ↓ Credit demand increases ↓ U.S. interest rate increases →	Credit enters the United States ↓ Dollar appreciates →	Central Bank sells dollars ↓ Dollar returns to previous value ↓ U.S. interest rate falls

FIGURE 15-6 FISCAL POLICY WITH FIXED EXCHANGE RATES. In this instance, fiscal policy works well. Intervention to keep the dollar from rising increases the dollar supply and prevents interest rates or exchange rates from offsetting expansionary fiscal effects.

Economic Lessons from the 1970s

Why was economic policy so depressingly unsuccessful in the 1970s? Part of the blame can be laid on the failure to adjust to changing exchange-rate regimes. Fiscal policies dominated the economic scene in the 1950s and 1960s; monetary actions were constrained by fixed exchange rates. Exchange rates became unstuck in the early 1970s, however, and the balance of power in economic policy changed, too.

The familiar prescriptions of fiscal policies that worked so well in the 1960s were almost useless in the 1970s. Battling inflation and unemployment with taxes and transfer payments made little sense under flexible exchange rates. Government deficits grew—borrowing forced the dollar up and reduced employment at home.

Monetary policy was suddenly free of the fixed-exchange rate constraint. Fiscal policies were ineffective, so monetary authorities tried to make up the difference. Combine frustrated fiscal policy and anxious monetary authorities with OPEC and other problems of the 1970s and you get a deadly brew that poisoned the world economy for much of the decade.

Economic Policy with Intervention

Exchange rates are neither firmly fixed nor freely floating in today's complex economic world. Exchange rates are flexible, but official intervention is a frequent fact of life. Economists call the current system a **dirty float.** Official

dirty float: a flexible exchange rate with frequent official intervention.

intervention makes life interesting because no fixed set of economic policies always works. Intervention makes economic policy a high-stakes crap shoot. Let us look at an example.

Exchange rates are flexible, but central banks around the world intervene when they think it is in their national interest. Suppose the FRS wants to stimulate RGNP at home, so it increases the U.S. money supply. This normally has the powerful results shown in Figure 15-3: aggregate demand rises due to increases in both investment spending and net exports. This policy, by itself, is effective.

Suppose, however, that the Japanese central bank views this policy as a threat—as a way of exporting U.S. unemployment to Japan. The expansionary monetary policy drives down the dollar's value, encouraging sales of U.S. exports (putting competing Japanese firms out of business). The falling dollar discourages sales of Japanese cars and other products in the United States, adding to Tokyo's unemployment woes. How can the Japanese central bank fight this aggressive U.S. policy? It intervenes on foreign-exchange markets, buying up dollars to keep the exchange rate fixed. The expansionary FRS policy now looks more like the fixed exchange rate case of Figure 15-5. The FRS creates money that the Japanese central bank takes off the market. American monetary policy is frustrated.

Is fiscal policy any better? Expansionary fiscal policy bids up U.S. interest rates, so the dollar appreciates as Figure 15-4 shows. This is good news for workers in Japan—they can export more to the United States and import less—but it is bad news for U.S. workers. The Japanese central bank does not have to intervene here, so the fiscal policy is weak. Falling exports and investment spending offset the stimulative government spending. The U.S. economy wallows.

Intervention of the kind illustrated here puts economic policy in a box; nothing works. Intervention offsets the otherwise effective monetary policy. Fiscal policy is ineffective anyway.

Oil and International Economic Policy

Oil is an important international commodity these days, and oil is priced in dollars. This means that foreign countries have a vested interest in keeping the dollar cheap so that they can buy oil cheaply—even if this costs the jobs of export workers. Assume that the Japanese central bank is willing to give up export jobs to keep oil prices low (an uncomfortable trade-off for an exporting country!). How do U.S.policies work now?

The FRS can expand the money supply without worry. Lower U.S. interest rates push the dollar down, making U.S. goods and oil cheaper for Japanese firms. No intervention prevents this exchange-rate change. Everything works just as Figure 15-3 showed.

Are fiscal policies effective, too? An expansionary fiscal policy drives up interest rates and increases the dollar's value. But the Japanese central bank intervenes and sells its dollar reserves to prevent this. The result? Increased government spending has been accommodated by an increase in the money supply—from the Japanese central bank, not the FRS! Both monetary and fiscal policies work here!

Interest Rate Wars

Does the fear of higher oil prices give the United States the upper hand in international economic policies? There are two reasons this is not the case. First, foreign central banks do not always intervene to push the dollar down. At some point the trade-off—lower net exports for cheaper oil—becomes too costly. Intervention ends and the dollar rises. The second reason is that we have looked only at expansionary policies so far. Contractionary policies introduce new problems.

The FRS adopted a restrictive monetary policy in the late 1970s, with the intent of reducing the United States' inflation rate. Interest rates rose in the United States, drawing credit from other countries. This had two important effects. First, it bid up interest rates abroad as credit supplies fled to the United States. Foreign firms and governments had to pay high interest prices for borrowed funds. Second, it forced the dollar's appreciation, making oil more costly for foreign buyers.

Foreign central banks found the best way to keep the dollar from rising was to raise their own interest rates and attract money back into home credit markets. The result? An interest-rate spiral that lowered world inflation rates but brought on worldwide recession, too. The interest-rate wars discouraged investment spending and damaged economic growth around the world.

ECONOMIC CONTROVERSY:

Defending the Dollar

All currencies are equal, but some currencies are more equal than others.

The dollar is a special currency. The central banks of major countries hold the dollar as a reserve currency—they trust its acceptance in payment of international obligations. Oil is priced in dollars and much international trade uses dollars as a convenient unit of account. Even Communist countries covet dollars because of their ability to purchase needed Western imports. The dollar is the linchpin of international finance.

The dollar's importance is both an advantage and a disadvantage for the United States. Dollars were readily acceptable to other countries during the 1960s, for example, so the United States was able to run balance-of-payments deficits and finance them with little effort. Foreign central banks were willing to hold paper dollars as payment for international debt. The United States exported dollars and imported valuable goods and services in this period—a great advantage.

The disadvantage of the dollar's central role is that the whole system lasts only so long as the dollar remains strong and accepted. The dollar's weakness during the mid-1970s worried central bankers around the world. The International Monetary Fund (a type of international central bank) considered plans to replace huge dollar stocks with an alternative in order to keep the system from being so sensitive to changing dollar values. No plan was adopted, but the message remained: international financial relations depend in intriguing ways on the health of the dollar.

Should the Federal Reserve defend the dollar—that is, should it intervene through currency transactions or high interest rate policies to keep the dollar's value high? Let us hear from three sides of this debate.

Defend the Dollar

The dollar must be defended. Look at the alternative. A falling dollar is inflationary. Import prices rise, directly boosting the CPI. Rising aggregate demand and falling aggregate supply (see Figure 15-1) push prices higher. Higher inflation rates, in turn, push the dollar still further down. Rising prices and falling dollar values create an economic maelstrom from which no country can escape.

Speculators make this cycle worse. Currency traders sense this problem and sell dollars before their value drops further. Their sales push the dollar's value down even more.

The falling dollar is dangerous for the United States and for the world. The OPEC countries demand payment in dollars. What do you think they would do if the dollar's value started dropping? Raise the price of oil? Right! Higher oil costs (coupled with higher import prices generally) would bring on more cost-push inflation like that experienced in the 1970s. Do you think the U.S. economy could stand another decade like the 1970s?

Foreign central banks hold many dollars as reserves. What will they do if the dollar plummets? They will unload their reserves—bringing on a real currency collapse. The dollar will be worthless and the world economy will be in peril.

Can we risk this collapse? No. We must defend the dollar to protect the world economy.

Fight Inflation First

What would you do if you had a 104-degree temperature? Would you take medicine to cure the disease or would you pack the thermometer in ice to bring down its reading? The dollar's decline is not a disease, it is a symptom of high U.S. inflation rates. Defending the dollar is like freezing the thermometer—it does nothing to solve the underlying problem.

What is the answer to the falling dollar? The United States must get its house in order. Balanced budgets and prudent monetary policies are needed to bring inflation down and secure the dollar's strength. Will this work? The early 1980s show this strategy's success. Tight monetary policy and high interest rates brought U.S. inflation under control and made the dollar strong again. These policies should be continued.

Will not these conservative plans cause high unemployment rates? In the short term, maybe. But in the long run, low inflation stimulates economic growth and creates many more jobs than are temporarily lost. Inflation is the real enemy. Stop inflation and the dollar's inherent strength must return.

Let the Dollar Fall

The dollar's value is nothing to get worked up about. The exchange rate is just a price that adjusts to bring supply and demand into balance. No government can hope to alter the market price for long without paying a high price.

What happens when the dollar falls? Cheaper dollars mean that U.S. goods and U.S. investments are cheaper to buyers abroad. This gives other countries an incentive to buy our goods and invest in our economy. We need these international injections to help the U.S. economy grow.

Defending the dollar is a revolting idea because it puts the burden of international finance on the backs of the poor and unemployed. Rising dollar values put people out of work in both export- and import-competing industries. Is the unemployment rate not high enough without this extra, artificial increase?

Let us take a lesson from the Germans and the Japanese. They have, at certain times, intervened to depreciate their currency—to force its value down! Why? Jobs are the answer. A falling dollar is bad for inflation but good news to workers. Would you rather have a job with moderate inflation or starve with stable prices? If the FRS must intervene in foreign-exchange markets, its purpose should be to drive the dollar down, not prop it up.

What is the real reason for all this talk about defending the dollar? Is it economic wisdom? No, just egotistical national pride. The United States is not numero uno any more. We should accept economic interdependence and learn to treat the dollar as a currency, not some macho symbol of national power.

SUMMARY

1. Trade and financial flows link the nations of the world like an interconnected system of bathtubs. One country's actions disturb the entire system.

2. Exchange rates affect the economy in many ways. A change in the exchange rate alters many prices, changes the distribution of income, and shifts aggregate demand and supply.

3. Interest rates are important international links. The credit markets of the world are tied together by credit flows. National interest rates are affected by international forces. Interest rates are important, too, because credit flows bring exchange-rate changes.

4. Eurodollars are an indication of international economic interdependence. Eurodollars are dollar-denominated accounts in foreign banks. Eurodollars pay a higher return because foreign banks are not subject to strict U.S. bank regulations. Eurodollar accounts allow investors to have higher foreign returns and keep their dollars, too. Eurodollars flow in and out of the United States as relative interest returns change.

5. What economic policy works the best with flexible exchange rates? The open-economy effects must be considered. Expansionary monetary policy forces dollar depreciation. Investment spending and net exports both rise, boosting aggregate demand. Fiscal policy is less effective. Lower investment and net export spending offset the fiscal injection.

6. What economic policy works best with fixed exchange rates? The fixed exchange rates tie the hands of monetary authorities, but they ensure accommodating policy for fiscal planners. Fiscal policy is more powerful in this instance.

7. We live in the world of the dirty float—nations frequently intervene to alter exchange rates. Which policy works best here? It depends on the pattern of intervention and whether the goal is to increase or decrease aggregate demand. Interest-rate wars erupted in the early 1980s as contractionary U.S. monetary policy met foreign resolve to keep the dollar from rising.

8. Should the FRS defend the dollar? One speaker claimed that defending the dollar was the key to fighting inflation. Another said that fighting inflation was the only way to keep the dollar's value high. The last speaker thought the dollar should fall to create U.S. jobs. What do you think?

DISCUSSION QUESTIONS

1. Compare and contrast the effectiveness of contractionary monetary and fiscal policies under flexible exchange rates. Which policy is more effective? Explain.

2. Compare and contrast the effectiveness of contractionary monetary and fiscal policies under fixed exchange rates. Which policy works best? Explain.

3. The Japanese central bank is considering a contractionary monetary policy. Explain how this would affect the U.S. economy under a system of flexible exchange rates. Is this good news for the United States? Explain the reasoning behind your answer.

4. The FRS began a contractionary monetary policy in 1979. At the same time, Congress increased spending, financing the deficit by borrowing from the public. How would this combination of policies affect a closed economy? How would it affect an open economy with flexible exchange rates? What is the difference, if any, between your two answers? Explain.

5. Should the FRS defend the dollar? Defend your answer.

TEST YOURSELF

Circle the best response to each question.

1. Exchange rates are flexible. Assume that interest rates in the United States rise. Which of the following events would *not* result from this action?

(W) the dollar would appreciate
(X) U.S. exports would increase
(Y) U.S. aggregate demand would increase
(Z) U.S aggregate supply would decrease

a. none of the above would result
b. (W) would not result
c. (X) and (Z) would not occur
d. only (W) would happen, the rest would not occur
e. (X) and (Y) would not happen

2. Exchange rates are fixed. You read that an increase in government spending is to be financed by borrowing. Which of the following events should you expect to observe?

(X) the FRS would increase the credit supply
(Y) the dollar would appreciate
(Z) U.S. exports would fall

a. all the above would happen
b. none of the above would happen
c. only (X) would occur
d. (Y) and (Z) would occur
e. exchange rates are fixed, so (X) and (Z) are true, but (Y) is not

3. Exchange rates are flexible. You read that the Japanese central bank has just decided on an expansionary policy. You should expect U.S. interest rates to ________ and the dollar to ________ against the yen (choose the answer that best fills in the blanks):

a. increase/appreciate
b. increase/depreciate
c. decrease/appreciate
d. decrease/depreciate
e. decrease/impossible to tell

4. The United States is an open economy. This changes the way monetary policy affects the economy. Monetary policy is:

(X) more effective in changing income because it influences both investment spending and exchange rates
(Y) less effective because it is less able to alter U.S. interest rates due to international credit flows
(Z) more effective because the FRS can control Eurodollars as well as the U.S. money supply

a. all the above are correct
b. only (X) and (Y) are correct
c. only (Y) and (Z) are correct
d. only (X) is correct
e. none of the above are correct

5. Exchange rates are flexible. Which of the following policies is most likely to increase inflation rates and reduce the unemployment rate (look at both national and international effects)?

a. an increase in the money supply
b. an increase in government spending
c. a decrease in the money supply
d. a decrease in government spending
e. an intervention to increase the dollar's value

SUGGESTIONS FOR FURTHER READING

The *Wall Street Journal* now publishes a detailed analysis of international economic news every day (on the first "inside" pages of the second section). Do not miss it. The best source of international economic analysis is still the British weekly, *The Economist.* A good theoretic presentation is provided by Rudiger Dornbusch's *Open Economy Macroeconomics* (New York: Basic Books, 1980). Interdependence is the theme of "Europeans Gripe When Dollar is Strong, Even Louder than When Dollar is Weak" by Richard F. Janssen (*Wall Street Journal,* March 9, 1981).

16

PROBLEMS, GOALS, AND TRADEOFFS

Preview

What are the goals of economic policy?
Are national goals all that count?
What trade-offs must be made?
Can we achieve all our goals at once, or must we give up a goal?
What problems make economic policy difficult?
Why can we not find an easy answer to our economic problems?
What about the future? Are things getting better or is the economy going down the drain?

IT IS time to look back at what you have learned about macroeconomics and then peer ahead at the future. This book began with a discussion of macroeconomic problems, goals, and trade-offs. Let us see what we have learned.

Goal 1: Full Employment

Full employment remains an unfulfilled promise. What is full employment? Why has the economy not created jobs for people who need them?

Full employment is a moving, changing target. Unemployment is not just one problem; it is a package of troubles from many sources. Most government policies and FRS actions aim at one side of the problem: cyclical unemployment. This makes sense, since cyclical problems loom large today. But frictional and structural unemployment cannot be ignored. These more subtle, but equally crippling, forms of unemployment are not solved by fiscal stimulus or monetary expansion. These difficult human problems cannot be cured by simply throwing money at them.

The full-employment puzzle grows more difficult when we consider the natural-unemployment-rate possibility. A growing body of evidence suggests that government policies cannot alter the unemployment rate for long. Expectations and institutional problems drive the jobless rate back to its equilibrium level. According to this theory (discussed in Chapters 3 and 12), fiscal and monetary policies aimed at reducing unemployment just make inflation rates rise. If you buy the natural-rate hypothesis, then government is powerless to reduce cyclical unemployment rates.

Does this mean we should just throw up our hands and learn to live with high unemployment rates? No. It means that we have to carefully reconsider government policies. Aggregate demand policies that worked well in the Great Depression might not be right for today's complicated, high-inflation, expectations-dominated world.

Goal 2: Stable Prices

Stable prices and high purchasing power are the second goal of modern macroeconomics. Are low inflation rates possible? One problem is that the inflation rate responds to expectations, as well as to the tools of monetary and fiscal policy. People who expect high inflation rates get them—their actions keep prices rising.

Can we bring inflationary expectations down? Expectations are sometimes hard to change. The inflation rate tumbled in 1982, for example—the CPI even fell for a month or two. Did lower inflation mean lower expectations of inflation? It is hard to measure expectations (surveys and questionnaires try). Credit markets are one indicator of expectations. Credit demand and supply are particularly sensitive to changing expectations. Did interest rates tumble when the inflation rate fell? No. High inflation expectations (among other things) kept real-interest returns high.

The lesson of the 1970s was that inflation is often unexpectedly high. The facts changed in the early 1980s, but individuals trained in the school of hard knocks did not quickly forget the lessons of high inflation rates. Expectations based on 10 years of high inflation rates were not forgotten in the enthusiasm over a brief month or year of price stability. This makes the goal of low inflation even harder to achieve.

Inflation is a hard problem to solve by itself; add high unemployment rates and you have got a real mess. Suppose that the natural-unemployment-rate theory is correct (it is still controversial among economists). This means the long-run Phillips curve is vertical, as Figure 16-1 shows. What happens when traditional economic policies try to fight inflation and unemployment together?

Presidents and Congress often finger either inflation or unemployment as "public enemy #1" and aim their weapons at a single target. Suppose they decide to fight unemployment first. Tax cuts and spending increases temporarily reduce jobless lines but at the cost of higher inflation rates. These gains

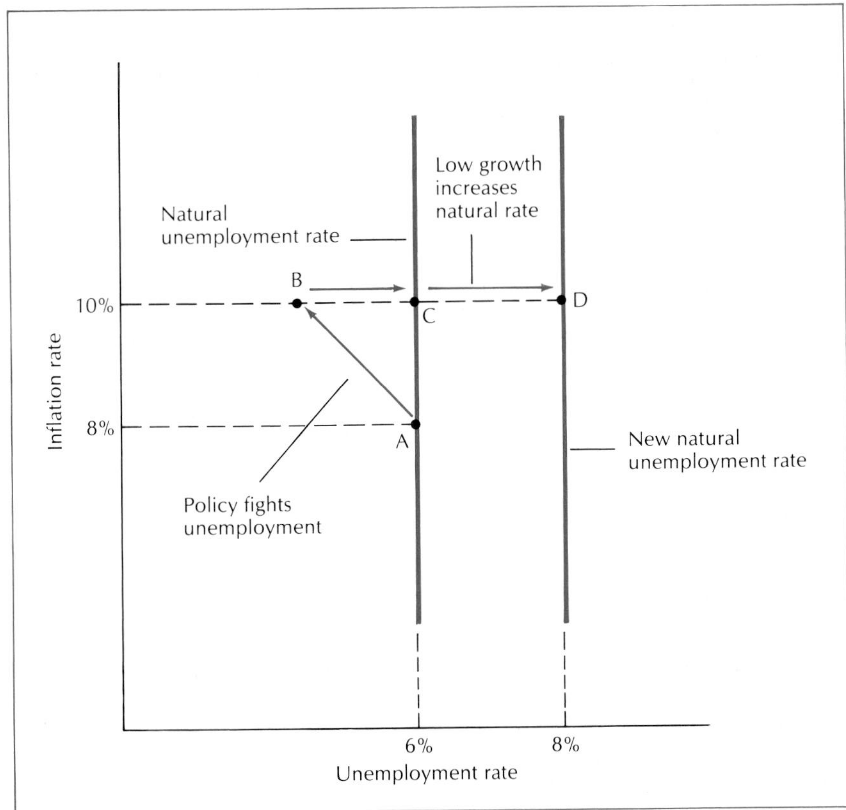

FIGURE 16-1 THE NATURAL-RATE PUZZLE. Is there a "natural rate of unemployment"? If there is, then anti-unemployment policies are difficult. Government policies increase inflation rates in the short run, with no long term effect on unemployment. High deficits from fighting joblessness reduce employment opportunities and "shift" the natural rate, making problems worse.

are short lived, however. Workers and employers adjust expectations to the accelerating inflation and the unemployment rate returns to its old level. The result? The Economic Discomfort Index (discussed in Chapter 1) creeps higher and neither problem is solved. Bigger problems call for bigger policies, so Congress boosts spending and makes deeper tax cuts to bring down unemployment. Huge deficits drive interest rates up, discourage investment, and hurt export sales; as a result, the natural rate of unemployment increases. Now the underlying inflation and unemployment rates are both worse. What a mess! This scenario looks suspiciously like the experience of the 1970s.

Goal 3: Economic Growth

How does an economy grow? Aggregate demand policies increase RGNP in the short run, but capacity roadblocks eventually appear. Economic growth in the long run means growth in aggregate supply.

The biggest obstacle to economic growth is its long-run nature. Few short-term policies bring capacity growth. Investment, innovation, education, and training are the keys to economic growth in the long run. But who is willing to sacrifice today for potential future gains? Economic policies that fight unemployment in the short run with high-interest deficits or try to lower inflation with tax increases get in the way of long-run economic growth.

Walt Kelly's cartoon character Pogo said, "We have met the enemy and it is us." Our own desire to reduce short-term problems makes long-run ills worse. But, as Keynes noted, "In the long run we are all dead." Temporary depression and hyperinflation are also obstacles to economic growth.

Full employment, stable prices, economic growth. The emerging view is that these are not three separate economic goals. They are of a piece. It is impossible to find full employment or stable prices without the economic growth that builds factories, creates jobs, gives opportunity to discouraged workers, and keeps down prices. But economic growth is difficult with high inflation rates and anti-unemployment deficits that force interest rates up and discourage or crowd out investment borrowing. Inflation and unemployment dance a tango that keeps economic policymakers spinning.

Other National Goals

Full employment, stable prices, and economic growth are not the only national economic goals. Other goals guide policymakers at the same time.

1. BALANCED BUDGET. Federal deficits over the years have accumulated a national debt of over $1 trillion. The burden of this debt weighs on conservatives who see it as an obstacle to lower taxes and on liberals who view it as a roadblock on the path to social goals. Both sides of the aisle think the deficit should be reduced. Toward this end, a constitutional amendment has been proposed to require the federal government to balance its budget the way most state and local governments do.

Balancing the budget forces more severe government trade-offs. Any plan to expand spending must come equipped with new taxes to raise the money. Tax cuts require spending reductions to offset the monetary loss. The government's ability to influence aggregate demand suffers. When forced balanced budgets are coupled with a fixed exchange rate (discussed in the last chapter), both monetary and fiscal policies are handcuffed. Keynesians and disequilibrium macroeconomists view this prospect with alarm; monetarist, supply siders, and rational expectations theorists might favor such an action.

2. EQUITABLE DISTRIBUTION OF INCOME. The size of the pie makes little difference to those who do not get a piece. Extremes of wealth and poverty are undesirable. One goal of economic policy is to fight poverty and improve the distribution of income. This antipoverty goal is full of uncomfortable trade-offs.

How does society best aid the poor? Two strategies come to mind. The first reduces the income gap by taxing the rich in order to make transfer payments to the poor. This Robin Hood plan improves equality, but reduces economic efficiency. The rich have less incentive to invest and produce income and wealth when the tax man takes a big bite. Poorer transfer recipients are encouraged to stay on the dole rather than train and work. The slices are more equally cut, but the pie shrinks, making all worse off.

Economic growth is the second plan, and evidence suggests this is an effective way of helping the poor. It is easier to increase the poor's share of national income in a growing economy. But economic growth's theoretical advantages are often offset by two practical problems. Economic growth that helps the poor also helps the rich. The rich get richer when the poor get richer, so the gap between the two groups grows. Reduced poverty means growing inequality of income. The second problem is that helping the poor in the long run often means subsidizing wealthy groups in the short run. The poor find it hard to save, invest, or innovate. Encouraging aggregate-supply growth means tax breaks and other benefits for those who already have money. Government attempts to innovate and invest are not uniformly successful. We must take one step away from the equality goal before we take two steps in the right direction.

3. EQUALITY OF OPPORTUNITY. Prejudice prevents even economic growth from solving the poverty problem. Equality of opportunity is another economic goal (the list can be expanded). We move toward this goal in the short run by outlawing outright discrimination, but this is only a first step. "Why do you not hire more black and women engineers?" the bureaucrat asks. "Because there aren't any" is the frequent answer. Equality of opportunity means a whole slew of goals for income, education, and the like. This problem is easy to legislate but difficult to really solve.

4. NONECONOMIC GOALS. Economic goals are important, but they are not the only ones that guide policy. Environmental quality, personal liberty and justice, national defense, and foreign-policy concerns all affect economic policy. International trade is used as a carrot to attract political allies and a stick to punish those who disagree with U.S. foreign-policy views. International trade is restricted by national-defense concerns. Policies that fight inflation or unemployment have environmental costs. Wage and price controls reduce individual freedom. This discussion focuses on the purely economic goals, but all these other concerns have an economic side.

International Economic Goals

International economic goals add to the problem of prosperity. Full employment, stable prices, and economic growth are hard to accomplish with a balanced budget and equality of income and opportunity. But open economies cannot afford to ignore external problems. Three international goals intrude.

1. **EXCHANGE-RATE GOALS.** Exchange rates are important to economic policy these days. The dollar is a key currency for the United States and the world. One goal of economic policy is to keep the dollar strong so that it can continue to play its vital world role. Does this mean that the dollar must constantly appreciate? No. But the dollar should not continually depreciate since this increases U.S. inflation, threatens higher oil prices, and reduces the value of world currency reserves.

This international exchange-rate goal is at odds with the national aim to reduce unemployment. Depreciation adds to export- and import-substitute jobs, at least temporarily. A short-run trade-off between jobs and the dollar's value seems inevitable.

2. **INTERNATIONAL-TRADE GOALS.** The United States has gone from an exporting country to one that imports more and more goods. We buy goods, like televisions and radios, that we once proudly sold. A second international goal is to balance imports and exports. Why is this goal so difficult? Why has production jumped to other countries? Lower wage rates (the comparative advantage is at work here) and foreign subsidies are part of the answer, but the reasons go deeper than this. The United States traditionally exported agricultural and manufactured goods. Agriculture in the United States has continued to innovate and invest and sell abroad. Some other innovative industries keep up exports, too. The largest single U.S. exporter in 1981 was the Boeing airplane company—another firm at the forefront of technology. The high-tech gurus of California's Silicon Valley show that innovation and research increase productivity and create export jobs.

Investment and rising productivity are the exception, not the rule, these days. High taxes, higher interest rates, and low investment and research outlays have taken away the United States' comparative advantage in many areas. Restoring the international-trade position of the United States is a complex problem, related to inflation, unemployment, and economic growth.

3. **BALANCE-OF-PAYMENTS GOALS.** The third international economic goal is a balance-of-payments equilibrium. No nation can escape the consequences of payments deficits forever. The strength and acceptance of the dollar made U.S. deficits easy to finance in the past, but the future will be different. The United States must bring its payments account into balance.

How can balance-of-payments deficits be cut? The deficit has four faces. The first is the balance of trade. More exports and fewer imports help solve the problem. Transfer payments are the second side. Economic and military aid to other countries helps achieve political and social goals but makes payments problems worse. Credit flows are part of the payments dilemma, too. We can reduce the deficit by attracting funds from abroad and limiting U.S. investments in other countries. Official reserves make up the last piece of this puzzle. The U.S. deficit can be financed for short periods by paying out the gold and currency the United States has accumulated through the years. This attracts a money flow into the country on the credit side of the payments ledger. Reserves movements are not a long-term solution, however.

Trade-Offs: Give Up a Goal?

Are these goals mutually exclusive? Must we give up one or more goals to achieve the rest? Two points of view prevail here. Trade-offs are a hard fact of life in the short run. Fighting unemployment means a worsening inflation problem. Economic growth suffers from both inflation and unemployment. National economic goals and international aims set up a deadly cross fire. In the short run, then, some goals must be forsaken.

But the long-term view is different. Look back at the goals discussed so far: prices, income, equality, and the rest. How can we attain any one of them without achieving them all?

Economic growth is the key to all of these goals. A growing economy reduces unemployment, fights inflation, and makes possible the stable dollar, strong exports, and payments equilibrium that the international economy requires. In the long run we must achieve all goals or none of them. But economic policies that fight specific fires in the short run bring us no closer to long-run solutions.

Three Questions in Search of an Answer

Let us examine today's policy problem. Assume that we are concerned with just three problems: high inflation, high unemployment, and balance-of-payments deficit. What tools are available? How do these tools work? Can all three woes be cured at once, or do we have to give up a goal? Let us look at the policy menu.

1. **THE CLASSICAL MEDICINE.** The classical cure for balance-of-payments woes is deflation. Government policies reduce aggregate demand and bring on recession. This shrinks import demand and brings the payments accounts back into line. Does this policy work today? The deficit cure is purchased with long unemployment lines. But fewer imports mean a smaller supply of dollars on international exchange markets. The dollar appreciates, reducing exports, too. Fewer imports are purchased (the recession's goal), but fewer exports sales (the exchange-rate effect) reduce this policy's effectiveness. There is no guarantee that payments problems are actually solved.

Interest rates are likely to fall in the United States, too. This drives credit out of the country, making payments deficits larger. The classical medicine tries to cut imports by causing recession, but credit exit and exchange-rate changes weaken this policy today.

2. **EXCHANGE-RATE INTERVENTION.** A second option is to go directly to the exchange markets and intervene to depreciate the dollar. In this instance, the FRS will sell dollars (giving up the strong dollar goal) to drive the dollar down, discourage imports, and encourage exports. The payments deficit is reduced in the short run and jobs are created in export and import substitute industries. Is this a perfect policy?

Exchange-market intervention has several flaws. The FRS can only change the exchange rate if other central banks cooperate and stay out of currency markets themselves. Reserves in the United States are limited, so intervention cannot be sustained for long periods. Intervention can also backfire. Dollar depreciation improves payments problems and increases employment, too, but at the cost of higher inflation. A 10 percent fall in the dollar's value soon leads to a 10 percent increase in U.S. inflation rates. Why? Imports are more costly and export prices are bid up by foreign buyers. The inflation rate soon pushes the exchange rate back to its old relative value and more intervention is required. In addition, international investors sometimes balk at tying up funds in a falling currency. This limits balance-of-payments gains.

3. **HIGHER INTEREST RATES.** Balance-of-payments deficits can be financed by attracting credit from abroad. Higher U.S. interest rates (and restrictive FRS policies) create a credit inflow to balance the trade deficit. This policy has been a frequent choice in recent years. Does it work?

There are several flaws in this gem. Raising interest rates only works if real rates rise above foreign returns. Foreign central banks can offset U.S. actions by pushing up their own interest rates. The interest rate wars of the early 1980s were the result of many countries all using this policy to fight payments deficits. Higher interest rates work if just one country uses the tool; no one wins when everyone competes for the same credit solution.

Exchange rates get in the way, too. Higher interest rates force dollar appreciation. This is good for inflation (it drives import prices down) but bad for unemployment. Higher interest rates and the rising dollar make for long unemployment lines, as U.S. workers found out in 1982. Dollar appreciation encourages imports and discourages exports, making trade deficits worse. Will credit inflows outweigh the balance-of-trade deficit? There is no way to tell. Higher interest rates might not even solve the payments crisis.

4. **TARIFFS AND QUOTAS.** Trade restrictions directly reduce payments for exports and help solve the balance-of-payments deficits. Tariffs and quotas shift spending from foreign goods to domestic production, increasing employment at home. Are tariffs and quotas the solution to this economic puzzle?

Trade restrictions are a dangerous policy for several reasons. First, they try to solve problems in the United States by shifting them to other countries. Fewer U.S. imports means fewer exports and fewer jobs in other countries. You can count on a fight for the shrinking trade pie. Retaliation is the rule. Higher trade barriers make all sides worse off. Export industry jobs are sacrificed to preserve import substitute work. There is no guarantee of a net employment rise.

Cost-push inflation is a threat here, too. Higher import prices increase production costs and boost prices. Wages rise to match higher prices and costs rise again. Tariffs are less effective when home prices start to rise toward the higher import cost.

Exchange rates work against this policy. Tariffs and quotas reduce the demand for foreign exchange. The dollar appreciates, making U.S. exports even more expensive. Tariffs keep imports out, but exchange-rate changes keep export sales down. Restrictive international trade policies frequently lead to higher inflation, longer unemployment lines, and worse balance-of-payments problems. International trade is replaced by damaging trade wars and all countries lose.

5. WAGE AND PRICE CONTROLS. Price controls are another option. Price controls directly reduce inflation, making U.S. goods a better buy abroad. But rising costs keep production from expanding to meet domestic and export demand. Shortages and uncertainty keep investment low. Effort goes into getting around government regulations rather than into innovation and production. This policy might work if it brought a real change in expectations. Wage and price controls have failed to alter anticipation in the past, however.

6. SUPPLY-SIDE TAX CUTS. What about the supply-side solution? Tax cuts reduce production costs and increase aggregate supply. This looks, at first glance, to solve all three problems at once. Rising aggregate supply bids down inflation and creates jobs that reduce unemployment. Lower costs and extra investment lead to more U.S. exports and fewer imports. High profits in the United States attract investment from abroad. Balance-of-payments problems are over.

The Reagan tax cuts of the early 1980s were supposed to have these effects, but they did not. What is the problem? Tax cuts cannot work immediately. High deficits in the short run bid up interest rates. Higher interest costs pushed prices higher and forced layoffs in the interest-sensitive automobile, wood products, and housing industries. Higher interest rates pushed the dollar's value up, too. Dollar appreciation made imports cheaper and discouraged exports. Inflation came down, but the unemployment ranks swelled and the U.S. trade position suffered. Higher interest rates diluted the planned benefits of lower taxes.

Policy Problems

Inflation, unemployment, balance-of-payments equilibrium. These are just three of the many goals of macroeconomics, yet none of the policies just discussed guarantees success. Trade-offs and interdependence make economic goals difficult to achieve. Four more problems complicate matters.

1. POLICY LAGS. Lags are a policy headache. The variable lag between interest-rate movements and investment decisions was discussed in Chapters

10 and 11. Fiscal policy suffers lag, too, as Chapter 8 noted. Lags also prevail in international trade. Today's exchange-rate shift does not change all import prices immediately. If the yen appreciates this afternoon, the price of Toyotas and Datsuns will not rise for days, weeks, or months. Cars already on dealer lots are not directly affected by exchange-rate changes. Exchange-rate effects are felt eventually, but a lot can happen in the meantime.

Lags distort economic-policy choices. Are current policies working? Do we need to do more? Should new plans be tried? Lags add to uncertainty and lead economic forces in the wrong direction.

2. MEASUREMENT. Measurement is the second problem. What policies are necessary? Which problem is most important? What is happening in the economy? We need facts to answer these questions. But uncertainty and inaccuracy plague the important task of economic measurement.

How serious is unemployment? Chapter 3 showed the errors of the unemployment rate. Unemployment numbers fail to count underemployed and discouraged workers but include the voluntary unemployed and underground-economy workers. According to Chapter 5's analysis, the underground system makes RGNP conclusions difficult. Chapter 4's inflation discussion pointed to problems with price indexes.

Measurement is important. Faulty readings of economic gauges lead Congress and the FRS to apply the right solutions to the wrong problems.

3. INTERNAL ECONOMIC CONFLICT. Economic policy suffers from conflict between the President, Congress, and the Federal Reserve. These three groups frequently disagree. Their conflicting actions let the economy drift in the short run, as Chapter 11 showed, with sometimes dreadful long-run consequences.

Internal economic debate runs deeper, however. Competing theories, discussed in Chapter 12, confuse business people and policymakers. Keynesians do not always agree with each other. Some fear inflation more than unemployment, for example. But when we add monetarist, supply-side, rational expectations, and disequilibrium theories together, who knows what is right? Is it any wonder that people are confused?

4. INTERNATIONAL ECONOMIC CONFLICT. We are not alone! Foreign governments and central banks make economic policies that affect us, just as our policies influence events in their economies. The delicate plans of one nation can be crushed by the aggressive monetary, fiscal, or exchange-rate policies of another. Conflict is not the only theme played by the international band, however. Common-Market countries have taught us the tune of cooperation. But even these united Europeans cannot completely escape policy conflicts.

Questions? Answers! Answers? Questions!

What is the moral of this long story? You started reading this book looking for answers. Why is the unemployment rate so high? Why is there so much inflation? Why can government not solve these problems?

Have you found the answers to these questions? Do you now have the key to prosperity? No. Why not? The economic world is complex and interdependent. If there were a quick fix it would have been quickly fixed years ago.

So what now? Do we give up? What good is macroeconomics if it does not give easy answers? Sometimes answers are not as important as knowing the right questions. You understand how the world works a little better now. You have an idea of how goals, problems, policies, and nations are interrelated. You can ask better questions and see why easy answers do not work. That is an important beginning to economic understanding.

There is just one question left: What of the future? That is the subject of this chapter's Economic Controversy.

ECONOMIC CONTROVERSY:

Where Are We Going?

Economic problems are not easy to solve. Will our problems grow worse in the future or are we heading for better times? Let us hear from both sides.

Gloom and Doom

Kontratieff was right 70 years ago when he said that capitalist nations go through cycles of prosperity and collapse. We are heading into an economic Dark Age and there is little we can do about it.

Why the dismal attitude? The inflation–unemployment trade-off is more severe than ever before. The natural unemployment rate, if it exists, is high. Political and social unrest must follow.

What do Americans do when unemployment rates get too high? They blame their problems on others—OPEC sheiks, Japanese car producers, European steel makers. And other countries blame their problems on us: high U.S. interest rates are blamed abroad for world recession.

Internal economic conflicts erupt into international economic wars. Already the Common Market shows symptoms of ripping itself apart. Greece, recently admitted to the EEC, already thinks it wants out. Nations that pledged free trade now freely restrict imports and exports. If the cooperative EEC nations cannot keep the peace, how can the United States and Japan, competitors in many markets, hold to an economic cease fire?

Compounding economic problems have produced a confusing thicket of new economic theories. Keynesians and monetarists have been joined by a gaggle of economists spouting different policy prescriptions. People grasp at any theory that promises a painless cure. Supply-side theory has little theory and almost no supporting evidence. Yet voters took it to their hearts and Congress passed huge tax cuts based on this famous un-theory. Can you imagine that? It is as if a new religion that promised Heaven to everyone who eats beets were to sweep the country! This is just evidence of how far down the road to collapse we have come!

What next? More crackpot theories, conflicting policies, and angry voters. And another Great Depression.

Don't Panic

There is no need to panic. Our economic problems are serious, but the world economy is strong and flexible. There is no reason to believe that economic collapse is due.

You are living through interesting economic times. The world economy is adjusting to new problems and institutions. The old problem was unemployment in a world of expanding frontiers. Resources are scarcer, now, and inflation adds to the problem. The international financial system is adjusting to different conditions, too. The old pattern of trade and payments is changing and it simply takes time for economic institutions to adjust.

These changes explain the controversy in economic theory. We need new answers to old questions in this changing world. The conflict in today's economic theory is much like the Keynesian revolution of the 1930s and 1940s. Keynes' ideas were thought to be "crackpot" and radical by many. It took years for a Keynesian synthesis to form. Today's new theories follow the Keynesian tradition of question and challenge.

The key to macroeconomics is economic growth. Investment, innovation, and effort are motivated by personal desire more than by government regulation and incentive. Even bad government policy cannot halt economic growth in market economies like the United States. The answer lies in individual action, not public policy. So long as individuals are willing to work, risk, and sweat, the promise of prosperity can be fulfilled.

SUMMARY

1. What are the goals of economic policy? National goals include full employment, stable prices, and economic growth. This list is expanded to include balanced budgets, income equality, and equality of opportunity. Each of these goals is difficult to achieve. Noneconomic goals like national defense, justice, and foreign policy influence economic choices, too. Trade-offs among goals are often necessary.

2. International goals add to policy problems. A strong dollar, an improved international-trade position, and a solution to the balance-of-payments problem are goals, too.

3. How are all these goals to be achieved? One view is that some goals must be given up—the various aims of economic policy are mutually exclusive. A different view is that there are not many goals, just one—economic growth. None of the other goals is possible without growth.

4. What is the best way to reduce inflation, lower unemployment rates, and reduce balance-of-payments deficits? Several policies were analyzed: clas-

sical medicine, exchange intervention, monetary policy, trade barriers, wage and price controls, and supply-side tax cuts. Each was found failing in some aspect.

5. Four more problems plague policy: lags in economic policies, measurement error and uncertainty, internal economic disagreement, and policy conflicts among nations.

6. What are the solutions to our macroeconomic problems? Easy solutions are scarce. The study of macroeconomics teaches you the right questions to ask, not pat answers to world problems.

7. Is the world going down the drain? One side of the Economic Controversy claims collapse is unavoidable. History, bad policy, and international trade wars are to blame. Is doom our fate? The other side of the debate counts on the strength and flexibility of the free-market economy to pull us through. The disequilibrium in theory and national affairs is a sign of change as the economy adjusts to new institutions and conditions.

DISCUSSION QUESTIONS

1. You are a member of the President's Council of Economic Advisors. The economy is experiencing high inflation, rising unemployment, a falling dollar, and a substantial balance-of-trade deficit. The President just called—he wants a plan to reverse these problems on his desk in the morning. What would you recommend? Sketch your plan and explain why you have picked this policy.

2. Are policy trade-offs any better when exchange rates are fixed? Assume that exchange rates are fixed. What policy best fights inflation and unemployment while reducing the balance-of-payments deficit? (Hint: consider the policies discussed in the text example.) Explain.

3. This chapter listed several national and international economic goals. What other economic, social, or political goals guide national policy? Explain your reasoning.

4. What are current government and Federal Reserve policies? Which goals do they aim to achieve? Which goals do they give up? Explain.

5. Is the future full of depression and economic collapse? What are the arguments on each side of the issue? Where do you stand?

TEST YOURSELF

Circle the best response to each question. Assume flexible exchange rates for all these questions.

1. The federal government has just increased spending (financed by borrowing from the public). Which of the following is *not* a probable result of this policy?

a. aggregate demand rises in the United States
b. credit flows into the United States
c. the dollar appreciates
d. net exports increase
e. aggregate supply is discouraged in the long run

2. The Federal Reserve has just increased the money supply. Which of the following is *not* a likely result of this action?

a. interest rates fall in the United States
b. the dollar depreciates
c. net exports rise
d. aggregate supply grows in the long run
e. credit flows into the United States, improving the balance of payments

3. The FRS has just intervened, selling dollars on foreign exchange markets. Which of the following is a probable result of this act?

(X) U.S. balance of trade improves
(Y) the inflation rate falls in the United States
(Z) the unemployment rate falls in the United States

a. all of the above
b. none of the above
c. (X) and (Z)
d. (X) and (Y)
e. (Y) and (Z)

4. Appreciation of the dollar tends, all else being equal, to:

(W) improve balance of payments
(X) create balance-of-payments deficits
(Y) increase inflation in the United States
(Z) increase unemployment in the United States

a. (W) and (Y)
b. (X) and (Z)
c. (X) and (Y)
d. (W) and (Z)
e. (Y) and (Z)

5. Which of the following is *not* a policy that would improve balance-of-trade deficits?

a. give tax cuts to U.S. consumers
b. raise additional trade barriers
c. intervene to cause dollar depreciation
d. increase U.S. interest rates
e. pay subsidies to U.S. import-substitute producers

SUGGESTIONS FOR FURTHER READING

Arthur Okun's *Equality and Efficiency: The Big Trade-off* (Washington, D.C.: Brookings Institution, 1975) discusses many of the problems outlined here. Lindert and Kindleberger's *International Economics* presents a clear view of balance-of-payments policies in today's world. Is the world coming to an end?

Paul Erdman destroyed the world in his novel, *The Crash of '79*. This fiction combines sound international economics with espionage and a little sex. What more can you ask?

SUGGESTIONS FOR FURTHER READING

Interested in what you've read? Want to learn more? Want to dig deeper into the problems, policies and ideas presented in the text? Here's your chance. This section provides a list of readings that build on the topics presented in the text. These articles and books should be available at most college libraries.

These readings are just a beginning. If you are interested in economics you need to begin a daily reading program to keep up with changing events. What should you read? Start with a good daily newspaper. The *New York Times*, *Washington Post*, *Chicago Tribune*, and *Wall Street Journal* all provide excellent reports and analysis of economic events. Magazines like the weekly *Time*, *Newsweek* and the British *Economist* are good sources, too. Of this list, the author especially recommends the *New York Times*, *Wall Street Journal*, and *Economist* for solid analysis of current events.

CHAPTER 1: MACROECONOMIC PROBLEMS

Where can you go for information about the economy? The periodicals listed above are all good sources. Here are some others. The Council of Economic Advisor's *Economic Report of the President* comes out each year in January. These reports present current statistics, the "official" analysis of current problems, and the President's plan for dealing with them. A different view is often presented in the Brookings Institution's *Setting National Priorities*. This thoughtful reaction to the President's plans usually appears in May or June. The Federal Reserve's perspective is published in its monthly *Federal Reserve Bulletin*. Martin Feldstein edited a good analysis of current conditions: *The American Economy in Transition* (Houghton Mifflin, 1980). Are we heading for another great depression? See Benjamin J. Stein's "A Scenario for a Depression?" *New York Times Magazine* (February 28, 1982).

CHAPTER 2: SUPPLY AND DEMAND

Any good microeconomics text will help you go further in the study of supply and demand. Try the author's *Introductory Microeconomics* (Academic Press, 1981). Want to see the personal side of a market? A particularly interesting view is R. A. Radford's "The Economic Organization of a P.O.W. Camp," *Economica* (1945).

CHAPTER 3: THE PROBLEM OF UNEMPLOYMENT

The current unemployment problem is analyzed in the Labor Department's *Monthly Labor Review*. Harvard economist Martin Feldstein has written an interesting article analyzing the changing nature of unemployment in America: "The Economics of the New Unemployment," *Public Interest* (Fall 1973). The *New York Times* reviewed the changing face of unemployment in a series titled "Out of Work" that appeared beginning with the January 10, 1982 issue. Where does unemployment come from? A theory of inflation and unemployment based on search costs is presented in Arthur Okun's influential *Prices and Quantities* (Brookings, 1981).

CHAPTER 4: UNDERSTANDING INFLATION

Robert Solow's "The Intelligent Citizen's Guide to Inflation," *Public Interest* (Winter 1975) remains one of the best discussions of inflation's effects. Wall Street Journal writer Lindley H.

Clark's *The Secret Tax* (Dow Jones Books, 1976) provides a good discussion of inflation, too. What happens when inflation slows down? See "Some People, Firms Feeling the Pain that Goes with Declining Inflation" by Ralph E. Winter in the *Wall Street Journal* (January 22, 1982).

CHAPTER 5: MEASURING ECONOMIC ACTIVITY

The details of GNP accounting are provided in the monthly *Survey of Current Business*. How big is the underground economy? See Peter M. Gutmann's "Statistical Illusions, Mistaken Policies" in *Challenge* (November–December 1979). What's happening to RGNP around the world? The September–October *World Bank Report* analyzes this question. Many other World Bank publications look at poverty and income around the world. Interested in the debate over the value-added tax? See the discussion in the author's *Public Finance* (Reston Publishers, 1984).

CHAPTER 6: KEYNESIAN AGGREGATE DEMAND

It's tough reading, but John Maynard Keynes' *General Theory of Employment, Interest and Money* is a classic! Not ready for that yet? Try a good intermediate macroeconomics text. One of the best is *Macroeconomics* by Rudiger Dornbusch and Stanley Fisher (McGraw-Hill, 1978). Also useful is Alvin Hansen's *A Guide to Keynes* (McGraw-Hill, 1953).

CHAPTER 7: AGGREGATE SUPPLY AND THE ECONOMY

Nobel Prize winner Lawrence R. Klein talks about the importance of aggregate supply in "The Supply Side," *American Economic Review* (March 1978). Walter Heller and Charles Schultz debate wage and price controls in an exchange published by the *Wall Street Journal* (February 27, 1980) and reprinted in the author's *Coursebook for Introductory Economics* (Academic Press, 1981). Leading indicators are discussed in Alfred L. Malabre, Jr.'s "Tracking a Trend" in the *Wall Street Journal* (December 22, 1981). Francis Bator's solutions to current macroeconomic problems are presented in "The Sins of Wages," *Economist* (March 21, 1981).

CHAPTER 8: FISCAL POLICY

The Brookings Institution has long been a center for the study of government and the economy. *Setting National Priorities* looks at fiscal policy every year. A conservative view can be found in yearly volumes of *Contemporary Economic Problems* (American Enterprise Institute). *How Taxes Affect Economic Behavior* (Brookings, 1981), edited by Joseph Pechman and Henry J. Aaron, tells the current tax story. Aaron and Michael S. Boskin's (eds.) *The Economics of Taxation* (Brookings, 1980) is an excellent tax primer. The author's *Public Finance* (Reston Publishers, 1983) is another good reference. Jude Wanninski is a famous popularizer of supply-side economics. This view is well presented in his *The Way the World Works* (Simon and Schuster, 1978).

CHAPTER 9: MONEY AND BANKING

John Kenneth Galbraith has written an interesting and understandable history of the whole money business: *Money: Whence It Came, Where It Went* (Houghton Mifflin, 1975). Lawrence W. Ritter and William L. Silber have put out an amusing little book that puts cash in perspective. It's called simply *Money* (Basic Books, 1977). The gold standard is the topic of Tom Bethell's "Hard Money Men" in *Harper's* (February 1981). This issue is further debated in an interview, "Should We (and Could We) Return to the Gold Standard?" *New York Times* (September 6, 1981) and "The Point of Linking the Dollar to Gold," by Arthur B. Laffer and Charles W. Kadlec in the *Wall Street Journal* (October 13, 1981).

CHAPTER 10: CREDIT MARKETS AND MONETARY POLICY

Your best bet for analysis of money and credit is the daily *Wall Street Journal*. Check the editorial page and the section labeled "Credit Markets." Government influence on the credit markets is explored in "America's Other Budget" by William Barry Furlong, *New York Times Magazine* (February 21, 1982). The debate over credit market ceilings rages still. Helen Frame Peters presents a good discussion of the pros and cons in a particular credit market in "The Mortgage Market: A Place for Ceilings," *Federal Reserve Bank of Philadelphia Business Review* (July–August 1977).

CHAPTER 11: MONETARY VERSUS FISCAL POLICY

There are many views of the FRS, government, and their policy combinations. Chapters 3 and 4 of the *Economic Report of the President*, 1982 give one view. "The Budget and the Economy" by Joseph Pechman and Barry Bosworth and "Long Term Budget Strategies" by Charles Schultz, both in *Setting National Priorities* (Brookings, 1983), present a different view. "The Budget Deficit is a Red Herring" by Paul Craig Roberts in the *New York Times* (February 14, 1982) gives one view of crowding out. "The Reagan Deficit and Investment" by Benjamin M. Friedman in the *Wall*

Street Journal (January 13, 1982) takes the other side of this issue.

CHAPTER 12: THE CHALLENGE TO KEYNESIAN ECONOMICS

Daniel Bell and Irving Kristol are editors of an excellent volume that analyzes the theories discussed in this chapter: *The Crisis in Economic Theory* (Basic Books, 1981). Daniel Bell's "Models and Reality in Economic Discourse" is particularly interesting. Mark W. Willes presents "Rational Expectations as a Counterrevolution" and Allan H. Metzler's article, "Monetarism and the Crisis in Economics," presents the monetarist view. Milton Friedman argues his monetarist views in "A Memorandum to the Fed," *Wall Street Journal* (January 30, 1981). An amusing and scholarly discussion of rational expectations is given in "A Child's Guide to Rational Expectations" by Rodney Maddock and Michael Carter, *Journal of Economic Literature* (March 1982).

CHAPTER 13: INTERNATIONAL TRADE

Comparative advantage and the gains from trade are discussed in more detail in the author's *Introductory Microeconomics* (Academic Press, 1981), Chapter 2 and *Introductory Economics* (Academic Press, 1981), Chapter 18. The auto import debate is well presented in "Car Wars: Protectionism Battle Over Imports of Autos May Head for Congress," an article on the front page of the *Wall Street Journal* (February 15, 1980). A different perspective is provided by "Quality: When Better Cars Are Built, Will America Be Building Them?" by Rich Ceppos, *Car and Driver* (March 1981). The changing balance-of-payments stages are illustrated in "The Saudis Build a Pittsburgh," by Douglas Martin in the *New York Times* (January 31, 1982).

CHAPTER 14: THE FOREIGN-EXCHANGE MARKET

Flexible and fixed exchange rates are discussed in *The Great Wheel: The World Monetary System* by Sidney E. Rolfe and James L. Burke (McGraw-Hill, 1975). Peter Lindert and Charles Kindleberger's textbook, *International Economics* (Richard D. Irwin publishers, 1982) has one of the best presentations of foreign exchange markets. What's the FRS up to in foreign exchange markets? The Fed reports its actions in its monthly *Federal Reserve Bulletin.* The world monetary system is analyzed by Gerald M. Meier, *Problems of a World Monetary Order* (Oxford University Press, 1982).

CHAPTER 15: INTERNATIONAL ECONOMICS

The *Wall Street Journal* now publishes a detailed analysis of international economic news every day—the first "inside" pages of the second section. Don't miss it. The best source of international economic analysis is still the British weekly *Economist.* A good theoretical presentation is Rudiger Dornbusch's *Open Economy Macroeconomics* (Basic Books, 1980). Interdependence is the theme of "Europeans Gripe When Dollar is Strong Even Louder than When Dollar is Weak" by Richard F. Janssen, *Wall Street Journal* (March 9, 1981).

CHAPTER 16: PROBLEMS, GOALS, AND TRADE-OFFS

Arthur Okun's *Equality and Efficiency: The Big Trade-off* (Brookings, 1975) discusses many of the problems outlined here. Lindert and Kindleberger's *International Economics* presents a clear view of balance-of-payments policies in today's world. Is the world coming to an end? Paul Erdman destroyed the world in his novel, *The Crash of '79*. This fiction combines sound international economics with espionage and a little sex. What more can you ask?

GLOSSARY

Absolute advantage: the ability to produce absolutely more with given resources.

Accommodating monetary policies: FRS policies that have the same affect on aggregate demand as do fiscal actions.

Adaptive expectations: expectations that change in light of new information.

Administrative-cost premium: interest rate due to cost of administering loan.

Aggregate demand: desired total spending in the economy; the combined demand for all goods and services.

Aggregate supply: total intended production of goods and services.

Allocation function: the role of government in allocating scarce resources to their best use.

Appreciate: increase in the relative value of a currency.

Arbitrage: riskless speculation; buying currencies on one foreign-exchange market to sell at a profit elsewhere.

Automatic stabilities: government programs that automatically react to changes in income and unemployment.

Average propensity to consume (APC): the fraction of total income spent on consumption.

Balanced-budget multiplier: change in aggregate demand when government spending and taxes change in the same direction by the same amount; the balanced budget multiplier equals one (1) multiplied by the change in government spending.

Balanced growth: equal increases in demand and supply.

Balance of payments: the record of all payments of a country; total inflows of money minus total outflows.

Balance-of-payments deficit: total money outflows exceed total inflows for a nation.

Balance-of-payment surplus: total money inflows (for exports, transfers, investment, and profits) exceed total outflows for a nation.

Balance of trade: the record of international trade payments; exports minus imports.

Barriers to occupational entry: institutional factors that limit one's ability to enter a job market.

Barter: a system where goods are exchanged directly without the use of money.

Base year: arbitrarily chosen year, used to construct the price index market basket.

Bond market: market where bonds (IOUs) are bought and sold.

Bottleneck aggregate supply curve: aggregate supply in an economy with rising marginal costs and production bottlenecks.

Business cycle: periods of economic expansion followed by recession.

Capacity: the physical ability of the economy to produce, limited by the stock of factories, machines, tools, and so on.

Capital gains: profits from the sale of assets.

Circular-flow model: a description of the flow of spending and income between the business and household sectors.

Closed economy: an economy with no interaction with other countries.

Collateral: items held as security for a loan.

Command economy: an economic system where production and distribution choices are made by central planners.

Commodity markets: markets where futures contracts for agricultural, mineral, and financial assets are exchanged.

Comparative advantage: the ability to produce at lower opportunity cost.

Complements: goods that are used together.

Complete crowding out: increased government borrowing leads to an equal decrease in private investment.

Conflicting policies: monetary and fiscal policies that are not intended to have the same effect on aggregate demand.

Consumer burden: the part of a tariff paid by consumers as higher price.

Consumer price index (CPI): a measure of inflation based on goods purchased by consumers.

Consumption spending: household spending on consumer goods.

Contractionary monetary policy: FRS policies that reduce credit supply to reduce aggregate demand.

Cost-push: a price increase caused by decreased supply.

Credit: the temporary exchange of money among individuals, as when loans are made.

Credit markets: markets where loanable funds are exchanged.

Customs union: groups of nations having free trade among themselves and unified tariff barriers with other countries.

Cyclical unemployment: unemployment resulting from falling aggregate demand.

Deadweight loss: loss due to wasted effort and resources.

Decrease in demand: a decrease in the quantity demanded at each price; shift to the left in the demand curve.

Decrease in supply: a decrease in the quantity supplied at each price; shift to the left in supply curve.

Deficit: the condition where money paid out by a sector is more than money received.

Deficit spending: government borrowing; spending in excess of tax receipts.

Deflation: falling price levels.

Demand: the buyer side of the market; a description of the kinds and amounts of goods people want to buy.

Demand curve: a graph showing the relationship between quantity demand and the price of the good.

Demand deposits: checking account balances.

Demand-pull: a price increase caused by increased demand.

Depreciate: decrease in the relative value of a currency.

Depreciation: the wearing out of machines and other productive resources.

Depression aggregate supply curve: aggregate supply in an economy with many unemployed resources.

Derived demand: demand for one good based on demand for its complement.

Devalue: to lower a currency's fixed exchange rate.

Direct relationship: the relationship between A and B, when A and B consistently move in the same direction.

Dirty float: a flexible exchange rate with frequent official intervention.

Discount: goods sold for less than their face value.

Discount rate: interest rate on FRS loans to member banks; a signal of FRS policies.

Discouraged workers: people who leave the labor force when unable to find work.

Disequilibrium theory: the school of economics that thinks markets fail to clear; macroeconomics based on problems of disequilibrium.

Disinflation: falling inflation rate.

Disintermediation: situation where savers take funds out of banks and deposit them directly in credit markets to avoid interest rate ceilings.

Disposable income: income available for spending; income after direct taxes have been paid.

Distribution function: the role of government in improving the distribution of income and wealth.

Dividends: corporate profits paid to stockholders.

Double-counting: a potential GNP error; counting production more than once.

Dow Jones average: an index that measures prices of major stocks on the New York Stock Exchange.

Economic discomfort index: a measure of the magnitude of national economic woes; the sum of the inflation and unemployment rates.

Economic efficiency: the best use of scarce resources.

Economics: a social science dealing with the production and distribution of goods and services in a world of scarcity.

Elastic demand: demand relatively responsive to price changes; characteristic of goods with many close substitutes.

Equation of exchange: the simple monetarist view of the economy; $M \times V = P \times Q$ where M equals money supply, V equals velocity of money, P equals price level, and Q equals RGNP.

Equilibrium price: the price at which quantity demanded equals quantity supplied.

Equity: ownership of an asset.

Eurodollars: dollar-denominated accounts held in foreign banks.

European economic community (EEC): a customs union composed of major European nations; also called the Common Market.

Excess demand: shortage.

Excess reserves: bank reserves over and above the reserve requirement; generally used for loans.

Excess supply: surplus.

Expansionary monetary policy: FRS policies that increase credit supply to stimulate aggregate demand.

Exports: sales of items to the residents of other countries.

Externalities: actions by one person or group that affect others.

Federal funds market: market for short-term government securities.

Federal Reserve System: the organization that regulates the national banking system and controls monetary policy in the United States.

Final good: a good purchased by its ultimate user.

Financial intermediaries: firms that act as go-betweens for savers and borrowers; banks, insurance companies, and credit unions are examples.

Financial investment: purchase of stocks, bonds, or other financial instruments that do not directly increase production.

Financial sector: the part of the economy that deals with borrowing, lending, and the exchange of assets like stocks and bonds.

Fiscal policy: government policies that influence aggregate demand.

Fixed exchange rates: exchange rates set by central banks.

Flexible exchange rates: exchange rates set by supply and demand.

Float: the time when two individuals temporarily own the same asset.

Foreign exchange: foreign currencies.

45-degree line: a line showing all the possible income levels where macroeconomic equilibrium can occur; points where spending equals income.

Forward exchange rate: a contractual agreement that sets the exchange rate for a specific transaction at a future date.

Fractional reserve banks: modern system of banking where only a fraction of deposits are held as reserves, the rest are used for loans and investments.

Frictional unemployment: unemployment resulting from imperfections in the labor market such as poor information about jobs and lack of mobility.

Full capacity aggregate supply curve: aggregate supply in an economy that has reached production limits determined by finite capacity.

Full employment: a goal of macroeconomic policy; the minimum normal unemployment rate in a healthy economy.

Futures contracts: contracts promising future delivery of an asset at a set price.

GNP index: a measure of inflation for the entire economy.

Gross national product (GNP): the total market value (in current dollars) of all final goods and services produced in an economy in a year.

Housing starts: number of new homes begun in a given period; a leading indicator of production.

Hyperinflation: very high rates of inflation.

Identification lag: the lag in fiscal policy that occurs while transfer payment recipients are identified and certified eligible.

Immature creditor nation: a nation with a balance-of-payments surplus from sales of raw materials and natural resources.

Immature debtor nation: a less developed nation with a balance-of-payments deficit resulting from high investment and transfer inflows.

Impact lag: the lag in fiscal policy that occurs before consumer spending responds to policy.

Implementation lag: the lag in fiscal policy that occurs while government policies are put into effect.

Imports: purchases of goods produced in other countries.

Income effect: a change in buying that results from changing purchasing power.

Increase in demand: an increase in the quantity demanded at each price; shift to right in the demand curve.

Increase in supply: an increase in the quantity supplied at each price; shift in the supply curve to the right.

Index of leading indicators: an index that foretells future changes in the RGNP.

Indexation: linking money payments to a price index.

Induced-consumption spending: changes in consumption spending resulting from fiscal policy.

Inelastic demand: demand relatively unresponsive to price changes; characteristic of necessity goods or goods with few close substitutes.

Inflation: a substantial, sustained increase in the general level of prices.

Inflation premium: interest rate due to expected future inflation.

Inflation rate: rate of increase in inflation index.

Injections: sources of spending that increase income.

Inputs: goods and services used to produce other goods and services; the ingredients of production.

Intermediate good: an item used as an input; not counted in GNP.

Intervention: government or central bank foreign-exchange transactions intended to alter the exchange rate.

Inventories: stocks of goods that firms hold for future production or sale.

Inverse relationship: the relationship between A and B and when A and B consistently move in opposite directions.

Investment in human capital: investments in training and education that increase worker productivity.

Investment rule: firms invest in projects with expected rates of return greater than or equal to interest rates of bonds of equal period and risk.

Investment spending: purchase of long-lasting inputs like factories, machinery, and structures.

L money supply definition: broadest measure of money; includes M3 plus short-term government securities held by the public.

Labor force: all those involved in the labor market; people working and those actively seeking work.

Laffer curve: graph showing the relationship between tax revenues and tax rates.

Laissez faire: a policy of minimum government interference in market actions.

Law of comparative advantage: the theory that international trade and production specialization are based on differences in opportunity cost.

Leading indicator: a statistic that foretells future changes.

Leakages: uses of income that reduce spending.

Legislative lag: the lag in fiscal policy that occurs while legislators formulate policy.

Long-term capital gains: profits from investment owned for one year or more.

M1 money supply definition: currency and demand deposit balances.

M2 money supply definition: currency, demand deposits and time deposits, and money market fund balances.

M3 money supply definition: M2 money definition plus large certificates of deposit.

Macroeconomic equilibrium: level of income where desired total spending equals income; leakages equal injections.

Macroeconomics: the study of the functioning of the national economy.

Marginal costs: the cost of producing additional units of a product, given the producers' current production rate and capacity.

Marginal propensity to consume (MPC): the fraction of any change in disposable income spent on consumption.

Market: the general term for institutions where goods and services are exchanged.

Market basket: list of types and quantities of goods and services purchased in the base year.

Market economy: an economic system where production and distribution choices are made by individuals acting without government direction.

Mature creditor nation: a nation with a balance-of-payments surplus from export of manufactured goods.

Mature debtor nation: a nation with a balance-of-payments deficit from credit and investment outflows.

Merchantilists: eighteenth century merchants and economists who favored trade restrictions to protect gold accumulations.

Microeconomics: the study of how individual economic choices are made, focusing on producers, consumers, and markets.

Minimum wage laws: laws that specify a minimum legal wage rate for workers in many job markets.

Mixed economy: an economic system where some choices are made by individuals and others are made by central planners.

Models: simplified descriptions of real-world processes that increase the understanding of the real world.

Monetarism: the school of economics that views economic theory as money demand and money supply; monetarists disagree with Keynesians about fiscal policy and the monetary transmission mechanism.

Monetary policy: FRS policies that affect aggregate demand and aggregate supply by regulating money and credit supplies.

Monetary transmission mechanism: the link between changes in interest rates and investment spending; the key to monetary policy.

Money: anything generally accepted in exchange for goods and services and in payment of debt.

Money illusion: the illusion that workers can buy more because they have more dollars (workers ignore inflation's effects).

Money market funds: investments in short-term government and corporate bond pools.

Money multiplier: the relationship between a new deposit and change in the money supply.

Money value: value expressed as the number of dollars, not purchasing power or real value.

Monopolies: firms that are able to control market price.

Mortgage credit market: market for long-term loans used for housing loans.

National debt: total federal government indebtedness.

Natural unemployment rate: the level of unemployment that occurs in an economy without government action.

Near money: assets with high liquidity that sometimes take the place of money.

Negative income effect: purchases of some good vary inversely with income.

Net exports: exports minus imports; a component of aggregate demand.

Net investment: investment over and above that necessary to compensate for depreciation.

New entrants: individuals who enter the labor force for the first time.

Nominal interest rate: interest rate expressed in money terms.

Nominal value: value expressed in money terms.

Normative economics: economic analysis based on values, judgment, or philosophy; statements that are a matter of opinion, not fact.

Open economy: an economy that trades with other countries.

Open market operations: FRS purchases and sales of bonds on the open market; used to regulate money and credit supplies.

Opportunity cost: the value of the best foregone opportunity when a choice is made.

Outputs: the items that firms produce.

Over-valued: an exchange rate above market equilibrium.

Paradox of thrift: saving makes any individual better off, but everyone suffers if everyone saves.

Payroll tax: a tax deducted directly from paychecks.

Per capital RGNP: RGNP adjusted for change in population.

Phillips curve: a curve showing an inverse relationship between inflation and unemployment rates.

Positive economics: economic analysis that can be proved right or wrong.

Price ceiling: the maximum legal price.

Price floor: the minimum legal price.

Price index: mathematical measure of price increases.

Price stability: zero inflation rate.

Prime interest rate: interest rate on short-term, low-risk loans.

Producer burden: the part of a tariff paid by sellers as lower net price.

Producer price index (PPI): measure of inflation based on goods used by business firms.

Product life cycle theory: the theory that newly invented goods are first exported then imported when standardized and produced abroad.

Production possibility curve (PPC): a graph showing the maximum amounts of two goods a nation can produce with scarce resources.

Productivity: the relative ability of a resource to produce goods and services; often measured by the amount of production per man-hour.

Progressive tax: a tax whose burden increases with income; the rich bear a higher tax burden than the poor.

Property tax: a tax based on the value of land and structures.

Proportional tax: a tax that imposes the same burden on all income levels.

Public-choice function: the role of government in making social choices.

Public goods: goods that, once produced, yield benefits that can be shared by all.

Purchasing power: the value of money measured in the amount of goods and services that it purchases.

Quota: a physical limitation on the quantity of imports.

Random walk theory: the theory that changing stock market prices have no systematic cause.

Ratchet effect: condition where economic policies result in ongoing increases in inflation with no permanent effect on unemployment.

Rational expectations theory: a macroeconomic theory built on microeconomic behavior; assumes individuals base rational behavior on expectations.

Real gross national product (RGNP): a measure of the total annual production in an economy, adjusted for inflation.

Real interest rate: interest rate adjusted for inflation rate.

Real value: statement of value adjusted for inflation.

Recession: a sustained period of declining production and income.

Regressive tax: a tax whose burden increases as income falls; the poor bear a higher tax burden than the rich.

Regulation Q: FRS regulations that limit bank interest payments.

Relative prices: price of goods compared to one another.

Reserve requirement: fraction of bank deposits that must be held as reserves.

Risk premium: interest rate due to uncertainty of loan repayment.

Rules policy: Milton Friedman's suggested FRS policy; money supply should grow at a constant rate to match AS growth.

Sales tax: a tax based on the value of purchased goods.

Say's law of markets: Jean Baptiste Say's statement that supply creates its own demand.

Scarcity premium: interest rate due to relative scarcity of loanable funds.

Sectors: parts of the economy that respond to different economic events.

Shortage: the quantity demanded exceeds quantity supplied at a particular price.

Social Security tax: tax on wages and salary income used to finance the social security system.

Special drawing rights (SDRs): an international central bank reserve; sometimes called "paper gold" because SDRs can be used like gold for central bank transactions.

Spending multiplier: the total effect of a change in spending; change in aggregate demand equals $\frac{1}{1-\text{MPC}} \times$ change in spending.

Stabilization function: the role of government in fighting inflation and unemployment.

Stagflation: high inflation rates accompanied by high unemployment rates; a stagnant economy with inflation.

Sticky wages: inflexible wages; wage rates that do not fall in response to labor surplus.

Stock markets: markets where shares of ownership in corporations are exchanged.

Structural unemployment: unemployment caused by poor matching of worker skills and job needs.

Subsidies: government payments to individuals or firms to encourage specific activities.

Substitutes: goods that perform the same function.

Substitution effect: buying more of a relatively cheaper good due to a price change.

Supply: the seller side of the market; a description of production and sale choices.

Supply curve: a graph of the relationship between the quantity supplied and the price of a good.

Supply-side economics: policies that try to increase aggregate supply by cutting tax rates.

Surplus: the quantity supplied exceeds quantity demanded at a particular price.

Surplus: the condition where money received by a sector exceeds money paid out.

Tariff: a tax on imported goods.

Tax burden: the fraction of total income going to a tax; tax divided by income.

Tax expenditures: special tax reductions given for individual spending on approved items.

Technology: the process by which goods are produced.

Terms of trade: the ratio of two goods in international trade.

Time deposits: savings account balances.

Time preference: interest rate due to the preference for present over future consumption.

Trade-off: the situation where one good or goal must be given up to gain another.

Trade possibility curve (TPC): a graph showing the combinations a nation can trade for with given terms of trade.

Trickle down: the idea that benefits given to high income groups eventually help poorer groups.

Underemployed workers: part-time workers seeking full-time jobs and people working in occupations that do not use their training or skills.

Underground economy: illegal markets; the part of the economy that sells illegal goods or acts to hide activity from taxation.

Under-valued: an exchange rate below market equilibrium.

Unemployed worker: a person willing and able to work, actively seeking work, but unable to find a job at the going wage rate.

Unemployment rate: a measure of unemployment calculated by dividing the number of people unemployed by the size of the labor force.

Unintended inventory accumulations: increases in inventory levels that occur when demand falls behind production.

Unintended inventory reductions: decreases in inventory levels that occur when demand rises above supply.

Usury laws: laws that set maximum legal interest rates.

Value-added: increase in value of inputs in production.

Value-added tax (VAT): a tax on value-added at each stage of production.

Variable lag: the uncertain lag in the monetary transmission mechanism between changes in interest rates and investment spending.

Velocity of money: the average number of times the money supply is spent in a year; GNP divided by the money supply.

Voluntary unemployment: unemployment that is by choice; the opposite of forced unemployment.

Wage and price controls: laws that freeze or control most wages and prices in an economy.

Wage-lag theory: an hypothesis concerning the cause of the Phillips curve that holds that inflation can temporarily increase business profits and so cause firms to increase employment.

ANSWERS TO "TEST YOURSELF"

CHAPTER 1: MACROECONOMIC PROBLEMS

1. C 2. B 3. E 4. C 5. A

CHAPTER 2: SUPPLY AND DEMAND

1. B 2. E 3. C 4. A 5. C

CHAPTER 3: THE PROBLEM OF UNEMPLOYMENT

1. A 2. B 3. B 4. B 5. A

CHAPTER 4: UNDERSTANDING INFLATION

1. C 2. B 3. B 4. E 5. C

CHAPTER 5: MEASURING ECONOMIC ACTIVITY

1. D 2. C 3. C 4. C 5. B

CHAPTER 6: KEYNESIAN AGGREGATE DEMAND

1. D 2. B 3. C 4. B 5. D

CHAPTER 7: AGGREGATE SUPPLY AND THE ECONOMY

1. D 2. D 3. D 4. B 5. C

CHAPTER 8: FISCAL POLICY

1. A 2. D 3. E 4. C 5. E

CHAPTER 9: MONEY AND BANKING

1. D 2. B 3. C 4. A 5. E

CHAPTER 10: CREDIT MARKETS AND MONETARY POLICY

1. C 2. D 3. A 4. B 5. D

CHAPTER 11: MONETARY VERSUS FISCAL POLICY

1. B 2. A 3. B 4. A 5. B

CHAPTER 12: THE CHALLENGE TO KEYNESIAN ECONOMICS

1. A 2. C 3. D 4. D 5. C

CHAPTER 13: INTERNATIONAL TRADE

1. C 2. C 3. C 4. E 5. A

CHAPTER 14: THE FOREIGN-EXCHANGE MARKET

1. C 2. B 3. E 4. C 5. C

CHAPTER 15: INTERNATIONAL ECONOMICS

1. D 2. C 3. C 4. B 5. A

CHAPTER 16: PROBLEMS, GOALS, AND TRADE-OFFS

1. D 2. E 3. C 4. B 5. A

INDEX